2004

LITERARY
CHARACTER

LITERARY CHARACTER

The Human Figure in Early English Writing

ELIZABETH FOWLER

CORNELL UNIVERSITY PRESS

ITHACA AND LONDON

First published 2003 by Cornell University Press

Printed in the United States of America

Library of Congress Cataloging-in Publication Data
Fowler, Elizabeth
    Literary character : the human figure in early English writing / Elizabeth Fowler.
        p. cm.
Includes bibliographical references and index.
    ISBN 0-8014-4116-1 (acid-free paper)
    1. English literature—Middle English, 1100–1500—History and criticism.   2. Characters and characteristics in literature.   3. English literature—Early modern, 1500—1700—History and criticism.   4. Literature and society—England—History—16th century.   5. Spenser, Edmund, 1552?–1599—Political and social views.   6. Chaucer, Geoffrey, d. 1400—Political and social views.   7. Literature and society—England—History—To 1500.   8. Spenser, Edmund, 1552?—1599—Characters.   9. Chaucer, Geoffrey, d. 1400—Characters. 10. Human beings in literature.   I. Title.
    PR275.C42F69 2003
    820.9'27'0902—dc21   2003003909

Cornell University Press strives to use environmentally responsible suppliers and materials to the fullest extent possible in the publishing of its books. Such materials include vegetable-based, low-VOC inks, and acid-free papers that are recycled, totally chlorine-free, or partly composed of nonwood fibers. For further information, visit our website at www.cornellpress.cornell.edu.

Cloth printing   10   9   8   7   6   5   4   3   2   1

This work is dedicated to my teachers, whose minds and acts
are inscribed on my heart. I am especially grateful for what I
have learned from Donna Lee Fowler and Joseph Michael
Fowler, Susan Fowler Zehnder, Peter John Fowler, Beverly
Tharp, William Lamont, Elizabeth Kirk, Michael Harper,
Susanne Woods, Barbara Lewalski, Helen Vendler, Derek
Pearsall, Roland Greene, Sacvan Bercovitch, Hermine Makman,
Charles Donahue, Jr., Stanley Cavell, Amartya Sen, W. V.
Quine, John Pope, Mary Carruthers, Gordon Braden, A. C.
Spearing, and, nearest my soul, Victor Ernest Luftig.

Charlottesville, Virginia
May 2002

Contents

viii   *Contents*

Acknowledgments

This book has involved me in many happy conversations. Thanks for help in its making are owed to my teachers, fellow doctoral candidates, and students in the English department at Harvard, to the junior and senior fellows at the Society of Fellows, to my colleagues and students (especially Andrew Zurcher) at Yale and the University of Virginia, and to the many institutions that have invited me to present this work in public. Such invitations are among the best rewards of scholarship. Librarians have risked my use of many rare book and manuscript collections in the United States, England, and Ireland; their open-handedness can be felt throughout the book. I am fortunate that, in its many stages, this project was sustained by grants from Harvard University, The Whiting Foundation, The Fulbright Foundation, Dame Frances Yates and The Warburg Institute, Yale University, The Harvard Society of Fellows, The American Council of Learned Societies, and the University of Virginia. The manuscript was polished and protected from many slips by the careful research assistance of Nicola Masciandaro, Emily Steiner, Cristina Cervone, Samara Landers, Lee Manion, Jennifer Hughes, and Ellen Malenas. Many other generous scholars have also read, heard, and commented upon parts of this project, and I warmly appreciate all their efforts. Among them, David Aers, Paul Alpers, Nicholas Canny, Roland Greene, Suzanne Keen, Barbara Lewalski, Derek Pearsall, Anne Lake Prescott, Maureen Quilligan, A. C. Spearing, Helen Vendler, John Watkins, and especially Victor Luftig will not be dismayed, I hope, to see their names inscribed among those most involved in the writing of this book. I thank Bernhard Kendler of Cornell University Press for his shepherding and cheerful faith in the manuscript. Finally, in hope that all these efforts will yield fruit, I thank my readers to be.

E.F.

A Note on Textual Debts

Biblical passages are taken from the Douay-Rheims Version. The medieval Canterbury pilgrim badge of the Frontispiece is reproduced by kind permission of Dr. Michael Mitchiner; the image appears as Figure 69 in his *Medieval Pilgrim and Secular Badges* (London: Hawkins, 1986), 49. I quote from manuscripts at the Bodleian Library, Oxford, with the permission of the Keeper of Special Collections and Western Manuscripts, and I cite passages from the manuscript archives of the Worshipful Company of Brewers by the permission of their Clerk and the courtesy of the Guildhall Library, Corporation of London, where the Brewers' records are held. With the permission of Houghton Mifflin Company, Geoffrey Chaucer is quoted throughout this book from Larry D. Benson's third edition of *The Riverside Chaucer*, copyright © 1987 by Houghton Mifflin Company. An early version of chapter 2 was published as "Civil Death and the Maiden: Agency and the Conditions of Contract in *Piers Plowman*" in *Speculum* 70 (1995): 760–92 and is used by permission of the Medieval Academy. An early version of the first half of chapter 3 was published as "Misogyny and Economic Person in Skelton, Langland and Chaucer" in *Spenser Studies* 10 (1992): 245–73; it is drawn upon here by the permission of AMS Press. Early versions of passages in chapter 4 appeared as pp. 48–54 and 67–71 of "The Failure of Moral Philosophy in the Work of Edmund Spenser," *Representations* 51 (1995): 47–76, copyright © 1995 by the Regents of the University of California, and are reprinted by permission of the University of California Press. Early versions of passages in chapter 4 appeared as pp. 71–83 of the essay "The Rhetoric of Political Forms: Social Persons and the Criterion of Fit in

Colonial Law, *Macbeth*, and *The Irish Masqve at Covrt*" in *Form and Reform in Renaissance England: Essays in Honor of Barbara Kiefer Lewalski*, ed. Amy Boesky and Mary Thomas Crane (University of Delaware Press, 1998), 70–103; that material is printed here with the permission of the Associated University Presses. My thanks to all these good keepers and publishers.

LITERARY
CHARACTER

❦ *Introduction* ❧

The Arguments of Person

Social Persons and Cognition

A medieval pilgrim to the shrine of St. Thomas Becket at Canterbury Cathedral might have bought there a souvenir badge to commemorate the ritual journey. She would have kept it on her person, pinned to a cloak or a hat, for instance. The Frontispiece shows a badge with a pin fastener; it was dug up near Billingsgate, London, is measured at 86 by 59 millimeters, and is thought to date from the same century as Geoffrey Chaucer's *Canterbury Tales*.[1] Though the left arch and side do not survive, there remains a beautiful and complex image of a tonsured figure in robes kneeling before an ornamented table that supports a huge goblet. Behind him are several armored knights suspended in space, carrying shields and brandishing swords at the head of the central figure. Another tonsured figure is leaning wide-eyed from a ledge that hangs over the cup and bears a Calvary scene. At the bottom of the badge a ribbon of squares reads "† THOMAS."

If we set aside what we know about Thomas, we can see how the badge draws on at least three familiar kinds of scenes: a scene of liturgical worship, a scene of public execution, and a scene of clandestine murder. We may refer to this notion of scene by the useful rhetorical term *topos* (from

---

1. Michael Mitchiner, *Medieval Pilgrim and Secular Badges* (London: Hawkins, 1986), 49. Most of his collection, Mitchiner informs us, was dug up on the Thames foreshore by a group of metal detector enthusiasts who felicitously call themselves the "mudlarks" (7). Thomas's shrine appeared soon after his death in 1170 and was much visited until (and after) the abolition of pilgrimage shrines in the 1530s by Henry VIII.

the Greek for *place* and, metaphorically, *topic*), which in its range of reference includes not only images and scenes but also arguments, issues, and
turns of phrase that are recognizably conventional. Any single use of a
topos invites a reverberation of memory, so that we must collate and compare it with other remembered examples of the convention.[2] On the badge,
the bodily attitude or pose of Thomas has an enormous cultural resonance
that activates all three topoi. In the terms of the liturgical scene, we may
see him kneel as a celebrant of the Christian mass; the monk may be a
preacher and the knights the defilers of a sacred ritual. In the murder scene,
he prays, and we perceive him as a victim caught in a pious moment; the
monk is a surprised witness and the knights are criminals in an ambush.
The terms of the execution scene invite us to see Thomas as the condemned
criminal offering his neck in submission to the swords of his justicers, with
their heraldry as their warrant and the monk as a goggle-eyed spectator.
The three topoi activate entirely different sets of personae: Thomas is a
priest, a *victim*, or a *criminal*; the monk is a *preacher*, a *witness*, or a *spectator*; the knights are *defilers*, *murderers*, or *agents of the law*.

Such representations I shall call *social persons*; they are the central topic
of this book.[3] Social persons are models of the person, familiar concepts of
social being that attain currency through common use. The viewer and
reader rely on them as ways of understanding figural representation,
whereas the artist relies on them as compositional tools or guides. Yet in
an important sense they are not "there," not in the picture at all, but only
in our minds and in the air of culture—phantoms of the cognitive process
of perception. As conventional kinds of person, social persons are very
much like literary genres, because they depend upon the recognition of
convention. They are better regarded as cumulative and changing sets of

2. On topos as a collation, see Mary Carruthers, *The Book of Memory: A Study of Mem-
ory in Medieval Culture* (Cambridge: Cambridge University Press, 1990), 61–68. See V. A.
Kolve, *Chaucer and the Imagery of Narrative: The First Five Canterbury Tales* (Stanford:
Stanford University Press, 1984) for readings of poetic images collated with visual traditions.
The concept of the literary topos came into importance in medieval studies with the publica-
tion of Ernst Robert Curtius, *European Literature and the Latin Middle Ages*, trans. Willard
R. Trask (New York: Pantheon, 1953).

3. I use the term "social person" (coined in an analogy to "legal person," which it includes) to describe something that social psychologists such as Gerard Duveen and Serge
Moscovici would call a "social representation" of the person. Mine is a general term meant
to indicate *a paradigmatic representation of personhood that has evolved historically among
the institutions of social life*. My thinking about social person draws on ideas suggested by
Marcel Mauss, "A Category of the Human Mind: The Notion of Person; The Notion of
Self," trans. W. D. Halls, in *The Category of the Person: Anthropology, Philosophy, History*,
ed. Michael Carrithers, Steven Collins, and Steven Lukes (Cambridge: Cambridge University
Press, 1985), 1–25. This essay was the Huxley Memorial Lecture of 1938, first printed as
"Une Catégorie de l'Esprit Humain: La Notion de Personne, Celle de 'Moi,'" *Journal of the
Royal Anthropological Institute* 68 (1938).

resemblances than as susceptible to definition by a list of features.[4] Social persons are sets of expectations built in the reader's mind by experience, and they are notions of what it is to be a person. The badge invokes its phantom social persons by its topoi, by the postures and array of its figures, by its use of letters, heraldry, and furniture, and by its allusions to history and ritual. The power of the image comes from the disposition of its human figures, a disposition that can call up such a crowd of ghosts. The image invites us to understanding by means of a process of sorting, collating, comparing, choosing, combining, and rejecting representations of the person.

The characters that inhabit fiction summon the same kind of specters by some of the same means; in demonstrating the importance of social persons in representation, this book offers a new method of analysis for the human figure in words. Our tools for the study of literary character are surprisingly primitive compared to those we have developed for, say, narrative, historical allusion, genre, rhetoric, iconography, plot, prosody, and other formal aspects of fiction. Previous studies of literary character have largely concerned the technical means authors employ to represent and shape forms of consciousness or subjectivity (e.g., E. M. Forster, Hélène Cixous, Dorrit Cohn, Martin Price, Katharine Maus), engineer plot (e.g., Vladimir Propp, Roland Barthes, James Phelan), propose ideas (e.g., D. W. Robertson, Kate Millett, Amélie Rorty), transmit literary genres and sources (Northrop Frye, Harold Bloom), or fuel the market for books (Deidre Lynch).[5] Critics have traced the histories of certain types and kinds

---

4. I should like here to affirm Stanley Cavell's perception of genre; he writes, "It will be natural in what follows, even irresistible, to speak of individual characteristics of a genre as 'features' of it; but the picture of an object with its properties is a bad one." He suggests that the important thing that is shared by members of a genre cannot be described by Ludwig Wittgenstein's notion of "family resemblance." Instead, he offers the idea that "the members of a genre share the inheritance of certain conditions, procedures and subjects and goals of composition, and that in primary art each member of such a genre represents a study of these conditions, something I think of as bearing the responsibility of the inheritance." Stanley Cavell, *Pursuits of Happiness: The Hollywood Comedy of Remarriage* (Cambridge: Harvard University Press, 1981), 28–29.

5. E. M. Forster, *Aspects of the Novel* (New York: Harcourt, Brace, 1927); Hélène Cixous, "The Character of 'Character,'" trans. Keith Cohen, *New Literary History* 5 (1974): 383–402; Dorrit Cohn, *Transparent Minds: Narrative Modes for Presenting Consciousness in Fiction* (Princeton: Princeton University Press, 1978); Martin Price, *Forms of Life: Character and Moral Imagination in the Novel* (New Haven: Yale University Press, 1983); Katharine Eisaman Maus, *Inwardness and Theater in the English Renaissance* (Chicago: University of Chicago Press, 1995); Vladimir Propp, *Morphology of the Folktale*, trans. Laurence Scott, 2d ed. (Austin: University of Texas Press, 1968); Roland Barthes, *S/Z*, trans. *Richard Miller* (New York: Hill and Wang, 1974); James Phelan, *Reading People, Reading Plots: Character, Progression, and the Interpretation of Narrative* (Chicago: University of Chicago Press, 1989); D. W. Robertson, Jr., *A Preface to Chaucer: Studies in Medieval Perspectives* (Princeton: Princeton University Press, 1962); Kate Millett, *Sexual Politics*

of literary character: the vice figure, the tragic hero, the penitent knight, the hard-boiled detective, and their familiar ilk.[6] Writers such as Warren Ginsberg, Susanne Wofford, John Watkins, and Andrew Galloway have added to our knowledge of form by showing how characters such as Achilles, Lucretia, Vergil, or Dido can be a kind of trope carrying intellectual history.[7] From all this work we know a great deal about source study, literary influence, and the interaction of genre and character. Yet rarely do theorists and critics acknowledge or attempt to explain how readers recognize these various techniques as figuration, how they integrate the scraplike details of characterization into coherent persons, or how authors exploit the powerful appeal figures make to readerly identification. These larger conditions of characterization will be among our concerns here.

Rarely too are theorists and critics able to treat character as a social form among others; we shall see that the theory of the social person will allow us to do so. Of course, scholarly writing on literary characters has been enriched by borrowings from the psychologies, moral philosophies, and medical theories of various periods, but we have lacked a method for coping appropriately with the differences between these modes of thought or even, oddly enough, with the differences between characters and living bodies. These differences have legal, aesthetic, moral, and mental consequences; they are not to be taken lightly. Perhaps this is why the twentieth century saw the decline of interest in the human figure in so many different fields. It is typical of the impoverished state of thought about characterization that even psychoanalytic theory has exiled characters. There are no characters in the writings of Jacques Lacan; figures like "Dora" disappeared together with the genre of the case study as the discourse developed in the years after Sigmund Freud. Literary scholars interested in psychological approaches to texts have followed suit, sometimes even excluding character as a potential location for psychoanalytic process. This book at-

---

(Garden City, N.Y.: Doubleday, 1970), Amélie Rorty, "Characters, Persons, Selves, Individuals," in *Mind in Action: Essays in the Philosophy of Mind* (Boston: Beacon, 1988), 78–98; Northrop Frye, *The Anatomy of Criticism: Four Essays* (Princeton: Princeton University Press, 1957); Harold Bloom, *Shakespeare: The Invention of the Human* (New York: Riverhead Books, 1998); Deidre Lynch, *The Economy of Character: Novels, Market Culture, and the Business of Inner Meaning* (Chicago: University of Chicago Press, 1998).

6. E.g., Gordon Braden, *Renaissance Tragedy and the Senecan Tradition: Anger's Privilege* (New Haven: Yale University Press, 1985), Andrea Hopkins, *The Sinful Knights: A Study of Middle English Penitential Romance* (Oxford: Clarendon, 1990).

7. Susanne Wofford, *The Choice of Achilles: The Ideology of Figure in the Epic* (Stanford: Stanford University Press, 1992); Andrew Galloway, "Chaucer's *Legend of Lucrece* and the Critique of Ideology in Fourteenth-Century England," *English Literary History* 60 (1993): 813–32; Warren Ginsberg, *The Cast of Character: The Representation of Personality in Ancient and Medieval Literature* (Toronto: University of Toronto Press, 1983); John Watkins, *The Specter of Dido: Spenser and Virgilian Epic* (New Haven: Yale University Press, 1995).

tempts to revive our interest in the human figure in part by specifying the form of its relation to the history of the disciplines, so that figuration's manifold uses of models of the person drawn from other disciplines can be described and made accessible, thus, to heterogeneous kinds of analysis.

But not all persons are "models" or "representations." What is the relation between the human figure in words and the human figure in flesh? Fiction always asks us to believe in the meaningfulness of the identity between the two, even if it rarely specifies the nature of that identity. Literary scholarship itself speaks of characters as if they were real people and, just as frequently, warns us that they are not. Students often notice the apparent contradiction and make their teachers aware that we lack a theoretical account of the relation between the literary character and the human being. The following chapters begin to provide such an account by describing the habituation of the reader during the recognition of social persons (chapter 1), the intrinsic capacity of social persons simultaneously to refer to individual bodies and to personify social relations (chapter 2), the effects of historical and disciplinary discontinuities on figural art's ability to produce meaning (chapter 3), and the politics of the embeddedness of social persons in legal and constitutional locations (chapter 4). Throughout this book, I emphasize the strong arguments that representations of the person make about the intellectual, institutional, and political practices of social life.

I shall begin here with the examples of the Knight and the Prioress, familiar characters in Chaucer's General Prologue to *The Canterbury Tales*, in order to introduce a central feature of all characterization: that it makes meaning through reference to social persons. It will be important to demonstrate precisely how formal aspects of poetry produce our recognition of social persons.

On the badge, we recognize a human figure kneeling; in the General Prologue, we apprehend the Knight as a man riding when we notice repeated uses of the verb *riden* (to ride) and realize that posture and activity to be a synecdoche for his military adventures:

> A KNYGHT ther was, and that a worthy man,
> That fro the tyme that he first bigan
> To *riden* out, he loved chivalrie,
> Trouthe and honour, fredom and curteisie.
> Ful worthy was he in his lordes werre,   *war*
> And therto hadde he *riden*, no man ferre,   *farther*
> As wel in cristendom as in hethenesse,
> And evere honoured for his worthynesse;
> At Alisaundre he was whan it was wonne.
> Ful ofte tyme he hadde the bord bigonne   *sat in honor*

> Aboven alle nacions in Pruce;
> In Lettow hadde he *reysed* and in Ruce,   ridden on raids
> No Cristen man so ofte of his degree.
> In Gernade at the seege eek hadde he be
> Of Algezir, and *riden* in Belmarye.[8]

The figure riding a horse invokes a number of social persons as it moves through the portrait: one is the *crusader*, a mainstay of, for example, chronicle, sermon, and manuscript illumination. The stark global landscape divided into "cristendom" and "hethenesse" suggests the early English romance and its fabulously belligerent protagonist, the *romance knight*; the catalog of heathen places that follows, as Jill Mann has shown, is a feature of the chanson de geste and puts us in mind of its somewhat different hero-knight, the *knight of the chanson de geste*.[9] Two social persons here, then, are drawn from literary tradition and conjured by landscape.

Both posture and landscape—figure and ground—can call up social persons and the discourses out of which they grow, social persons that jostle together with those provided by means of simple nomination in the first line of the portrait: *knight, man*. In the context of the catalog of persons that is the General Prologue, "knight" in line 43 must refer to a person of a certain social class or estate; "worthy man" is its own broadly construed social person, evoking a kind of masculinity. Neither should we neglect the ideological discourse encapsulated in the second couplet's description of the Knight's love for chivalry: his embrace of the ethical values of chivalry describes a particular kind of knighthood that reveres riding horses and fighting as heavily coded moral and spiritual practices. This ethos strives to fashion its adherents into its own social person that is yet another model of *knight* that can be distinguished from the others present here. Let us call him the *chivalric ideal*. In the course of the portrait, as we discover our man's extraordinary success, we may add to this crowd of social persons that of the *victor*:

> At Lyeys was he and at Satalye,
> Whan they were wonne, and in the Grete See
> At many a noble armee hadde he be.
> At mortal batailles hadde he been fiftene,

8. Lines 43–57; italics mine. Unless otherwise noted, all quotations from Chaucer have been taken from *The Riverside Chaucer*, ed. Larry D. Benson, 3d ed. (Boston: Houghton Mifflin, 1987). "Reysed," from Middle Dutch and Middle Low German, is another word for "to ride" that is a specialized term for raiding campaigns. *Middle English Dictionary*, s.v. "reisen."

9. Jill Mann, *Chaucer and Medieval Estates Satire: The Literature of Social Classes and the General Prologue to the "Canterbury Tales"* (Cambridge: Cambridge University Press, 1973), 110–11.

And foughten for oure feith at Tramyssene
In lystes thries, and ay slayn his foo.   *formal duels*
(58–63)

Here we come close to the *triumphator* of Roman equestrian statuary and
civic procession, the social person that Theseus explicitly embodies in the
opening procession of the Knight's Tale. From this pinnacle of description
we both ascend and fall into the next four lines:

> This ilke worthy knyght hadde been also
> Somtyme with the lord of Palatye
> Agayn another hethen in Turkye;
> And everemoore he hadde a sovereyn prys.
> (64–67)

In line 47, we discovered our man in the person of the *feudal retainer*
through the evocation of relation in the phrase "his lordes werre";
throughout the catalogue of places nothing has moved us from the
thought that the riding was in knight-service to a Christian lord fighting
against heathen enemies or, possibly, in the mention of "Ruce," against
Christian heretics. Our sense of his prowess mounts as we find his theater
of war expanding to Turkey; however, with this expansion comes the new
knowledge that he has fought beside "the lord of Palatye," a heathen warring against another heathen. This war in Turkey appears to have no
Christian motive; nor are we told that he is there according to any feudal
obligation. The lack of explanation and the idiomatic phrase "sovereyn
prys" (which means he was "highly valued" in the non-economic sense of
having a superb reputation, yet uses economic diction) raise the somewhat
uncomfortable specter of the *mercenary soldier*, uncomfortable because it
is incompatible with the motive inherent in the social person (if not every
historical instance) of the *crusader*, who fights as a Christian religious
practice.

We need not embrace the portrait as satire or severe critique, as Terry
Jones and others have done, in order to perceive the character growing out
of these evocations of quite different models of the person, for as readers
we are engaged in a process of measuring the character by means of these
social persons.[10] That the social person of the mercenary has been evoked
in his portrait is a first-order judgment that admits, I think, of little con-

---

10. Terry Jones, *Chaucer's Knight: The Portrait of a Medieval Mercenary* (Baton Rouge:
Louisiana State University Press, 1980). For a rebuttal of Jones that gives an account of aristocratic crusading in the fourteenth century, see Maurice Keen, "Chaucer's Knight, the English Aristocracy and the Crusade," in *English Court Culture in the Later Middle Ages*, ed.
V. J. Scattergood and J. W. Sherborne (London: Duckworth, 1983), 45–61.

troversy. Whether the Knight's identity is that of a mercenary, however, is a second-order critical judgment and controversial. In assessing the role of the social person of the mercenary, it helps to compare this evocation to others, for example, that of the *mayde* in line 69:

> And though that he were worthy, he was wys,
> And of his port as meeke as is a mayde.   *deportment*
> (68–69)

The social person of the *mayde* comes to us in the form of a simile. The Knight is attributed meekness, a quality (unlike worthiness or wisdom) inappropriate to the social person of a knight—not, I stress, necessarily inappropriate to knights, but inappropriate to the social person. Insofar as it means unaggressive, weak, soft, lowly, abject, submissive, docile, or pliant, "meeke" suggests the opposite of the hardy, upright, aggressive nature of a knight. The near-paradox of a meek knight might have resulted in a satire of the kind suitable for Terry Jones's illustrious non-Chaucerian productions. Here, of course, its potential for hilarity is mastered by the evocation of the *mayde*, and meekness becomes a virtue we may admire in a fighter. Although the Middle English word "mayde," by virtue of implying chastity, can refer to men, as a social person it is overwhelmingly female.[11] No critic has yet written a book arguing that the character is a woman, perhaps because the simile instructs us to measure our character against the mayde, and thus to take an attribute that *is* a virtue in the latter *as* a virtue in the former. But the poem does leave open the question whether the character is a *mayde*—at least until the next portrait where we meet his son in the person of the Squire.

Similarly, the poem's description of the Knight's behavior in Turkey asks us to consider his prowess as geographically wide and highly prized. It leaves aside (and open) the question whether he is a mercenary and, further, whether such an identity is incompatible with his other identities, and whether that therefore makes him vicious and false. The role of the social person of the mercenary in the portrait is circumscribed by the description of the extent of his reputation. In my judgment, we are not explicitly invited to wonder whether he is really a mercenary or a woman, though we may wish to; the appearance of these social persons is not the true revelation of identity that overturns all the previous ones. Instead, these models of the person appear as outlying marks on the map of his character, as radar signals from further away than the others, as coordinates in terms of which we may chart the Knight's own place. They partic-

---

11. *Middle English Dictionary*, s.v. "maiden," sense 2d.

ipate in carefully structured ways in the process of characterization, but they are not properly referred to as among the Knight's identities. I would put the mercenary—together with the mayde and the *speaker of "vileynye"* (which appears under negation in line 70)—in the category of social persons that do not qualify as full-blown identities of the character, despite the fact that they figure prominently in his characterization. My point here is that the difficulty we experience in sorting out the degree of attribution in each case causes us to feel a density in the character, no matter which judgment we make. Social persons are, by definition, simple and thin; positioned among a number of them, a character takes on complexity and weight. The process of reading begins with recognition and moves quickly to deliberation.

The most important turn in the course of the portrait is not the swerve to Turkey, but the change in register that comes with the lines I will quote again:

> And though that he were worthy, he was wys,
> And of his port as meeke as is a mayde.
> He nevere yet no vileynye ne sayde
> In al his lyf unto no maner wight.   *person*
> He was a verray, parfit gentil knyght.
> But for to tellen yow of his array,
> His hors were goode, but he was nat gay.
> Of fustian he wered a gypon   *coarse cloth, tunic*
> Al bismotered with his habergeon,   *stained, coat of mail*
> For he was late ycome from his viage,
> And wente for to doon his pilgrymage.
>   (68–78)

The central figure of the portrait, the man riding, we now view against the animating background of Christian penitential theology, together with its ritual actions, virtues, and grooming of the body. Whereas social space provided the main parameters of the first half of the portrait, here we move to another world, that of habitus and manners: comportment, speech, ideological code (gentillesse), dress, and practice. Habitus and its shorthand, clothing, as so often in fiction and life, send a signal to us, and in receiving that signal we recognize the social person of the *pilgrim*. Because the holy land was the primary destination for Christian pilgrims as well as for crusading knights, the figures of the *crusader* and the *pilgrim*, two men riding, were indeed pervasive (and sometimes even made identical) in medieval ethical deliberations on the relation of the Christian West to its Eastern neighbors. The crusader and the pilgrim are the two primary evocations of the portrait. The tension between these social persons is high; they identify very different ideals, modes of dress, bodily practices, attitudes to others, places in the social fabric, experiences of the passions, postures before other cultures, uses of property, obligations, and even notions of time and space. That Chaucer is not the only medieval writer to bring these two social persons together takes none of this tension away; rather, we may see the power generated by such a catachrestic collocation in theologians such as St. Bernard of Clairvaux, who uses the two social persons together to make war nearly a sacrament, and in early romances such as *Sir Isumbras*, which find a spiritual process and basis for worldly property and power.[12]

The riding figure holds together the entire portrait, but it vacillates before us through many models of the person (I have counted at least thirteen distinct social persons in the portrait of the Knight). The process of vacillation itself develops the character—neither a crusader nor a pilgrim, alone, but something made of the alternation, like a flip-page book or a film that we perceive as integral, though it comes of many distinct still frames racing by our eyes. We experience Chaucer's Knight as if the many social persons that appear in his portrait were separate lenses of different distortion and each produced a flat image that combined with the others to construct the illusion of depth. These social persons are phantom templates by which we measure the Knight: they are in tension with one another and with our other senses of the character, and, as we apprehend him, we move out from the words to the social persons and back to the single described figure, in a kind of dialectical shuttle. With such mental acts of recognition and measuring, each of us locates the figure of the Knight in terms of whatever medieval and modern frameworks or maps of meaning comprise her or his learning. Insofar as we are readers, we welcome the richness of art that registers on such multiple sets of coordinates, and we embrace the opportunities art offers us for puzzling, for deliberation, and for judgment.[13]

The act of locating the character and reading its meaning against the co-

---

12. For Bernard, see Mann, *Chaucer and Medieval Estates Satire*, 108–9. For a consideration of the penance-oriented romance as a genre, see Hopkins, *The Sinful Knights*, especially 20–31.

13. The appreciation of multiplicity in art is surely one of the areas of deepest consensus in the aesthetics of the last century. From William Empson's ambiguity to Stephen Orgel's textual openness, literary critics have felt at home with undecidability. Openness is not an exclusively modern aesthetic value, of course, but in the pre-modern period it can look very different. I have already cited Carruthers' description of the topos as tool for an ethical process of thought. Warren Ginsberg uses Cicero's presentation of the rhetorical exercise "disputatio in utramque partem" (arguing an issue from both sides) to describe how Boccaccio and Chaucer represent personality in literary character in *The Cast of Character*, 98–133.

ordinates of social persons is a process of recognition and identification that moves in two directions.[14] We position the Knight on our maps of social meaning, and, in this same act, we are also positioning ourselves—responding in some way to an Althusserian "hail."[15] Figural representations draw us into their social landscapes: the act of cognition is the double act of finding our way around that social space and of finding ourselves there. Like other ritual experiences, reading "fashions" us, in Edmund Spenser's famous phrase.[16] Like other kinds of looking at images of people, I shall argue at length in chapter 1 that reading the human figure in words *habituates* us to social persons.

Because it is an activity designed to be repeated, we may aptly consider reading poetry a habitual practice, one that may produce the disposition of the student, the scholar, or the avid lay reader. According to Aristotle and his followers (I might mention Thomas Aquinas, Edmund Spenser, Marcel Mauss, and Pierre Bourdieu), such habits develop a durable disposition of the person that shapes character as well as the body.[17] By the term *habitus*, I shall refer to this shaped disposition of the body, brought about by frequent practices and functioning. Habitus, I shall argue, is a kind of glue that helps fit the body to the social person. We have glimpsed how the habitus of Chaucer's Knight is made up of his beliefs, actions, comportment, speech, expression, familiarity with and use of his possessions, his

14. On recognition as a constituent feature of image perception, see Michael Podro, chap. 1 in *Depiction* (New Haven: Yale University Press, 1998) and Kathy Eden, chaps. 1 and 3 in *Poetic and Legal Fiction in the Aristotelian Tradition* (Princeton: Princeton University Press, 1986). For a political treatment of recognition, see Charles Taylor, *Multiculturalism and "The Politics of Recognition": An Essay* (Princeton: Princeton University Press, 1992).

15. For "hailing" and the notion of interpellation, see Louis Althusser, "Ideology and Ideological State Apparatuses (Notes Towards an Investigation)," in *Lenin and Philosophy and Other Essays*, trans. Ben Brewster (New York: Monthly Review Press, 1971), 127–88. Judith Butler addresses the paradoxes of this topic in chap. 4 in *The Psychic Life of Power: Theories in Subjection* (Stanford: Stanford University Press, 1997).

16. Spenser gets his verb, ultimately, from Aristotle's notion of habituation; see the discussion in chapter 1.

17. Aristotle treats the process of habituation and its relation to the good state in the *Nicomachean Ethics*, ii.2. See also Aristotle, *The Categories of Interpretation*; Thomas Aquinas, *Summa theologica*, 2.1.50–54 and *Commentary on the Nicomachean Ethics*; Peter Abelard, *Collationes*; Edmund Spenser's letter to Walter Ralegh; Pierre Bourdieu, *Outline of a Theory of Practice*, trans. Richard Nice (Cambridge: Cambridge University Press, 1977), *The Logic of Practice*, trans. Richard Nice (Cambridge: Polity Press, 1990), or his essays in *Rethinking the Subject: An Anthology of Contemporary European Social Thought*, ed. James D. Faubion (Boulder: Westview, 1995); and Carruthers, *Book of Memory*, 180. Nicola Masciandaro has alerted me to the variety within this tradition; see especially Augustine's *Confessions* for a view of the durability of habit that is quite different from Aristotle's. Marcel Mauss, "Techniques of the Body," *Economy and Society* 2 (1973): 70–88 is a good introduction to the bodily shaping accomplished in the habitus.

dress. The habitus is the human being socialized—the shapeless, fleshy mass that has been licked into a bear cub by its mother, to use the traditional anecdote. The habitus is formed in part by the institutional contexts of our lives and in part by a psychological and aesthetic process of deliberate bodily postures and movements. We cultivate habits (including reading) in part as a process of identification with and against social persons, be it forced or voluntary, conscious or unconscious. We cultivate habitus as a mode of making ourselves understood in the social world; thus, too, habitus is cultivated in us by that world's understanding.

Chaucer captures more of the process of the habitus in his engaging portrait of the Prioress, who seems to see herself in terms of two social persons that are perhaps less compatible than the Knight's conqueror and pilgrim. Lexis is one of Chaucer's means of raising the two phantoms. Let us call them the *nun* and the *lady* and so assign them to their estates.[18] The two social persons share the cultivation of the practices of singing and speaking. Although we know that the practices are linked to different values and aims in the two persons, Chaucer stitches them together by choosing words that the reader can only just manage, with a bit of a stretch, to assimilate to both the nun and the lady:

> Ther was also a Nonne, a PRIORESSE,
> That of hir smylyng was ful symple and coy;
> Hire gretteste ooth was but by Seinte Loy;
> And she was cleped madame Eglentyne.   *called*
> Ful weel she soong the service dyvyne,
> Entuned in hir nose ful semely;
> And Frenssh she spak ful faire and fetisly,   *elegantly*
> After the scole of Stratford atte Bowe,
> For Frenssh of Parys was to hire unknowe.
>   (118–26)

As most readers have noticed, simplicity, coyness, seemliness, fairness, and elegance are all bursting at the seams here, strained by their double use. Similarly, the topoi suggested by the two social persons refer to different settings and have their historical counterparts in different insti-

---

18. The long-recognized tension in the Prioress between the nun and the courtly lady was first articulated by John Livingston Lowes, *Convention and Revolt in Poetry* (Boston: Houghton Mifflin, 1919), 60–67. Jill Mann's reading of the portrait places this tension within the rich traditions of estates satires and ideals. Mann stresses Chaucer's use throughout the portrait of "value-words" that "can be differently defined from different standpoints" (*Chaucer and Medieval Estates Satire*, 128–37); my stress upon the links among social person, habitus, language, value, and estate develops this early work of hers. For a reading of the Prioress's portrait as performing femininity, see Priscilla Martin, *Chaucer's Women: Nuns, Wives, and Amazons* (London: Macmillan, 1990), 30–35.

tutions. The lady of romance inhabits a courtly topos that has its counterpart in the aristocratic household. Prioresses, though, inspired the
writing of an administrative literature that represents space liturgically in
a way designed to govern the spiritual life of the convent. Though actual
households and priories are barely recognizable in the conventions of the
topoi, the two topoi have even less in common than do their institutional
counterparts. The two worlds, despite their differences, are knit together
in Chaucer's portrait by language and practices that can shift between
them: charity, pity, and *amor* are ideals of both the nun and the lady,
though they may suggest quite incompatible practices in each setting.[19]
For example, the object of the lady's pity is likely to be the wooing
courtier; the nun's pity, should it seek out the same object, would be scandalous indeed.

A topos and a corresponding social institution are stocked not only with
indigenous social persons but also with a repertory of such valued and depreciated passions, actions, plots, and genres. Weeping is a valuable action, under certain conditions, in both court and convent. If those conditions do not obtain, weeping can become—as it threatens to do in the
Prioress's portrait—comic, degraded, or vicious. Actions bind a character
to a topos through the habitus appropriate to the social person; weeping
binds the Prioress insecurely to both the habitus of the nun and the habitus of the lady. As the Prioress enacts her double process of identification,
like the Knight she cultivates the bodily habits of her social persons—
speaking, singing, weeping, and, especially, eating:

At mete wel ytaught was she with alle;	*dinner*
She leet no morsel from hir lippes falle,	
Ne wette hir fyngres in hir sauce depe;	
Wel koude she carie a morsel and wel kepe	
That no drope ne fille upon hire brest.	
In curteisie was set ful muchel hir lest.	*pleasure*
Hir over-lippe wyped she so clene	
That in hir coppe ther was no ferthyng sene	*i.e., drop*
Of grece, whan she dronken hadde hir draughte.	
Ful semely after hir mete she raughte.	*reached*
And sikerly she was of greet desport,	*deportment*
And ful plesaunt, and amyable of port,	*bearing*
And peyned hire to countrefete cheere	*a countenance*
Of court, and to been estatlich of manere,	
And to ben holden digne of reverence.	*worthy*

(127–41)

19. Here I repeat Jill Mann's point about diction in order to place it within the context of
social persons and topoi.

The posture or sculptural attitude of the figure is again important as we are invited to see the Prioress at table. The image refers not only to the table she heads as the leader of a spiritual community under an ecclesiastical rule of life that places ritual eating and fasting at the center of its symbolic order, but also to the banquet table at which ladies are trained to show exquisitely mannered styles of eating in order to express class status and intelligence. Such training and grooming for table manners is undergone especially by young women who contemplate the marriage market.[20] The poem does not instruct us to view the Prioress's attention to manners as vicious or virtuous. Instead, it alerts us to the rift between her manners and the usual social purpose of such behavior.[21] The habitus fashions the body, by means of a plenitude of minor and major practices, so that it fits into a particular social person, institution, and set of present and future social bonds. A lack of fit between habitus and office provides common fodder for poets.

Social persons, as we shall see throughout this book, depend not only upon their contexts of topoi and institutions, but also upon their positions in networks of social relationships. The social person of the nun is not simply one of the many hats an individual might interchangeably wear. *Amor vincit*—love chains one to and triumphs over—very particular others.[22] Nuns and ladies bond with and sever themselves from entirely different classes of persons. A lady presents herself well for a lover; a nun abjures lovers for her god. A lady's generosity might well fall upon exotic domestic pets, but we expect the object of a nun's charity to be the suffering poor. Social persons come in configurations with others, not on their own.[23] This thesis is pursued by my second chapter, which explores the consequences of the human figure's ability to personify social bonds.

Each of the following chapters describes how, by referring to social persons, single characters are able to convey arguments about larger social structures. Characterization also has a special ability, through mobilizing social persons, to engage the reader with ideas, propositions, and ideolo-

20. As Lowes notes, Chaucer takes the description of the Prioress's table manners from the *Roman de la Rose* (*Convention and Revolt in Poetry*, 63).

21. As A. C. Spearing points out, the images of food-spilling Chaucer uses to describe what the Prioress's manners carefully avoid ("no morsel . . . no drope . . . no ferthyng," 128–34) give a disgusting picture of what might result from a break in her self-control (personal communication, 19 October 2000). The cultivation of habitus, though it is often largely unconscious, requires effort and can fail.

22. For *vincit* as "binds," see John M. Steadman, "The Prioress' Brooch and St. Leonard," *English Studies* 44 (1963): 350–53.

23. In this sense, social persons work in ways analogous to the discursive positions described by various theorists: for instance, consider Michel Foucault's "enunciative function," as defined in *The Archaeology of Knowledge*, trans. A. M. Sheridan Smith (New York: Pantheon, 1972), 88–103.

gies. It is in good part due to our perceptions of social rules that remnants of the Prioress seem to obtrude beyond the margin when we see her through the lens of either social person. Despite the narrator's persistent appreciative use of the word "semely," it is difficult to assimilate the lavish spoiling of pets with meat and milk (146–47) into the social person of the nun or, conversely, to assimilate the vows of chastity and poverty into that of the lady. The ideological problems of fit have a fleshly expression in her description: the Prioress somehow seems to be a character whose animal body has not been properly shaped for the two persons—nun and lady—it aspires to occupy.

> Ful semyly hir wympul pynched was,
> Hir nose tretys, hir eyen greye as glas,   *well formed*
> Hir mouth ful smal, and therto softe and reed.
> But sikerly she hadde a fair forheed;
> It was almoost a spanne brood, I trowe;   *believe*
> For, hardily, she was nat undergrowe.
> Ful fetys was hir cloke, as I was war.
> Of smal coral aboute hire arm she bar
> A peire of bedes, gauded al with grene,   *set, beaded*
> And theron heng a brooch of gold ful sheene,
> On which ther was first write a crowned A,
> And after *Amor vincit omnia.*
>
> (151–62)

The slight misfiring of the habits designed to fit the Prioress into two social persons becomes a surplus of body that culminates in her ornament, the beads and brooch. This stage prop, whether we classify it (according to social person) as a rosary or as jewelry, brings the potential conflict between her social persons to a propositional crux: the motto *Amor vincit omnia* suits both perfectly but unsettles us nonetheless. Like her hyperbolic forehead, *omnia* includes too much and provides the reader with a way of unraveling the smooth weave of dominant cultural understandings of women, to see how ideals contain internal contradictions that allow us to measure, choose, and alter them. Chaucer's interest in the social form of the human figure generates the plan of the General Prologue, where portraits identified primarily by their social persons make up a long sequence. It is notable that he brings these concepts of the person before us as simultaneously, in the terms canonized by E. M. Forster, "flat" and "round," as nearly allegorical in their reference to abstract categories and as individuated instances of mixed success in the acquisition of habitus and the accession to multiple social persons.[24] Chaucerian characterization makes espe-

---

24. Forster, *Aspects of the Novel*, chap. 4, "People (continued)."

cially explicit the position of human beings within the overlapping force fields of cultural institutions and their forms of personhood. The feeling of ideological strain that we experience in *Amor vincit omnia*, produced by the tensions among social persons as they are embodied in a single character, is an effect loved by all four of the authors I treat here, though they turn it to different uses. Pictorial or verbal, then, human figures make claims upon us through a process fraught with passions and arguments.

Of course characterization is complexly woven into many formal features of literature and not accomplished by verbal portraiture alone, for nearly all the details and structures of texts are capable of contributing to characterization. A list of the textual cues for social persons that we have seen interpreted in my examples to this point would include bodily posture and gesture, topos, title, nomination, attribution, built space, mapped space, landscape, allusion, ritual, ceremony, specialized lexis, genre, ethos, ideology, iconography, social relations and bonds, values, virtues and vices, ideals and rules, narratorial attitude and tone, metaphor and other tropes, simile and other figures of speech, habitus, representations of the passions, allusions to social institutions and historical events, and literary conventions of characterization. In the chapters that follow, we will add to this list of prominent devices that evoke social persons.

The Four Parts of the Argument: Habituation, Social Bonds, Historical Time, the Polity

The familiar meanings of the term "person" are many: the human understood as an individual human being, as a somebody (a personage), as body (as in "on his person"), as role (particularly in acting), as grammatical point of view (as in "first-person narration"), as uniquely or intimately distinguished (what is "personal" to us), as a mode of deity (the three-personed god), as a legal fiction (the corporation), as a theological construct (the soul), and as variations on these themes.[25] Language has numerous subtle ways of referring to the human, and we use all of these kinds of reference to signify social persons.

Let me further define my main term. It is important that my Chaucerian examples not restrict us to the view that the social person is merely a new term for occupation or role. If that were so, we would need no new term. Social persons are abstract figurations of the human; the term refers to all figurations that attain recognizable, conventional status through use. The

25. The *Oxford English Dictionary*, 2d ed., s.v. "person," cites definitions for all these meanings, plus the technical zoological term designating "each individual of a compound or 'colonial' organism, having a more or less independent life . . . a zooid."

category of the social person includes many kinds: for instance, "legal persons" such as the corporation, the crown, and the privy council make up an important subset of social persons. So do civic agents such as council, sheriff, and the City of London; corporate entities such as guild and university; economic persons such as alewife, merchant, and buyer, but also labor and market; kinship designations such as mother, family, and heir; races and ethnicities such as Moor, Scythian, and Briton; and literary persons such as senex amans, author, and allegorical personification.[26] Social persons provide a shorthand notation that gives us enormous leverage in reference. Indeed, literary characters are largely cobbled together out of allusions to a number of social persons. In this way, social persons are like genres: they are abstract conventions that never actually "appear" in any pure form, but are the implied referents by which characters are understood. They are the collective imaginative technology that allows language to make a literary character (as well as to make the figures familiar in other discourses and disciplines), but, like chisels, scaffolding, and plans that have left their marks on a monument but since disappeared, social persons must be inferred from their artifactual traces if characterization is to be understood.

The four chapters of this book develop ways of thinking about the human figure in words that open up both formal and historical topics specific to poetry and that, nonetheless, draw strongly on the history of law, theology, economics, and political philosophy. Let me return to the little pilgrim badge of the Frontispiece as I begin to explain how. In the pilgrim's badge, we can readily see how the different social persons invoked by the figure of Thomas carry radically different ascriptions of intention. These ascriptions shape our interpretation of the action and the character of Thomas. If he is a condemned criminal, we must consider his actions in the light of disobedience to the crown, and his bowing of his neck to the swords then becomes a penitent admission of guilt and a submission to fate. The juridical process of killing is designed, like the guillotine, to absorb intention entirely in process so that the ritual stroke is given not by a human being but by a legal fiction, an intentionless agent of the state. If Thomas is, in the second view, the victim of murderers, his innocent intentions are displayed in his pious attitude of prayer, and the murderers' intentions are the object of our scrutiny. If he is, in the third view, a celebrant priest, his action is ritualistic and to be interpreted in the light of

26. On the history of the author, see A. J. Minnis, *Medieval Theory of Authorship: Scholastic Literary Attitudes in the Later Middle Ages* (London: Scolar Press, 1984) and Kevin Pask, *The Emergence of the English Author: Scripting the Life of the Poet in Early Modern England* (Cambridge: Cambridge University Press, 1996).

sacramental theology, which distributes intention among at least three persons: the priest's proper performance of the sacrament, God's grace, and the state of the receiving souls. The priest's interior state, theologians determined, is (within limits) irrelevant. The sacramental topos (like the topos of murder and unlike the topos of execution) shifts the weight of horror firmly away from the character of Thomas to crush the offending knights. These three alternative views of intention are all present in the image, though they are not equally weighted, of course, by its internal disposition. Rather, the disposition of the image invites the reader to measure the three constructions of intentionality against one another, even as it weights the evidence it provides.

Like the power of Chaucer's Pardoner's Prologue and Tale, which is the subject of the first chapter, the power of the badge depends not upon the correctness of the reader's choice but upon the process of his or her deliberation as the apparitions of social persons are considered according to the instruction of the details of the figure. My first chapter, "Character and the Habituation of the Reader: The Pardoner's Thought Experiment," investigates the habituation to social persons that may be accomplished through literary characterization.[27] In the Pardoner's case, that habituation concerns the experience of interior states, especially of intention. The conflicting social persons of the Pardoner—for example, the confessing sinner and simoniac minister—will serve to demonstrate the important role of social persons in the analysis of human intention. Like the classification of Thomas as a victim, which subjects the scene to a common law definition of how to construe intention in the case of murder, the classification of the Pardoner as a confessing sinner brings with it an entire intellectual discipline of intention: penitential practice and its codification in canon law. The classification of him as a simoniac minister brings with it a nearly reversed, though equally learned, construction of intentionality. I have already suggested that social persons serve Chaucer throughout *The Canterbury Tales* as ways of summoning complex configurations of meaning. In chapter 1, I consider the Pardoner frequently in the light of the Parson, who carries with him into the *Tales* a carefully elaborated index to the social persons that belong to the sacrament of penance. I also aim to describe how Chaucer's use of multiple intentional states within the form of characterization requires considerable technical innovation and makes important claims for poetry. In the Pardoner's Prologue and Tale, espe-

27. A thought experiment is an exercise of reasoning and imagination, rather than of empirical research; it is undertaken, usually by theoretical physicists or philosophers, as a kind of test or proof. I use the phrase throughout this book as a good description of the deliberative exercise in which fiction invites us to engage.

cially when paired with the Parson's Tale and the Retraction, Chaucer offers poetry as a third, new construction of intentionality and, with it, a new technology for producing interior experience.

Classifications like that of Thomas as victim and the Pardoner as a confessing sinner, together with their discursive contexts in common law and canon law, make clear not only how social persons shape our notions of intention and other interior states, but also how they organize our understanding of relations between people and distribute capacities among interlocked sets of persons. In the badge's pair of murderer and victim, common law notions of intention direct our focus to the murderer's action and volition. In the pair made up of justicer and criminal, our focus is shifted the other way—toward an assessment of Thomas's culpability. The second chapter, "Persons in the Creation of Social Bonds: Agency and Civil Death in *Piers Plowman*," considers this role of social persons in distributing capacities, agency, and roles across the population. The opening section of the fourteenth-century allegory *Piers Plowman* begins with a marriage plot concerning a female personification of the money economy; it ends instead with the surprising marriage of two male personifications of government. I argue that the allegory demonstrates the profoundly interdependent nature of social persons: they are not discretely individual, but fitted building blocks in the larger structure that is the polity. Social persons should be considered in light of their interdependence. "Baron" and "wife," for instance, are not intelligible except in a pair, and in that pair the two social persons juggle a complex division of labor. Langland, we shall see, depends on this binding function of the attribute of gender in the course of his political satire. The chapter explains that we do well to interpret even a single figure as the personification of a standpoint within larger configurations of social bonds. The implications of this axiom for the analysis of character are many. The primary role social persons play in the composition and interpretation of art is echoed and confirmed by their paramount role in the constitution of society. Social persons are instrumental in the process of fitting human beings into the positions offered by the polity and in the process of sorting and distributing people across the constitution. Thus, the history of social persons provides a record of the continual process of shaping the polity and making its parts fit together.

As the polity undergoes this process of continuous revision and remaking, the history of social persons is registered in the archeological traces of the centuries. Writing, because it richly employs figures of the human, gives us access to the temporal transience of social persons and to their double reach—their effects upon people's bodies (such as those detailed in chapter 1) and their effects upon people's bonds to others (such as those described in chapter 2). Having begun with Chaucer's Pardoner, my movement directly from Langland's Mede to Skelton's Elynour permits me to carry through an increasingly complex analysis of how economic thought depends upon the semiotics of gender. This analysis illuminates how social persons are instrumental in shaping the relations among groups or classes of human beings. The third chapter, "The Temporality of Social Persons: Value in 'The Tunnyng of Elynour Rummynge,'" concerns a poem that reveals how theories of economic value silently depend upon particular representations of the person that, if altered, have devastating effects upon the theories.

Skelton deftly evokes topoi as various as those we saw in the pilgrim badge. He depicts the topos of the market that is the mainstay of early economic thought, but he replaces the figure of economic person—the social person indigenous to that topos—with one drawn from clerical antifeminism. The two social persons represent entirely opposite theories of value. Economic person is a productive laborer; antifeminist person, to coin a term for that familiar figure of vice, is an incontinent wife. Each discourse employs habitus to suggest the practices we should expect from economic actors, but these practices too are sharply opposed: production for the economists, consumption for the antifeminists. The comically degraded topos of the market portrayed by Elynour's ale selling, I shall argue, amounts to an ingenious critique of the money economy. As it is in the little pilgrim badge, so too, in the poem, the notion of what is valuable is inextricably linked to particular social persons.

Further, the critique embodied in Skelton's poem has been lost, because the social person of the garrulous, incontinent wife that grew out of clerical antifeminist discourse necessarily underwent a transformation in the Reformation as the English church changed. The meanings of the pilgrim badge are also subject to the changing institutional history that preceded and followed its creation. The popular understanding of Thomas's death as a martyrdom rather than a just execution reflects in part (and is in part caused by) the shifting relations of church and state that precipitated the incident. The positive or negative charge that characterization can carry is a crucial weapon in the arsenal of writers and artists as they make political arguments. Like the charges that swirl around Thomas's figure, the negative charge of clerical antifeminist portraits of women needs to be placed within both social and intellectual history if we are to understand its persistence.

Social persons and their topoi are associated not only with particular eras, but also with particular landscapes: a bishop with a cathedral and a see, a criminal with a territory and a scaffold, an earl with a shire and a seat. Yet what happens when the landscape changes under the person? What happens when a set of social persons is transported not into new epochs, but new lands? Chapter 4, "Architectonic Person and the Grounds of the Polity in *The Faerie Queene*," considers some of the ways that social persons were altered and engineered by the English crown's attempts to solidify its control over sixteenth-century Ireland. I show how the relation between social persons and the nature of the polity, an important topic of early modern political philosophy and poetry, relies upon the criterion of *fit* to measure the justice of social relations throughout the polity. Literary character and the trope of personification, in particular, can test social arrangements against this criterion of justice. The chapter argues that contemporary legal strategies for creating and transforming social persons permeate Thomas Smith's constitutional philosophy and Edmund Spenser's poetics. The forms of the person we can trace among these related kinds of cultural production—legal history, poetry, and political philosophy—produced and were produced by the same historical events. The island of Ireland in the sixteenth century was full of people struggling over what social persons they would occupy, what the nature of their social relations would be, what kind of government they would answer to or participate in, what social landscape—what polity—would be the grounds of their dominion. The forms of person and the forms of space—geography and polity—are closely related in these records; both are felt intensely to be, as Smith and Spenser put it, mutable. The causes, the conditions, and the limits of that mutability of person and polity are a subject of jurisprudential and ethical importance both for sixteenth-century Europe and for us.

Consider again the example of the little badge. The interdependence of social person and place is clear: the figure of Thomas as a celebrant priest genuflects in a space we understand as before an altar; the murder victim falls in a dark place of ambush; the condemned criminal kneels upon a public scaffold in the place of his last repentance. Only the frame clarifies the place of the badge's scene by providing ornamental arches that indicate a cathedral roof. The protective, ominous arches hover scarcely a tiny hand's breadth above the heads of the figures. The badge thus contains a series of fictional spaces and constitutes part of a larger, moveable ritual of built space: a pilgrim obtained such a badge in Canterbury to mark a visit to the holy shrine. By wearing it, the pilgrim remained under the canopy of Ecclesia, within the corporate body of the church, even upon the journey home.

The badge's historical use may persuade us that the frame of the badge controls the meanings of the scene. That is, it unifies the tension between the three topoi by a pictorial frame that clearly represents church architecture (undoubtedly it was whole before the badge's left side was broken). However, there is another space that explodes out of the cathedral scene like a footnote or a hypertext button. On the ledge that supports the monk in cantilever over the altar is a tiny carved Calvary scene. The ledge itself is either a pulpit, an altar retable that provides a hiding place, or a witness box—depending on the social persons that we ascribe to the monk. Three crosses and three hanging figures protrude from the ledge in reverse hieratic scale: they are smaller than Thomas's hands. The space of Calvary, so important a point on the church's historical map of the world, is here both an allusion and a simile. It argues about the scene by inviting us to compare its plot with the scene around it, making a martyrdom and *imitatio Christi* out of Thomas's fate. So too does the ground of the badge's frame, where the symbol of the cross and the six letters of Thomas's name appear. Like many contemporary stained glass windows and illuminations, the badge provides a verbal foundation for the meaning of images.

The badge is a miniature, wearable piece of architecture designed to establish someone's participation in social space. The fictional space of the badge makes an argument about the most pressing issue that faced the English constitution in the time stretching from the middle ages to the beginning of the modern era: the relation between ecclesiastical and royal dominion. English thought about the relative claims to dominion of church and crown often had recourse to the scene of the slain Thomas, which provided a kind of limit case or test of the extent of royal power. The retelling of this story in the particular case of the badge places us under the cathedral roof, in the social space controlled by the church, and argues that our deliberations should be controlled by the church's claims—that Thomas's death takes place in the church and therefore our deliberations should proceed within the context of ecclesiastical dominion. This kind of spatial and institutional persuasion is what I have in mind when I compare Spenser's Ireland to the badge (and this is what I will elaborate in my fourth chapter, when I will discuss dominion further in relation to Spenser). In the space of art, and in how that space measures up to the ghostly real and imagined spaces invoked by social persons and their topoi, we see artists struggle with the configurations of established social structures, remapping the world according to their own arguments.

Poetry, though it is seldom possible to pin it on one's breast, is similarly designed to establish one's participation in social space. I have chosen two episodes of *The Faerie Queene* that imagine the polity in terms of fictional landscapes anchored firmly in geography: the estuary downriver from London where the Medway runs into the Thames (IV.xi–xii) and the landscape around Spenser's castle, Kilcolman, in Munster, Ireland (*Two Cantos of Mutabilitie*). Each episode generates a global, even cosmic, geography that is wildly political and inventive; each also employs social persons to connect that geography to accounts of the constitution so deeply in conflict that their jurisprudential drama takes on a tragic cast. The issue of dominion, that state of mixed person-and-polity, is brought before the reader with deliberative force that requires us to feel and think about our own existence in space as dangerously politically vexed. In the space of art, we become conscious of our own positions at the brink of the terrifying chasms between social spaces, spaces like polity and geography that claim to occupy the self-same place.

Social Persons among the Disciplines

In all, the chapters ahead take four issues that might normally be said to belong to philosophy (intention, agency, value, and dominion) and study them from a number of other points of view at once, but seldom in the contexts that we would now consider to be their natural habitat. My license for this peculiar behavior has been my interest in following questions when they lead out of their usual sphere of business. When one asks a philosophical question and looks for literary, legal, or economic answers, one risks fully satisfying the evidentiary requirements of no one. Yet directing such inappropriate questions is what my authors do so well. The four primary texts studied here contain extremely powerful characters, representations that have the capacity to cut across a vast number of cultural spheres and to assess the different models of person indigenous to each. Though today we treat these texts, produced between the mid-fourteenth century and the end of the sixteenth, as if they were written to further the literary canon, it is not at all clear that their authors understood themselves to be practicing the single discipline we call literature. What they do have in common is their profoundly figural quality: meaning develops in all four cases by means of an intense formal dependence on character. To take a question from one field and pose it to another is one of the special capacities of figural art and can, as I hope to show, enable a deep analysis of the forms of knowledge and of social life.

In late medieval and early modern England, we find the most imaginative representations of the person in poetry and the law, discourses that encourage the rethinking of concepts of personhood by abstraction, formal innovation, and responsiveness to social crisis. The focus of this book is upon problems that occur in the endowment of the person with the attributes of intention, agency, value, and dominion. My four main texts address controversies about the representation of the person in marriage doctrine, economic thought, antifeminism, moral philosophy, and jurisprudence—all parts of the legal canon of late medieval and early modern thought. I have sought to explain how forms of the person incorporate and regulate social relations, and how, through competing social persons, ideas and disciplines struggle for explanatory power. Such power is, I think, always the power to explain and establish authority over what is urgent and vexed in the experience of people at the time. A strong explanation is necessarily an action that changes human experience. It may well justify or incite action of less textual kinds, as the strong social analysis in *Piers Plowman* appears to have been important to the participants in the Rising of 1381.[28]

Both literary and legal representations of the person deliberate the language, standards, and concepts by which we understand social categories. Poetry has a pronounced tendency to use the allegorical function of language, which, as we shall see, enables it to bring together and assess many discursive models of the person despite their differing origins. Law has its own powerful conceptual habits, and all of the four main authors treated in this study draw strongly upon those special powers of legal representation. When characters appear in legal discourse, they are personifications of social relations. Law personifies social relations in order to perpetuate social structures, to facilitate judicial decision, to apply doctrines to particular people and so to naturalize judicial decision, or sometimes to avoid decision and dislodge an act from its conventional penalties. Legal terms such as "wife," "monk," "clerk," "bastard," "the reasonable man," and "feoffee" plainly do not refer to the natural bodies of particular human beings. It is not true that legal discourse simply makes its terms by abstracting our neighbors, our rulers, and us; the relations among social persons are paramount in such representations. Legal discourse also gives rights or accords agency to some things that are not human: for example, the crown, the church, guilds, cities, other corporate bodies, and even god (in trial by ordeal, god is asked to make a decision). These personified entities also stand for social relations rather than for particular people. The crown stands not for a particular Richard II, but for a particular set of institutional arrangements, for the set of relations between the particular Richard II and the particular people who are, for example, his councilors, his tenants, the City of Westminster, his subjects.

Legal conventions in the treatment of the person recognize this fictional quality. F. W. Maitland frequently uses the term "personification" while writing the history of the law of corporations, finding the origins of the process of legal personification called "incorporation" in the relation between medieval "persons" or parsons and their parsonages, the forms of universities and convents, and in kingship. He traces personification through English political theory as lawyers found ways of making distinc-

---

28. On this question, see Steven Justice, chap. 3 in *Writing and Rebellion: England in 1381* (Berkeley: University of California Press, 1994).

tions between forms of property and dominion associated with the crown.[29] Ernst Kantorowicz's influential *The King's Two Bodies*, a study in what his subtitle calls "mediaeval political theology," continues this line of inquiry, showing the theological origins of certain modes of personification in the English theory of kingship.[30] We might view the Christian trinity itself as an elaborately defined agency relation, separating a single god into three persons with complementary faculties; we should study debates about that relation together with the history of other controversies about social relations.

Three technical terms (legal persona, juridical person, and natural person) help to distinguish between levels of "incarnation" in the legal use of the term person. Legal persona is a position in a network of human relations, made "human." *Black's Law Dictionary* defines it and quotes a related legal maxim:

> **Persona.** Lat. In the civil law. Character, in virtue of which certain rights belong to a man and certain duties are imposed on him. Thus one man may unite many characters, (*personae,*) as, for example, the characters of father and son, of master and servant. . . .
> **Persona est homo cum statu quodam consideratus.** A person is a man considered with reference to a certain *status*.[31]

"Persona" is a term of reference for that kind of legal person that is openly acknowledged to be of a constructed nature, yet is grounded in so-called natural person. "A man" (natural person) has "a status" or "many characters" (personae, or what we might call roles). Persona, then, has a dual status that is both socially constructed and natural, as opposed to juridical person that in itself is wholly spiritual or disembodied.

"Juridical person" specifically indicates corporations, entities that in spite of a lack of human physiology are treated through a well-established legal fiction as having certain rights and responsibilities due to persons. "Natural person" means simply "human being," the term meant to get furthest away from legal fiction. In fact, the idea of the juridical person is not fully distinguished from the concept of the natural person in English law until the work of theorists such as the sixteenth-century law reporter Edmund Plowden.

The relational nature of social persons makes personification instru-

---

29. E.g., Frederick Pollock and Frederic William Maitland, *The History of English Law Before the Time of Edward I*, 2d ed. (Cambridge: Cambridge University Press, 1923), 1:486–526.

30. Ernst H. Kantorowicz, *The King's Two Bodies: A Study in Mediaeval Political Theology* (Princeton: Princeton University Press, 1957).

31. *Black's Law Dictionary*, rev. 4th ed. (St. Paul, Minn.: West, 1968).

mental in the process of building social structure and distributing capacities and faculties across the culture. The legal persons "wife," "parson," "baron," "master," and "ward," for example, point to established models of affiliation in pre-modern English society, defined respectively in the legal "coverture" established by marriage, the forms of ecclesiastical corporations, and the feudal relations of tenure, of indenture, and of wardship. These relations, like many others, involved a specially structured agency in which the ability of one human being to act or intend was in many or all of its capacities transferred to another. The second person, by a kind of conceptual incorporation, stood for the first in a political and social sense: the husband for the wife, the baron for the tenant, the master for the indentured servant, the lord for the ward. The rights of one to the use of the labor, property, or body of the other, along with certain responsibilities toward him or her, were granted to some definite extent in all these cases. Those rights and responsibilities were passed on to the next occupant of the social person in the case of the lord who held tenants and wards, and to a lesser extent in the cases of husbands (children complicated matters) and of masters of indentured servants. In the Year Books of Henry VI it is stated that " 'the chapter is *covert* by the dean as the wife is *coverte* by her husband.' "[32] Marriage was a well-understood model that could be employed to explain other kinds of relations. Langland's king employs a parallel logic when he proposes, as we shall see in chapter 2, that the character Mede should be married to, and thus be *coverte* by, Conscience in order that the economy be *covert* by moral reason. Legal persons serve many purposes in juridical practice; they are the means of fitting people into the structures of the polity.

A catalog of a society's dominant forms of social person would describe not only its members, but also its constitutional shape, because the forms should fit one another and fit the institutional arrangements of the polity. Jurisprudence relies heavily on social persons: positive law accords legal person a privileged role as the gateway by which human beings come under legal control or jurisdiction. The paramount status of person in ancient Roman jurisprudence establishes the literary form of the western legal treatise, in which the "law of persons" constitutes the first major category and section. Such treatises conceive of law as primarily relating to persons rather than geographical regions, political territories, or religious institutions. Endowed with this centrality of person, Roman law became a primary source for the canon law of the medieval church and then for modern codifications of western customary law, reinforcing the predominant status of the concept of person in these canons of thought and prac-

---

32. Pollock and Maitland, *History of English Law*, 1:491.

tice. The primary form taken by the law's social persons is fundamental to the deep structure of our own political economy. Corporations qualify as legal persons, and can act, be imputed intentions, carry blame, and make contracts apart from their shareholders. Family law began only in the nineteenth century to imagine married women as endowed with rights attributed to the individual; for centuries in the West, the married couple had been treated by the law and tax systems as one person, incorporated in the husband, under the doctrine of "unity of person." (Marital *unity of person*, a complex social person crucial not only to law but to theology and political philosophy, will be discussed in chapters 2 and 4.) Social persons that have their origins in legal thought can be found exerting their power over many apparently unrelated areas of the culture.

The amount of legal history in this book raises a question about the nature and origin of social persons: are they a kind of rule in themselves? Are they inherently oppressive? They are, I would venture, inherently socializing. There is no social life without powerful representations of the human. Like language, social persons are quasi-consensual: if no one finds a representation of person convincing or meaningful, it fades away and never attains the paradigmatic, conventional status that qualifies a figure to be a social person. However, this consensual quality of social persons must not distract us from the fact that nobody ever chooses or even knows exactly what she is consenting to when she recognizes or accedes to a given social person. Still, to some certain extent, circumscribed by all kinds of material and immaterial conditions, it is hers to reinvent. The figure of a wife, for instance, has a predominantly practical existence—an existence in practice. It is not wrong to say that "a wife" is the sum of what everyone acts as if it is. Like genre, the social person is a custom honored most powerfully in a thousand breaches—a cognitive projection that helps explain specific connections between thought, language, and action, but that is never itself completely explained as thought, language, or action.

Throughout history, we continually make, dispute, and re-make social persons in the course of our cognitive and practical organization of the world. What does a society personify and endow with agency and intention? What personifications can produce value or claim dominion? The category of person does not include all human beings, nor does it consist only of human beings. Remembering that debates on the law of slavery consider whether a slave is "person" or "property" reveals how much can be at stake in such definitions.[33] One might assume that the individualism

---

33. Orlando Patterson's work shows how slavery is a relation that constructs the person "owner/master" as much as it constructs the human object of that ownership (e.g., *Slavery and Social Death: A Comparative Study* [Cambridge: Harvard University Press, 1982]). See

so strongly underwritten by contemporary culture solves this kind of problem easily, but controversies over the legal and medical technologies of birth, abortion, intelligence, death, and murder prove that the definition of the person cannot be regarded as simple, natural, or settled in any age, no matter how individualist its culture. Neither are our ideas about corporate persons more stable: political groups from the level of the voting district to the continent are painfully difficult to define with a clear sense of just principles. Individualism suggests that endowing as many biological organisms as possible with the gift of independent humanity is just, but it is not always sufficient or desirable to recognize as persons all the individuals who need to be protected by the sphere of rights and immunities that humanity should confer. Daily life, both private and public, is full of such dilemmas. Power and stewardship must be gained, conferred, limited, transferred; trade and collaboration must be encouraged and made just; participation in the polity as well as protected retreat and dissent must be fully possible; independence and responsibility must be equally full. All of these ideals and paradoxes present themselves to us continually. The arguments of person—the arguments made by particular social persons as well as those that are made about them—are at the heart of such questions of social justice. This book is an attempt to raise our level of expertise in assessing figures of the human by offering formal tools for use across disciplines and historical periods.

The Aims of This Book

I wish to extend the range of our formal and historical treatment of character. "Character" is the literary representation of person, and we should understand it as comparable to the representations of person in other spheres of cultural practice. In other words, "character" is to literary discourse what "economic person" is to economics, what "legal person" is to the law, what a "Christian soul" is to theology, what the "female nude" is to painting: each is a dominant model of person that has grown out of a social practice—a practice that has its own institutions, behaviors, artifacts, motives, social effects, audiences, and intellectual issues.

In this book I propose that "character" is how literature expresses the human figure in its social form. Literature is not the only verbal art; all

---

also Patricia Williams, "On Being the Object of Property," in *The Alchemy of Race and Rights* (Cambridge: Harvard University Press, 1991), 216–36. Post-colonial theory posits a similar dual construct; see Frantz Fanon, *Black Skin, White Masks*, trans. Charles Lam Markmann (New York: Grove Weidenfeld, 1967); and Ashis Nandy, *The Intimate Enemy: Loss and Recovery of Self under Colonialism* (Oxford: Oxford University Press, 1983).

discursive practices, including the sciences, use some of the resources of fiction and personification to shape their own representations of the person. This is why formal literary analysis is a powerful tool for understanding the process of figuration when it occurs in any disciplinary context. Conversely, our literary acts of understanding the human figure in words continually involve us in placing characters against the background of social persons drawn from the entire palette of the disciplines. Genre helps us understand what a particular sonnet is doing; similarly, social persons help us understand a particular human figure as making certain kinds of alterations against a background of conventions, a background as wide as the entire culture.

Together with this broadened view of what character is, this book proposes that we treat the details of all such forms of representing the person with a strengthened literary attention. It will already be apparent from the pages on legal persons that this book, under the influence of F. W. Maitland and others, considerably expands the sense and capacities of the rhetorical term "personification." The marks of historical and political life are etched upon fictional characters by their uses of social persons and become accessible through an analysis that is able to treat the complex structure of those marks. The nature of social persons of all kinds is, as we shall see in chapter 2, inherently allegorical: social persons personify positions in the network of social structures. This quality makes them susceptible to what literary theorists call "allegoresis," and this book will propose a method (especially in chapter 2) and a theory (especially in chapter 4) of figural meaning that has personification at its core.

My analysis depends upon and extends previous thought about allegory and personification. Like other scholarship, mine offers an historical warrant in authors like Edmund Spenser and John Harington. Unlike literary theories that have grown out of biblical exegesis, mine does not preselect contexts for the poem's "levels" of meaning. Instead it requires us to trace the specific verbal cues of the poetry, thus satisfying what we might call the "Alpers criterion" after Paul Alpers' eloquent call to tie interpretation firmly to the textual details of Spenserian allegory.[34] On the other hand (of rhetorical analysis), unlike Maureen Quilligan's careful account of allegory as arising out of specific language (in the extension of puns), Rosemund Tuve's account of it as arising out of specific iconography (in conventional images), or R. W. Frank's account of it as arising out of specific names (in kinds of personification), my account allows us confidently to

---

34. Paul J. Alpers, *The Poetry of "The Faerie Queene"* (Princeton: Princeton University Press, 1967).

interpret a broad range of the literary, social, and institutional references of the form, placing them in history.[35] Like Quilligan and Stephen Knapp, I hope to revive the interest of critics and historians of post-1800 culture in forms of personification.[36] Further, in my exposition of the habituation to social forms achieved by characterization, I intend to provide a fuller account of the consequences of readerly cognition and experience than those put forward by C. S. Lewis, Angus Fletcher, Rosemund Tuve, D. W. Robertson, Morton Bloomfield, Paul de Man, and Mary Carruthers.[37]

Of course, this book might have been a history of characterization or charted literary characterization in relation to the history of dominant social persons. Here and there, fascinating trails of literary history have intersected with the present book's trajectory and have been difficult to resist. It has seemed to me, however, that working out some of the formal, theoretical, and methodological problems that attend representations of the person is a condition of our ability to write the histories of literary

35. Maureen Quilligan, *The Language of Allegory: Defining the Genre* (Ithaca: Cornell University Press, 1979); Rosemund Tuve, *Allegorical Imagery: Some Mediaeval Books and Their Posterity* (Princeton: Princeton University Press, 1966); Robert Worth Frank, Jr., "The Art of Reading Medieval Personification Allegory," *English Literary History* 20 (1953): 237–50.

36. Steven Knapp, *Personification and the Sublime: Milton to Coleridge* (Cambridge: Harvard University Press, 1985).

37. C. S. Lewis, *The Allegory of Love: A Study in Medieval Tradition* (Oxford: Oxford University Press, 1936); Angus Fletcher, *Allegory: The Theory of a Symbolic Mode* (Ithaca: Cornell University Press, 1964); Tuve, *Allegorical Imagery*; Robertson, Jr., *A Preface to Chaucer*; Morton W. Bloomfield, "Allegory as Interpretation," *New Literary History* 3 (1972): 301–17; Paul de Man, "The Rhetoric of Temporality," in *Blindness and Insight: Essays in the Rhetoric of Contemporary Criticism*, 2d ed. (Minneapolis: University of Minnesota Press, 1983), 187–228; Mary Carruthers, *The Book of Memory* and *The Craft of Thought: Meditation, Rhetoric, and the Making of Images, 400–1200* (Cambridge: Cambridge University Press, 1998). Other influential accounts of allegory include Erich Auerbach, "Figura" [1944], trans. Ralph Manheim, in *Scenes from the Drama of European Literature* (Minneapolis: University of Minnesota Press, 1984), 11–76; Thomas P. Roche, Jr., *The Kindly Flame: A Study of the Third and Fourth Books of Spenser's "Faerie Queene"* (Princeton: Princeton University Press, 1964), 5–15; Elizabeth Salter and Derek Pearsall, introduction to *Piers Plowman*, ed. Salter and Pearsall, York Medieval Texts (London: Edward Arnold, 1967), 3–28; Michael Murrin, *The Veil of Allegory: Some Notes Toward a Theory of Allegorical Rhetoric in the English Renaissance* (Chicago: University of Chicago Press, 1969); Stephen A. Barney, *Allegories of History, Allegories of Love* (Hamden, Conn.: Archon Books, 1979); Jon Whitman, *Allegory: The Dynamics of an Ancient and Medieval Technique* (Cambridge: Harvard University Press, 1987); Theresa M. Kelley, *Reinventing Allegory* (Cambridge: Cambridge University Press, 1997). Important corrections to the recovery of historical practices of allegoresis are made by Mary Carruthers, who urges us to see the levels of biblical exegesis as referring to steps in an ethical process of reading rather than a set of propositions (*The Book of Memory*). Gordon Teskey calls such a focus on readerly practice "allegorical aesthesis" in his excellent brief introduction to the history and theory of allegory in *The Spenser Encyclopedia*, ed. A. C. Hamilton (Toronto: University of Toronto Press, 1990), 16–22, developed in his *Allegory and Violence* (Ithaca: Cornell University Press, 1996).

characterization and of other forms of person. I have, therefore, resisted the temptation to follow not only the story of medieval forms of fictional character as they led into modern kinds, but also the similar stories of sexual persons, legal persons, economic persons, and racial persons. All of these topics appear frequently in the chapters ahead and will, I hope, encourage other scholars to consult again those histories that have been written and to write new histories with new ways of working in mind. This book is a book of theory and method, soaked in the historical details that will test and demonstrate its principles. I have tried to bridle the book's impulses to historical narrative so that I could provide myself and others with a better theoretical foundation for producing such narratives. I have attempted, for similar reasons, to handle carefully the book's explorations of philosophical materials. I intend to clarify and explicate the process of deliberation that is embodied in human figures, not merely to enact that process or, worse, to resolve it.

For it is the process of deliberation that is paramount here. These chapters show how, as we begin to experience words, images, emotions, and ideas according to the instructions of the text, the authors invite us to undertake figuration as a species of philosophical thought experiment. This is not only a literary experience but a political one. In the experiment of deliberation, we consider what seems good from the position of each social person, always in conjunction with justice as it is exemplified by an entire system of social life. Rather in the way that the *demande d'amour* leads us to deliberate about the amusing situations hypothesized in romance, all fiction puts its readers in the position of evaluating the social persons that fashion its characters. By means of character, fiction tests the forms, both ethical and political, of social life. This cognitive, moral process, I submit, gives fiction its literary shape, its ethical habituation, and its political force.

Chapter One

Character and the Habituation of the Reader: The Pardoner's Thought Experiment

A rt is the habituation of bodily experience. The feelings and thoughts that fiction stirs up in us are signposts upon a map of the world that offers to tell us where we are, and who we are. The strongest habituator among all the shapes that language can conjure is character, because the figural representation of the person carries an explicit invitation to imagine the social shape of the human. When the human figure appears in words—in the tiniest evocative detail or the most generalized type—it offers the reader something like a pair of sleeves and a neck opening, a doorknob, a mirror, a climbing rope and a foothold, a deictic marker that allows the matching of voice to voice and epistemological standpoint to epistemological standpoint, or an X on the map that allows one to calculate the direction and distance between one's body and the treasure of meaning. The task of interpreting the figure requires each reader to align herself or himself, cognitively and affectively, with the world that is conjured by words.

Every reader of English is aware that poets use representations of the person in order to produce a strong experience of interiority, a sense of the richness of the inner life. But nothing about words on the page or verse in the ear suggests particularly that they might provide the means to such an experience. And nothing about, say, reported speech or personification allegory seems necessarily suited to a description of belief, cognition, passion, or intentional states.

In this chapter, I investigate how poetry uses social persons to make claims upon our inner lives.[1] First, the case of Geoffrey Chaucer's *Canterbury Tales* allows us to compare poetry to other cultural practices of interiority, because it seems to challenge the power over subjective experience wielded by fourteenth-century devotional practice. Throughout the chapter, the Pardoner's portrait, Prologue and Tale and the Parson's Tale will exemplify Chaucer's renovation of fiction. We shall search the Pardoner's Prologue and Tale for representations of interior life, especially states of intention, and discover how carefully they are tied to the complex social person of the medieval pardoner. Then the long middle section of the chapter traces the origins and habitat of that social person in canon law, theology (here, the Parson helps), and the commercial practices of the institutional church. Equipped with a thicker description of the social person and its legal, intellectual, and ecclesiastical history, we then return to the peculiar portrait of the Pardoner in the General Prologue and derive Chaucer's depiction of habitus from the origins and history of the social person.[2] We are then in a position to return to a reading of the Pardoner's Prologue and Tale and the Parson's Tale that can properly consider the process of habituation, the fitting of the human body to the social person by means of habitus. In the final section of the chapter, this time under the influence of Chaucer's Retraction, we search out the historically evolving role that the practice of reading plays in the habituation of the reader to social persons.

I am drawn to the example of *The Canterbury Tales* by the prominent role of persons in the poem. Chaucerian character invites us to perform a set of ethical exercises or thought experiments about the representation of the person. Every word of the *Tales* is attributed to someone, and many words are assigned to more than one voice; Chaucer himself occasionally appears within the fiction in the persona of a reporter present at the scene.[3] Speaking characters seldom bear proper names, but, rather as if they were all sent by central casting, they are called by the names of their occupations and social types. Each has the unmistakable air of deriving from at least one familiar sphere of culture or estate: the tavern, war, the

1. See the Introduction for my term "social person," which is central to the argument of the book.

2. Here I use the Aristotelian and scholastic term "habitus" revived by Marcel Mauss and, later, Pierre Bourdieu. See the Introduction for more on the habitus.

3. The limits of this pervasive attribution are also important, as A. C. Spearing's work on the range of subjectivity-effects in medieval poetry shows, e.g. "Prison, Writing, Absence: Representing the Subject in the English Poems of Charles d'Orléans," *Modern Language Quarterly* 53 (1992): 83–99. I attempt here to account for the power and the function of persons in Chaucer without using that topic as a warrant to convert all other aspects of the poem (particularly its presentation of ideas, affect, and sensual experience) to the psychological portrayal of the pilgrims.

court, the feudal household, the convent, commerce, the university, the law, the manor, the guild, medicine, marriage, the parish, agriculture, the church courts, and so on. On one side, these characters are representations of the bodily dispositions produced by the practices of those spheres and estates—the manners, affect, grooming, dress, gestures, and other shaping habits that engineer the character's habitus. On the other side, Chaucerian characters derive from social persons, the powerful conventional forms of the person that populated and were reproduced by the same institutions of medieval life.

Character, as we shall repeatedly find, is built out of a collection of details, fragments that are traceable to their lexical or iconographical locations in one or more sphere of culture. Understanding the source materials of character allows us to explain how powerfully referential it is and how it can reflect upon and assess a society's institutions and ideals. Character's social reference is accompanied by an equally powerful capacity to invade our most private experience: character appeals to affect and cognition, and thus it brings into being our interior experience as we read.

Psyche's Priests: Chaucer's Project and the Pardoner's Intention

> Yes, I will be thy priest, and build a fane
>   In some untrodden region of my mind,
> Where branched thoughts, new grown with pleasant pain,
>   Instead of pines shall murmur in the wind.
>   John Keats, "Ode to Psyche"

One of Chaucer's greatest achievements is his fashioning of fictional character into a technology for the experience of what Augustine directs us to find "in interiore homine" (in the inward man): the kind of experience that, for centuries before Chaucer, had been the domain of religious practices.[4] What is interior need not be individual (indeed, in the *Confessions* Augustine warns it must not be) but is defined by opposition to an inherently social exterior. The interior is usually conceived of as a world

4. "Noli foras ire, in teipsum redi; in interiore homine habitat veritas," Augustine, *De vera religione,* in *Patrologia Latina,* ed. Jacques-Paul Migne, 34:154. Charles Taylor, who uses the phrase "in interiore homine" as the title of a chapter on Augustine and inwardness, translates this maxim as "Do not go outward; return within yourself. In the inward man dwells truth." Charles Taylor, *Sources of the Self: The Making of the Modern Identity* (Cambridge: Harvard University Press, 1989), 129. Though I am frustrated by Taylor's approach to history, his book's philosophical interests have richly influenced this chapter (see the Afterword, note 2). For more on the self, see my "Chaucer and the Elizabethan Invention of the 'Selfe,'" in *Approaches to Teaching Shorter Elizabethan Poetry,* ed. Patrick Cheney and Anne Lake Prescott (New York: Modern Language Association, 2000), 249–55.

apart from some "exterior" social world, and it may well offer its own institutions and politics—as do Augustine's inward "veritas" and modern
feminism's "personal" consciousness, each a form of inwardness that issues in a politics. The movement of experience from the interior to the exterior of the person is often closely regulated by a society: when social conflicts can be resolved "inside" bodies they needn't be understood as
conflicts between people or as requiring changes in social arrangements.[5]

Psychology, which is today's strongest competitor for the territory "in
interiore homine," has mapped and renamed it the "mind." Modern psychological paradigms can explain the characters of the *Tales* "retroac-
tively," as it were, translating the characters for contemporary readers by
means of references to a new set of figures. Although I aim to identify medieval representations of the person in these characters, that makes me no
more immune to the charge of retroactivity. In analyzing the histories and
workings of social representations of the person, including literary character, my task is not to purge us of our own categories of thought and feeling, but to give a history to them by tracing the changing intellectual and
institutional shapes of medieval and early modern social life.

Medieval Christianity offered itself as a supremely satisfying form of interior experience by providing techniques for the cultivation of the soul,
an ancient and powerful representation of the person.[6] In the recorded experiences of model personages (for example, in Bible stories and drama,
exercises built around Christ's passion, liturgical rituals, hagiography,
books of hours, and conversion narratives such as Augustine's *Confessions*), Christians had access to richly emotional and ideational experiences centered upon the repetition of the interior lives of others whose
souls had been earnestly cultivated. Another form of exercise of the soul,
the sacrament of penance, became increasingly widespread and affectively
oriented during the thirteenth century, as penitential theology became
more concerned with interior experience. At the time of Chaucer's birth,
penitential discourse had perhaps the most authoritative claim of all forms
of English cultural practices to explain the meaning of what was "in interiore homine."

Sacramental theology no longer dominates English language culture,
and in literary history Augustine's *Confessions* has come to be seen not as

---

5. This is a central issue for Tibetan societies, according to Robert R. Dejarlais, *Body and
Emotion: The Aesthetics of Illness and Healing in the Nepal Himalayas* (Philadelphia: University of Pennsylvania Press, 1992).

6. Though it can also refer to a part of a person (in opposition, say, to the body), "the
soul" is indeed a social representation of the person, a figure for the human. A "soul" is a
synonym for an individual in colloquial English, and it possesses its own visual convention:
the soul often appears as a (tiny) human figure in pre-modern painting.

a founding constitution for the armies of workers cultivating and organizing the territory of the interior, but, somewhat bathetically, as an autobiography—merely one of the early glimmers of a literary genre centered on the self rather than the soul. Psyche's territory is no longer controlled by the ecclesiastical discipline of the soul; in the late middle ages and the Reformation, with Chaucer's help, psyche's territory was partly captured by the explanatory power of literature.

As we shall see, *The Canterbury Tales* stretch and expand the capacities of the device of character, the poet's representation of the person. In the *Tales*, all that has belonged to the domain of literary character in the past, together with the newly claimed interior, becomes an arena for flexing the muscles of character. Chaucer's poetry suggests that fiction-makers—not canonists, or moral theologians, or parsons—are the truly expert analysts of the human character, of human motive, action, passion, belief, and intention. He presents poetic character as a more moving and compelling vehicle for these insights than is the theological discourse about penance.

Not that Chaucer abandons confessional and penitential discourse; indeed, we have long recognized that Chaucer depends upon them, especially upon penance's legal jurisdiction, the confessional. Aptly named the law's "internal forum" by the church, the confessional was distinguished from the law's "external forum," the ecclesiastical courts. The last tale of *The Canterbury Tales*, that of the Parson, is a penitential manual based on two widely read and translated Latin works by the monks Raymund of Pennaforte and William Peraldus.[7] The Retraction that then follows, itself a penitential scene, formally imitates a confession. We shall visit that scene at the end of this chapter.

Scholars have also situated the Pardoner's Prologue among its sources in penitential literature.[8] Though I shall argue here that Chaucer's use of the tropes and vocabulary of confession is antagonistic, I do not mean to suggest that Chaucer is against confession or that he is not a "believer."

---

7. Raymund of Pennaforte's treatise is incorporated in Gratian's *Decretum*, the authoritative compilation of the canon law. The *Decretum* occupies the first volume of *Corpus iuris canonici*, ed. Emil Friedberg (Graz: Akademische Druck- u. Verlagsanstalt, 1955); the first part of the *Decretum* has been translated as *Gratian: The Treatise on Laws (Decretum DD. 1–20) with the Ordinary Gloss*, trans. Augustine Thompson and James Gordley (Washington: Catholic University of America Press, 1993).

8. See Mary Flowers Braswell, *The Medieval Sinner: Characterization and Confession in the Literature of the English Middle Ages* (Rutherford, New Jersey: Fairleigh Dickinson University Press, 1983); and Lee Patterson, *Chaucer and the Subject of History* (Madison: University of Wisconsin Press, 1991), 367–421. Rita Copeland writes about the discipline of the Pardoner's rhetoric: "The Pardoner's Body and the Disciplining of Rhetoric," in *Framing Medieval Bodies*, ed. Sarah Kay and Miri Rubin (Manchester: Manchester University Press, 1994), 138–59. I build upon their work here.

Rather, I will argue that Chaucer's work narrows the meaning of confessional discourse, reduces the sphere of its explanatory power, and further—the particular thesis of this chapter—that in the Pardoner's Prologue and Tale Chaucer demonstrates the incoherence of the canon law's command over the interior in order to claim this territory for poetry.[9]

I do not mean to suggest that the truth-value attributed by the poem to the Parson's Tale is in any way compromised. But the status of the Parson's Tale as literary fiction is extremely pale (A. C. Spearing voices a familiar sentiment when he calls it "tedious"[10]), and this pallor serves, among other things, to make us aware of the high standard of characterological vivacity that the *Tales* put forward. According to Chaucer's standard of figural representation, the Parson's doctrinal abstractions have lost their status as the best explanation of what people are like inside. When we accept that the territory "in interiore homine" has been mapped by Chaucer *as character*, the map that views it *as soul* no longer seems to afford us as deep an experience of the interior. The Parson's arguments become true in a second sense, now alienated; a truth one step removed, they stand outside of the project of describing the newly conceived interior.

The *Tales* share their project with Gower's *Confessio Amantis*, a poem that explicitly seeks to connect the penitential soul with the fictional persona. However, the *Tales* are more successful in constructing a serviceable third-person literary character that can bear the weight of fiction's power to explain interior experience without retreating from the busy, mundane world of human interaction.[11] Indeed, Chaucer's serviceable new version

9. Britton J. Harwood stresses the importance of notions of interior and exterior to the portrayal of the Pardoner in "Chaucer's Pardoner: The Dialectics of Inside and Outside," *Philological Quarterly* 67 (1988): 409–22.

10. Introduction to Geoffrey Chaucer, *The Pardoner's Prologue and Tale*, ed. A. C. Spearing (Cambridge: Cambridge University Press, 1965), 25.

11. See Braswell's *Medieval Sinner* for the argument that penitential discourse profoundly influenced the characterization deployed by the "belletristic literature" (16) of the late fourteenth century (Langland, Gower, the *Pearl*-poet, Chaucer). Chaucer does not perform these feats without precedent or company; we can trace how enthusiastically he borrows his project from writers in French and Italian. It has long been recognized that the most important literary source for the Pardoner is the wicked, persuasive, self-exposing Faus Semblant, an allegorical character in the *Roman de la rose* who passes himself off as a confessor. Among Chaucer's London contemporaries, the author of *Piers Plowman* is also concerned with the territory of the interior. His intensely experimental characterization continually transforms interior to exterior experience by personifying mental faculties and affects as bodies outside the subject. The allegory claims nothing for literary and fictional discourse; on the contrary, it is skeptical about literature both as a vocation and a cultural product and sees itself as a spiritual exercise. In the case of the *Confessio Amantis*, Gower's claim for poetry should be understood as an Aristotelian view that identifies ethics and political philosophy as the highest or architectonic science, but that also sees poetry as a worthy vehicle for these highest pursuits. On Gower's view of the disciplines, see James Simpson, *Sciences and the Self in Me-*

of character has borne that weight elegantly for some centuries. His characterization habituates its readers to imagining the person as a bodily container for interiorized conflicts among different social representations of the person: as we saw in the Introduction, the Prioress's personality is produced for us (and perhaps "for her") by the clash between the nun and the romance heroine. His satirical representations dissuade us from practicing the hypocrisy these conflicts seem to diagnose, yet at the same time they persuade us that such conflicts make up the very nature of the person. For Chaucer, and for much of the English writing of the following six centuries, character stands at the meeting point of social conflict and interior experience. Who would have thought, knowing English poetry before Chaucer, that its representations of the person would be able to provide the intense diagnostic acumen that the interior requires?

English descriptions of the interior of the person centrally concern the concepts of intention, will, belief, and emotion. Many of the *Canterbury Tales* involve difficulties in enacting, confirming, or discerning these interior states, yet among the frequent eruptions of such issues, the most important occur in the confessional prologues attributed to the Wife of Bath, the Pardoner, and the Canon's Yeoman.[12] These prologues are often acknowledged as the most compelling full-bodied deployments of character in the *Tales*, and sometimes in the history of English poetry.[13] The bravado of their execution rewards the reader who credits Chaucer's project of wresting away some of the canon law's discursive control of the territory of the interior. Doctrine can be preserved, as the inclusion of the Parson's Tale reassures us. But if granting literary fiction a license for authoritative description "in interiore homine" provides access to such ambiguous, emotionally moving, morally complex, socially explosive experiences of

---

dieval Poetry: Alan of Lille's "Anticlaudianus" and John Gower's "Confessio amantis" (Cambridge: Cambridge University Press, 1995).

12. Elizabeth Archibald finds Chaucer increasingly occupied by the notion of intention after he reads Boethius. See her "Declarations of 'Entente' in *Troilus and Criseyde*," *Chaucer Review* 25 (1991): 190–213.

13. For example, H. Marshall Leicester, Jr., *The Disenchanted Self: Representing the Subject in "The Canterbury Tales"* (Berkeley: University of California Press, 1990), an important precedent for my project here. And Lee Patterson writes: "Moreover, the Wife of Bath became the means to bring together two ideas that have subsequently been definitive for our literary tradition, the ideas of character and of literature. Put too explicitly, literature is here defined as a form of writing capable of representing, with specificity and understanding, the irreducible selfhood that constitutes the essence of human life." Patterson, *Chaucer and the Subject of History*, 422. Under the influence of Dante and the *Roman de la Rose*, Chaucer connects reading, ethics, and the development of habitus most directly in his dream visions, in the Wife of Bath's Prologue, and in moments like Dorigen's complaint in the Franklin's Tale. The present chapter must focus on the Pardoner in order to trace how Chaucer captures the power of penitential theology's main social person, the soul, and uses that power to animate literary character.

the interior as Chaucer provides in his characterization of the Wife, the Pardoner, and the Canon's Yeoman, then we must recognize that reading these narratives produces an experience of interiority accessible through careful attention to the formal details of character. The prologues of the three tales share much in terms of sources and approach, but they differ in their social reference. The portrait of the Wife focuses Chaucer's assessment of person in the social institution of marriage and the portrait of the Canon's Yeoman in that of service, whereas, as we shall see, the portrait of the Pardoner is the locus of Chaucer's assessment of person in the canon law's two primary institutions.

Steeped in confessional forms and diction, morally perplexing, and full to the brim with his boiling will, the figure of the Pardoner remains one of the most puzzling and compelling characters in English. He infamously couples a confession of his sinful motives together with an attempt to fleece the pilgrims despite their knowledge of his deceit. He confesses with richly passionate wit, yet he disclaims the corresponding inner state of contrition and impresses us as hollow. He elaborates possessively upon his motives, yet his speech has an undeniably automatic quality. The form of his speech is fundamentally equivocal: it is both a sermon and a confidence game.

The Pardoner's dizzy equivocation invites us to consider the intention *behind* his revelation of intentions. In the brief one hundred thirty-four lines of his Prologue, he employs the word "I" fifty-four times and the words "me" and "my" twenty-one times; in the latter half of the Prologue, he uses the words "entente" or "entencioun" four times and attributes to himself the emphatic verb "wol" nine times (seven instances occur in the course of merely twelve lines). Counting is only to quantify what all readers feel reading the Prologue: that the Pardoner declaims his own will and intention, and his firm control of them, very loudly indeed:

> For myn entente is nat but for to wynne,   *profit*
> And nothyng for correccioun of synne.
> (403–4)

> But shortly myn entente I wol devyse:
> I preche of no thyng but for coveityse.
> Therfore my theme is yet, and evere was,
> *Radix malorum est Cupiditas.*
> (423–26)

> But that is nat my principal entente;
> I preche nothyng but for coveitise.
> (432–33)

For though myself be a ful vicious man,
A moral tale yet I yow telle kan,
Which I am wont to preche for to wynne.
(459–61)[14]

Language about will and intention suffuses the Pardoner's Prologue and Tale, directing our attention to elements of psychological and moral character and also to character as it is produced by means of the social person.[15]

The Pardoner's Prologue divides into three parts: in lines 329–88 he describes his professional acts, in lines 389–434 he describes his intentions, and in lines 435–62 he describes the consequences of his acts for himself and others. These three sections correspond to a tripartite assessment of the person that is typical of penitential discourse. The Pardoner's theme, *radix malorum est cupiditas* (the root of evils is cupidity), provides an image—a tree rather than a human figure—that controls the tripartite analysis and links it to the Parson's Tale. The tree is a familiar medieval diagrammatic device designed to display, in the process of botanical life, an organic continuity between parts: here roots, branches, and fruit suggest intention, act, and effect. The image of the tree unifies the Pardoner's utterance, controlling the shape of both the prologue and tale. In the tale, the concluding image—a tree with gold at its roots and the strange fruit of dead rioters fallen beneath its branches—memorializes the *radix malorum* theme of the preceding sermon with iconic visual force.

The notion of fruitfulness is crucial to both sacramental theology and sexual ideology, providing a nexus of meaning for two important aspects of the Pardoner's person. The issues of the prologue burst into narrative development in the tale, which is centrally plotted around the slippery problem of the performance of intention and its results or fruits. The plot of the Pardoner's Tale hinges on a faulty personification of death: is it a

---

14. Geoffrey Chaucer, *The Canterbury Tales*, in *The Riverside Chaucer*, ed. Larry D. Benson, 3d ed. (Boston: Houghton Mifflin, 1987). All references to Chaucer's works are to this edition.

15. While most criticism written on the Pardoner concerns character in some way, his social persons have been most thoroughly investigated by those interested in him as a pardoner, preacher, or homosexual. The best work on medieval pardoners remains Alfred L. Kellogg and Louis A. Haselmayer, "Chaucer's Satire of the Pardoner," *PMLA* 66 (1951): 251–77. See also J. J. Jusserand, "Chaucer's Pardoner and the Pope's Pardoners," *Chaucer Society Essays* 13, pt. 5 (1889): 423–36. Alastair Minnis develops the role of the preacher as a background to the Pardoner in "Chaucer's Pardoner and the 'Office of Preacher,'" in *Intellectuals and Writers in Fourteenth-Century Europe*, ed. Piero Boitani and Anna Torti (Cambridge: D. S. Brewer, 1986), 88–119, and the early landmark on the homosexual identity of the Pardoner is Monica E. McAlpine, "The Pardoner's Homosexuality and How It Matters," *PMLA* 95 (1980): 8–22.

person or an action? The three rioters make two vows, to be brothers and to find death:

> Herkneth, felawes, we thre been al ones;
> Lat ech of us holde up his hand til oother,
> And ech of us bicomen otheres brother,
> And we wol sleen this false traytour Deeth.
> He shal be slayn, he that so manye sleeth,
> By Goddes dignitee, er it be nyght!
>
> (696–701)

Death, the predicate object of the rioters' action, makes them into his own object when their actions become avaricious. Death's frightening vacillation is triggered by their embrace of sinful intention. They begin by seeking to conquer death, but they abandon that quest when a tempting substitute object appears. What determines whether the rioters' quest is a heroic *imitatio Christi* (Christ is often described as conquering death) or a group murder? The tale returns to the tree, in the end, to find the answer in the intentional state of their souls. They become the wasted fruit underneath it.

There are different kinds of intentions; the agent is more aware of some than of others. Chaucer translates Boethius as saying: "Ne I ne trete not here now of willeful moevynges of the soule that is knowyng, but of the naturel entencioun of thinges . . . For certes, thurw constreynynge causes, wil desireth and embraceth ful ofte tyme the deeth that nature dredeth. (That is to seyn as thus: that a man may be constreyned so, by som cause, that his wille desireth and taketh the deeth whiche that nature hateth and dredeth ful sore)" (*Boece*, Book III, Prosa 11, 153–68). The phrase "the naturel entencioun of thinges" suggests that intention is inherent *in* the body (as a thing among things), but also that intention lies *outside* the person proper, outside the soul and the will. It lies instead in "nature," which is endowed by pathetic fallacy with a will and affect of its own ("nature hateth and dredeth ful sore"). The will is capable of leading the natural body to embrace a death that the flesh dreads: this horrible state is suffered by the mysterious old man who appears in the rioters' path.[16] In that apparition, which seems to shimmer before them in an altered ontological

---

16. I shall consider the old man at more length in the section on Habitual Action and the Person below. Cf. the sociologist Bourdieu on the habitus: "In other words, being produced by a *modus operandi* which is not consciously mastered, the discourse [of the virtuoso] contains an 'objective intention,' as the Scholastics put it, which outruns the conscious intentions of its apparent author and constantly offers new pertinent stimuli to the *modus operandi* of which it is the product and which functions as a kind of 'spiritual automaton,'" Pierre Bourdieu, "Structures, *Habitus*, Practices," in *Rethinking the Subject: An Anthology of Contemporary European Social Thought*, ed. James D. Faubion (Boulder: Westview, 1995), 36.

state, the rioters are unwittingly confronted with a choice between striving against death and embracing it. Their avarice produces actions that utterly transform their bodies. Thomas Aquinas describes the "avarus" as a man who guts himself: "Thus, as to *Ecclesiasticus*, the statement that the greedy man *setteth his own soul to sale* is given as a reason, namely because for money he exposes his own soul, i.e. his life, to peril. So the text goes on, *Because while he liveth he hath cast away*—i.e. held to no account—*his bowels* [intima sua], in order to make money."[17] Under the tree, the culminating image of the unity of intention, action, and consequence, the three who felt they were heroically seizing their fate are ignobly subjected to it.

Yet the unity of intention, act, and fruit is complex and elusive. The prologue is focused on the distinctions and disconnections for which the image of the tree is a foil. Out of the divisions between act, intention, and effect, the Pardoner makes his living and his person. He claims to offer a tidy whole: in the first section of the Prologue, the Pardoner describes his acts and quotes himself preaching about avarice; in the second section, he claims to act according to a motive of avarice; and in the third section he describes the effects produced by these doubly avaricious acts. He closes the Prologue neatly with this summary:

> For though myself be a ful vicious man,
> A moral tale yet I yow telle kan,
> Which I am wont to preche for to wynne.
>
> (459–61)

But it is the very sameness of man, moral tale, and intention—they are all identified as cupidity—that produces our recognition of the great disparities among them. Whereas the tale is against cupidity, the intention is for it. (This conflict is a result of the vicious quality of cupidity; the virtue of charity, for example, would not produce the same divisive effect.) The discontinuous migration of avarice from the Pardoner's theme to his speech act and its avowed intention, then to its effects, and then to his person owes something to the paradoxes of the logicians.[18]

As it is in the Pardoner's Prologue and Tale, lying is both an attribute of action and an attribute of person in the famous ancient paradox attributed in one of its forms to Epimenides, the Cretan who said that all Cretans

---

17. Thomas Aquinas, *Summa theologica*, 2.2.118.5 (Cambridge: Blackfriars, 1964–76), 41:254–55. I shall refer to this Latin-English edition as Blackfriars.

18. The collection of Paul Vincent Spade, *The Mediaeval Liar: A Catalogue of the Insolubilia-Literature* (Toronto: Pontifical Institute of Mediaeval Studies, 1975), attests to a widespread medieval fascination with the liar's paradox from the beginning of the thirteenth century to a few decades after Chaucer's death.

were liars. The paradox relies upon the capacity of behavior to be constitutive of the identities of persons and upon the capacity of categories of
the person to indicate acts: Epimenides' act of attribution contradicts the
sense of the attribution. When the Pardoner's preaching against avarice is
motivated by avarice, an equivocation is produced that begins in a pun on
the Middle English word "of." "Of avarice and of swich cursednesse / Is al
my prechyng," (400–401) can mean "all my preaching is about avarice
and such cursedness" (and therefore aims to eradicate it) or "all my
preaching is done out of avarice and such cursedness" (and therefore
serves to perpetuate it). Since both meanings are true in the fiction, we
have a paradox: the sermon is both against and for avarice; therefore it is
a true sermon and a false sermon. If he enlightens us as to how he is deceiving us, is the Pardoner no longer deceiving us? He says "this is how I
am deceiving you," but what he says is true if and only if it is false.

What kind of truth can Christian doctrine claim when it is wielded in an
act of deception by a vicious agent? The liar's paradox is cited by Paul in
his letter to Titus. (The Pardoner's text, *radix malorum*, comes from Paul's
first letter to Timothy, 6:10.) The modern theorist of paradox, W. V.
Quine, has suggested that Paul missed the point of the paradox, but the
epistle states each side of the paradox clearly and emphatically.[19] Paul
urges Titus, whom he has ordained Bishop of Crete, to consider the sort of
person that a bishop must oppose:

> For a bishop must be without crime, as the steward of God; not proud, not
> subject to anger, not given to wine, no striker, not greedy of filthy lucre . . .
> For there are also many disobedient, vain talkers, and seducers; especially they
> who are of the circumcision:
> Who must be reproved, who subvert whole houses, teaching things which they
> ought not, for filthy lucre's sake.
> One of them, a prophet of their own, said: The Cretians are always liars, evil
> beasts, slothful bellies.
> This testimony is true.   (Titus 1:7 and 10–13)

Paul goes on to explain the paradox:

> All things are clean to the clean: but to the defiled, and the unbelievers, nothing
> is clean; but both their mind and their conscience are defiled.
> They confess that they know God, but in their deeds they deny him; being
> abominable, and incredulous, and to every good work reprobate.
> (Titus 1:15–16)

19. W. V. Quine, "The Ways of Paradox," in *The Ways of Paradox and Other Essays*
(New York: Random House, 1966), 8.

Here Paul assimilates corrupt preachers to the liar's paradox. In his account, a propositional statement (the teaching about God) has been contradicted by the act of teaching (because the deed denies God). His judgement is that the Cretan's report of God, even if it is a true proposition, should be repudiated because the Cretan's deeds (which include that report) deny God. To Paul, the report of this prophet presents no puzzle, because, at least in this moment of writing, the church administrator firmly subordinates teachings and other truth locutions to the persons who profess them. Is the speaker a defiled unbeliever or one of the clean? That is the primary question in assessing the locution.

Intentions and acts, we might say, are both controlling attributes of persons. The liar's paradox asks us to equate acts and persons: two contradictory attributes of the Cretan ("he is a liar" and "he is saying he is lying") are presented to us as the same paradoxical attribution ("a Cretan said Cretans are always liars"). Yet are these attributes of equal weight? The paradox invites us to measure them. How deeply do acts and intentions penetrate our definitions of person? If our notion of the person governs our understanding of his acts, the content of the speech act can be regarded as having little propositional force, because we should not listen carefully to liars and, as Paul advises, should "contend not in words: for it is to no profit, but to the subversion of the hearers" (2 Timothy 2:14). He counsels us to "shun profane and vain speeches: for they grow much towards impiety: And their speech spreadeth like a cancer" (2 Timothy 2:16–17), a piece of advice that is echoed by the Parson's Prologue (32–34). If we admit such philosophical cancer, deciding that intentions and acts (including speech acts) should take precedence in our understanding of persons, we can inflect our notion of the liar to include the possibility of occasional fits of truth telling. But that would be to weaken the status of the person as the first premise of the paradox and, perhaps more importantly, to underestimate what the paradox demonstrates: that social persons control our interpretation of witnessed figures and actions both.

In order to approach the paradox, the philosopher of logic needs, as Quine says, a method of distinguishing "a hierarchy of truth locutions"; the ordinary language philosopher needs (and J. L. Austin and P. F. Strawson provide) a method of distinguishing between descriptive and performative aspects of expression.[20] But neither of these methods considers one of the most forceful aspects of the paradox: that it concerns not only acts,

20. Quine, after Bertrand Russell and Alfred Tarski, distinguishes levels of reference by noticing what is true or false and what is meaningless or ungrammatical ("Ways of Paradox," 9–10); P. F. Strawson develops J. L. Austin's work by stressing the performative aspects of truth locutions in "Truth," *Analysis* 9 (1949): 83–97.

language, and reason, but a speaking social category—a speaking social person—the Cretan Liar.[21] Bare as it can be—the mere collocation of two attributes (Cretanness and lying)—the figure carries a force that is at once ethical and political. It shapes our understanding of individual human beings (Epimenides); it shapes our understanding of polity and race (the Cretan); and it also shapes our understanding of action and intention (lying). We need the term *social person* to describe the class of figures that, like the hypothetical example Epimenides puts before us, can make these kinds of claims upon a culture's cognitive practices. (The term "person" would suggest only the single, embodied Cretan, not the whole race or nation.)

Typical philosophical discussions of the paradox slide too quickly away from all categories of the person. The consummate logician Quine dismisses the appearance of the person in the paradox as a kind of untidyness or "loophole": "We can even drop the indirectness of a personal reference and speak directly of the sentence: 'This sentence is false.' Here we seem to have the irreducible essence of antinomy: a sentence that is true if and only if it is false."[22] Yet complicating the "personal reference" is, in my view, the point of the paradox. The self-avowed vice figure, the object of its own racist, camp mockery, contributes more to the paradox than local color, for in embracing that figure, Epimenides drives a wedge into self-possession by simultaneously differentiating *and* identifying the speaking subject and the social person. The Cretan's avowed deceit, like the Pardoner's embrace of anti-clerical satire, is a prosopopeia of a social person.[23]

Once we grant that in such a thought experiment there are at least two orders of person speaking (say, the social person and the character), then questions arise about the Pardoner's insistent ascription of intention to himself. The paradox sets up a *mise-en-abîme* that generates something like a hierarchy of intention-locutions (to echo Quine's formulation). The performative quality of the expression of the Pardoner's "entente" necessarily distracts us from accepting his avowed intention as pure description of intent (what is he trying to *do* by telling us his intentions are vicious?);

21. We may concede that perhaps the Cretan Liar is a hypothetical or fictional social person conjured by Epimenides: if this were true, his utterance, as a speech act, brings into being (yet not, it pretends, for the first time) a representation of the person that claims to be normative. In any event, Paul's letter suggests a widely held concept of the Cretan Liar and may indeed be considered evidence of a well-worn representation of the person, a social person in historical fact.

22. Quine, "Ways of Paradox," 9.

23. We could include here the second great example of the Wife of Bath's embrace of antifeminist rant. The jurisprudence of hate speech would benefit by distinguishing people, representations of the person, and social persons, an argument I hope to pursue elsewhere. See Judith Butler, *Excitable Speech: A Politics of the Performative* (New York: Routledge, 1997) for an analysis of the performativity of hate speech.

the perlocutionary effects of his act keep us from believing that his avowed intention is pure description of completed effects upon others (what is all this doing to his *listeners* now?); the characterological implications of that act of expression prevent us from taking his avowed intention as pure description of the act it performs (what kind of *person* is he to try to do that?); and the socially constitutive force of that act of making the person deflects us from understanding his avowed intention as pure description of character (what kind of *society, race, nation* produces persons like that?). Meanwhile, back on the pilgrimage, we think about what kind of author makes persons like that—and what he means to do to us with them.

Intention, then, is best defined as situated among acts, persuasive effects, persons, and cultures. It has an uncanny ability to collapse into its surroundings: thus the intention to lie can create a liar, a lie can reveal an intention to lie, and a translation of habitus can newly categorize a statement as a lie. Was Paul's Cretan making a statement, a joke, a philosophical point, an anthropological judgement, a political stratagem, or a fraud designed to defile Christian doctrine? Our answers to this question depend in large part upon the way we interpret the representation of intention, the way we think of it as housed.

The Pardoner's representation of intention is itself paradoxical. On the one hand, the Pardoner insists he knows and possesses his own will, calling it "avarice" and frequently repeating "I wol," the declarative epitome of the Prologue. He seems to think, too, that no matter what the predicated action is, the dominant subject "I" is in a position to prosecute that action without being the object of it. Unlike the cancerous talk Paul worries about, the Pardoner's acts do not disembowel the agent. In his view, they issue from it and enlarge its parameters:

> I wol nat do no labour with myne handes,
> Ne make baskettes and lyve therby,
> By cause I wol nat beggen ydelly.
> I wol noon of the apostles countrefete;
> I wol have moneie, wolle, chese, and whete,
> Al were it yeven of the povereste page,
> Or of the povereste wydwe in a village,   *widow*
> Al sholde hir children sterve for famyne.
> Nay, I wol drynke licour of the vyne
> And have a joly wenche in every toun.
>   (444–53)

This attempt to enrich his interiority and live out his will at the expense of others requires a special kind of abnegation of control, an indifference to the consequences of his words and acts that sets a limit to his interior experience. It is of no account to him, he says, what the results for others are:

> I rekke nevere, whan that they been beryed,
> Though that hir soules goon a-blakeberyed!
> For certes, many a predicacioun   *preaching, predicate*
> Comth ofte tyme of yvel entencioun.
>
> (405–8)

He excuses himself by hiding in a crowd of other bad preachers. What are the consequences of preaching that comes of "yvel entencioun"? He says "I rekke nevere," although his Tale then shows that the results of evil intentions can be much more than the will bargains for.

No reader doubts that the Pardoner presents us with a defiled ethics. There is also a political, institutional side to the Pardoner's concept of intention. He evokes a formal and non-subjective notion of intention—that preaching about *cupiditas* may cause repentance—by claiming that intention does not fix the perlocutionary consequences of his speech acts. The Pardoner says that he can get rich, and that people can be improved or damned, and that there is no necessary connection between his evil intention and what happens to his audiences:

> Thus kan I preche agayn that same vice
> Which that I use, and that is avarice.
> But though myself be gilty in that synne,
> Yet kan I maken oother folk to twynne   *turn*
> From avarice and soore to repente.
> But that is nat my principal entente;
> I preche nothyng but for coveitise.
> Of this mateere it oghte ynogh suffise.
>
> (427–34)

He asserts a slip or a hinge between his "yvel entencioun" and its results, and, the Pardoner seems to boast, we may recognize that hinge as parasitic upon the church's method of immunizing the sacraments from the sinfulness of its officials, namely, in terms of the notion of *ex opere operato*. This doctrine allows valid sacraments to be conferred by ministers in a state of sin by locating the efficacy of the sacrament in its ritual form, rather than in the intention of the agent. The Pardoner's revelations frighten his audience with a moral dilemma: does his "yvel entencioun" interfere in the workings of the opportunity for *caritas*, indulgence, and absolution that he offers?[24] Is the sacrament of penance truly immune from such cancer? As we shall see in the next section, this dilemma had special institutional and doctrinal consequences for the late medieval church. What is the status of the assertion of intention in speech acts, especially in the sacramental acts that are designed to create persons? Canon lawyers and theologians developed a number of ways of approaching this matter, and all of them raise important issues for our understanding of the medieval social person of the pardoner.

The Pardoner's Intentions in the History of the Church

If we trace the details of Chaucer's use of characterization into the history of ideas, we can see the Pardoner as the conjunction of two ways of thinking about intention and the person. The first way asserts that intention reigns entirely over acts in determining the value of the person. We might associate this view with the fact that the concept of intention became increasingly important in twelfth-century theology after Peter Abelard insisted on its primacy. In his *Ethics* (c. 1135), he set forth a radical position: "Works in fact, which as we have previously said are common to the damned and the elect alike, are all indifferent in themselves and should be called good or bad only on account of the intention of the agent [intentione agentis]."[25] As Abelard no doubt knew, this is an idea that was inimical to the jurisprudence of existing medieval legal jurisdictions, which took what we will treat as the opposed view and considered behavior and consequences before affect or, more usually, instead of it. Peter Lombard found internal penitence for sin as powerful as did Abelard and limited the role of priestly absolution in penance.[26] Though theologians such as Hugh of St. Victor (and in the thirteenth century, William of Auvergne and, most radically, Duns Scotus[27]) countered Abelard's extreme position by stressing the necessity of the priest's absolution for salvation, the newly theorized importance of intention survived and was supported by the creation of a new jurisdiction that specialized in intentions: confession took place in what was called the "internal forum" of the canon law.

---

24. Minnis, "Chaucer's Pardoner," 92, and see Alan J. Fletcher, "The Topical Hypocrisy of Chaucer's Pardoner," *Chaucer Review* 25 (1990): 110–26, for the importance of this issue in the poem and Lollard polemics.

25. *Peter Abelard's Ethics*, trans. D. E. Luscombe (Oxford: Clarendon, 1971), 45. See also D. E. Luscombe, *The School of Peter Abelard: The Influence of Abelard's Thought in the Early Scholastic Period* (Cambridge: Cambridge University Press, 1969).

26. Peter Lombard, *Sententiarum quatuor libri*, 1.18.1–7.

27. Duns Scotus, *On the Sentences*, 4.15.1.7.

By the end of the century, confession was considered to be a formal legal jurisdiction complementary to that of the external forum of the ecclesiastical courts, and the distinction between the internal and external fora was the primary institutional division of the canon law. The internal forum's traffic was assured in 1215, when the canon *Omnis utri usque sexus* of the Fourth Lateran Council institutionalized the regulation of the interior by requiring all Christians to undertake confession and absolution at least once a year. The same council set out the first regulations for the office of the pardoner or *quaestor*, as he is called in church Latin. In following years, Thomas Aquinas attempted to synthesize the two theological positions on efficacy with help from Aristotle, combining the importance of the acts of the penitent or the "quasi-matter" of the sacrament with its "form," performed by the priest: "Completeness is ascribed to anything whatsoever because of its form. Now it has been said that this sacrament is completed [perficitur] by what is done by the priest. Hence it must be that those things which are done by the penitent, whether they be words or deeds [sive sint verba, sive facta], are as it were the matter of this sacrament, but those things which are done by the priest take the part of the form."[28] Thomas's explanation became the generally accepted view of the sacrament of penance. Duns Scotus's position, that the sacrament itself consists in the priest's absolution and that contrition is merely its condition, persisted as a minority view and was not condemned by the Council of Trent.

Twelfth-century philosophy's orientation toward the interior encouraged the rapid growth of penitential literature. Earlier medieval penitentials were stark schedules of sins and objective penalties meant to be employed in confession and absolution but once in a lifetime. The literature was transformed by the infusion of affective philosophical inquiry and became an often flowery discourse of guidance for priests and penitents. At the end of *The Canterbury Tales*, Chaucer's Parson presents his audience with a penitential manual of his own. He conveys the directive to an annual sacrament in a manner that looks back to the springtime opening of the General Prologue: "And certes, oones a yeere atte leeste wey it is laweful for to been housled, for certes, oones a yeere alle thynges renovellen" (Parson's Tale, 1027). To be "housled" means to receive the Eucharist; beforehand, one should be "shriven"—confessed and given absolution in the sacrament of penance. The Parson's call to contrition gives the baggy structure of the *Tales* a strong feeling of closure that is capped by a coda

---

28. Thomas Aquinas, *Summa theologica*, 3.84.3.5, Blackfriars, 60:12–13. The statement to which Thomas refers is covered in 3.84.1–2. See the *New Catholic Encyclopedia* for a succinct history of the sacrament to modern times.

that begins, "Heere taketh the makere of this book his leve."[29] By the end of the fourteenth century, confession offered the kind of familiar cycle that, like the calendar of seasons, could reinforce the unity of an ambitious, motley poem like Chaucer's *Tales*.

Though the internal forum and the external forum operated with completely different methods and developed distinct sets of problems, strategies, and favorite concerns, nevertheless ideas could travel between the two jurisdictions; workers and writers sometimes played roles in both jurisdictions and frequently drew upon the same bodies of texts. In its juridical development, the concept of intention was mainly confined to the internal forum. But deliberation about intention is taken out of that context and used for a case in the ecclesiastical courts by Pope Urban III, whose decretal letter *Consuluit* (1187) applies the technical criterion of intention to the judicial evaluation of two cases of commercial debt transactions.[30] Urban cites the words of Jesus in Luke 6:35: "Date mutuum, nihil inde sperantes" or "lend; hoping for nothing thereby." The stress on the interior state of hope in this teaching allowed the role of intention to be expanded as scholastic economic theory developed. Comparisons were made between areas in which intention was determinant, such as sins against charity, and those in which intention had not previously played a role. William of Auxerre, for example, writes that "a usurious will makes the usurer" and compares usury to lust, a sin that can be committed by a solely internal experience even when it never results in any action of the body.[31]

The changing thought about usury applied more stringent standards of conscience but, paradoxically, accommodated more variety of behavior. If a merchant did not intend to profit from a loan, he could sometimes licitly benefit. Intention became increasingly important in twelfth-century treatments of usury; consonantly, as John Noonan has shown, usury was recognized as a sin of injustice rather than merely a sin of avarice.[32] Classifi-

29. This coda appears in nearly all manuscripts of the *Tales* that contain the complete Parson's Tale: *The Riverside Chaucer*, ed. Benson, 965; *The Text of "The Canterbury Tales," Studied on the Basis of All Known Manuscripts*, ed. John M. Manly and Edith Rickert (Chicago: University of Chicago Press, 1940), 2:471–72.

30. "Consuluit" (1187) appears among the decretals collected for Pope Gregory IX (X 5.19.10) in *Corpus iuris canonici*, ed. Friedberg, 2:814. See John T. Noonan, Jr., *The Scholastic Analysis of Usury* (Cambridge: Harvard University Press, 1957), 19–20, 32, 90–92.

31. William of Auxerre, *Summa aurea in quatuor libros sententiarum* (Paris, 1500, composed c. 1210–1220), III:21, fol. 224r:b, quoted in Noonan, *Scholastic Analysis*, 33.

32. Noonan, *Scholastic Analysis*, 18–20, lists Gratian's *Decretum*, decretals of Alexander III and Urban III, and Canon 25 of the 1179 Third Lateran Council among the uses of intention in considerations of usury.

cation of the sins mattered in a material way, because sins against charity, such as avarice, required penance but not restitution; sins against justice, however, could not be satisfied by penance without restitution, even if they were considered solely in the confessional.

Usury lurks about the edges of the Pardoner's sham miracles in his association of the fertility of his relics with Jews, who were conventionally reviled for lending money for profit:

> Thanne have I in latoun a sholder-boon　　　*a brass-like alloy*
> Which that was of an hooly Jewes sheep.
>
> (350–51)

> Taak kep eek what I telle:
> If that the good-man that the beestes oweth　　　*owns*
> Wol every wyke, er that the cok hym croweth,
> Fastynge, drynken of this welle a draughte,
> As thilke hooly Jew oure eldres taughte,
> His beestes and his stoor shal multiplie.　　　*stock*
>
> (360–65)

The introduction of the theme of usury invites us to consider whether the Pardoner's confessed avarice has led him into more than a sin against charity. His abuse of *caritas* expands before his audience into an abuse of justice as he describes not only his intention of covetousness but also his defrauding of the poor. His interior vice grows into crime against others that is fully exterior and social; his infractions call out for remedies from both jurisdictions. Whereas his institutional role grows out of the internal forum and the sacrament of penance, that same role, as we shall see, subjects him no less securely to the jurisdiction that properly handled crimes of commercial fraud: the external forum of the ecclesiastical courts.

As the transforming notion of usury shows, when the concept of intention was imported into the external forum, it could alter adjudicative practice by granting immunity to a wider range of behaviors and fueling or damping financial innovation as well as corruption. The office of the pardoner itself is an example of a good deal of ideological and institutional creativity that left its holder in a set of double binds: the pardoner was simultaneously inside and outside church structures. He was directed to announce his business during the mass after the Gospel was read, and his proceeds were surely related to his eloquence; however, he was prohibited from preaching.[33] He conveyed indulgences that were granted by the

---

33. In the canon "Cum ex eo," Innocent III disallows preaching, and the later papal form letter for indulgences (incipit "Si iuxta sententiam") reiterates the prohibition. "Cum ex eo" was promulgated at the Fourth Lateran Council; for the text, see Joannes Dominicus Mansi,

pope or bishop together with an appeal for funds, yet he was in direct, unwanted competition with local clergy for any disposable assets to be
gained.[34] He had the astonishing power to excommunicate persons who
presented obstacles to his collection, yet he was liable to forfeit his possessions and his freedom without legal recourse should he not meet the
amount of his bond.[35] He could licitly convey an indulgence for the remission of the penalties of sin only to persons who were contrite as well as
confessed, yet he was not trained or empowered to examine, confess, or
absolve them.[36] The position of the pardoner's office expresses a deep ambivalence on the part of an institutional church that had to collect funds as
enthusiastically as it had to despise their collection.

Pardoners were essential to the business of raising money as efficiently
as possible for the support of hospitals and other large building and main-
tenance projects. Under this charge they were rather like the development
officers of the modern university, who are not engaged in or accredited
with the intellecutal work of the faculty but who must represent that work
in proposals and praise to potential donors. Such persons inspire both
hope and distrust in the way medieval pardoners did, though they target
the rich rather than the poor. Pardoners, however, were really more like
external subcontractors. They received no salary from the authorizing
church; instead, each paid himself his expenses and his salary out of his
collections, and many further subcontracted the work of fundraising to
other agents. While it was a potentially lucrative position (at least according to sàtire), it was also risky and financially demanding, because the pardoner was required to post bond in order to be licensed to collect money.
He might also need to post bond in exchange for his letters of introduction.

In a real sense, then, the pardoner bought the pardons and retailed them.
His activities were inherently commercial even when he was not abusing
his patent. They resemble nothing so much as those of the medieval tax
collector, who was also required to post bond to receive his license and
who collected taxes in order to refill his own pocket. Imagine that you, as
an agent of, say, the U.S. Internal Revenue Service, must post a personal
bond for the amount of money the government thinks your town will contribute to support public medical benefits, food programs for the poor, and

---

ed., *Sacrorum conciliorum nova et amplissima collectio* (Graz: Akademische Druck- u. Verlagsanstalt, 1961), 22:1050. "Si iuxta sententiam" is printed in Michael Tangl, *Die päpstlichen Kanzleiordnungen von 1200–1500* (Innsbruck, 1894), 280–82. Kellogg and Haselmayer, "Chaucer's Satire," 253, 255 n. 35.

34. *Corpus iuris canonici*, ed. Friedberg, 2:1190.

35. Kellogg and Haselmayer, "Chaucer's Satire," 262–64.

36. "Si iuxta sententiam" in Tangl, *Die päpstlichen Kanzleiordnungen*, 282.

the construction of far-away government works projects. You must pay sums to various officials for letters of recommendation and licenses. You must travel about your town displaying these credentials, collecting all the money your neighbors can be cajoled and threatened into giving you in exchange for certificates that promise a tax immunity for imaginary penalties far in the future. You are trying to pay off the loans you have taken out in order to get your license; at the same time, you must try to make a living by skimming off the top of your collections. Is it possible to imagine a position more beleaguered by the pressures of commerce?

Despite these institutional pressures upon pardoners, the popular literature and the canon law are full of protests that pardoners should not be commercial. The division of the labor of the interior that gave rise to the pardoner created commerce as his only specialty; thus the regulations that attempt to extinguish the commercial cast of his work are as contradictory as is Chaucer's Pardoner himself. They declaim their good intentions loudly—the canon law is against corruption—but the attempt to attribute the commercial nature of the pardoner's work to the misbehavior of those occupying the office is doomed from the start. The pardoner's livelihood grows out of the technology of the interior forum, yet he is not allowed to engage in the practices of the sacrament of penance but only to exchange a secondary commodity, the pardon, for money. The regulations that surround his office do nothing to preserve the link between the external indulgence and the internal state of intention that is so crucial in the transaction with which the pardoner is charged. Neither do they confront the institutional contradiction at the heart of his existence.

Chaucer bares this contradiction for his readers by portraying a type specifically condemned in canon law. According to conciliar decree, pardoners and their subcontractors should not preach, should be modest and discreet, should not stay in taverns or other inappropriate places, should not make useless or sumptuous purchases, and should not deceptively dress in religious clothing.[37] The language of the regulations concerns only conduct; it does not put forward a standard for the work of pardoners in the interior, because they are not considered qualified to do such work. Still, they are mysteriously qualified to distribute indulgences. Chaucer takes advantage of this tension between the ideology of the interior, in which the Pardoner publicly trades, and the commercial nature of his office, which he has taken to heart. We see his financial duties penetrate his

37. See the requirements laid down by the Fourth Lateran Council of 1215 in *Decretales Gregorii IX*, X 5.38.14 (*Corpus iuris canonici*, ed. Friedberg, 2:889). See also John T. Noonan, Jr., *Bribes* (New York: Macmillan, 1984), 220, and Kellogg and Haselmayer, "Chaucer's Satire."

interior experience, and we fear his sins threaten to penetrate into those who receive his pardons and his words. The division of labor that invented the office of the pardoner has not preserved the distinction between commerce and sacrament; in the character of the Pardoner we can see how these purposes erode each other. The erosion extends back beyond the institutional division into the ideological division that sponsored it. Something has gone horribly wrong in the church's attempt at an institutional solution for its ambivalence about collecting money. The Pardoner's character embodies a conflict between the two primary jurisdictions of the canon law: the internal and the external fora. Thus, in Chaucer's representation of the social person of the pardoner, we see a monstrous production of the divided structure of the canon law itself.

From the point of view of the exterior forum, the regular ecclesiastical courts, Chaucer's Pardoner's crime is simony. Coined as a reference to Simon Magus, who offered to pay for the power of laying on of hands (Acts 8:9–24), the term *simony* can be strictly construed as the purchase of spiritual goods, but it usually includes its companion crime, the sale of spiritual goods.[38] Chaucer's Parson defines simony traditionally, with a heavily affective emphasis: "Espiritueel marchandise [commerce] is proprely symonye, that is *ententif desir* to byen thyng espiritueel; that is, thyng that aperteneth to the seintuarie of God and to cure of the soule. / This desir, if so be that a man do his diligence to parfournen it, al be it that his desir ne take noon effect, yet is it to hym a deedly synne" (Parson's Tale 781–82).[39] Similarly, according to John Wyclif, "the definition of simony that the laws of the church give is: an eager will to buy or sell anything spiritual or connected with the spiritual."[40] Wyclif's is one of the most strenuous definitions of simony; it makes up the tenth of twelve theological works on dominion composed between 1375 and 1382. In this treatise, Wyclif accuses pardoners specifically, declaring that "simony is present in those who illicitly sell indulgences and absolutions from punishment and sin along with other spiritual gifts" (49). The argument of the treatise is designed to explain the consequences of the definition of simony as heresy, in order to support Wyclif's general proof that the church had been corrupted by its immersion in worldly property-holding relationships since the Donation of Constantine.[41] Simony holds an important place in

38. They can be distinguished as simony and *gesia*, after the sinner Gehazi (2 Kings 5:20–27).

39. My emphasis. See Gratian's last comment on the first case of his *Decretum*, which considers simony: C. 1 q. 7 c. 27 (*Corpus iuris canonici*, ed. Friedberg, 1:438).

40. John Wyclif, *On Simony*, trans. Terrence A. McVeigh (New York: Fordham University Press, 1992), 48.

41. Treating simony as a heresy is by no means original to Wyclif. Simony is heretical according to Augustine (*De haeresibus*), Gregory the Great, and Cardinal Humbert (Noonan, *Bribes*, 142–43). See Gratian, *Decretum*, C. 1 q. 7 c. 27 (*Corpus iuris canonici*, ed. Friedberg,

Wyclif's thought, because it stands at a crossroads between the large institutional question of ecclesiastical dominion and the topic of interior, subjective states such as intention.[42]

The canonists did not usually treat the acts of pardoners as potentially simoniacal; rather, the normative discussion of simony concerns those in holy offices. Neither did the canonists treat pardoners as sympathetic subjects with complex interiors, so perhaps it is not surprising that pardoners did not leap to the fore in considerations of a sin in which intention is important. In the canon law collections, censures of the pardoners' abuses appear in general treatments of penance and the remission of sins, whereas simony is given its own category and collected with other kinds of financial misbehavior, such as usury. When simony is considered a sin against religion rather than a sin against justice, its character is automatically inflected by intention as it would not be, for example, in a case of theft.[43] The importance of intention in the case of simony is so definitive that, as we have seen, it was used analogically by scholastic theorists who wished to press the claims of intention elsewhere.

An emphasis on intention intrudes into some curious decisions in cases that revolve around the issue of simony, itself an indecorous commercial by-product of the spiritual institution of the church. For example, in a decretal written to the archbishop of Canterbury, Pope Alexander III allowed the collection of money by means of pardons for the purpose of building bridges. It is difficult to see how exchanging indulgences for money that will pay for a bridge can be cleared of simony, but the case was also justified by Thomas Aquinas, who assures us that an indulgence can be made "for temporal things ordered to spiritual things, such as . . . the construction of churches and bridges." He states that "simony does not occur there, because the spiritual is not given for the temporal but for the spiritual."[44] He manages to classify the bridge as spiritual, rather than temporal, by resorting to its purpose. In such a broad definition of what constitutes a spiritual purpose for raising money, there is a willingness to go to great conceptual lengths to protect that lucrative product of the internal forum of canon law, the indulgence. John Noonan writes: "By the

---

1:437–38). Thomas Aquinas says simoniacs are commonly regarded as heretics after Augustine and explains why in *Summa theologica*, 2.2.100.1.

42. His insistence upon working out the relationship between the two standpoints, the interior and the institutional, is a particular strength of Wyclif's thought. In this approach and its reinvention of ecclesiastical social persons, Wyclif's work provides an interesting parallel to Chaucer's project of reinventing literary character.

43. Noonan, *Scholastic Analysis*, 158. Theft is also justified in the case of extreme need, but it is the circumstance, not the intention, that absolves the thief.

44. A letter of Pope Alexander III to the archbishop of Canterbury in *Decretales Gregorii IX*, X 5.38.4 (*Corpus iuris canonici*, ed. Friedberg, 2:885) and Thomas Aquinas, *Scriptum super quatuor libros*, quoted in and trans. Noonan, *Bribes*, 222.

extraordinarily simple move of categorizing as spiritual every temporal act ordered to the spiritual, the sin of simony no longer endangered the exchanges by which crusades were organized, churches built, and civic improvements financed. An economy was validated in which one of the most spiritual of objects, the fate of the soul after death, could be affected by cash laid out on earth, and the exchange would not count as an exchange of the earthly for the heavenly."[45] In Thomas's slippery interpretation, the criterion of intention is applied not to the pardoner and penitent who are making the deal but to the improbable and entirely impersonal project of the bridge. The purpose of the bridge stands in for the intentions of the agents making the trade, protecting the church's economic move from vulnerability to its own criterion of interior, human intention, but potentially legitimizing all kinds of financial arrangements that remained controversial.

Simony is closely associated with affective interior states. The Parson, as we have seen, considers simony to be a most serious sin:

> Certes symonye is cleped of [named for] Simon Magus, that wolde han boght for temporeel catel the yifte that God hadde yeven by the Hooly Goost to Seint Peter and to the apostles. / And therfore understoond that bothe he that selleth and he that beyeth thynges espirituels been cleped symonyals . . . That oother manere is whan men or wommen preyen for folk to avauncen hem, oonly for wikked flesshly affeccioun that they han unto the persone, and that is foul symonye. . . . [Simony] is the gretteste synne that may be, after the synne of Lucifer and Antecrist. (Parson's Tale, 783–88)

Simony is a favorite theme of anti-clerical writings throughout the later middle ages, and the sale of spiritual benefits by pardoners was an abuse that occasioned popular satire. Cupidity, avarice, covetousness—these interior states of sin are declaimed by the Pardoner as his reason for preaching. These same sins result in acts of simony according to the Parson and to the writings of theologians and canon lawyers. Though the canonists do not diagnose it in the *quaestor*, the crime that is confessed by Chaucer's Pardoner is clearly characterized as the crime of simony: the exchange of spiritual goods for temporal ones.

The Parson's phrase "ententif desir" echoes the discussion of simony in the *Summa theologica* (2.2.100) where Thomas Aquinas defines the sin by means of *studiosa voluntas*: "Simony is fittingly defined in terms of the will [*per voluntatem*]. This act is furthermore described as *express* [*studiosa*], in order to signify that it proceeds from choice, which plays the

45. Noonan, *Bribes*, 222.

leading part in every virtue and vice."[46] The Pardoner's frequent declarations of willfully chosen bad motives are reinforced by his visual self-characterizations, which also invoke the idea of *studiosa voluntas*:

> Thanne peyne I me to strecche forth the nekke,
> And est and west upon the peple I bekke,   *nod*
> As dooth a dowve sittynge on a berne.
> Myne handes and my tonge goon so yerne   *eagerly*
> That it is joye to se my bisynesse.
>
> (395–99)

His hands and his tongue are so busy that their business is the external sign of his eager will.

The image of the dove resonates in the context of simony, because it recalls the often-cited biblical story in which Jesus throws dove-sellers, along with money-lenders, out of the temple. To the exegete, the "dove-seller" was a type of the simoniac like Simon Magus, Gehazi, and Judas. The Venerable Bede is cited in the *Decretum* as saying:

> Dove-sellers who make the house of God a house of business are not only those people who seek holy orders by giving money, praise, or even an office, but also those who use their rank or spiritual gift which they have received from the Lord's generosity not with a pure intention [*non simplici intentione*] but to obtain some kind of human reward contrary to the Apostle's urging: "If anyone speaks, let it be as with words of God. If anyone ministers, let it be as from the strength that God furnishes; that in all things God may be honored."[47]

Part of the work of exegetes is to translate biblical passages out of the context of alien and archaic social persons and into contemporary ones. With a freedom typical of textual interpretation now as then, Bede not only translates the now culturally anomalous "dove-sellers"—those who sold animals for sacrifice outside of synagogues—by "candidates for holy orders," he also adds a general application of the term that goes beyond the passage's institutional critique to emphasize an ethical lesson that concerns the interior experience of intention. In Bede's exegesis the dove-sellers metamorphose into aspiring clerics, and they are censured for the character of their intentions, as well as for selling spiritual things too near a now entirely metaphorical altar. Not only should the house of God exclude sales transactions, but the desire for human reward should be abol-

46. Thomas Aquinas, *Summa theologica*, 2.2.100.1.2, Blackfriars, 40:130–31.

47. Trans. Terrence A. McVeigh in his edition of John Wyclif, *On Simony*, 52. Gratian, *Decretum*, C. 1 q. 3 c.11 (*Corpus iuris canonici*, ed. Friedberg, 1:417).

ished from everyone's use of office. In Chaucer's portrait, the Pardoner sees himself as both the "ententif" businessman and the dove; he seems to be wittingly or unwittingly selling himself in his simony.[48] At the same time, in a homely, countrified perversion of one of the figures for the inspiring holy spirit, he nods upon the people, "as dooth a dowve."[49] He speaks the words of God but, against Wyclif's urging, without divine strength or inspiration.

Chaucer's emphasis on intention throughout the prologue has the effect of insisting that we use the criterion of intention as we evaluate the Pardoner. Will we agree that his sin is merely avarice, an interior sin against charity? Is it simony, a sin against religion that threatens the institution of the church? Is it theft and fraud, a crime against the property of others, and thus against justice?[50] The Parson's Tale presents simony in this third way, as a subcategory of "deceite bitwixe marchaunt and marchant" (777): it is a ghostly trade, a traffic in things "that aperteneth to the seintuarie of God and to cure of the soule" (781). His definition appears under the general heading of avarice, the patron sin of the Pardoner.[51]

Decisions about how to classify sins involve determining how deeply intention cuts into the person, into exchanges and sacraments, and into social institutions; conversely, they require us to define how deeply social institutions and roles reconfigure or create the interior. If we were to apply the logic of the Parson's Tale to the case of the Pardoner, the various aspects of the Pardoner's sin would not be distinct but extensive: he sins against charity, against religion, and against justice; his sin penetrates his interior, his social person, his office, the sacrament of penance, other people, other people's property, and the institutional church. The Parson's discourse requires every party to take the utmost responsibility, but wields so broad a brush that, were we to apply it to the case of the Pardoner, it would obscure the institutional critique waged by the Pardoner's portrait. The Parson's renunciation of fictional modes blurs his moral analysis, which is incapable of perceiving the social details of the Pardoner's corruption.[52] Chaucer's new literary mode of describing the interior provides

48. Cf. "*Ecclesiasticus* says, *Nothing is more wicked than a covetous man*, and continues, *There is no more wicked thing than love of money, for such a one setteth his own soul to sale*," Thomas Aquinas, *Summa theologica*, 2.2.118.5.1, Blackfriars, 41:252–53.

49. Minnis, "Chaucer's Pardoner," 106–08, explores the images of the dove and the serpent with respect to the office of the medieval preacher; see also Patterson, *Chaucer and the Subject of History*, 398.

50. Thomas Aquinas includes simony in his treatment of theft in *De decem praeciptis*.

51. Under the rubric of avarice, the Parson's description of simony forms part of a subsection devoted to tyranny, the violation of the duty of stewardship that accompanies lordship.

52. For an argument that fictional modes can enhance ethical analysis within penitential discourse itself, see Mark Miller, "Displaced Souls, Idle Talk, Spectacular Scenes: *Handlyng Synne* and the Perspective of Agency," *Speculum* 71 (1996): 606–32.

not only a better analysis of the experience of sin than that offered by the penitential manual, but has, in addition, the capacity to wage an institutional analysis of the canon law.

Simony is important not just because it helps us classify the Pardoner's crimes and gives us a method of assessing intention, but also because it is an enormous threat to the church's ability to reproduce itself throughout the middle ages. A simoniacal minister endangers the stable reproduction of the church and a just distribution of its benefits. Simony describes another direct link between the organization of the inner states of social persons and their immediate embedding in institutional and political architectures. As the sacraments became ever more firmly established to be legal ceremonies conveying institutional position and personality upon their recipients, they were made vulnerable by the Abelardian expansion of intention. How were penitent recipients to be assured that the sacraments that they received were valid when the intentions of their minister were not? Each recipient could vouch for her own intention, but what control did she have over the states of sin experienced and tolerated by those in authority?

Augustine settled the first major crisis of this kind, the Donatist controversy. Ordination and baptism had been particularly disrupted by the emperor Diocletian's persecution of Christians, especially in North Africa where many bishops defected from the church under political pressure, yet continued to ordain and to baptize. A council at Arles in 314 decided that these sacraments were valid and accepted the bishops back into the church, but followers of Donatus, the bishop of Carthage, did not accept this finding. The Donatist controversy persisted and was addressed by Augustine at length, especially in a treatise on baptism.[53] He located the efficacy of the sacrament in the ritual, rather than in the minister's purpose or status. When a sacrament was effected by a proper rite, it bestowed what he called a "seal" or indelible character. However, other spiritual benefits of that sacrament, called its fruits or God's grace, might not be conferred or sustained if sin presented an obstacle. A licit sacrament was thus distinguished from a valid one. The effect of the valid sacrament could be impaired by the receiver and the minister, but only within certain impermeable limits.

Despite the theoretical settlement that Augustine's distinctions achieved, the vulnerability of the sacraments was to reappear critically in different moments throughout the history of the church. Humbert of Silva Candida wrote in 1057 that orders conferred on or by simoniacs were automatically invalid. In a response to such controversy, the Synod of Rome issued a general amnesty in 1063 for those who had been ordained by simoniacs

53. Augustine, *On Baptism against the Donatists*.

but who had not themselves paid for the privilege. It described its purpose not as justice but mercy, implying that a stricter interpretation might have exposed many more ordinations to invalidity.[54] It was theoretically, as well as practically, difficult simultaneously to preserve the invulnerability of the sacraments and to pursue the culpability of the ministers.

The history of penitential theology and legal thought is inextricable from the church's fortunes throughout the transition into the Reformation. In 1517, in the town where a famous worrier about intention, Hamlet, would be said to have attended university, Martin Luther nailed to a door a list of ninety-five points upon which he was willing to dispute canonical doctrine; he emphasized sacramental theology and the pardoners' trade in indulgences.[55] Medieval clerical satire, including Chaucer's excoriations of the Pardoner's vicious methods, was taken by sixteenth-century English reformers to be an important harbinger of their own fight against Rome. By 1567, Pope Pius V had cancelled all indulgences meant to be exchanged for money; the pardoner's office had been abolished by the Council of Trent; and the pardon, that legal document conferring spiritual rewards for charitable largesse, had lost its official role.

In Chaucer's times, of course, such reforms were still far in the future. The valid or licit nature of the sacrament of penance or "shrifte" is treated by Chaucer's Parson as subject to two conditions:

> Also the verray shrifte axeth [true penance requires] certeine condiciouns. First, that thow shryve thee by thy free wil, noght constreyned, ne for shame of folk, ne for maladie, ne swiche thynges. For it is resoun that he that trespaseth by his free wyl, that by his free wyl he confesse his trespas, / and that noon oother man telle his synne / but he hymself; ne he shal nat nayte ne denye his synne, ne wratthe hym agayn the preest for his amonestynge to lete [admonishing to abandon] synne. / The seconde condicioun is that thy shrift be laweful; that is to seyn, that thow that shryvest thee and eek the preest that hereth thy confessioun been verraily in the feith of hooly chirche, / and that a man ne be nat despeired of the mercy of Jhesu Crist, as Caym or Judas. (Parson's Tale 1012–15)

The first condition concerns the interior state of the penitent, who must have a will or intention to repent that is constrained neither by external factors such as social pressure or distress, nor by internal states such as denial or "wratthe." The second condition concerns both parties to the sacrament: the minister as well as the penitent. Interior states are crucial to

54. Noonan, *Bribes*, 141.

55. For intention as a primary topic of English renaissance theater, see Luke Wilson, *Theaters of Intention: Drama and the Law in Early Modern England* (Stanford: Stanford University Press, 2000).

this condition, but no longer relate to intention in its role in the working of the sacrament. In the last clause, the Parson makes a curious shift away from second-person address to the vague and apparently inclusive locution "a man": both parties are expected to have taken on the responsibilities of church membership in good faith and not through a species of despair. Importantly, the primary sense of the phrase "in the feith of hooly chirche" is legal and institutional, and requires the two to be members in good standing of the church, not excommunicates. It is never suggested among the conditions of the true sacrament that the priest must not administer the sacrament out of despair; his inner state is a condition of his ecclesiastical position but not a condition of the sacrament in any more specific, instrumental way.

In other words, in Chaucer's version of the penitential manual by Raymund of Pennaforte—a manual that had been incorporated into the canon law—the priest's internal states impinge on the penitential process only insofar as they threaten his qualifications as a priest. In contrast, both the penitent's interior and exterior acts are closely linked to the workings of the sacrament. The pardoner, who might well convey a pardon to the penitent as part of the last stages of penance, is not mentioned at all in the Parson's treatment of the sacrament. This omission is typical; pardoners are discussed not as part of the process of penitence, confession, and absolution, but in connection with their regulation and with financial crimes, as pertaining to the external rather than the internal forum. The subtle but often urgent question of the attribution of intention is absent from the church's regulation of pardoners.

All the late medieval sacraments needed to be surrounded by a sphere of immunity that could protect their validity from some of the pressure caused by penitential discourse and its stress upon intention. The problem of intention is difficult to contain within the interior of the penitent. Among all those involved in the process of the sacrament of penance, which person should we designate as the possessor of the operative intention? God whose grace confers absolution? The bishop who signs and seals the pardon? The pardoner who "communicates" it? The letter of indulgence itself? The Christian who receives it as a reward for giving money? How do these intentions interpenetrate and affect each other? All of these persons should have good intentions, of course, but what if they do not? Is there no Augustinian core inside the process of the sacrament that is out of the reach of these representations of the person? One can see many reasons to tear up the pardon in rage, as Piers the Plowman does. While the theologians clearly place the emphasis upon the authentic contrition of the sinner and the absolute judgement of God, this pinning down of the extremes of the process only shifts the responsibility away from the church and the tough question of how the institutional apportionment, embodiment, and expression of intention should be understood to operate in acts and social transactions.

According to canon law, a pardoner is merely an agent distributing an indulgence; he is prohibited from claiming to effect absolution. Chaucer's Pardoner makes such illicit claims repeatedly:

> He wol come up and offre a Goddes name,
> And I assoille him by the auctoritee   *absolve*
> Which that by bulle ygraunted was to me.   *license*
> (386–88)

> I yow assoille, by myn heigh power,
> Yow that wol offre, as clene and eek as cleer
> As ye were born.
> (913–15)

> It is an honour to everich that is heer
> That ye mowe have a suffisant pardoneer
> T'assoille yow in contree as ye ryde,
> For aventures whiche that may bityde.
> (931–34)

> Looke which a seuretee is it to yow alle
> That I am in youre felaweshipe yfalle,
> That may assoille yow, bothe moore and lasse,
> Whan that the soule shal fro the body passe.
> (937–40)

In addition to the contrition required on the part of the penitent, the success of the pardon is effected by the intention of God and the church, not the intention of the minister and certainly not the intention of the pardoner. Sacramental doctrine, expressed in the shorthand *ex opere operato*, places intention outside of the human agent in its model of ministration, insulating the sacrament from injury. Gratian's *Decretum* explains, citing Gregory and Isidore, that the sinfulness of ministers does not prevent the working of the sacraments: "divine virtue works secretly in them [sinful ministers], and this virtue or power is only of divine, not of human efficacy."[56]

In the middle of the twelfth century, Peter Lombard systematically synthesized much received wisdom about the sacraments in his *Sententiarum*

---

56. Gratian, *Decretum*, C. 1 q. 1 c. 84 (*Corpus iuris canonici*, ed. Friedberg, 1:388). The quotation is translated by Elizabeth Frances Rogers in *Peter Lombard and the Sacramental System* (1917; reprint Merrick, New York: Richwood, 1976), 44.

libri quatuor, an influential treatise that became a kind of theological counterpart to Gratian's legal sourcebook. In the fourth book, Peter discusses the problem of sin's interference in the sacraments and reiterates the distinction cited by Gratian. In connection with the Eucharist, he writes: "We are also often asked whether wicked priests can administer this sacrament.—To this we may answer that some priests, although they are evil, consecrate truly, that is, those who are within the Church in name and in sacrament, even if not in life; because the consecration is effected not by the merit of the consecrant, but by the word of the Creator."[57] The question is complicated by many details, but Peter's position is that a divine agent, not the minister of the sacrament, is the true worker of sacramental grace. Human agents, properly authorized by the church, are indispensable, if not entirely pure conveyors of grace:

> It is necessary that there be a priest, and the intention must be felt that he intends to perform it [the sacrament of the Eucharist].—But if he does not believe the truth concerning this mystery, do you suppose he can intend to perform it? And if he does not intend, do you suppose he performs it?—Some even say, that if he does not think rightly of this mystery he can intend not indeed to perform it, which would then be to believe rightly, but to do that which is done by others when the mystery is performed, and thus the intention is present; and even if the intention of performing this mystery may be said to be lacking, nevertheless inasmuch as he intends to say and do things, which are done by others, the mystery is accomplished.[58]

As it entertains an exterior conception of intention for the minister, Peter's language here approaches the traditional treatment of commercial transactions by canon law. Obsessed with the threatening subtleties of intention, penitential discourse wrapped priests and the sacraments inside a sphere of immunity by polarizing intention at two relatively inscrutable extremes of the sacramental process: God and the recipient soul were the agents that bore the burden of intention. Otherwise, the efficacy of penance lay in the "form," in the ritual's acts and words. Penitential discourse does not describe an interaction between the intentional states of the penitent and the priest; instead it concentrates solely on the education of the priest and the examination of the penitent. As it was produced by the theologians, thinking about intention reinforced the gap between the internal and the external fora.

The pardoner's role was to embody the insulation that protected the sacrament of penance from the ravages of intention. He stood dumbly and

---

57. *Sententiarum quatuor libri* 4.13.1, trans. Rogers, *Peter Lombard*, 148.
58. Ibid., 150.

deafly—without making judgements or hearing confessions—between the intending church and the intending recipient of grace; he made the collection of money and the distribution of pardons an event separate from the other meaningful steps in the process of penance. The social person called "the pardoner" was invented to help absorb the intentional conflicts in the commerce of salvation, to embody and preserve the gap between the internal and external fora. This makes him the perfect figure for Chaucer's investigation of how social persons locate intention within the architecture of social rituals and institutions.

Despite his role insulating the sacrament from the doubtful nature of intention, the Pardoner repeatedly speaks in a framework that invites us to assess his intentions. We have seen his extensive use of "wol" and other grammatical and syntactical habits that stress intentionality. Questions of intention are also embodied in the nature of his speech acts. It happens that preaching is especially fraught with issues of intention in the fourteenth century. According to treatises like the *Ars componendi sermones* by Ranulph Higden (c. 1340), preaching requires an upright intention (*intentionis rectitudo*) to suit its proper end or final cause.[59] Some writers say that reward may be kept in mind as a secondary intention during the act of preaching, but for others money is an entirely illegitimate motive. In his explication of the Pardoner's Prologue and Tale, Alastair Minnis brings scholastic thought to bear upon what he incisively calls "the Pardoner's implicit *quaestio*, whether or not a sinful preacher can perform a proper act of preaching."[60] In fact, the *quaestor* (as we have seen) was prohibited from preaching, and the Pardoner's infraction of this rule invites us to expand Minnis's parsing of Chaucer's deliberative thought experiment. Can a sacrament be efficacious if its agents are in a state of sin? Can any act be efficacious if undertaken in an intentional state that contradicts its formal purpose?

Chaucer's Pardoner, of course, says that his principal intention is avarice, and that the salvation of his audience, should it occur, is a side effect:

> Yet kan I maken oother folk to twynne
> From avarice and soore to repente.
> But that is nat my principal entente;
> I preche nothyng but for coveitise.
> (430–33)

59. Margaret Jennings, "The *Ars componendi sermones* of Ranulph Higden," in *Medieval Eloquence: Studies in the Theory and Practice of Medieval Rhetoric*, ed. James J. Murphy (Berkeley: University of California Press, 1978), 112, 116.
60. Minnis, "Chaucer's Pardoner," 92.

As the Pardoner exercises his office, he deliberately turns his intentions to counter the intentions that are meant to be embodied in the office itself. A conflict emerges that disturbs us more than that which might result from a simple dereliction of duties. Instead, he forces his audience to fall back (or perhaps to be rudely dropped) upon the idea expressed in *ex opere operato*, upon the church's assurance that the sacraments cannot be harmed by sinful ministers. Anti-clerical satire shows that many fourteenth-century Christians felt this was a dubious or insufficient protection.[61] The Pardoner's voice enacts not only a wicked sermon but also a swindling call to confession, a set of suspicious indulgences, and a false promise of absolution. If all these acts are counterfeit, what remains of the sacrament of penance? Does the Pardoner's vicious nature intrude into its core? He claims that he can make "oother folk . . . soore to repente," but even if he can we may well worry that their absolution might be fatally compromised.

If someone is a contributing cause of the good results of such events as confession and absolution, what happens when these events become the occasion of his vice? This question prompted a line to be drawn in numerous practical discussions of whether sinful priests should preach or effect the sacraments. It was thought that when the vices of a priest became well known, or "notorious" (in legal language), it was a source of scandal for him to continue. In other words, at the point that his sin became an occasion of sin for others, he should cease in his duties. The Pardoner's publication of his own vices leaves no doubt about his notoriety. The curious aspect of his case is that the sacrament of penance is itself the occasion of his sin. Secondly, his office is the occasion of sin for his audience: the church would have had no difficulty in censuring the Pardoner after hearing his prologue, but its formulas for censure could not adequately address the way in which the Pardoner manages to feed off the protective immunity wrapped around the sacrament itself. In Chaucer's presentation, the very notion of *ex opere operato* becomes a source of scandal.

The church could call upon three practical approaches to defining the relation between its members and its ideals. The first arises from the need for prescription: what are the proper attitudes and duties of preachers, priests, and pardoners? In discussions of pastoral care and manuals for priests an advisory standard is developed, an ideal that guides aspirants and those who evaluate them and that continues to assist acting officers of

---

61. For a literary introduction to anti-clerical satire, see Penn R. Szittya, *The Antifraternal Tradition in Medieval Literature* (Princeton: Princeton University Press, 1986) and Wendy Scase, *"Piers Plowman" and the New Anticlericalism* (Cambridge: Cambridge University Press, 1989).

the church to fulfill their roles. A second approach responds to the need to regulate the behavior of the church's officers. In what circumstances do their shortcomings and misdeeds require "exterior" or public assessment and correction? This is a legal, disciplinary question only partially related to the standards developed in pastoral discourse. Sacramental theology led to a third type of consideration of members of the institutions of the church. How is the sacrament of penance related to the various persons it involves? The series of requirements instated by the Fourth Lateran Council intensified just this third line of inquiry.

In assigning the pardoner to a kind of interface between the intentions of the church and its act, the Fourth Lateran Council reinforces the theoretical sphere of immunity around the sacraments of the church, creating an institutional role that embodies it. In Chaucer's portrayal (mimicking historical fact), the pardoner's role is precisely to embody this sphere of immunity: to act as an income gathering agent of others who are the source of the promise held out by his pardons. The church thus estranges itself from the monetary transaction so that the transaction seems less like a sale of spiritual goods for temporal ones. When the work of exchanging pardons for money is subcontracted out to the newly created office of pardoner, the person who confesses, absolves, and issues pardons is split into several persons. Similarly, the creation of the pardoner's office offers at least the illusion, if not the fact, that the grant of absolution and the receipt of money have become disconnected acts rather than a single, potentially simoniacal transaction.

Pardoners were licensed with a stipulation that they were unqualified to address the moral concerns of confession. The purpose of the ruling was the clarification and regulation of the cultural process of penance and the expansion of financial collections for projects outside of the purview of local church structures, but by the fourteenth century the results were perceived by Wyclif and others as antithetical to the proper aims of the sacrament. The church's separation of penance from fund-raising amounted to an intensification of commerce. Its separation of the offices of the man who pardoned and the man who distributed pardons, a version of the separation of intention from action, only exacerbated the problem of corruption. Once acts are insulated from intention by a sphere of immunity, the insulation itself becomes a possible occasion of vice.

Sexual Figuration and the Habitus

Having considered the social person of the pardoner in law, theology, and institutional history, we are in a position to return with some vigor to the details of Chaucer's treatment of the Pardoner. The General Prologue's

portrait of the Pardoner embodies the conceptual and institutional paradoxes I have described in ways that offer to expand our understanding of
the role of social persons in habituation. First I want to take up the heavily
sexualized portrait in this light. Then I will return to the Prologue and Tale
one last time, reading them together as they perform the Pardoner's habitual practices and show how his body is shaped to the lineaments of his
conflicting social persons and their ethical and institutional environments.

The General Prologue's portrait of the Pardoner (669–714), one of the
most famous descriptions in English literature, deserves careful attention.
Half devoted to his appearance and half to his "craft," the portrait is full
of antithesis, equivocal conjunctions, and hedging of various kinds; the
conjunction "but" begins seven lines in this short passage, including three
that make up the anaphora of 676–80. In the course of the visual description, fourteen of nineteen lines focus on the Pardoner's head. Only the
brief mention of his lap, in which his "walet" lies, directs the mind's eye
below the Pardoner's shoulders. Despite its concentration on the head,
which seems an unlikely way to convey sexuality, the description carries a
heavy sexual charge that is clinched at the end of the bodily portrait in the
form of a paradoxical identity that does make us think below the shoulders: "I trowe he were a geldyng or a mare" (691). This declaration is followed by the second half of the portrait, which is devoted to his "craft"
and has, surprisingly, no discernible sexual charge. What is the relation
between these two parts of his portrait, between the sexualized, top-heavy
figure and the list of professional acts? Like the other portraits of the General Prologue, the Pardoner's concentrates on describing habitus: the
shaping of the body that comes from practices and social environment. In
one direction, habitus alters the human body; in the other, it clings to the
social person. These two roles of habitus provide the structure of the portrait.

Let us now give the Pardoner the attention that in the Introduction I
gave to the Knight and the Prioress, considering how his portrait draws
upon social persons to produce its meaning. First, he is identified as "a
gentil Pardoner." As we have seen, by Chaucer's time institutional history
had elevated the construction of person that grew out of his office to a
place in the public imagination, and the word "pardoner" carried its own
distinctive set of attributes in the tradition of anti-clerical satire. The second social person evoked is that of the seducer. When we first see him, his
rowdily amorous singing with the Summoner comically scrambles the Pardoner's authority:

> With hym ther rood a gentil PARDONER
> Of Rouncivale, his freend and his compeer,

> That streight was comen fro the court of Rome.
> Ful loude he soong "Com hider, love, to me!"
>
> (669–72)

"Comen fro . . . Rome" quickly becomes an indecorously trumpeted "Com . . . to me." The "om" in "to me" links the two sentences together and softens the peculiarity of the broken rhyme by tying it into the three repetitions of "com." The antithesis "fro . . . to" suggests his transformation along the road to a seducer, and the parallel drawn between the actions by their common verb "com" produces an effect of tight, uncomfortable comparison between the officer of the church and the seducer. The Summoner "bar to hym a stif burdoun" (673), vocally contributing a bass line, but also, literally, carrying a stiff burden to his friend.[62] Insofar as the lyrics declare seduction, the two men are bodily accomplices, just as if a painter represented them in complementary, compromisingly linked postures.

Our seducer's attention to his stylish dishevelment, a paradoxical combination of care and "jolitee" (680), is both narcissistic and an invitation to be viewed or touched. The reader's attention is drawn, with the narrator's, to the Pardoner's head—his singing voice, his hair, his head coverings, his eyes, his beardlessness. His grooming and lack of it both seem to fascinate the narrator. Like the Prioress, he evokes a personification of vanity inappropriate to an officer of the church. Four similes and a metaphor compare his features to two domestic commodities (wax and flax) and three animals (a hare, a goat, and two kinds of horse). The wax and flax give the head an over-dressed, baffling, inhuman aura: for a moment, the poem invites us to think of a funeral effigy or a doll, two peculiar social persons that invite repulsion and tenderness. All three of the animals to which he is compared are part of medieval sexual iconography and might well have been expected to appear in a pictorial image of a figure associated with sexual behavior.[63] I shall say more about the animals in turn, but first consider the larger structure of combination.

Chaucer's similes accomplish the same glossing function as do iconographical props in visual portraiture, though he puts his things and ani-

---

62. The *Oxford English Dictionary*, 2d ed., shows confusion between the two senses, musical and weight-bearing (2 and 9), as early as the tenth century (s.v., "burden"). "Burdoun" could also mean "pilgrim's staff" (*Middle English Dictionary*, s.v. "burdoun," sense 1), though the primary sense here is clearly "low-pitched undersong," sense 2.

63. On the sexual iconography of hares, goats, and horses, see M. C. Seymour et al., eds., *On the Properties of Things: John Trevisa's Translation of Bartholomaeus Anglicus, "De proprietatibus rerum"* (Oxford: Clarendon, 1975), 2:1220–21 (hare), 2:1162–63 and 2:1208–09 (goat), 2:1186–89 (horse); and Beryl Rowland, *Animals with Human Faces: A Guide to Animal Symbolism* (Knoxville: University of Tennessee Press, 1973), 88–93 (hare), 80–86 (goat), 103–112 (horse).

mals much closer to the body than, for instance, a tapestry or painting would, making a kind of grotesquely composite character. The mix of human, vegetable, and animal parts has the rowdy energy of a cross-species illumination in the margin of a medieval manuscript and is kin to the descriptions of bodies in the fabliaux. In such a visually oriented, nearly ecphrastic passage, we are invited to see the Pardoner, if only for fleeting moments, in terms of a range of conventional figures: the carousing seducer, the vain man, the fabricated effigy, the doll, the animal-like body from the fabliaux, the courtly eunuch. Figural details evoke the conventions of social persons and at the same time set forth the specific variance of this complex Pardoner from each of those conventions. As sexual conventions, the images exercise a powerful push and pull upon the reader, eliciting our curiosity and appealing to our erotic responses of attraction and repulsion.

Character is such a powerful fiction in *The Canterbury Tales* that it can stuff the most motley crowd of figurations into a single body, merely by unifying them under the rubric of a single name and a pronoun. The disunity is a necessary product of description in words: unlike the media of clay or paint, words are an impossible medium in which to map the human body with any correspondence of scale. Without ecphrastic conventions, even the most realistic verbal description is more spatially deranged than any Picasso, because the spatial orientation of words in narrative has no similarity to our visual, tactile, and aural experience of bodies in space. The Pardoner is an odd set of objects moving and ticking near the man carrying that stiff burden: a loud song; some hanging hair, yellow wax, and flax; a pair of shoulders spread with thin locks; a bare-naked, unpinned rider in a cap; a pair of hare's eyes; a beard and close shave that aren't there; a high-pitched bleating goat; a hot wallet; a gelding; and a mare. Thought of as unrelated objects in a field these are odd enough; brought together into a patchwork single body, we have something more monstrous than Dr. Frankenstein's creations.

But few readers find the description incoherent in the least, because we are skilled at working the bumps of figurative language (here, idioms, similes, and metaphors) into the smooth fabric of propositional statement, and because we know how to catch the conventional signals that set up the topos of the two buddies and the genre of the portrait. Yet we miss the main formal feature of these lines until we say that, at a midlevel between rhetorical tropes and genre, readers also recognize a set of heterogeneous figural and characterological conventions that manage the process of meaning by recourse to social persons.

Bodies, matter, and space are, in verbal accounts, entirely figurative: this body is not meaningfully organized in material, geographical space (that space between London and Canterbury to which the process of narration encourages us to give priority) but rather in multiple dimensions of social space. The fragmentary details are taken from their places in old patterns of signification and, like a collage, evoke those patterns synecdochically in order to help us reassemble meaning in a new figure. The spatially incoherent conglomeration made by the newly collected fragments—a shape projected by the text—alternates in our minds with the outlines of figures remembered in the allusions of the details. Here stands the lineup of all the social persons that readers have found were evoked by the passage: the jolly seducer, the preening cleric, the vice figure, the animal-like body from the fabliaux, the courtly eunuch, the sodomite, the homosexual, the hermaphrodite, and the pardoner of anticlerical satire. (The satirical pardoner of anticlericalism is, if at all, evoked solely by name until the second half of the portrait, which abandons the sexual characterization and speaks instead of "his craft.")

It is as if the attempt to conjure a body by reciting words has the effect of raising a dozen ghosts. Readers see the Pardoner's body, no matter how differently, only by means of those ghosts. Without the templates their social persons provide, he would be unintelligible to us. Good readers perform the instructions and supply the ghostly social persons so easily that it is often difficult to make them aware of how very abstract and peculiar an operation it is. When reading instructs us to imagine the visual experience of the Pardoner's body, we must think first and picture second. As the narrator moves from the account of his sensual perceptions to the conclusive statement of belief, "I trowe he were a geldyng or a mare," he imitates the reader's experience in reverse, and "sees" before he "thinks." In this way, the poem encourages us to imagine the priority of the Pardoner's body over the verbal description and the cognitive instructions it encodes; but without the mediation of social persons, no meaning and no coherent picture can be produced. The description cannot create a body in our minds unless we can attach the detail of wax to some glimmer of human meaning (and it need not be the effigy I have specified: any figuration of the human can start the process). Thus social persons have a kind of creative ontological priority over the bodies that fiction presents as prior to them.

The obvious fact that many of the social persons invoked by the portrait are incompatible invites us as readers to deliberate about their applicability to the Pardoner. Important distinctions and qualifications arise out of this critical activity as we begin to think about how social persons need to be understood in historical terms. For example, could "mare" mean "homosexual"? That depends, of course, on what "homosexual" is taken to mean. Exactly when "the homosexual" becomes an intelligible category of the person is a matter of dispute, a dispute that has deepened our sense of the grey area between behaviors and identities, reinvigorating the importance of social history to philological analysis.[64] I suppose that sexual behaviors we now find sufficient to identify someone as the social person "homosexual" were frequent in the fourteenth century. However, I am of the camp that thinks the social person of the homosexual is an invention of the late nineteenth and early twentieth century. The important point for interpretation, however, is that for Chaucer's living readers the modern category determines how sexuality is understood; therefore, any analysis we make of medieval sexuality must be accountable to both medieval and modern categories of the person, explaining medieval social persons through our own.[65] We have hardly begun to understand the relation of sexual activity to medieval social persons, and until we do, banishing the category of "the homosexual" risks incurring greater historical inaccuracy than its anachronism can cause. Like other analytical acts, the history of the social person requires a challenging and imperfect task of translation.

The point I want to make is that social persons haunt the portrait of the Pardoner and invite our identificatory discoveries and disagreements, so as to engage us in the process of deliberation that is central to the exercise—or thought experiment—of fiction. Figuration in art causes us to deliberate about social persons. A particular character, such as Chaucer's Pardoner, evokes a multitude of social persons and, with them, all kinds of values and expectations we can bring to our evaluation of the character and of ourselves. All are available, and some better than others engage the instructions of the poem. Even the most tightly ideologically controlled kinds of characterizations, such as those D. W. Robertson was wont to describe, become open to multiple standards as they circulate among audiences. The use of a common and heterogeneous language makes this cir-

64. The question was pointed for the present generation by Michel Foucault in the three-volume *The History of Sexuality* [*Histoire de la sexualité*] (1976–84); see Carolyn Dinshaw, *Getting Medieval: Sexualities and Communities, Pre- and Postmodern* (Durham: Duke University Press, 1999), 22–38 for an important assessment of Foucault, John Boswell, and others on this question.

65. There is a fast growing body of writing on what we now call the queerness of the Pardoner; see, for example, Steven F. Kruger, "Claiming the Pardoner: Toward a Gay Reading of Chaucer's Pardoner's Tale," *Exemplaria* 6 (1994): 115–39; Glenn Burger, "Doing What Comes Naturally: The Physician's Tale and the Pardoner," in *Masculinities in Chaucer: Approaches to Maleness in the "Canterbury Tales" and "Troilus and Criseyde,"* ed. Peter G. Beidler (Cambridge: D. S. Brewer, 1998), 117–30; and especially the sustained and subtle attention Carolyn Dinshaw has devoted to the text in *Chaucer's Sexual Poetics* (Madison: University of Wisconsin Press, 1989), 156–84, and *Getting Medieval*, 100–142. I hope the notion of the social person will contribute to the increasingly important historical questions raised by the relation between sexual behavior, sexual ideology, and identity.

culation inherently possible; authors like Chaucer increase the probability of such circulation by mixing lexicons and cross-pollinating topoi, genres, and characterizations.

What does this deliberation look like? Centuries of good readers have made the Pardoner into a particularly full demonstration of the ethical process that figural representation initiates. Types, discourses, diagnoses have all been adduced to help explain how we should imagine him, and plenty of resistance to the authority of various interpretive schemes has also been recorded. The role of detail in simultaneously evoking social person and recalling us to the specificity of the portrait is richly performed in the history of Chaucer criticism. This is an explicitly ethical and even political process: each ghostly social person brings with it values, standards of evaluation, a configuration of attributes, a sense of possible actions and plots, an orientation toward social institutions. When the Pardoner is identified as a eunuch (Curry, Dinshaw), it leads to different ethical evaluations of the character than when he is identified as a homosexual (MacAlpine), a sodomite (Frantzen, though disavowing), a queer (Dinshaw, Burger, Sturges), a preacher (Minnis), a master rhetor (Copeland), a vice figure (Peterson, Neuss), a philanderer (Benson, Green), or (yet another sexual type, this one associated with 1950s America) a salesman (Pearsall).[66] The deliberation about the relation of the Pardoner to these proposed social persons requires us to test historical evidence, to produce new readings, to search out the compatibilities and incompatibilities among social persons, to consider them in terms of predication, of social practices, and of institutions. *The Canterbury Tales* represents such deliberation as it records the responses of its characters to one another; it is

---

66. This exuberant and inexhaustive list refers to Walter Clyde Curry, *Chaucer and the Mediaeval Sciences* (New York: Oxford University Press, 1926), 54–70; Dinshaw, *Chaucer's Sexual Poetics*, 156–84; McAlpine, "The Pardoner's Homosexuality"; Allen J. Frantzen, "The Pardoner's Tale, the Pervert, and the Price of Order in Chaucer's World," in *Class and Gender in Early English Literature: Intersections*, ed. Britton J. Harwood and Gillian R. Overing, (Bloomington: Indiana University Press, 1994), 131–47; Carolyn Dinshaw, "Chaucer's Queer Touches/A Queer Touches Chaucer," *Exemplaria* 7 (1995): 75–92; Glenn Burger, "Kissing the Pardoner," *PMLA* 107 (1992): 1143–56; Robert S. Sturges, *Chaucer's Pardoner and Gender Theory: Bodies of Discourse* (New York: St. Martin's, 2000); Minnis, "Chaucer's Pardoner"; Copeland, "The Pardoner's Body and the Disciplining of Rhetoric"; Joyce E. Peterson, "With Feigned Flattery: The Pardoner as Vice," *Chaucer Review* 10 (1976): 326–36; Paula Neuss, "The Pardoner's Tale: An Early Moral Play?" in *Religion in the Poetry and Drama of the Late Middle Ages in England*, ed. Piero Boitani and Anna Torti (Cambridge: D. S. Brewer, 1990), 119–32; C. David Benson, "Chaucer's Pardoner: His Sexuality and Modern Critics," *Mediaevalia* 8 (1982): 337–49; Richard Firth Green, "The Sexual Normality of Chaucer's Pardoner," *Mediaevalia* 8 (1982): 351–58; and Derek Pearsall, "Chaucer's Pardoner: The Death of a Salesman," *Chaucer Review* 17 (1983): 358–65.

also designed to produce such deliberation and has done so plentifully for many generations.

I hope to deflect our attention from the attempts to identify the Pardoner with a single social person and to describe, instead, how the conflict among social persons generates ethical deliberation about his body and his preaching that then leads us into political deliberation about the ideals and institutional arrangements of society. There is a still closer connection than I have yet described between the Pardoner's conflicting array of social persons and the paradoxical descriptions of intention that arise out of the canon law's two fora, and this connection helps to explain the powerful sexualization of his portrait. As we have seen in the Pardoner's Prologue, the philosophical issue of Chaucer's thought experiment chiefly concerns intention: how far does intention extend outside the person and into others? The question of intention's extensivity arises easily in terms of the sexual body and sexual behavior, because sexuality is something both carnal and social, something that (like the sacrament of communion, pregnancy, the eating of flesh, and murder) can involve the interpenetration of bodies.

The issue of intention is indelibly associated with Abelard for philosophers because, as you will remember, he posits the most radical situating of meaning within intention, denying the relevance of acts. Whether or not this argument is related to Abelard's traumatic castration by the family of his lover Heloise (but why not?), the mapping of intention, act, and consequence onto the sexual body was widely recognized. A sense of the intellectual content of sexual behavior developed alongside the importance of the internal forum. The legal historian James A. Brundage writes: "The late twelfth century was a period in which attitudes toward homosexual behavior were beginning to change. Sexual practices and preferences in this period commenced to be taken as indicators of doctrinal orthodoxy; deviance from the dominant sexual preference was thought to manifest deviance from accepted doctrine."[67] Sexuality, that is, became a way of thinking about intention.

The General Prologue employs sexual configurations of the body as tropes for intention in its portrait of the Pardoner. There, Chaucer memorably speculates:

> A voys he hadde as smal as hath a goot.
> No berd hadde he, ne nevere sholde have;
> As smothe it was as it were late shave.
> I trowe he were a geldyng or a mare.
> (688–91)

---

67. James A. Brundage, *Law, Sex, and Christian Society in Medieval Europe* (Chicago: University of Chicago Press, 1987), 313.

These descriptions employ a map of the body that stresses the bodily signs of sexuality in order to suggest something about the capacity of the Pardoner to accomplish his will. Horses are a traditional symbol for the will and the passions, which must be trained and "bridled."[68] Chaucer compares the Pardoner to two kinds of horses that are sexual opposites in three ways. First, they are of opposite genders. Second, females carry their reproductive organs largely on the inside; males carry them largely on the outside, so that it is easy to see if a male horse has been castrated. And third, of course, a "mare" is a sexually potent animal meant for breeding, whereas a "geldyng" is a castrate. The paradoxical relationship between the Pardoner's cupidinous will and his spiritual impotence is corporeally registered as a cluster of contradictory sexual attributes. The disturbance of an effective link between intention and action is conveyed by the pervasive theme of bodily dismemberment, present both in the Pardoner's relics and in the narrator's and the host's interest in castration—a bodily sign of an interruption between seed and fruit, between the will and satisfaction, between intention and act.[69]

In the sexual characterization of the Pardoner, Chaucer draws upon a wider discourse of anticlericalism. A sexual metaphor for the simoniac also appears in the Lollard condemnation of such clerics for serving two masters, the temporal and the spiritual: "hermaphrodite or ambidexter would be good names for such men of double estate."[70] Here genital and manual iconography are both invoked to describe an illicit activity. Wyclif takes his sexual diagnosis of the sin of simony from the same thinker Chaucer relies upon in the Parson's Tale, William Peraldus: "Whence the Parisian in his treatise *On Avarice*, in listing eight reasons to detest this sin [simony], expresses its terrible nature by calling it spiritual sodomy. For just as in carnal sodomy contrary to nature the seed is

---

68. For example, John Bromyard, *Summa predicantium*, quoted in G. R. Owst, *Literature and Pulpit in Medieval England*, 2d rev. ed. (Oxford: Basil Blackwell, 1961), 89–90.

69. In her essay "Eunuch Hermeneutics" Carolyn Dinshaw is eloquent on the relation of loss and sexuality in the Pardoner, connecting the economy of relics in his own discursive world with a kind of spiritual fetishism. She explains this valence of Chaucer's sexual figuration, writing of the Pardoner's origins in the *Roman de la rose*: "So human language was seen, by many medieval thinkers, to be *essentially* partial. This is why Raison's narration of castration leads to a discussion of language and relics: 'coilles,' 'reliques,' 'paroles,' they're *all* fragments" (171). Dinshaw demonstrates that Chaucer figures his poetics through a gendered, bodily sexuality throughout his work, and that to do this he draws on ancient and medieval discussions of meaning and language already saturated with sexual tropes. My understanding of the Pardoner depends upon this essay, which also moves from a consideration of the Pardoner's Prologue and Tale to the Retraction. *Chaucer's Sexual Poetics*, 156–84.

70. Quoted in *Heresy and Authority in Medieval Europe*, ed. Edward Peters (Philadelphia: University of Pennsylvania Press, 1980), 279.

lost by which an individual human being would be formed, so in this sodomy the seed of God's word is cast aside with which a spiritual generation in Christ Jesus would be created." In this passage the conjunction between the interior state of avarice and the act of simony is developed as sexual waste. He goes on to draw a typological and historical relation between sodomy and simony: "And just as sodomy in the time of the law of nature was one of the most serious sins against nature, so simony in the time of the law of grace is one of the most serious sins against grace. And since the devil's adherents sin more seriously in the time of the law of grace than they had sinned in the time of the law of nature, Christ expressly says to the simoniacs in Matthew 10:15 that it will be more tolerable for the land of Sodom on judgment day than for a people who reject worthy rulers."[71] Chaucer takes these sexualizations of simony and embodies them in the Pardoner in a way that stresses the complex relation of vicious interior states of intention and will to exterior behavior such as usury and fraud. This complex relation is expressed in the two-part description of habitus (again, the disposition of the body and soul that results from habitual practices) delineated by the portrait: the sexualized style attributed to the Pardoner describes the habitus shaping his animal body; his craft and practices describe the fit between the habitus and the social person. The following sections concern this war on two fronts. First, one final pass through the Pardoner's Prologue and Tale will investigate why particular practices and speech acts are chosen by Chaucer to make up the habitus of the Pardoner. Then I shall argue that the Retraction, a little appendage to the Parson's Tale and so the very end of the poem, explicitly transforms the social persons of penance into literary persons that embody a new theoretical structuring of intention. Thus Chaucer brings *The Canterbury Tales* to a stunningly meta-disciplinary close. Thus he also brilliantly cashes in on the project epitomized by the Pardoner sections but pursued throughout the *Tales*: the habituation of the reader to the explanation and experience of interiority by means of literary fiction.

---

71. Wyclif, *On Simony*, 36 (9:5). Wyclif is referring to William Peraldus (c. 1200–c.1271) and his treatises *Summa virtutum* and *Summa vitiorum*. Throughout *Getting Medieval*, Carolyn Dinshaw treats late medieval discourses on sodomy as important to the exclusion and inclusion of community. Her comments on the association between sodomy and simony appear at 61–64. Lee Patterson also connects the Pardoner's simony to sodomy and adds evidence to his earlier readings of the Pardoner as bearing essentially religious meanings in the course of an argument against psychoanalytic critical approaches, "Chaucer's Pardoner on the Couch: Psyche and Clio in Medieval Literary Studies," *Speculum* 76 (2001): 638–80. On sodomy, see Mark D. Jordan, *The Invention of Sodomy in Christian Theology* (Chicago: University of Chicago Press, 1997).

Habitual Action and the Person

Let us return to the poem to see how the Pardoner's commercial practices and acts dispose his body to be fit to his primary social person. His disposition, as Chaucer presents it, is formed by medieval economic thought, especially its peculiarly intimate and, indeed, personal accounts of money. The Pardoner's habitual acts—his habitus in action—are the source of his fascination for his audience both inside and outside the poem. Chaucer creates an exquisite *modus operandi* for him: to make a literary confession function as both a sales pitch and a sermon. By exposing his interior, he creates a spellbinding intimacy with his audience. The object of confession is to reveal one's own intentions; the object of a sales pitch and a sermon is to create intentions in others. The Pardoner combines these objects in his self-revelations and in the sacrifices that he encourages the audience to make:

> Goode men and wommen, o thyng warne I yow:
> If any wight be in this chirche now   *person*
> That hath doon synne horrible, that he
> Dar nat, for shame, of it yshryven be,
> Or any womman, be she yong or old,
> That hath ymaked hir housbonde cokewold,
> Swich folk shal have no power ne no grace
> To offren to my relikes in this place.
> And whoso fyndeth hym out of swich blame,
> He wol come up and offre a Goddes name,
> And I assoille him by the auctoritee
> Which that by bulle ygraunted was to me.
> (377–88)

This is a particularly egregious attempt to inculcate intentions inside an audience: under the lure of absolution, it both accuses his listeners of horrible sin and shame and, further, forces them to defend their innocence by giving money. The verb in the phrase "He wol come up and offre" is ambiguously declarative *and* imperative: it appears innocently as a description, "he wishes to offer," yet there is the undertone of blackmail in the command, "he will offer." This he admits to his present audience, boasting that his speech is a "gaude," or trick:

> By this gaude have I wonne, yeer by yeer,
> An hundred mark sith I was pardoner.
> (389–90)

The operation that the Pardoner tries to perform upon his audience here, with the rough and subtle instrument of the sales pitch, is the substitution of a notion of external for internal intention. In miniature, the passage tries to do as we shall see, what his sermon and tale attempt at large. And in the same move, Chaucer deftly connects his portrayal of the habitus directly to the poem's habituation of its readers.

Money is an excellent symbol of the connection between the portrayal and performance of habituation, because the thoroughly abstract character of money in scholastic theory paradoxically qualified it to act as a powerful social bond, linking persons and commodities in its role as the *general equivalent*.[72] Financial transactions depend wholly on social rules, though they pretend to follow naturalized, mathematical ones; medieval (like modern) discussions of money's attributes think about human behavior in a refracted, generalizing way that treats all human agents as roughly the same. Medieval theorists were in agreement with Aristotle that money civilized social differences by providing a medium for trade.[73] In order to perform this role as it was circumscribed by the scholastics, money was understood as something that owed no natural loyalty to its possessor: it was absolutely alienable from the person. The exchange of a product of personal labor for impersonal, abstract coin reveals the act of economic trade as the moment of the alienation of value from the person. Similarly, the exchange of negatively valued, personal sin for positively valued, impersonal grace reveals the sacrament of penance as the moment in which intention is alienated from the person.

Perhaps because its early punishments were monetary fines, penitential discourse draws heavily on the Bible's economic themes and commercial language of debt, exchange, redemption, and satisfaction. In the character of Chaucer's Pardoner, as in the case of Urban III and his handling of usury, the two worlds of the confessional and of commerce are combined, yet remain in conflict. When Chaucer uses the business of the Pardoner to think about how intention is alienable, he employs the theme of exchange that was shared by economic thought and sacramental theology. In the disquieting analogy between sales and penance, the Pardoner demonstrates a commercial exchange and a sacrament to be the same act, the same event, the same alienation. As a social person, a pardoner is a kind of corrupt intention disposed to corrupt economic practices.

---

72. The concept of the general equivalent will be developed at more length in chapters 2 and 3, where medieval economic thought plays an important role in my treatment of *Piers Plowman* and "The Tunnyng of Elynour Rummynge."

73. A good introduction to early economic theory is Odd Langholm, *Economics in the Medieval Schools: Wealth, Exchange, Value, Money and Usury according to the Paris Theological Tradition, 1200–1350* (Leiden: E. J. Brill, 1992). My analysis depends on his throughout this section and the following chapters.

Under the rubric *radix malorum est cupiditas*, Chaucer's portrait of the Pardoner evokes three precepts that were of great importance to the economic analysis of the canonists. These three principles permeated the theoretical discussion of money in the middle ages: its *sterility*, its *consumptibility*, and its *atemporality*. Each of these precepts declared a negative proposition: that money does not breed as animals do; that it does not survive its use, being more like wine than a house; and that it is not mutable over time. Thus usury, selling the use of money, was proscribed because it was impossible to sell produce when there had been no reproduction, fraudulent to sell something that was already consumed, and immoral to sell time, which, like the sale of knowledge by teachers, was the illicit sale of a resource that was a free gift from God. In this era, some Christian Europeans felt about time and knowledge the way some pre-conquest North Americans reportedly felt about land: it was sacrilegious to convert such valuables to commodities and to trade them in a money economy.

In scholastic thought, the idea of money's sterility draws a distinction between money and other fecund kinds of commodities, such as livestock and useful plants.[74] Among the benefits that the Pardoner offers to those who will give him money for the use of his relics are two kinds of usurious profit that miraculously result. If, in exchange for an offering, a sheep bone is dipped in a well and the farmer drinks of the well each morning, then: "As thilke hooly Jew oure eldres taughte, / His beestes and his stoor shal multiplie" (364–65). Similarly, the Pardoner offers a mitten into which a farmer may put his hand in order to "have multipliyng of his grayn, / Whan he hath sowen, be it whete or otes, / So that he offre pens, or elles grotes" (374–76). Coins do not bear young—unless, that is, they are entered into the Pardoner's confidence scheme. The sexual description of the Pardoner as a castrate gelding or a breedable mare maps a theme of fertility onto both parts of his double act: sterility and potential pregnancy are inappropriate not only to his apparent sex but to his role as a collector of money and a dispenser of pardons. The Pardoner should not be making a speculative economic exchange; thus he should not be profiting as his boasts claim he does. Nor should he be offering usurious returns on the money given him. He should, however, be assisting in the sacrament by allowing penitents to be rewarded for giving alms toward worthy projects. The sacrament itself should, as the canonists say, bear the fruit of God's grace. Thus, the sacrament administered by a vicious minister might be valid, but it could not convey sacramental grace. As we have seen, this was

74. For an example loved by poets, see Aegidius Romanus (1247–1316), *De regimine principum*, 2.3.11, which draws on Aristotle and Aquinas.

a way of acknowledging the damage such sin might cause without making the sacrament ineffective or illicit. The hint of sterility about the "geldyng" Pardoner expresses such a deprivation of the fruit called sacramental grace, a deprivation that he might cause in the sacrament of penance by abusing the pardon.

These sexual and commercial themes structure the Prologue, the Tale, and even the pilgrims' response to the performance. Though, according to the Pardoner, the "develes officeres" that appear in the tavern at the very opening of the tale—the female "tombesteres," "yonge frutesteres," and "wafereres"—all "kyndle and blowe the fyr of lecherye" (477–81), they are figures for sterile sexual transactions only.[75] This lively description of illicit sales is given a particular moral charge through sacramental associations: wafers and fruit are here wasted rather than being properly consumed in the rite of the Eucharist, in which they undergo transubstantiation and in which proper intention bears the fruit of sacramental grace. The Host seems to interpret the Pardoner accurately when he refuses to give money and offers to castrate him instead. For the host, the sterile financial transaction, rather than the fruitful sacrament, is the proper diagnosis of the Pardoner's double act.

> "Nay, nay!" quod he, "thanne have I Cristes curs!
> Lat be," quod he, "it shal nat be, so theech!   *I swear*
> Thou woldest make me kisse thyn olde breech,
> And swere it were a relyk of a seint,
> Though it were with thy fundement depeint!   *bottom*
> But, by the croys which that Seint Eleyne fond,
> I wolde I hadde thy coillons in myn hond   *testicles*
> In stide of relikes or of seintuarie.
> Lat kutte hem of, I wol thee helpe hem carie;
> They shul be shryned in an hogges toord!"
> (946–55)

Rather than the Pardoner's supposedly fecund relics, the Host asserts, we should take his severed testicles as the proper sign of his works. They should be enshrined "in an hogges toord" to show that they represent the dead waste of consumption, rather than a promise of generative abundance. Cupidity, the root of evil, is both over-fecund and sterile; as the tale

---

75. The appearance of the "tombesteres" or tumblers is followed quickly by an account of the tumble that Adam took; here the Pardoner somewhat bathetically accuses Adam of gluttony. If only he had been "moore mesurable / Of his diete, sittynge at his table" (515–16), the fall might have been prevented. Chapter 3 will discuss similar connections among gluttony, waste, and women in the poetry of John Skelton. ·

suggests, avarice leads to material rewards that seem to offer profit but produce only sterility.

The Pardoner's practices abuse not only what never properly was but also what already has been. According to the scholastic analysts, consumptibility, another frequently stressed theme in medieval economic thinking about fraud, is a quality of money that classifies it with wine.[76] Wine cannot be sold again after it is consumed; thus neither can money. In this view, of course, illicit financial transactions are associated with gluttony, waste, and sexual activity devoid of the intention to procreate. When treated synecdochically by satirists, money becomes a consuming force in itself, draining things of their value and corrupting souls.[77] Like the cooks of whom the Pardoner complains in a stunning philosophical and theological conceit, money turns "substaunce into accident" (539). Again, Chaucer shows this process—a kind of reverse transubstantiation—at work in the Pardoner's habitus, in the Tale, and in the audience.

The frequent mention of consumptible commodities draws an economic analysis of value into the Pardoner's world of words: they create an unsatisfying but tempting continuum that resembles what psychoanalysts call a signifying chain. Gold, silver, money, wool, cheese, and wheat will be converted by the Pardoner into liquid dissipation and sexual debauchery (448–53), even though they come from the poorest page or widow of the village. Such activities are rhetorically opposed to productive labor in the lines that frame his long list of consumables:

> I wol nat do no labour with myne handes,
> Ne make baskettes and lyve therby,
>
> (444–45)

> Nay, I wol drynke licour of the vyne
> And have a joly wenche in every toun.
>
> (452–53)

Expressed in the scholastic association between gold and wine that informs the ending of the Pardoner's Tale, the consumptibility of money weighs heavily in Chaucer's consideration of intention. He shows that both sacramental and other less exalted kinds of intention have a defining effect upon acts and persons. The intention to make money causes the Pardoner's actions to dissipate value rather than produce it; his own satisfaction is dissipated in the process.

76. See Noonan, *Scholastic Analysis*, especially 56; Justinian, *Digest*, 7.5, especially paragraph 7, which quotes Gaius; and Thomas Aquinas, *Summa theologica*, 2.2.78.1–3.

77. John Skelton's "Elynour Rummynge" is a brilliant example of such a satire and occupies our attention in chapter 3.

The power of money to consume is well deployed by the Pardoner in his tale when the ingenious opening sermon on gluttony is paired with the story of how gold led three tavern customers to their grisly deaths. This opening scene contains a parody of communion that is answered by another at the story's close. In the former, certain young folk of the great commercial center, Flanders, are described in a rich genre painting that mocks the Eucharist. They love riot, gambling, brothels, and taverns:

> They daunce and pleyen at dees bothe day and nyght,
> And eten also and drynken over hir myght,
> Thurgh which they doon the devel sacrifise
> Withinne that develes temple in cursed wise
> By superfluytee abhomynable.
> Hir othes been so grete and so dampnable
> That it is grisly for to heere hem swere.
> Oure blissed Lordes body they totere—   *tear apart*
> Hem thoughte that Jewes rente hym noght ynough—
> And ech of hem at otheres synne lough.
>
> (467–76)

At the close of the story, having abandoned the quest to kill the great thief death, the unholy trinity of revelers slaughters its youngest member, and then unwittingly but fatally shares the poisoned wine. Neatly severed from their quest and its *imitatio Christi* by the old man's Abelardian reduction of their acts to their intentions, the three characters take gold as a substitute object. As a metonym for their cupidity, gold turns substance into accident, persons into corpses, in a way that parodies the sacramental transubstantiation of wine into blood. The cupidity of their intention to find death is what brings death to them in this particularly vicious form. The parodies of the Eucharist stretch Abelard's position to a horrific extreme: even such gruesome acts as murder and cannibalism are to be deemed good or bad solely according to intention.

Sin is more than a behavior or a wish; it is, as we have seen in Abelard, an intention that leaves the soul in a persistently sinful state until it is redeemed by contrition and confession. This sinful state, induced by an intention, colors not only any behavior that might result directly from the intention but also any good behavior preceding the sin, as well as good behavior that is accomplished during the state of sin. The Parson describes such works as "dead" works: "Soothly, the goode werkes that he dide biforn that he fil in synne been al mortefied and astoned and dulled by the ofte synnyng. / The othere goode werkes, that he wroghte whil he lay in deedly synne, thei been outrely dede, as to the lyf perdurable in hevene. / Thanne thilke goode werkes that been mortefied by ofte synnyng, whiche goode werkes he dide whil he was in charitee, ne mowe nevere quyken agayn withouten verray penitence" (Parson's Tale 233–235). Sinful intention nullifies good works and separates the sinner from "lyf perdurable in hevene," a separation that is expressed in a temporal register. Good works do not persist in time under the pressure of sin unless they are revivified by penance and its special temporal process; conversely, the good works of saints continue to be accomplished by the relics of their bodies long after normal bodily action is possible. Thus, there is a paradoxical relation between the relics hawked by the Pardoner and their promises of life. Such a sinner is imagined by the Parson as a person who embodies a disturbed and morbid relation to living temporality.

There is an aspect of this morbidity in the Pardoner's effect on his audience. Scholastic theorists think of money as atemporal, but when the Pardoner sells pardons he attempts to trade time off purgatory for money; when he sells the action of relics he offers another temporal disturbance. The compulsive narrative temporal structure of the Pardoner's Prologue is itself frightening: he explains his usual "gaude" to the pilgrims, then tells his tale and performs the "gaude" on them, his exhibition of his methods thus creating an obsessional sense of atemporality through repetition and a blurring of reported actions with present ones. The compulsion to repeat the trick is a morbidity that the Pardoner's acts have inculcated in him. The effect provides an awful kind of gothic thrill as the narrative moves rapidly toward the audience, as if his corruption were involuntary, contagious, and fatal.

The simoniacal nature of all of these practices makes the Pardoner his own first victim. His financial scams cause him to take on the objective qualities of money from which he then suffers. Sterility, consumptibility, and atemporality become his very nature. While his spiritual commerce may seem to him to be the pursuit of unmitigated self-satisfaction, in the penitential logic of the poem such a pursuit cannot address his real needs. As Boethius is told in Chaucer's translation of *De consolatione philosophiae*: "Thanne mai nat richesses maken that a man nys [is not] nedy, ne that he be suffisaunt to hymself; and yit that was it that thei byhighten [promise], as it semeth" (Book III, Prosa 3, 52–55). The Pardoner suffers from both excessive self-assertion and increasing indifference, both rapaciousness and impotence, and this double nature is the embodiment of his habitus.

The "bisynesse" (399) of his practices promises to enrich and satisfy him, yet it seems instead to suspend him in perpetual repetition of his need. The Pardoner has already threatened his audience with the theologians' ideas about how sin presents an impediment to the enjoyment of the fruits of penance:

> Swich [sinful] folk shal have no power ne no grace
> To offren to my relikes in this place.
>
> (383–84)

As the word "power" indicates, sin is figured here as incapacitating and, as the word "grace" acknowledges, depriving. Instead of the satisfaction which has been figured sexually in the Prologue, where he claims that he will "have a joly wenche in every toun" (453), at the end of his tale the Pardoner receives only the insults of the host, who infamously wishes to castrate him.

Do the Pardoner's actions dismember or replenish him? Wyclif describes language's struggles with the mysteriously personifying and depersonifying force that sin wreaks upon the habitus:

> Generally sin is spoken of equivocally, either in regard to its form or in regard to its deformity, and thus every sin is a defect, not a positive entity, or if it is considered under its material cause, an inordinate act or habit is called sin. Indeed a sin sometimes is identified with the sinner, or the sinful offering is identified with the sin. But because the external acts of the soul are best known to us and therefore the church must have knowledge of simoniacal heresy, it is reasonable, therefore, to speak of it insofar as it is an act, and both the defect of sin as well as the vicious habit are inseparably connected with the act itself.[78]

In the strange continuum that is intention, action, and consequence, a continuum calcified by habitual action, persons are made and unmade.

Perhaps that effect accounts for the Pardoner's habitual fondness for apostrophe, a rhetorical figure that attempts to create and dissolve person. Chaucer builds the uncomfortably mixed spiritual and economic habitus of the Pardoner into the confidence man's speech acts. As a means for swaying an audience, apostrophe is frequent throughout both the prologue and tale. At the end of the story of the rioters, a string of apostrophes converts the Pardoner's exhortation to extortion. The voice moves frighteningly smoothly. An address to Murder too easily becomes a reported address to his past audiences and then a direct address to the present pilgrims and to us, Chaucer's living audience:

> O cursed synne of alle cursednesse!
> O traytours homycide, O wikkednesse!
> O glotonye, luxurie, and hasardrye!   *gambling*
> Thou blasphemour of Crist with vileynye

78. Wyclif, *On Simony*, 59–60.

> And othes grete, of usage and of pride!
> Allas, mankynde, how may it bitide
> . . .
> Now, goode men, God foryeve yow youre trespas,
> And ware yow fro the synne of avarice!   *warn*
> Myn hooly pardoun may yow alle warice,   *cure*
> So that ye offre nobles or sterlynges.
>   (895–900, 904–7)

This rhetorical attempt to place his audience in the position of the deadly sins is designed to make them want, in turn, to displace themselves from the uncomfortable state of personified sin. They can do this simply, the Pardoner explains, by the act of offering money.

Such a longing for exchange repeats the longing of the tale's old man:

> Ne Deeth, allas, ne wol nat han my lyf.
> Thus walke I, lyk a restelees kaityf,   *prisoner*
> And on the ground, which is my moodres gate,
> I knokke with my staf, bothe erly and late,
> And seye "Leeve mooder, leet me in!
> Lo how I vanysshe, flessh, and blood, and skyn!
> Allas, whan shul my bones been at reste?
> Mooder, with yow wolde I chaunge my cheste
> That in my chambre longe tyme hath be,
> Ye, for an heyre clowt to wrappe [in] me!"   *haircloth*
>   (727–36)[79]

The old man asks to trade his worldly possessions (the chest and his age) for spiritual ones (the shrift and shroud represented by the haircloth: repentance and death). He asks to be taken in by the earth, the second person addressed in his apostrophe and a personified substance alien to him yet figured as his mother. The awkward twist caused by the rhyme in the last line "an heyre clowt to wrappe in me," which reads "in me" or "me" where we expect "to wrap me in,"[80] conveys a sense of his suffering, longing and confusion about the relations between the few objects in his mental universe: the staff, the bones, the chest, the chamber, the haircloth. Each object has an ambiguous status in relation to his sense of himself. Each vacillates among three metaphorical meanings: each is alternately a part of his body, an instrument of his body, and a haven for his body. The

---

79. Cf. The Parson's Tale, 213–16.
80. Larry D. Benson chooses the "me" reading. The "in me" phrase appears in the groups of manuscripts he calls Egerton and Harley (Ha), and in the New College manuscript, and, among the editions cited by Benson, in Robinson's second and Baugh. See the "Textual Notes" section of *The Riverside Chaucer* (1130).

chest, for example, seems simultaneously to indicate the ribcage that holds his heart, the strongbox that holds his property, and the coffin in which he will give himself to the earth. These meanings equivocate and produce a kind of semantic aura around the riddle-like words of his wish.

Persisting and vanishing simultaneously, the figure of the old man itself hovers between life and death, carnality and spirituality, movement and immobility, without the ability to rest in the occupation of any of these states. Wishing to exchange the chest that holds his property for a penitential haircloth may suggest a desire to move away from the tortures of avarice, if not the state of considered repentance that might effect such a movement; thus we can see him as the evocation of a possible fate of the Pardoner. Thomas Aquinas writes that "while in *Mark* we read that the possessed man tore his clothes off, the greedy man [avarus] wraps himself up in unneeded possessions."[81] This passage appears in the article that questions whether avarice is a spiritual or a carnal sin. Thomas concludes that avarice, like Chaucer's old man, occupies a midpoint between spirituality and carnality: "Set upon an objective relating to the body, avarice is still not a quest for the pleasures of body but of soul, namely the experience wherein a person delights in his possession of riches. This is why it is not a carnal sin. Still, because of the objective, it is true that it [avarice] stands midway between purely spiritual sins, which pursue an inner delight in regard to some intangible objective—as pride does with regard to personal worth—and purely carnal sins, which pursue sheer physical pleasure in some objective related to body."[82] Hovering at the midpoint between states, longing for transformation, the old man is a pivot upon which more than the plot depends. He expresses the "ententif desir" (Parson's Tale 781) of simony to exchange spiritual things for temporal ones, and it causes his body to equivocate ever more wildly and abstractly between carnality and spirituality.

The old man longs to trade his age with some willing youth whom he futilely seeks and to exchange his possessions with a "yow" whom he believes to be his mother. Such "chaunge" is both transformation and exchange. On a more metaphysical plane, it recapitulates the trope of economic exchange, the event that is the purpose of the Pardoner's apostrophes. And once we read apostrophe as an attempted exchange, we may hold it to the standard expressed by the prohibition against simony. As Wyclif says, rephrasing the Aristotelian ideas of Thomas Aquinas: "Thus the sin [of simony] consists not in the exchange itself but in the extraordinary desire for the exchange, because it is not primarily a matter of

---

81. Thomas Aquinas, *Summa theologica*, 2.2.118.6, Blackfriars, 41:258–59.
82. Thomas Aquinas, *Summa theologica*, 2.2.118.6, Blackfriars, 41:256–59.

the extrinsic act but rather more deeply a matter of the act of willing. And because from this approach it would be possible for error to exist in the volitional power which is designated 'will,' simony therefore is said significantly to consist in an act of volitional power."[83] Apostrophe exposes the "deepness" of the act of simony, how far it cuts into the person, but also the paradox of the social relationship it forms. It expresses the subject's desire for a bond to and a severance from its object. Like a reversed mirror image of the old man, the Pardoner wishes not for union, but for satisfaction at the expense of others:

> I wol noon of the apostles countrefete;
> I wol have moneie, wolle, chese, and whete,
> Al were it yeven of the povereste page,
> Or of the povereste wydwe in a village,
> Al sholde hir children sterve for famyne.
>
> (447–51)

During the Pardoner's apostrophe to the sins, we recognize him as an emblem of his matter—*cupiditas*. His habitual practices are changing him into a vice personified, a figure we recognize from the dramatic and lyric traditions.[84] This hollow man urges us unabashedly to allow him to get away with his exchange. Will his audience sin by consent, or worse, by contribution? For the Pardoner as for the old man, apostrophe represents a failed exchange, a desired but as yet unaccomplished communion in the one case and severance in the other. Apostrophe promises to articulate their desires and bring them to triumphant satisfaction, but it equivocates with them and finally signifies their failure. For both characters the failed exchange expresses a loss that penetrates deeply into the habitus. There is no release for the old man, who longs to achieve a union with something *outside* the will; similarly, no plenitudinous closure is enjoyed by the Pardoner, who boasts of the satisfaction of will inside itself at the expense of what is outside. A similar character is described by Thomas Aquinas: "The incurableness of avarice, however, has its basis in the constant deterioration which besets our nature. Thus, the more needy a person becomes, the more he needs the relief afforded by temporal [*exteriorum*] things and so the more he slips into avarice."[85] Vicious acts habituate a person both to vicious intentional states and to vicious relations with the world.

Chaucer portrays the Pardoner's body as beset by sterility, con-

---

83. Wyclif, *On Simony*, 30. Cf. his *On the Acts of the Soul / De actibus anime*, in *Miscellanea philosophica*, ed. Michael Henry Dziewicki (London: Trübner, 1902), 1:25.

84. Peterson, "With Feigned Flattery," 326–36 and Patterson, *Chaucer and the Subject of History*, 399.

85. Thomas Aquinas, *Summa theologica*, 2.2.118.5.3, Blackfriars, 41:254–55.

sumptibility, and atemporality, suffering in consequence of his habitual practices. As he mixes sales pitch and sermon, apostrophe and threat, and as the purpose of collecting money suborns the formal intention of the sacrament of penance, we see that those practices attach his body to the social person of the medieval pardoner in a self-confirming circuit.

> I trowe he were a geldyng or a mare.
> But of his craft, fro Berwyk into Ware
> Ne was ther swich another pardoner.
> (General Prologue, 691–93)

As his avaricious habitus configures his body with the sterile, consumptible, atemporal attributes of money, it suits him well for the practices of his office. As his habitus creates him as social person, the social person creates his habitus. To say this is to observe, again and more complexly, what we saw at the beginning of the chapter: that the Pardoner's intentions are imposed from the outside (by the social person) and, paradoxically, that his intentions originate entirely in his interior and could not be more voluntarily or thoroughly embraced. We have, according to Quine's criteria, a true paradox. It can only be solved by understanding the relation of habitus to social person.

Reading, Writing, and Habituation

I have been arguing that *The Canterbury Tales* attempts to widen the possibilities of poetry to include the powerful diagnosis of human interiority; that the poem demonstrates the superior resources of fiction for probing the complexities of intention, the institutional and discursive environments of social persons, the indebtedness of interior experience to the habitus, and the paradoxical fit between habitus and social person. Speech act, simile, iconography, genre, apostrophe, paradox, character—these are fictional resources that were not off-limits to canonists and theologians but that in their uses were not directed toward the production of rich interior experience through representations of the person. In Chaucer's hands these resources bloom into a literary discourse that is capable of much more than analysis and prescription: it is capable of performing the experience of the interior and enlisting the reader in that performance. The text of the Pardoner's Prologue and Tale might not have worked as a manual for the confessional, but it works powerfully as a script for the affective experience of intention and its contradictory life. The poem tries to align our skill at interpreting literary language with our skill at interpreting others and ourselves. It teaches us to decode bodily appearance, behavior, and especially speech as signs of habitus and the evidence of both interior states and social positioning. This is Chaucer's new art, and its power is still evident in anglophone culture today.

Of course, legal and theological situations are not the only ones in which a need for describing intention developed. While the Pardoner's Prologue and Tale exploit the jurisprudence of the internal forum, other works of Chaucer consider intention in its other historical contexts. For instance, Biblical exegesis and the practice of rhetoric were other venues in which strong discussions of intention took place from antiquity through the middle ages. Chaucer explores those versions of intention in the Wife of Bath's Prologue, the Melibee, the Nun's Priest's Tale, and elsewhere. In Chaucer's work, intention and interpretation are linked in a different and much less stable way than they are in commentaries, in medieval invocations of the *intentio auctoris* and in Gratian's jurisprudential project of harmonizing discordant canons. As A. J. Minnis has shown, Chaucer most often gives himself the conventional authorial role of the compiler.[86] This social person conventionally seeks to minimize the problem of intention through modesty topoi, the imitation of sources, and a stress on the third person point of view, but Chaucer tends to tease us with these devices, inviting us to wonder about authorial intention, particularly in his disclaimers.

If, in *The Canterbury Tales*, literary fiction displaces the canonists and the theologians and attempts to describe the interior of the person by means of full-blown literary instruments (character, narration, image, plot, rhetoric), then literature must face the problem of intention in its own institutional setting without the practical and institutional contexts that were designed by the church to address the stresses of intentional states. The coda known as Chaucer's "Retraction" follows the Parson's Tale in nearly all manuscripts.[87] The Retraction acknowledges the old standards of the displaced discipline of the interior, even as it celebrates the achievements of literary fiction. It begins, "Heere taketh the makere of this book his leve" and responds to the Parson's penitential manual with a moving example of contrition. Yet when the topos of the internal forum reappears in the last act, as it were, of the poem, it evokes a profound

---

86. A. J. Minnis, *Medieval Theory of Authorship: Scholastic Literary Attitudes in the Later Middle Ages* (London: Scolar Press, 1984). For less precise but influential notice of the historical vicissitudes of the author, see Michel Foucault, "What Is an Author?" in *Textual Strategies: Perspectives in Post-Structuralist Criticism*, ed. Josué V. Harari (Ithaca: Cornell University Press, 1979), 141–60.

87. *The Riverside Chaucer*, ed. Benson, 965. For a range of work on how the Parson's Tale effects closure in the poem, see *Closure in "The Canterbury Tales": The Role of the Parson's Tale*, ed. David Raybin and Linda Tarte Holley (Kalamazoo: Medieval Institute Publications, 2000).

awareness of how radically the *Tales* have transformed the territory of the interior into the other-worldliness of literary fiction. Contrition as Chaucer knew it (through his creature the Parson and in the company of the writings of William Peraldus and Raymund of Pennaforte) is here reimagined in terms of the purposes of an entire literary career; it is not made insincere or irrelevant, but stretched to new meaning.

The form of the Retraction is profoundly mixed.[88] A combination of topoi, as so often in Chaucer, gives enormous power to the brief scene. One is evoked by the instruction to pray for the writer: "Wherfore I biseke yow mekely, for the mercy of God, that ye preye for me that Crist have mercy on me and foryeve me my giltes" (1084). This petition recalls the inscriptions on tombs and chantry chapels that instruct the visitor to pray for the dead. The figures we expect in that topos are the "speaking" corpse and the pious pilgrim; the act is one of commemoration. Insofar as we feel this topos behind the writing, the text of the Retraction issues from the position of the dead body, and the reader is in the position of the pious pilgrim.

A second topos, much more powerfully present, is the internal forum's scene of confession. This is evoked by the movement of the Retraction through the three parts of penance and by its position at the end of the Parson's Tale, as if it were a response to the Parson's instructions. The topos of confession leads us to expect certain representations of the person: the confessor and the penitent are indispensable to the scene. But there is no attending confessor who has the authority to grant Chaucer comfort, absolution, and indulgence (the pressure to do that falls upon the reader). The penitent too is partly missing. We expect the initial prayer to be directed to God or to the confessor; instead, the scene opens with a prayer addressed to "hem alle that herkne this litel tretys or rede" (1081). The prayer is not the expected utterance of the social person of the penitent soul, but rather a preface, a conventional piece of modesty topos, a list of acknowledgments (and disacknowledgments), a literary opening gambit that instructs the reader how to read and cites an authority or gives an epigraph. Contrition, the first part of penance (according to the Parson's scheme), is transformed into a prefatory address to the reader.

In the second part of the sacrament of penance, the action proper to the penitent soul is to confess a series of sins; instead, the "giltes" confessed in the Retraction are a series of compositions. The catalogue does not pertain to a life of deeds and purposes apart from writing; it is the *curriculum*

---

88. On the genre of the Retraction and Chaucer's death, see Derek Pearsall, *The Life of Geoffrey Chaucer: A Critical Biography* (Oxford: Blackwell, 1992) and Minnis, *Medieval Theory of Authorship*.

vitae of "Geffrey Chaucer," the "makere of this book," not the confession of a penitent soul who doubtless had offenses more rankling than poems to confess. The third part of penance, satisfaction, continues fast upon the second and is also represented by compositions: the good bibliography of philosophy, hagiography, homilies and other acts of "moralitee and devocioun" (1088). In closing, another prayer commends the speaker's soul to Christ in the manner of a dedication. The turning of the features of the topos of confession toward literary forms—the preface, the catalogue of works, the dedication—causes yet another topos murkily to emerge, that of the writer in the act of signing off his work. The utterance is bound by deictics to the time and place of writing, and may evoke the writer in an intimate study, burning midnight oil, conforming to a medieval convention of the visual arts.

Like the pilgrim badge of my Introduction, then, Chaucer's Retraction evokes sets of social persons embedded in topoi and thus presents us with a process of ethical deliberation. In this process, we try out different dispositions toward the figure of the writer and the act of reading. The penitent soul and the confessor, the corpse and the visitor to the tomb: these two pairs vie to influence our understanding of the pair that consists of the "makere" and the reader. The poetic maker comes before us as two figures: the effigy in the act of giving instructions and the penitent soul in the act of confession. We the readers are figured in terms of the confessor and the visitor to the tomb. While the Retraction is utterly devotional, it also rather radically captures the power of devotional practices for the literary topos. By evoking the topos of tomb inscription, Chaucer makes claims for poetry as a good habituator; like a chantry chapel, which urges visitors to consider the life, works, and death of the entombed and to pray for his soul, the poem urges our commemoration of its maker and our careful conservation of his works. A poem becomes a ritual memorial practice. By evoking the topos of confession, the text invites us to understand poems as acts with moral consequences and to imagine them as emanating from a maker and compiler whose intentions are of great interest and importance. A poem becomes a means to experience interiority and to diagnose intention.

So the concept of intention, tethered to the author and reader's fresh placement as social persons, serves as the linchpin of the Retraction's transformation of the confessional topos, just as it did in the Pardoner's Prologue and Tale, where Chaucer uses the intersecting associations of the Pardoner to examine the incoherent structuring of intention in the church's institution of canon law. In the literary forum incipient in the Retraction, intention is annexed to the person of the "makere" and explicitly refigured as authorial. The passage boldly extends to literary fiction all the scope and weight of the tradition of interpretive skills and quandaries that developed as medieval canonists and theologians used scripture for evidence in their arguments. When Chaucer describes his authorial intention (as maker) explicitly, writing that "oure book seith, 'Al that is writen is writen for oure doctrine,' and that is myn entente" (1083), every word of Paul's maxim for the interpretation of intention is suddenly resonant and disturbing. Now somewhat displaced from the confessional and the tomb, now acclimated to the expanded realm of literary fiction delivered by *The Canterbury Tales*, the reader can no longer easily know in what context Paul's words take their meaning. As a part of penitential discourse, these words had been a clear mandate and a foundational set of assumptions, but moved to the scene of the maker's subscribing of his work, they now appear as a profound crux.[89] They had promised a plenitude of meaning, but in place of this fullness we feel the absence left by a receding creator. What is "myn entente"? Which tales "sownen into synne" (1086)? These questions urge us to go back to the beginning of the tales and to read them again, to reevaluate the way they have habituated us.

For the human Chaucer, who fitted his own natural body to many social persons and died, it may be that canon law provided the most compelling understanding of intention and interiority; nevertheless, for the maker Chaucer the Retraction is not a moment of death but a new life conferred by a subtle and complex depiction of intention and interiority.[90] The Retraction invests its author with a dark and moving interiority just at the moment in which we anxiously feel we are losing him and desiring to know him more than ever. To assuage our loss, literary discourse offers us two consolations: a newly forceful mode of characterization and a re-created crux called authorial intention. Or, more properly, new constructions of the social persons *character* and *author*, designed to be able to represent and produce intense intentional states.[91]

89. Famously, of course, Paul's dictum also appears intensely ambiguous at the end of Chaucer's beast fable, the Nun's Priest's Tale, which comically and profoundly considers reading as interpretation with both very high stakes (life or death) and very silly controversies (the dreams of chickens).

90. Built upon fragments of the relationship between the penitent soul and the confessor, the new relationship between the author and the text becomes an important forum for the sophisticated interpretation of intention. For example, American constitutional legal theory, which has produced a rich discourse about intention, is more likely to cite a literary theorist than a theologian when arguing about intention and interpretation, and more likely to attribute intention to lawgivers as "authors" rather than as representations of person drawn from legal institutions.

91. For controversy on authorial intention, see *Against Theory: Literary Studies and the New Pragmatism*, ed. W. J. T. Mitchell (Chicago: University of Chicago Press, 1985), which treats intention as if it has no history and no relation to social persons. A more historically informed and equally theoretically subtle work is Minnis, *Medieval Theory of Authorship*. See also A. J. Minnis, " 'Authorial Intention' and 'Literal Sense' in the Exegetical Theories of

Whereas our sense of the character's intention habituates us to a formal mode of characterization and to genre, the poem's recreation of authorial intention shapes its readers in another way, as well. Our new understanding of the author's intention as richly problematic habituates us to a particular discipline. The language of the poem situates the maker's endeavor among the forms of reading and writing practiced by the culture; it accustoms us to requiring certain things of poetry and it changes our sense of the role of poetry among all the practices of thought and feeling available to us. If a description of the interior can be accomplished more meaningfully by fiction, that in itself does not diminish the power of the canon law's internal forum to pursue its other ends. The old saints do not disappear simply because they are unveiled as metaphorical by the instruments of a new science; yet their meaning changes as we become habituated to new configurations among the disciplines.

The poem depicts itself as an act of its maker that invites an act from its readers. As an instruction to action, it requires a reader to bring action into being. Poetry is designed for repetition, and placing our voices in the words of the text develops certain shapes in us—shapes of feelings, thoughts, sounds that "were" Chaucer's. As we take them (or rather make them ourselves in ways he could not entirely have imagined), they become a part of our experience of the world. Acting together with us, the poem shapes our bodies. Directed by it, we make feelings, thoughts, and voices live, and we become accustomed to their shapes, their spins, their suasion. We thus become habituated to a world in which person, passion, and cognition can work the way they do when we read Chaucer. As a practice, Chaucer's poem is powerful and inventive. Indeed it altered the habitus of poets and poetry readers in its time, and it continues to bring into being my own habitus, as I read, teach, and write about Chaucer and other writers to whom his work was important.

Why do we employ our bodies in the action of these words? We may be constrained to do so by a syllabus, but insofar as we experience meaning that is particular to the poem, we are drawn into the action simply by being moved. The paradoxical nature of the Pardoner as an agent of the internal forum run amuck in the external forum's world of fraud and commodity sales provokes the reader into thought and feeling—on the one hand, into deliberation about the relation of the economic and sacramental worlds and, on the other, into states of pain and pleasure, such as anger, amusement, disgust, curiosity, and exhilaration. As the Pardoner

---

Richard FitzRalph and John Wyclif," *Proceedings of the Royal Irish Academy* 75 C (1975): 1–31 and the exchange among H. Marshall Leicester, Jr., A. C. Spearing, and Victoria Kahn in *Exemplaria* 2 (1990): 241–85.

shifts from apostrophe to personification, the poetry probes and bullies us. Its vacillations between the carnal and the spiritual imitate the making and unmaking of the person in uncomfortable ways that offer the pleasures of liminality as well as its pains. These pleasures and pains move us to identify, diagnose, categorize—to situate ourselves among representations of the person. The thrill or disgust or amusement that avarice makes us feel can seduce us into speaking the lines, "myn entente is nat but for to wynne" (403) and "I preche agayn that same vice / Which that I use, and that is avarice" (427–28). In this sense, the tales may well "sownen into synne," as their maker worries in the Retraction (1086), giving us permission to enjoy vice.

But once we are performing the action of the poem—once we speak the words—then we are inside someone else: not another body, but another person. Because poetry makes its words available to any voice, and because it is the voice that conjures fictional persons, Chaucer's words are made inside us. Insofar as we make sense of them, we are making sense of other persons. This translation of the body into an alien interiority by means of voice is, in itself, an act with moral consequences. The exercise trains us in precisely those virtues that the Parson says are the remedy for avarice:

> Now shul ye understonde that the releevynge of Avarice is misericorde [mercy], and pitee largely taken. And men myghten axe why that misericorde and pitee is releevynge of Avarice. / Certes, the avricious man sheweth no pitee ne misericorde to the nedeful man, for he deliteth hym in the kepynge of his tresor, and nat in the rescowynge ne releevynge of his evene-Cristen. And therfore speke I first of misericorde. / Thanne is misericorde, as seith the Philosophre, a vertu by which the corage of a man is stired by the mysese of hym that is mysesed. / Upon which misericorde folweth pitee in parfournynge of charitable werkes of misericorde. (804–6)

The remedy for avarice is mercy and pity, virtues whose actions depend (the Parson says that Aristotle says) on the cognitive and affective capacity to imagine the states of others.

In reading, our corruption—the way the poem appeals to our pleasure in order to draw us into the avarice of the Pardoner's utterance—is at the same time an exercise of ethical transport that invites us to be "stired by the mysese of hym that is mysesed," to share the interior states of other persons and, then, to situate ourselves, to choose a position in the fabric of the polity, to make judgements about social persons. We might not choose with the Parson. But in the act of imagining the vicious Pardoner, we become accustomed to imagining other people, even ones who wish us harm, as having an interior life.[92] Though not as effective as penitential practice is at assessing the details of the reader's avarice, Chaucer's technology of the interior is better than penance at exercising and strengthening the reader's imaginative capacity for entering into the "mysese" of others— whether we are then stirred to mercy and pity depends on the habitus that we have cultivated.

Chaucer's reconfiguration of social persons offers the reader an intense experience of interiority that habituates us to the ethical process of deliberative conflict. Passions create intentions; intentions create actions; and actions, especially habitual actions, create persons. As we enter by turns into the voices of Chaucer, the Pardoner, and their "compeers," we create within ourselves the interior states of others. We experience the thrill of the Pardoner's avarice; but the condition of the thrill is to have taken an action that makes virtue possible. The power of the poem is generated by these opposed spins—the push and pull of poetic suasion. As we are moved by poetry to imagine the human figure, we create ourselves and are created as persons.

92. The old argument that reading fiction has ethical force because it enlists the imagination is a theme throughout the recent work of Elaine Scarry and Martha Nussbaum. Kathy Eden, *Poetic and Legal Fiction in the Aristotelian Tradition* (Princeton: Princeton University Press, 1986), identifies an Aristotelian tradition of the defense of fiction as deliberative in both literature and law that is important background both here and in chapter 4.

⊘ Chapter Two ⊘

Persons in the Creation of Social Bonds: Agency and Civil Death in *Piers Plowman*

> *In matrimonio animus debet gaudere plena libertate.*
> *Ubi non est libertas, ibi non est consensus.*
>
> —two legal maxims

With Chaucer's help, we have seen how social persons are instruments for composing and reading fictional characters and how, in the cognitive and emotional practice of reading, modes of characterization habituate the reader to the world of social persons. That process is as fully political as any in which literature participates, for social persons also provide a link between figural representations and the economic, legal, and institutional arrangements of the polities in which these figures are produced and apprehended. This chapter aims to describe this link and to explain the power of characterization to assess social life. I shall argue that although the social person appears to represent individuals, in fact it is best understood as the personification of social bonds. To investigate the complexity and range of representation inherent in the social person and the enormous analytic leverage it affords poets, it is best to turn from Chaucerian characterization, which became normative in later letters, to consider the wild variety of one of the masters of allegorical personification.

The long work in Middle English now known as *Piers Plowman* survives for us in fifty-three different texts that indicate wide circulation, and its alliterative verse deploys a greater variety of cultural forms than one might think possible: dream vision, ecclesiastical and social satire, sermon, anatomy of statecraft, scholastic grammatical analysis, legal formulae, penitential confession, faculty psychology, romance, apocalyptic prophecy, theological dispute, devotional transport, and (perhaps the best generic category for the baggy whole) personification allegory.[1] Rather than taking the items of this catalogue in turn, as Chaucer's tales seem designed to do, the manuscripts of *Piers Plowman* mix them more thoroughly and invent a thickly wrought patois grown out of the lexis and topoi of a large number of spheres of culture, including customary practices, discourses, institutions, disciplines, and iconographical traditions.[2]

There are no sharp divisions in the narrative, which uses the dream vision form to undermine the ontological status of all of its propositions. It has, however, two main parts, called the "visio" and the "vita," and their sections are called "passus," after the Latin for "step." In further contrast to the more clearly mapped *Canterbury Tales*, *Piers Plowman* is not interested in claiming new territory or technology for any particular institution. It never presents itself as a poem or as literature and never presents itself as having an "author" or a "compiler." Its first-person protagonist, Will the dreamer, figures the thinker who instigates the text. He is said in the C text to labor with his prayer book and its prayers for different occasions (C V.45–47), drawing on the social person of the laborer. This assimilation of the writer of *Piers Plowman* to the third medieval estate, often iconographically represented by the plowman, explicitly aims to organize our thinking about the practice of using the written word.

All of this makes *Piers Plowman* a notoriously difficult text for literary scholars to use and interpret. The capacity of the text to cast a wide net for cultural detritus of all kinds creates a chaotic reading experience. The manuscripts are grouped into three or four traditions by their editors (A, B, C, Z), but there is still no firm consensus about what the differences between the manuscripts represent—for example, whether the different versions of the text reflect the evolving opinions of an author in light of im-

---

1. In this essay, I quote the B text from *The Vision of Piers Plowman: A Complete Edition of the B-Text*, ed. A. V. C. Schmidt (London: J. M. Dent, 1984), the most accessible edition for classroom use. Most punctuation, including capitalization, has its source in the editor and not in the early manuscripts. In all quotations I have silently altered Middle English thorns to "th." Where indicated, I quote C text passages from *Piers Plowman by William Langland: An Edition of the C-Text*, ed. Derek Pearsall (Berkeley: University of California Press, 1978).

2. The legal diction of *Piers Plowman* has been most carefully excavated. John Alford's lexicography has laid the groundwork for much later analysis, and my own thinking here is much in debt to his labors. See John A. Alford, *"Piers Plowman": A Glossary of Legal Diction* (Cambridge: D. S. Brewer, 1988). Recent developments in the legal analysis of the allegory include Emily Steiner, "Medieval Documentary Poetics and Langland's Authorial Identity," in *Crossing Boundaries: Issues of Cultural and Individual Identity in the Middle Ages and the Renaissance*, ed. Sally McKee (Turnhout: Brepols, 1999).

portant historical events, or the opinions of multiple authors, or aesthetic revisions and refinements, or responses to the reception of the work, or the refitting of a stock of verse to persuade different audiences on different occasions.[3] The allegory explicitly tackles the problems of will, intention, and action and of continuous self-identity and authority; the reader is plunged into questions about these problems, their relation to one another, and their status in a given social context.[4]

Piers Plowman engages us in a complicated editorial and interpretive practice, but we must remember that what the text offers is, above all, a devotional practice. The story depicts Will stumbling repeatedly and falling from devotion to mere knowledge, a deflation of practice to propositional statement that urges the reader to "Do-bet," to practice truth, rather than merely to acknowledge the text's propositions as true. This invitation to agency is encoded at every level of the allegory's form. The cycle of rise-into-devotional-practice and fall-into-proposition habituates the reader to a cognitively and passionately stringent personal discipline, and it engages the reader in ethical and political deliberation about agency and its specific social forms. Those forms—economic, legal, and political—will help us develop the thinking begun in the preceding chapter. Indeed, it is in the delineation of such social forms, primarily forms of the

3. These issues have surfaced in editorial (what other fields would call "theoretical") controversies that have produced some of the most concrete, subtle, and practical investigation of the production of writing we have. For the current state of controversies regarding textual editing, see Jill Mann, "The Power of the Alphabet: A Reassessment of the Relation between the A and B Versions of *Piers Plowman*," *Yearbook of Langland Studies* 8 (1994): 21–50, and, for instance, Traugott Lawler, "A Reply to Jill Mann, Reaffirming the Traditional Relation between the A and B Versions of *Piers Plowman*," *Yearbook of Langland Studies* 10 (1996): 145–80, and Lee Patterson, "The Logic of Textual Criticism and the Way of Genius: The Kane-Donaldson *Piers Plowman* in Historical Perspective," chap. 3 of *Negotiating the Past: The Historical Understanding of Medieval Literature* (Madison: University of Wisconsin Press, 1997), 77–113. A list of contributions to the editing debate through 1988 can be found in Derek Pearsall, *An Annotated Critical Bibliography of Langland* (Ann Arbor: University of Michigan Press, 1990), especially 6–31 and 45–64.

4. The debate about the education and identity of the writer of the allegory continues. On the "author" of *Piers Plowman*, see Kathryn Kerby-Fulton, "Langland and the Bibliographic Ego," in *Written Work: Langland, Labor and Authorship*, ed. Steven Justice and Kathryn Kerby-Fulton (Philadelphia: University of Pennsylvania Press, 1997), 67–143; Anne Middleton, "William Langland's 'Kynde Name': Authorial Signature and Social Identity in Late Fourteenth-Century England," in *Literary Practice and Social Change in Britain, 1380–1530*, ed. Lee Patterson (Berkeley: University of California Press, 1990), 15–82; Andrew Galloway, "*Piers Plowman* and the Schools," *Yearbook in Langland Studies* 6 (1992): 89–107; John A. Alford, "Langland's Learning," *Yearbook in Langland Studies* 9 (1995): 1–17 (includes responses by Stephen A. Barney and Andrew Galloway). On Langland as a London poet, see Caroline M. Barron, "William Langland: A London Poet" in *Chaucer's England: Literature in Historical Context*, ed. Barbara A. Hanawalt (Minneapolis: University of Minnesota Press, 1992), 91–109; Derek Pearsall, "Langland's London," in *Written Work*, 185–207.

person, that *Piers Plowman* offers its most urgent deliberative challenges. The allegory's word for its criterion of judgement is "treuthe"; its name for the act of assessment is "mesure." In this chapter I will study the process of this deliberation, which will help me to explain how the representation of person—what I have been calling the *social person*—participates in the formation and testing of social bonds.

How does one assess the forms of social life? Practically and generally speaking, for one thing to be measured, some point of similarity with a second thing must be found: that point becomes a third, possibly abstract thing— length, color, inflammability, usefulness, monetary value, or the time required for manufacture. In fact, an economic transaction is an act of measuring, because for things to be exchanged, they must be made equivalent, made measurable. *Black's Law Dictionary* contains the following entry:

> **Measure of value.** In the ordinary sense of the word, "measure" would mean something by comparison with which we may ascertain what is the value of anything. When we consider, further, that value itself is relative, and that two things are necessary to constitute it, independently of the third thing, which is to measure it, we may define a "measure of value" to be something by comparing with which any two other things we may infer their value in relation to one another.[5]

"Whan alle tresors arn tried" says Holi Chirche in the first passus of *Piers Plowman*, "Treuthe is the beste" (I.85). This maxim describes a measurement, a trial, the weighing of all kinds of value, and the establishment of "the third thing," a general equivalent (that is, truth) that can serve as the general measure of all other value. Holi Chirche repeats her advice four times in the course of the passus (at lines 135, 137, 207). The act of measuring provides its own criterion, moderation:

> Mesure is medicine, though thow muchel yerne.
> Al is nought good to the goost that the gut asketh,
> Ne liflode to the likame that leef is to the soule.   *food, flesh, dear*
> (I.35–37)

As Holi Chirche's rhetoric elevates it to an ideal, the principle of measuring begins to constitute a somewhat threatening admonition; she quotes Luke 6:38 in two languages:

> For the same mesure that ye mete, amys outher ellis,
> Ye shulle ben weyen therwith whan ye wenden hennes:
> *Eadem mensura qua mensi fueritis remecietur vobis.*
> (I.177–78a)

---

5. *Black's Law Dictionary*, rev. 4th ed. (St. Paul: West, 1968).

The personification allegory of *Piers Plowman* works like such an act of measuring: the opening episodes of the text, devoted to the character Mede, serve as an experiment in which we measure various kinds of social relations—in psychological process, marriage, economic exchange, and the political constitution—against each other, generating a set of standards that can apply to all social bonds, because it involves the will's investment outside itself.[6]

Agency is a primary aspect of social bonds, for it is central to the circulation and practice of power among individual human beings and society. "Agency" can express an engagement of gears between will or intention and action, between one person (a principal) and another (the agent), between persons and an institution (an agency) established to effect their purposes, and between planning and executive parts of corporate bodies. The concept is central to spheres as diverse as the philosophy of mind and action, the law of persons, economic custom, and constitutional politics.

At the core of *Piers Plowman* is, I shall suggest, a struggle with the problem of agency. The dream-vision shape of the allegory itself expresses a detached torpor, a deep longing that cannot wholly rise into activity and accomplishment, a paradoxically insurmountable chasm between intention and action. The predominant first-person voice of the text belongs to a man called Will who is engaged in a search to overcome his distance from truth—an ideal state of *knowing* and of *doing*—and thus from satisfaction and salvation. He is always willing to try some new way to gain purchase upon that salvation, to "werchen His w[W]ille that wroghte me to man" (I.82): to work, as it were, a reversal of principal and agent—to become through his own agency the effected will of another.[7] In his encounters with other persons, he strives to develop a concept of a general equivalent that will allow him to do better at reaching truth. The entire process of alternating cognition and action is represented by the allegory as proceeding through human figures—when Will wants to do better, he looks for Do-bet, and when he worries about value, we see a Truth that lives in a castle like a lord. Meanings vacillate between states so that we are unsure whether they are actions or persons; this is like the vacillation between lying as an act and lying as a person that we saw in the first chapter's discussion of Epimenides' paradox. In *Piers Plowman*, personification is a tool that leads the reader through such transformations of the person again and again as an exercise designed to instigate moral agency.

6. For how medieval philosophical and grammatical notions of "relation" illuminate Langland's assessment of social bonds, see D. Vance Smith, "The Labors of Reward: Meed, Mercede, and the Beginning of Salvation," *Yearbook of Langland Studies* 8 (1994): 127–54.

7. On the reversal I mention, see Charles Taylor's discussion of Augustine's notion of the "perverse will" in *Sources of the Self: the Making of the Modern Identity* (Cambridge: Harvard University Press, 1989), 127–42.

As strongly as we are impressed by the faculty psychology that the characters dramatize, we must also recognize that Will is not only a familiar aspect of every human or a part of one thinking and writing man. The individuation of Will is slim indeed, though the brief, poignant passages that convey a taste and a smell so vivid as to feel autobiographical have been justly treasured by our author-needy criticism. "William Langland," long for Will, is the name we give to the putative author, but he is impersonal. Will is also a part of the body politic, the long land. He represents a will that is not just a feature of the human body, in the way that we expect each human animal to possess a hand, but something more communally held. Indeed, though individuals have access to will, the allegory figures this as an access to (or a refusal of) another's will, a divine will that exists in a controversial relation to the desires of the allegory's voice. As Will moves through the narrative, there are plenty of guides with whom he may converse along the way, and through these guides, external and internal, positive and negative, the allegory's ideals and promises of satisfaction continue to draw him onward.[8] Will's story becomes the story of the problem of agency, the problem of effecting an ideal connection between intention and action, between subjectivity and its fulfillment in the relational life of a political animal.

The primary treatment of agency in *Piers Plowman* concerns this relational will: even in its most individualist moments, the narrative imagines agency less as a state than as a relation. When Liberum Arbitrium (free will or capacity to "do or do nat gode dedes or ille" as Langland defines it below) appears in the C text, he appears outside of Will and explains himself in a long speech drawn from a much repeated (and altered) passage of Isidore of Seville's *Etymologiae*. This passage sets out to describe the capacities of consciousness, but it has the curious effect of alienating those capacities from the individual by suggesting that they are characters

---

8. For discussions of the way personification allegory works in *Piers Plowman*, see especially Jill Mann, *Langland and Allegory*, The Morton W. Bloomfield Lectures on Medieval English Literature 2 (Kalamazoo, Mich.: Medieval Institute Publications, 1992); Maureen Quilligan, *The Language of Allegory: Defining the Genre* (Ithaca: Cornell University Press, 1979), for a stress upon verbal wit and close reading; Mary Carruthers, *The Search For St. Truth: A Study of Meaning in "Piers Plowman,"* (Evanston: Northwestern University Press, 1973) for a verbal and cognitive approach derived from medieval rhetoric; and Elizabeth Salter's introduction to *Piers Plowman*, ed. Salter and Derek Pearsall, York Medieval Texts (London: Edward Arnold, 1967) for a figural approach influenced by Erich Auerbach; for comments on *Piers Plowman* in its social context, medieval categories of thought, and the nature of the personal, see especially David Aers, *Chaucer, Langland and the Creative Imagination* (London: Routledge & Kegan Paul, 1980) and *Community, Gender, and Individual Identity: English Writing 1360–1430* (London: Routledge, 1988); on the nature of the personal, see also Judith H. Anderson, *The Growth of a Personal Voice: "Piers Plowman" and "The Faerie Queene"* (New Haven, Conn.: Yale University Press, 1976).

(agents) who are distinct from the protagonist (principal), a role filled here by Liberum Arbitrium but implicitly offered to both Will and the reader.

> And whiles y quyke the cors ycald am y *Anima*,
> And when y wilne and wolde *Animus* y hatte,
> And for that y can and knowe ycald am y *Mens*,
> And when y make mone to god *Memoria* y hatte,
> And when y deme domes and do as treuthe techeth
> Thenne ys *Racio* my rihte name, Reson an Englische.
> And when y fele that folke telleth my furste name is *Sensus*
> And that is wit and wysdoem, the welle of alle craftes.
> And when y chalenge or chalenge nat, chepe or refuse,
> Thenne am y Concience ycald, goddes clerk and his notarie.
> And when y wol do or do nat gode dedes or ille
> Thenne am y *Liberum Arbitrium*, as lered men telleth.
> And when y louye lelly oure lord and alle othere
> Thenne is Lele Loue my name, and in Latyn, *Amor*.
> And when y fle fro the body and feye leue the caroyne
> Thenne am y spirit spechelees and *Spiritus* then y hote.
> Austyn and Ysodorus, either of hem bothe
> Nempned me thus to name; now thou myhte chese
> How thou coueytest to calle me, now thou knowest al my names.
>   (C.XVI.182–200)

Liberum Arbitrium offers a technical model of consciousness: this passage is an anatomy that distinguishes and identifies various aspects of human liveliness, mind, psyche, or, to use the historically correct social person, soul. (In fact, in the B text the speech is given to Anima.) Surely this passage is also an extraordinarily sophisticated and precise description of (indeed, a theory of) what literary criticism now understands to be "the subject."[9] Yet notice how the process that Langland describes cannot be confined within what we may feel is the natural territory of subjectivity, the individual human being. The voice and the repetition of the "I" unify the cast of characters in a single personification, and yet the relation between the "I," the collective voice, and the characters themselves as they go about their business is a relation of agency, fluidly extending both inside and outside of what we might designate "the individual." The speech introduces an entire crew of figures whose employment has always been to work Will's body, as well as the reader's. Liberum Arbitrium illustrates the permeability of the soul by relations of agency, a permeability that gives the passage a disturbing and invasive quality.

9. See David Lawton, "The Subject of *Piers Plowman,*" *Yearbook of Langland Studies* 1 (1987): 1–30.

This model of being and cognition thus not only distinguishes between a spiritual and a physical or biological level of existence but also presents consciousness in terms of social existence. According to Liberum Arbitrium, consciousness is a group of related persons with separate jobs, resources, skills, and even epistemological positions, drawn from different parts of the body politic. Reson appears to be a judge, as well as the faculty of judgement. Conscience acquires a particularly social role as "goddes clerk and his notarie" and is therefore at the heart of the conjunction between the psychological and the social. The social meaning of the passage is amplified when it is compared to its more abstract Latin source, which Langland quotes immediately following:

> *Anima pro diuersis accionibus diuersa nomina sortitur: dum viuificat corpus, Anima est; dum vult, Animus est; dum scit, Mens est; dum recolit, Memoria est; dum iudicat, Racio est; dum sentit, Sensus est; dum amat, Amor est; dum declinat de malo ad bonum, Liberum Arbitrium est; dum negat vel consentit, Consciencia est; dum spirat, Spiritus est.* (C.XVI.200a)[10]

In each dilation of the Latin, we can see how Langland's English animates its abstract nouns to the point where they become not only characters but actors in a relational world. Memory makes moan "to god"; Reson does "as treuthe techeth"; Sensus understands "that folke teleth"; Love loves "oure lord and alle othere"; even the spirit "spechelees" flees *from* the body and the "caroyne," and thus is defined in a negative relation.

Isidore's *Consciencia* is that which refuses or consents; Langland's Conscience expands the role of this faculty in two socially specific directions, the legal (to "chalenge or chalenge nat") and the economic (to "chepe or refuse"). Here Conscience's actions are defined as the actions that a principal may take with respect to a legal contract: to refuse or to consent, to challenge (claim or accuse at law) or to let stand, and to "chepe" (trade or act according to an economic agreement) or to "chepe" not. As we shall see, the early part of the text has the character Conscience presiding over a troubling evaluation of contract, in which the relations of agency, in its legal, economic, and political aspects, are at the forefront. The prominent

---

10. '*Anima* is known by different names according to its different functions: when it gives life to the body, it is Soul; when it expresses volition, it is Consciousness; when it has knowledge, it is Mind; when it recollects, it is Memory; when it judges, it is Reason; when it feels, it is Sense; when it loves, it is Love; when it turns from evil to good, it is Free Will; when it refuses or consents, it is Conscience; when it breathes (with the divine inspiration), it is Spirit' (trans. Pearsall). This passage is taken from Isidore of Seville, *Etymologiae* xi.i.13, but the phrase about Liberum Arbitrium is Langland's addition (see *Patrologia Latina*, ed. Jacques-Paul Migne, 82:399).

part that Conscience plays in this analysis is appropriate to the special association of conscience with equity in jurisprudence, and to the developing
association between conscience and the English court of chancery; Conscience is the king's chancellor in the allegorical kingdom.[11]

In what follows, I will show that *Piers Plowman* makes a complicated
argument about what kinds of agency belong in a just human society. The
conditions that make consent meaningful, the nature of just economic activity, the constitution of the political contract—these are all issues that
the verse deliberates by means of its portrayal of social persons as embodying models of agency. The allegory treats agency as a concept of social obligation that recognizes not only acts but also intentions, not only
faculties but also social relationships.

As the prologue opens, Will walks the Malvern Hills, hills so abruptly
high that being on them is like being in a box seat with a view of the social
world staged below, like occupying a real Archimedean point. Once there,
however, he falls asleep while looking into a stream, and in this most interior, asocial, un-Archimedean of circumstances, he dreams that he beholds
a tower rising upon a hill toward the eastern sun and, below, an ominous
fortress sunk deep in a dark valley. Between them spreads a social world:
a "fair feeld ful of folk" (17) of all types and estates, working, strutting,
buying and selling, praying, playing, begging, sinning, going on pilgrimages, preaching, accounting, lawyering, ruling. Holi Chirche comes to the
dreamer's aid in Passus I, interpreting the scene before him and advising
him in a mix of precepts, stories, maxims, threats, high oratory, sublime
metaphor, and abuse. From objective observation to dream-vision to the
edicts of church authority, the reader, like Will, approaches the allegory
from many epistemological vantages at once. Here, human figures are presented not as individuals with their own given names but as embodiments
of characteristic activities—social persons such as pilgrims, preachers, and
lawyers. This presentation is not a matter of distancing or obfuscation; it
is what makes them comprehensible and accessible to measurement. The

---

11. The traditional description of chancery as the "court of conscience" seems to have
been established by around 1370: see Robert C. Palmer, *English Law in the Age of the Black
Death, 1348–1381* (Chapel Hill: University of North Carolina Press, 1993), 107–10, 130. As
early as 1328, the chancellor's common law jurisdiction is referred to as a place of equity
(J. H. Baker, *An Introduction to English Legal History*, 3d ed. [London: Butterworths,
1990], 118–22). Like its sister-notion conscience, equity is necessary and accessible to all
judges (and indeed in a less effective sense to all human beings), but it is especially associated
with the chancellor's charge to issue writs and, when needful, to make new writs. In its specific meaning as a particular body of English law that complements but is separate from common law, the notion of equity grows out of the fifteenth-century work of chancery, but this
fact, as *Piers Plowman* itself proves, does not limit the association of the chancellor and the
jurisprudential concepts of equity and conscience to later periods.

project of the will, and thus the project of the narrative, is accomplished through a series of agency relations, a string of encounters between the dreamer and other characters who exist, like Liberum Arbitrium, both inside and outside of Will.

Sexual Agency: Contract, Coverture, and Legal Person

Will's desire for knowledge, poignantly expressed to Holi Chirche in Passus I, elicits three sections of social analysis, the story of the marriage litigation of Mede the maid (Passus II–IV).[12] It is here that the reader encounters Langland's governing model of agency relations: in the institution created by marriage and understood in law as the doctrine of "unity of person."[13] He uses this construction of person in order to measure and evaluate both the economic and the political form of fourteenth-century English society. Marriage is not a perfect model of just, contractually created relations of agency; indeed, Langland is interested in its faults. By the fourteenth century, the topic of marriage had generated an elaborate body of moral deliberation, in comparison with which the conceptions of person and agency in contemporary economic thought were still very thin. In the Mede section of the allegory, not only does Langland make the urgent objection that money has no conscience and takes on an immoral and corrupting life of its own (anticipating concerns of both Chaucer and Skelton), but he also develops a deeper investigation of the conditions surrounding transactions, drawing together three kinds of institutions that will not be collected in social thought under the rubric of "contract" until much later: marriage, economic exchange, and the political constitution.[14]

In the twelfth century, the legal entry into the contract of marriage had

12. The Middle English word "mede," later regularized as "meed," ranges in meaning from reward to compensation to bribe.

13. The legal doctrine held in English and American law until its abrogation by the Married Women's Property Acts in the nineteenth century.

14. For a tighter focus on the notion of contract, see the earlier version of this chapter, "Civil Death and the Maiden: Agency and the Conditions of Contract in *Piers Plowman*," *Speculum* 70 (1995), 760–92. On the early English legal history of contract, see Baker, *Introduction*; S. F. C. Milsom, *Historical Foundations of the Common Law*, 2d ed. (London: Butterworths, 1981); Frederick Pollock and Frederic William Maitland, *The History of English Law Before the Time of Edward I*, 2d ed. (Cambridge: Cambridge University Press, 1923); A. W. B. Simpson, *A History of the Common Law of Contract: The Rise of the Action of Assumpsit* (Oxford: Clarendon, 1975); C. H. S. Fifoot, *History and Sources of the Common Law: Tort and Contract* (London: Stevens, 1949); W. T. Barbour, *The History of Contract in Early English Equity*, ed. Paul Vinogradoff, Oxford Studies in Social and Legal History, vol. 4 (Oxford: Clarendon, 1914). It may be that here and elsewhere I am overestimating the achievement of *Piers Plowman* by underestimating the importance of civil law in England; civilians enjoyed a richer concept of contract gleaned from their Roman law inher-

been firmly established by decretals of the popes Alexander III and Innocent III to require nothing more than the willing consent of two eligible persons—canon law does not require the permission of parents, lords, rulers, or any necessary action by officials of the church or the government. Canonists did insist that couples should have the benefit of a church ceremony and the good will of those in authority.[15] Nevertheless, a simple, private exchange of words of present consent (*per verba de praesenti*), or sexual intercourse after an exchange of words of future consent (*per verba de futuro*), was sufficient to establish legal marriage and would be upheld by the ecclesiastical courts if proved.[16]

Most cases that came before the ecclesiastical courts in the thirteenth and fourteenth centuries concerned not divorce, support, or the custody of children, but the performance of promises to marry, the details of exchanges of consent, and the existence or non-existence of marriages. Consequently litigation centered on the moment of contract, as does Langland's scene. The allegory of the Mede passages exploits contemporary litigiousness over the enforcement of marriage contracts by overlaying a plot of marriage litigation onto economic concepts. What might constitute a proper exchange of consent, to what conditions is it subject, how should impediments and incapacities in the parties be understood and treated—all these topics were better developed in the marriage doctrine and cus-

---

itance. For a relevant example, see Vacarius's *Summa de matrimonio*, which treats marriage analogically as a kind of contractual conveyance.

15. Clandestine marriage was prohibited in over thirty pieces of English conciliar legislation and episcopal decrees between 1200 and 1342. See Michael M. Sheehan, "The Formation and Stability of Marriage in Fourteenth-Century England: Evidence of an Ely Register," *Mediaeval Studies* 33 (1971): 228–63. Something of the character of the English customs against which the church fought might be glimpsed in decrees such as that of Walter Reynolds, the Archbishop of Canterbury, at the Council of Oxford in 1322, cc. 22–23, as reported by William Lyndwood: "Marriage like the other sacraments should be celebrated with honor and reverence by day and in the face of the church, not with laughter and joking and contempt." *Constitutiones provinciales ecclesiae Anglicanae* (1679), 4.1.[1], at 270–1, trans. Charles Donahue, Jr. See D. Wilkins, *Concilia Magnae Brittaniae et Hiberniae* (London, 1737), 2:513. Langland's description of the celebration of Mede's wedding to Fals might have been written to illustrate this decree.

16. According to R. H. Helmholz, "Marriage was an institution which seemed, in the fifteenth century, to require a more truly free kind of consent than had been thought in the thirteenth," *Canon Law and the Law of England* (London: Hambledon, 1987), 154. For the history of English marriage formation and litigation in the period, see Charles Donahue, Jr., "The Canon Law on the Formation of Marriage and Social Practice in the Later Middle Ages," *Journal of Family History* 8 (1983): 144–58; R. H. Helmholz, *Marriage Litigation in Medieval England* (Cambridge: Cambridge University Press, 1974); Michael M. Sheehan, "Choice of Marriage Partner in the Middle Ages: Development and Mode of Application of a Theory of Marriage," *Studies in Medieval and Renaissance History*, n.s., 1 (1978): 3–33. These are my sources for the brief characterization of fourteenth-century litigation that follows.

toms of the common and canon laws than they were in medieval economic analysis and regulation. Just price doctrine had developed detailed approaches to fraud in land and commercial transactions, but common law concepts of what constituted propriety in fee-for-service transactions were much less comprehensive.[17] It is this richness of legal thinking about marriage that the allegory of *Piers* attempts to transfer to a consideration of economic practices.

Langland's analysis does find the authoritative precepts of Alexander III and Innocent III sufficient; he insists on a complicated structure requiring the consent of those outside the marriage to its constitution. The king treats Mede as his ward (despite her living father Fals), and Conscience and Reson are called upon to judge the proposed marriages. Medieval marriage is a model for exchange that stresses intention, consent, social control, and an understanding of economic value and exchange that (at least in theory) is controlled by spiritual concerns; the satirical charter of Passus II exemplifies this association between the commercial transaction and the moral value of the marriage exchange. Both Chaucer and Langland associate the amorality of monetary transactions with configurations of human sexuality: Chaucer describes the internal forum of the canon law as an inadequate cure for the socially perverse effects of commerce, and Langland describes marriage law as inadequate control of the promiscuity of money.

While we may think it is quite radical, sensible, and just to give women the power of consent in the arrangement of their own marriages (most of the alternative models of the regulation of marriage that were available to Alexander provided women with far less control over their own lives), nevertheless in studying marriage one must ask: under what conditions can genuine or meaningful consent obtain?[18] Despite the equal footing of their consent, the parties to a marriage contract do not consent to the same thing, whether in the twelfth or the twentieth century.[19] The equitable forms of entrance into marriage and of "sexual commerce" within marriage mask the asymmetrical nature of the contract itself.

Inequity in marriage arises in the fact that a marriage contract establishes an agency relation in which the wife undergoes a degree of "civil

17. The first legislation regulating the profession appears in 1275, in the Statute of Westminster I, chapter 29, according to Paul Brand, *The Origins of the English Legal Profession* (Oxford: Blackwell, 1992), 120.

18. John T. Noonan, Jr., "Power to Choose," *Viator* 4 (1973): 419–34.

19. For general discussions of women in medieval marriage see Henry Ansgar Kelly, *Love and Marriage in the Age of Chaucer* (Ithaca: Cornell University Press, 1975), and Dyan Elliott, *Spiritual Marriage: Sexual Abstinence in Medieval Wedlock* (Princeton: Princeton University Press, 1993), especially 132–94 on marital debt.

death." In order to understand her status and the status of the marriage, which is legally termed "coverture" (and which I discuss in the Introduction), it is worth comparing marriage to similar social relationships.[20] In the classic thirteenth-century treatise on English law, "Bracton" draws the analogy between the villein and the monk, who may both be described as civilly "dead," being under the power of their lords: *"Est etiam mors civilis in servo in servitute sub potestate domini constituto."*[21] Civil death does not mean loss of all power to intend or act but the fiction of such loss and therefore a corresponding degree of powerlessness and of immunity within a particular community and a particular jurisdiction. Blackstone explains the traditional doctrine of the unity of person in marriage and the legal structure termed "coverture" in a famous passage:

> By marriage, the husband and wife are one person in law: that is, the very being or legal existence of the woman is suspended during the marriage, or at least is incorporated and consolidated into that of the husband: under whose wing, protection, and *cover*, she performs every thing; and is therefore called in our law-french a *feme-covert*; is said to be *covert-baron*, or under the protection and influence of her husband, her *baron*, or lord; and her condition during her marriage is called her *coverture*. Upon this principle, of an union of person in husband and wife, depend almost all the legal rights, duties, and disabilities, that either of them acquire by the marriage. I speak not at present of the rights of property, but of such as are merely *personal*. For this reason, a man cannot grant any thing to his wife, or enter into covenant with her: for the grant would be to suppose her separate existence; and to covenant with her, would be only to covenant with himself: and therefore it is also generally true, that all compacts made between husband and wife, when single, are voided by the intermarriage. A woman indeed may be attorney for her husband; for that implies no separation from, but is rather a representation of, her lord.[22]

Likewise, rape and assault are difficult to argue within coverture, because such crimes require the wife's separate existence.

Statements attributed to chancellor Robert Stillington during a 1467 Exchequer chamber session illustrate the strange distribution of act, consent, and intention within unity of person: "And the Chancellor said that the wife could not consent during the marriage. If something was done out

---

20. Paul Strohm discusses the analogies posited by the 1352 Statute of Treason, which includes a wife killing her husband ("une femme qe tue son baron") in its definition of treason. "Treason in the Household," in *Hochon's Arrow: The Social Imagination of Fourteenth-Century Texts* (Princeton: Princeton University Press, 1992), 124.

21. Bracton, fol. 421b, quoted in Pollock and Maitland, *History of English Law*, 1:433, n. 1.

22. William Blackstone, *Commentaries on the Laws of England: A Facsimile of the First Edition of 1765-1769* (Chicago: University of Chicago Press, 1979), 1:430.

of dread or coercion, it could not be called consent; and whatever a married woman does may be said to be done for dread of her husband. And they should take no notice of the fact that the wife received the [purchase] money, because she could not have had the benefit of it."[23] Contrary to the convention that rape is legally impossible within marriage, this bald statement might suggest that all sexual relations within marriage are rape, since dread and coercion can be said to incapacitate the wife from consent. In the canon law, sexual "commerce" (as it is often called by theologians such as Hugh of St. Victor) has a primarily economic description where husband and wife are said to enter into a perpetual and equitable "marriage debt" initiated by consummation.[24] This language, derived from 1 Corinthians 7:3–4, serves as another resource for Langland's association of economic problems with coverture. He applies coverture broadly: the king's view is that Mede should be *coverte* by Conscience so that the economy be *covert* by moral reason.

The canonists' idea of marriage debt is impartial to gender, in contrast to the hierarchical metaphor of the individual body that often controls the idea of coverture. There the head is accorded a natural dominion. Chapter 2 of Genesis, on the creation of Eve, is often cited in both legal and theological argumentation:

> And Adam said: This now is bone of my bones,
> and flesh of my flesh: she shall be called Woman,
> because she was taken out of man.
> Wherefore a man shall leave father and mother, and
> shall cleave to his wife: and they shall be two in one
> flesh.
>
> (2:23–24)

The original creation of the category of person called "woman" and the creation of marriage, according to theology, are simultaneous, containing both hierarchy and equality. Hugh of St. Victor writes:

> For since she was given as a companion, not a servant or a mistress, she was to be produced not from the highest or from the lowest part but from the middle. For if she had been made from the head, she would have been made from the highest and she would seem to have been created for domination.

23. The case was argued before the chancellor and the justices of both benches. It is recorded in the Year Books of Edward IV (Y.B. Trin. 7 Edw. IV, fol. 14, pl. 8) and as *Anon.* (1467) in *Sources of English Legal History: Private Law to 1750*, ed. J. H. Baker and S. F. C. Milsom (London: Butterworths, 1986), 98–99. Bracketed clarification by Baker and Milsom.

24. E.g., Hugh of St. Victor, *On the Sacraments of the Christian Faith*, trans. Roy J. Deferrari, Medieval Academy of America Publications, no. 58 (Cambridge: Medieval Academy of America, 1951); Gratian, *Decretum*, C. 27, 32, and 33 (*Corpus iuris canonici*, ed. Emil Friedberg [Graz: Akademische Druck- u. Verlagsanstalt, 1955], 1:1046–78, 1:1115–59).

But if she had been made from the feet, she would have been made from the lowest and she would seem to have been subjected to slavery. She was made from the middle, that she might be proved to have been made for equality of association. Yet in a certain way she was inferior to him, in that she was made from him, so that she might always look to him as to her beginning and cleaving to him indivisibly might not separate herself from that association which ought to have been established reciprocally.[25]

Biblical creation defines "female" as "wife"; similarly, we shall see that Langland derives Mede's sexuality from the paradigm of unity of person in marriage, even though she is as yet still "Mede the mayde."

Coverture also creates a particular connection between gender and will. During a case in Chancery recorded in the Year Books for 1478, John Vavasour successfully argued the following, citing a writ that had been in use much earlier than the late fifteenth century: "The law will not allow anything done by her [the wife] during the marriage to be good [i.e., valid]. If she makes a feoffment of her land during the marriage, it is void: and this well proves that nothing done by her during the marriage concerning any inheritance is good. For the writ of *cui in vita* says, 'whom in her lifetime she could not gainsay', and this proves well that her act and will is void during the marriage."[26] In a parallel passage, the English canonist William Lyndwood quotes the legal maxim that claims the monk has no will of his own (*non habet velle, neque nolle*), because he is subject to the will of another—legally, the abbot (168).[27] F. W. Maitland compares the monk's vow of obedience to the legal form of slavery, and then, somewhat later in the same essay, to the common law construction of marriage.[28]

What these kinds of legal arguments attempt are precisely drawn structures of agency. They model agency and control its variables; they distribute faculties and facilities to people. In all these instances, there is a social circulation or redistribution of such faculties as "will" according to the processes of personification at work. Changes in status such as birth, maturity, and death, and the formation and dissolution of institutions such as marriage, indenture, and tenure entail carefully negotiated and regulated structures of agency that are applied to, and constitutive of, social rela-

25. Hugh of St. Victor, *On the Sacraments*, 2.11.IV (Deferrari, 329). For more comment on Genesis 2, see Hugh's *De beatae Mariae virginitate*, in *Patrologia Latina*, ed. Jacques-Paul Migne, 176:862–65 and Peter Lombard's *Sententiarum quatuor libri*, 4.26.

26. Anon. (1478), in *Sources*, ed. Baker and Milsom, 100.

27. Quoted in Pollock and Maitland, *History of English Law*, 1:433.

28. Pollock and Maitland, *History of English Law*, 1:433, 438. See also *The Reports of Sir John Spelman*, ed. J. H. Baker, Publications of the Selden Society 94 (London: Selden Society, 1978), 2:321: "The case of the monk was thought to be analogous to that of the married woman."

tionships. The redistribution of "will" in these relationships means that they partake of a degree of coverture and involve a degree of civil death for certain parties and a corresponding dominion for others.

The parameters of such structures of agency are subtle and various. Like marriage and entrance into holy orders, many of these models are contractual and require consent on the part of those about to suffer civil death. From the twelfth century on, ecclesiastical law increasingly emphasized the voluntary consent of the individual to both marriage and entry into orders, and by the fourteenth century it is no longer fully acceptable for parents to push children into monastic civil death under the age of consent. The term civil death has rather severe connotations that although accurate are also relative.[29] Marriage may well be experienced by most women as an enhancement of their capacities, rather than as a partial death, because it is a movement from parental control into a voluntary contract.[30] As Blackstone claims, coverture provides a degree of immunity and protection for women that needs to be accounted for without losing sight of the explanatory power of the term civil death.

How can these forms of socially constructed agency be evaluated? The terms of evaluation will be different, but related, in the different realms of individual psychology, marital unity of person, and the polity. How hard or soft is the distinction between the planning faculty and the implementing action? (It is true, for example, that an abbot supervises the labors of his monks in more detail than a husband oversees the labors of his wife.) How far does the power to delegate extend? (If a wife is allowed to incur debt on behalf of her husband, can she designate an agent in her lover who is also allowed to incur debt on behalf of her husband?) Under what conditions is the principal responsible for the agent's actions?[31] (If a man is out of the room and his wife incites the tavern to rebellious statements, can anyone be prosecuted?) What constrains the agent's responsibility for the results of the principal's bad faith? (Can an indentured servant be absolved of his actions by his master's culpability?) What mobility is there between positions? (Can an agent, through acquiring the authority of skill, become a principal?) Is the agency terminable, and by whom? If

29. I assume that a full capacity for legal and political agency is naturally due to women as a matter of justice, but of course that state was not the pre-marital condition of four-teenth-century Englishwomen.

30. But see Judith M. Bennett, *Women in the Medieval English Countryside: Gender and Household in Brigstock Before the Plague* (Oxford: Oxford University Press, 1987), who shows that single women and widows indeed enjoyed more civic responsibility and capacity than did wives in this period. See also the discussion of women's agency in Elliott, *Spiritual Marriage*, 195–265.

31. See, for example, the discussion of felonious possession in Baker, *The Reports of Sir John Spelman*, 2:319–23.

these questions seem to summon the world of farce or the fabliau, it is because farce often mines the no-man's-land between social fictions and social rules.

The case of coverture involves a curious reversal. In marriage the will of the husband covers the will of the wife, so that her will, as it is expressed in contracts that she undertakes, is void: we thus might describe the wife's will as being deeded to the husband. But in the legal expression of unity of person, as we have seen in the Year Books and Blackstone, it is the wife who is described as an agent for her husband. She is "representative" of him, rather than he of her: "A woman indeed may be attorney for her husband; for that implies no separation from, but is rather a representation of, her lord."[32] At a semiotic, cultural level, her interests are displaced ("voided") in the identity of his acts and her will, and precisely the *representative* quality of this identity becomes invisible: his actions are sufficient in themselves, without referring to her will. In contrast, her actions always make reference. In cases where she acts on her own behalf, she is construed as acting on behalf of him, his person, his will. When Mede appears before Will, he wants to know whose wife she is in order to understand how to interpret her social meaning; the question of her affiliation will become a driving force of the plot. The first question about a mysterious male character, however, is unlikely to be whose husband he is. Though the male is a prominent component of the female's social meaning (she is, as it were, "Mrs. Him"), she is an invisible, trivial part of the interpretation of the male (he is, as it were, a self-referential "Mr. Him").

The doctrine of unity of person allows Langland to distinguish between will and agency by means of gender. While the husband is head of the body that is the married couple, the potential (if infrequently constituted) status of the wife as "attorney," in Blackstone's term, associates a woman with the agency relation itself: thus it is the agent who represents agency, despite the fact that the principal dominates. In such a relation, the feminine can be seen as an expression of "pure" agency, agency without intentionality, and indeed this is the femininity with which Langland endows Mede the maid. She does not represent any natural agency specific to women: she is not pregnant or nursing. Instead, the allegory explores the feminine character of agency that is derived from the doctrine of unity of person, taking deeply ambivalent attitudes toward it. As we shall see, Mede experiences a reversal similar to the transfer and disappearance of the wife's will under coverture. Her marked passivity is an occasion for the corrupt actions of men, yet when Conscience analyzes the situation for the king, he sees her not as the agent of men's corruption, but as corruption it-

32. Blackstone, *Commentaries*, 1:430.

self. While the capacity to act (to choose) is a necessary condition of morality, nothing about this capacity, nothing about agency itself, predisposes that the act will be good. Good must come from the principal, from intention. Conscience argues that Mede's incompleteness is vicious in itself and incapable of remedy. His arguments prevail, leading the government to conclude that banishing her banishes corruption.

The Case of Holi Chirche

In the semiotic shell game that marriage provides, not only does the wife stand for agency, but, because the doctrine of unity of person takes sexual union as its primary proof and image, she can also stand for sexuality. The division by gender of the "one flesh" that is unity of person into principal and agent newly invents sexuality in the guise of the eroticization of coverture. Feminine sexuality thus begs the question of coverture in that it is produced by the structure of coverture itself. It has often been noted that among its many purposes, the institution of marriage serves to control women's sexuality, and thus reproduction, in the interests of paternity, men and the church. Here I am making the further point that the writings of theologians and jurists invented a particular sexuality—available, promiscuous, violent, corrupting—and assigned women to be its possessors in order to help rationalize the need for the sovereignty of husbands. The notion of the "one flesh" creates the perception of the need it proposes to satisfy: that women be married. Any waywardness of feminine sexuality can therefore always be interpreted as this known, indeed predicted, waywardness, an argument, finally, for the necessity of the model, for the necessity of marriage.

Unity of person, then, is a social institution. But it is also a template for understanding the world. Conscience "knows" Mede is sexually vicious before he has any experience of her, despite Theology's defense of her neutrality, and despite the text's attribution of all the sexual adventurism in these scenes to men (Holi Chirche's sexual aggression is the exception, as we shall see shortly). In this form, sexuality is an eroticized social division of action from intention, and of civil death from dominion. For the narrative to resolve these divisions, it must banish women's sexuality from coverture—impossible as a policy, but achieved at the end of Passus IV by means of an argument waged through personification.

Still, *Piers Plowman* is surprisingly and profoundly ambivalent about women's sexuality. In Passus II, Holi Chirche herself displays an active sexuality that she asserts in competition with Mede. The two female figures are clearly meant to be compared, as Mede's appearance at the opening of Passus II echoes the appearance of Holi Chirche at the opening of

Passus I, and the dreamer responds with a similar awe to each. His vision of Mede "the mayde" is an advertisement of wealth that is tinged with political, moral, and sexual danger. Her array is so rich—a crown as good as the king's and ruby rings as "rede as any gleede" (glowing coal)—that it leaves the dreamer "ravysshed" (II.12, 17). Mede is the personification of reward, compensation, and recompense—all terms that are morally ambiguous.

The dreamer turns to Holi Chirche for an interpretation of the figure of Mede:

> I hadde wonder what she was and whos wif she were.
> "What is this womman," quod I, "so worthili atired?"
> (II.18–19)

Holi Chirche responds in a fit of irritation and sexual jealousy:

> "That is Mede the mayde," quod she, "hath noyed me ful ofte,   *harmed*
> And ylakked my lemman that Leautee is hoten,   *disparaged, lover, called*
> And bilowen hym to lordes that lawes han to kepe.   *lied about*
> In the Popes paleis she is pryvee as myselve,   *as intimate*
> But soothnesse wolde noght so—for she is a bastard,
> For Fals was hire fader that hath a fikel tonge,
> And nevere sooth seide sithen he com to erthe;
> And Mede is manered after hym, right as asketh kynde: *nature*
> Qualis pater, talis filius. Bona arbor bonum fructum facit.
> [Like father, like son (proverbial). Good tree yieldeth good fruit (Matthew 7:17).]
>   "I oughte ben hyere than heo—I kam of a bettre.
> My fader the grete God is and ground of alle graces,
> Oo God withouten gynnyng, and I his goode doughter,
> And hath yeven me Mercy to marie with myselve;
> And what man be merciful and leelly me love   *loyally*
> Shal be my lord and I his leef in the heighe hevene;   *beloved*
> And what man taketh Mede, myn heed dar I legge   *wager*
> That he shal lese for hire love a lappe of *Caritatis*."   *portion*
> (II.20–35)

Sympathetic and comical, Holi Chirche whines and boasts by turns; she complains that her lover Leaute has been slandered by Mede, then accuses Mede of interfering with law enforcement and of being as close to the pope as she herself is. These intrusions into Holi Chirche's territory are particularly offensive because, as she says petulantly, she deserves better than a bastard like Mede—coming of such a prominent father, being a good daughter, and having married extremely well. During the course of her tirade, a farcical gap develops between her righteous posture and her sexual behavior. We learn that Holi Chirche not only has a husband

(Mercy) *and* a lover (Leaute), but, competing with her rival Mede, she angles for new conquests with promises and threats, offering any interested man sexual dominion over her. Any man who becomes her lover, she promises, will be promoted to heaven; but she is willing to bet her head that men who take Mede for a lover will lose divine favor. Holi Chirche advises the dreamer to inform himself about Mede by observing her marriage to Fals, the man just named as the bride's father. At the wedding, planned for tomorrow, he may understand "alle / That longen [belong] to that lordshipe, the lasse and the moore" (II.45–46). In the event, Mede's domain is conveyed by a marriage charter which includes "al the lordshipe of Leccherie in lengthe and in brede" (II.89).

The poem's emphasis on Mede's sexuality has been linked by scholars to the commodification of desire, but Holi Chirche's virtuous promiscuity has been neglected.[33] Her aggressively sexual nature suggests that Langland is creating a rather complex misogyny. By personifying social relations, Langland forces his readers to confront the implications of a set of unresolved tensions in the politics of sexuality and religion. According to Holi Chirche, the social form of the two characters' sexuality is identical: they are both promiscuous, though one in a good and the other in a bad way. Thus the dreamer (the reader's proxy) is presented with a necessary choice of sexual relationships. In offering that choice, the allegory insists that these personifications require of us not merely understanding or even particular moral behaviors, but also commitment to a kind of sexual bond with the church or with commercial institutions, and thus a placing of ourselves within one or another of two structures of social relations.

The sexuality of Holi Chirche in the B text should be understood in the context of late medieval affective theology; in effect, it prevents the reader from dismissing Mede as evil *per se*.[34] Indeed it is the character Theology who interrupts Mede's marriage to Fals, beginning the marriage litigation by arguing on Mede's behalf. The sexuality attributed to the church must also be read as a diagnosis of hypocrisy and corruption, though this reading conflicts with the appeal to affective theology. Perhaps, like many readers, Langland felt uncomfortable with a sexual Holi Chirche; in any

33. Clare A. Lees, "Gender and Exchange in *Piers Plowman*," in *Class and Gender in Early English Literature: Intersections*, ed. Britton J. Harwood and Gillian R. Overing (Bloomington: Indiana University Press, 1994), 112–30, and David Aers, "Class, Gender, Medieval Criticism, and *Piers Plowman*," in *Class and Gender*, 59–75. M. Teresa Tavormina notes that changes in the C version of Holi Chirche's speech reduce her resemblance to Mede: *Kindly Similitude: Marriage and Family in "Piers Plowman"* (Cambridge: D. S. Brewer, 1995), 11.

34. See James A. Brundage on the twelfth-century sexualization of Jesus in *Law, Sex, and Christian Society in Medieval Europe* (Chicago: University of Chicago Press, 1987), 228.

event the farcical nature of her sexual jealousy is vastly toned down in the C text. Or perhaps the sexual appeal of Holi Chirche is not sustained because that would have required working it into the political allegory: if the "marriage plot" of Passus II through IV had ended with the marriage of Holi Chirche to the king, it would no doubt have made *Piers Plowman* even more attractive to its attentive Reformation audience, but it would have carried a very different political force.

The legal details of the dreamer's vision of Mede's marriage are well worked out allegorically.[35] Mede and her bridegroom are offered an outrageously sinful *maritagium*, and the baldly financial character of the transaction satirizes the commercialization of the marriage sacrament among the landed aristocracy. However, these complaints are not the basis of Theology's objection to the marriage. In his speech to the officiating civilian lawyer Cyvyle, whose presence emphasizes the commercial aspect of the exchange over its spiritual aspect, Theology contradicts Holi Chirche's allegation of Mede's illegitimacy:

> Now sorwe mote thow have—
> Swiche weddynges to werche to wrathe with Truthe!
> And er this weddynge be wroght, wo thee bitide!
> For Mede is muliere, of Amendes engendred;   *legitimate*
> And God graunted to gyve Mede to truthe,
> And thow hast gyven hire to a gilour—now God gyve thee sorwe!   *deceiver*
> . . .
> Wel ye witen, wernardes, but if youre wit faille,   *deceivers*
> That Fals is feithlees and fikel in hise werkes
> And as a bastarde ybore of Belsabubbes kynne.
> And Mede is muliere, a maiden of goode,
> And myghte kisse the Kyng for cosyn and [if] she wolde.
> (II.116–21, 129–33)

Although he disputes Holi Chirche's charge, Theology reveals yet another impediment to the proposed marriage: Mede is previously betrothed to Truthe. Since neither exchange appears to have been consummated, marriage litigation might be expected to ensue, as Theology warns it must. He further complains that Mede and Fals are of different stations. Disparagement (marriage between classes) was not grounds for dissolution at canon law, but an "error of condition" might be argued and considered to negate Mede's consent if it could be proved that the difference in their status was

---

35. For a guide to legal references in *Piers Plowman*, see Alford, *"Piers Plowman": A Glossary of Legal Diction*.

fraudulently hidden from her, and that is suggested by Theology's objection.[36]

The vows themselves are problematic. The narrative suggests strongly that an exchange of consent has taken place but represents that exchange ambiguously:

> Ac Favel was the firste that fette hire out of boure
> And as a brocour broughte hire to be with Fals enjoyned.
> Whan Symonye and Cyvylle seighe hir bother wille,   *both of their*
> Thei assented for silver to seye as bothe wolde.
>
> (II.65–68)

The phrases "hir bother wille" and "as bothe wolde" insist that the consent of both parties has been obtained, but "both" is allowed to refer ambiguously either to Mede and Fals, or to Fals and Favel. The contract cannot legitimately take place without Mede's consent; thus the question of whether it is Mede or her broker whose "will" the marriage represents prepares us for Theology's interruption of the celebrations. Mede herself is not directly reported to do or say anything until Passus III; she is thoroughly passive and compliant. When the company rouses itself to change venues, Mede's passivity casts further doubt on whether her consent is meaningful, as Favel instructs Gile to "feffe Fals-witnesse with floryns ynowe, / For he may Mede amaistrye and maken at my wille" (II.147–48). The rout of well-wishers reassures Fals and Favel of their good faith, claiming that it too has mastered Mede's will:

> Tho this gold was ygyve, gret was the thonkyng
> To Fals and to Favel for hire faire yiftes,
> And comen to conforten from care the False,
> And seiden, "Certes, sire, cessen shul we nevere,
> Til Mede be thi wedded wif thorugh wit of us alle;
> For we have Mede amaistried with oure murie speche,
> That she graunteth to goon with a good wille

36. For disparagement, see Tavormina, *Kindly Similitude*, 9 nn. 21–22, and Anna P. Baldwin, *The Theme of Government in "Piers Plowman"* (Cambridge: D. S. Brewer, 1981), 32–34. See Helmholz, *Marriage Litigation*, 100, 160, 212–14 for the error of condition as a type of impediment. Canon law had jurisdiction over marriages, but, as Tavormina points out, statutory law legislated against marriages of feudal wards to enemies of the lord guardian or those of lower social station (27–28). Yet Scott Waugh shows that thirteenth-century English kings and barons "largely accepted the Church doctrine of consent" and were willing to compensate those impoverished by clandestine marriage or refusals, to stipulate the necessity of consent (though not necessarily choice), and to punish enforced marriages. Scott L. Waugh, *The Lordship of England: Royal Wardships and Marriages in English Society and Politics, 1217–1327* (Princeton: Princeton University Press, 1988), 60–61.

To London, to loken if the lawe wolde
Juggen yow joyntly in joie for evere."

(II.149–57)

The refashioning of Mede according to the will of these men seriously compromises the voluntary nature of her consent, notwithstanding her compliance: she seems to have no will of her own in Passus II, an incapacity that canon law does not enumerate but that becomes more flagrantly outrageous to morality in Passus III.

By questioning whether the marriage contract is valid and binding, Theology succeeds in moving the entire entourage to court. It proceeds, however, to the king's courts at Westminster. Theology had said "Londoun" (II.135) and no doubt meant to send them, for legal reasons as well as his own interests, to the church courts there.[37] For his are questions about impediments, including the prior contract. The impediment of incest is not openly discussed, perhaps because it may have proved less metaphorically resonant than other impediments, and therefore the author diminished its role. In the C text, the name of Mede's father is Favel and her bridegroom Fals Faythlesse. In the B text, as we have seen, Mede is the daughter of Fals with a fickle tongue (II.25) and is to be married "to oon Fals Fikel-tonge" (II.41).[38] Kinship does prove metaphorically instrumental in a further sense, however, because here Mede's ability to call the king "cosyn" and her importance as a property-holder allow her to appear before the king as his ward, despite canon law and its jurisdiction over marriage, thus preserving the political level of the allegory.[39]

At Westminster, Mede is led by the nose and by everyone. With justices at the head of the procession, a parade of well-wishers comes to greet her in her room at court:

Gentilliche with joye the justices somme
Busked hem to the bour ther the burde dwellede,
Conforted hyre kyndely by Clergies leve,
And seiden, "Mourne noght, Mede, ne make thow no sorwe,
For we wol wisse the Kyng and thi wey shape   *inform*
To be wedded at thi wille and wher thee leef liketh
For al Consciences cast or craft, as I trowe."

(III.13–19)

37. The mention of the advocates, "vokettes of the Arches" (II.61), makes it clear that the author knew that the Archbishop of Canterbury's provincial court was in London at St. Mary le Bow, and not in Westminster.

38. On the significance of kinship in the episode and on the complicated differences between the texts regarding Mede's birth, see the discussion in Tavormina, *Kindly Similitude*, chapter 1.

39. For the king's feudal rights concerning wardship and marriage (which were the concern of the chancellor), see Waugh, *The Lordship of England*, 15–63.

Next come the clerks, who "beden hire be blithe—'For we beth thyne owene / For to werche thi wille the while thow myght laste'" (III.27–28). The submission of these male characters to her "wille" in this passage becomes increasingly comical and somewhat disturbing, because Mede has evidenced no will of her own. She is little more than a projection screen, or an actor who takes her lines from others. She responds to those who offer themselves to her will by granting their will in abundance. As matters escalate, she allows the confessor in friar's robes even more wicked permissiveness that he sought leave to have. When she has her first audience with the king, he uses the word "unwittily" to describe her action literally as mindless action, as agency lacking intention:

> Unwittily, womman, wroght hastow ofte;
> Ac worse wroghtest thow nevere than tho thow Fals toke.
> But I forgyve thee that gilt, and graunte thee my grace;
> Hennes to thi deeth day do so na moore!
> I have a knyght, Conscience, cam late fro biyonde;
> If he wilneth thee to wif, wiltow hym have?
>
> (III.106–11)

Mede's inappropriate answer epitomizes her passive responsiveness; she is as willing to do what the king wants her to do as to be the pawn of Fals's designs: "'Ye, lord,' quod that lady, 'Lord forbede it ellis! / But I be holly at youre heste, lat hange me soone!'" (III.112–13). Mede gives the answer that Cordelia refuses to give to her own king and father. Being wholly at anyone's "heste," she cannot be moral, nor, as Theology has argued, can she in herself be immoral. She can, however, be the agent of others' immorality. Mede embodies action loose from its intention or subjective source—femininity in need of masculinity, a woman in need of a husband to control her agency with an intentional source, a moral center, a male conscience. If Mede seems neutral in Theology's eyes, it is because she lacks such a capacity to be a full subject. To the extent that conscience is linked to will, to soul, or to the various guises described by Liberum Arbitrium, Mede is empty and void. To the extent that she lacks a conscience, she is judged immoral and a source of evil, as Conscience judges her. Her character makes a telling analogy to the workings of money. Her sexuality, her femininity, the problem of her being only half of the unity of person that is marriage, being out of intention's control: this image of feminine sexuality out of coverture provides the allegory with an analytical tool that reveals how much the economy needs moral agency.

Economic Agency: Just Price and Mede Mesurelees

The level of the allegory that narrates the marriage litigation explains why Mede must be married, but it does not explain why the king thinks she must be married to Conscience. Besides its sexual meanings, Mede's characteristic instrumentality also bears an economic connotation. She is a financial instrument: in part, "mede" stands for money, which in itself is morally neutral but can certainly be the instigator of vice. As we can see by now, the measure or determination of value—how to know what things are worth—is a central problem of the entire narrative, a facet of the search for truth that holds together the affiliative, economic, and political lexicons of the text's language. The crises that Langland perceives in marriage, the economy, and the government are structured as analogous. The allegory describes a circulation of vicious surplus value in what we would now call the service economy of Westminster, a system of bribes and kickbacks that is the consequence of a monetary commutation of courtesy and duty. The uncontrollable nature of this surplus circulation of payment is portrayed as feminine, and through this portrayal the text claims that the economy must be morally analyzed and socialized by strict controls, just as marriage controls women and sexuality.[40]

The invocation of social persons allows us to see the way the allegory connects the project of bridling Mede's excess sexuality to the problem of determining a just measure of value in economic exchange. When the character Conscience makes his clinching argument before the king, he distinguishes between two types of meed or reward in an attempt to separate unjust from just transactions according to the kinds of social person who undertake them:

> Ther are two manere of medes, my lord, by youre leve.
> That oon God of his grace graunteth in his blisse
> To tho that wel werchen while thei ben here.
> The Prophete precheth therof and putte it in the Sauter:
> *Domine, quis habitabit in tabernaculo tuo?*
> Lord, who shal wonye in thi wones with thyne holy seintes
> Or resten in thyne holy hilles?—This asketh David.

---

40. The economic status of women in late medieval England is the subject of much important current work; Judith Bennett reviews its premises in "Medieval Women, Modern Women: Across the Great Divide," in *Culture and History, 1350–1600: Essays on English Communities, Identities and Writing*, ed. David Aers (Detroit: Wayne State University Press, 1992), 147–75.

And David assoileth it hymself, as the Sauter telleth:
Qui ingreditur sine macula et operatur iusticiam.
[He that walketh without blemish, and worketh justice (Psalm 14:2).]
Tho that entren of o colour and of one wille,
And han ywroght werkes with right and with reson,
And he that useth noght the lyf of usurie
And enformeth povere men and pursueth truthe:
Qui pecuniam suam non dedit ad usuram, et munera super innocentem &c;
[He that hath not put out his money to usury, nor taken bribes against the
    innocent (Psalm 14:5).]
And alle that helpen the innocent and holden with the rightfulle,
Withouten mede doth hem good and the truthe helpeth—
Swiche manere men, my lord, shul have this firste mede
Of God at a gret nede, whan thei gon hennes.

(III.231–45)

There is a characteristic shift in these lines from individuals ("who shal
wonye in thi wones?") to intentions and other faculties ("tho that entren of
o colour and of one wille") and then to social structures and relations ("he
that useth noght the lyf of usurie / And enformeth povere men and . . .
helpen the innocent and holden with the rightfulle"). For Langland, the
question is not "who shall be saved?" so much as it is "what habitus gives
us access to salvation?"

Similarly, corrupt economic activity has its source in social persons,
practices, and inequitable relations of agency:

Ther is another mede mesurelees, that maistres desireth:
To mayntene mysdoers mede thei take,
And therof seith the Sauter in a salmes ende—
In quorum manibus iniquitates sunt; dextra eorum repleta est muneribus;
[In whose hands are iniquities; their right hand is filled with gifts (Psalm 25:10).]
And he that gripeth hir gold, so me God helpe,
Shal abien it bittre, or the Book lieth!   *pay*
Preestes and persons that plesynge desireth,
That taken mede and moneie for masses that thei syngeth,
Taken hire mede here as Mathew us techeth:
Amen, amen, receperunt mercedem suam.
[They have received their reward (Matthew 6:5).]

(III.246–54)

This second kind of recompense is condemned by the Bible and described
as meed "mesurelees." The agency relation between lords and the misdoers they support is expressed in the iconography of the hand, a bodily sign

of agency.[41] The hands are held out, full of iniquity and bribes. They present an invitation to others to "grip" and so they conjure the bodily sign of social bonds, clasped hands—but the narrator tries to stop the reader from such grasping, from the contract built upon the corrupting power of gold. There is a faint current of Mede's sexual power returning to the scene in line 252, where the narrative describes how priests and parsons "that plesynge desireth" all "Taken hire mede" in this world and are at risk of receiving no reward in the next. Such evil, measureless meed is contrasted with appropriate payments for services:

> That laborers and lewede leodes taken of hire maistres,   *people*
> It is no manere mede but a mesurable hire.
> In marchaundise is no mede, I may it wel avowe:
> It is a permutacion apertly—a penyworth for another.
>
> (III.255–58)

These lines hover between the descriptive and the prescriptive, the actual and the ideal. The writing seems to multiply clauses and become more emphatic than analytic, amounting to a contention that lacks proof. Here Conscience insists, perhaps too loudly, that wage labor and commerce operate without meed.[42]

Conscience sets these cases aside because the allegory wishes to direct our attention to areas of economic life that lack, as yet, cogent formulations of right and wrong. Medieval economic thought depends primarily upon such legislation as the Statutes of Laborers and the doctrines of just price and of usury, modes of understanding that are insufficient for Langland's model of the economy, with its predominantly service-based, professional transactions.[43] However, his exceptions make a distinction that

41. For the hand as an icon of agency, see the rich history in Katherine Rowe, *Dead Hands: Fictions of Agency, Renaissance to Modern* (Stanford: Stanford University Press, 1999).

42. On the relation of this passage in B and C to the scholastic theological distinction between *meritum de condigno* and *meritum de congruo*, see James Simpson, "Spirituality and Economics in Passus 1–7 of the B Text," *Yearbook of Langland Studies* 1 (1987): 93–97. He cites Samuel A. Overstreet, "Grammaticus Ludens: Theological Aspects of Langland's Grammatical Allegory," *Traditio* 40 (1984): 251–96. Simpson represents Conscience's distinction as satisfactorily resolving the controversy over meed (see especially 97, n. 23); in my view neither Conscience nor the theological distinction succeeds in so doing.

43. Late medieval economic theory is primarily embodied in canon law: see John Gilchrist, *The Church and Economic Activity in the Middle Ages* (New York: St. Martin's Press, 1969). On just price, see John W. Baldwin, "The Medieval Theories of the Just Price: Romanists, Canonists and Theologians in the Twelfth and Thirteenth Centuries," *Transactions of the American Philosophical Society*, n.s., 49, pt. 4 (1959) and Odd Langholm, *Price and Value in the Aristotelian Tradition: A Study in Scholastic Economic Sources* (Bergen:

is patently false: Conscience's untenable declaration that there is no profit in wages or sales unsatisfactorily closes a question that recurs throughout the text in different forms. How can we determine legitimate or (in the language of the canon lawyers) *just* price and a just wage?[44] Wage labor and commercial transactions could be, and were, regulated, though not very effectively. The multiple enactments of the Statutes of Laborers, for example, suggest what economic historians have confirmed: that such laws were difficult to enforce and that transactions of these kinds continued to generate controversy. The allegory attempts to extend the realm of its analysis to the kind of economy epitomized by the Westminster courts, a site of complex financial transactions that could not be classified as homage, as sales, or as wage labor. While convention and competition must have had some regulating effects, there was no policy that allowed for redress in cases of excess (or insufficient) fees. Conscience's distinction between measurable and immeasurable things proves no sharper than a simple verbal comparison between moderation and immoderation. Worse, wage labor and sales are in theory no more clearly "measurable" than fees for services. While Langland's gender semiotics allows him to make a distinction between agency with a controlling intention (married women) and agency without (unmarried women), the distinction does not transfer with any precision to economic analysis and cannot provide a razor with which to divide just economic exchange cleanly from fraud.

In part, Mede's characterization embodies the fragile social framework of the money economy, in which wages, when commuted into quantities of money, are wrenched from their context in familiar and regulated social bonds. The allegory of Mede's marriage litigation argues that exchange outside of its context in fealty is morally dangerous, robbing wage labor of some of its appeal. In this view, the freedom and portability that are conveyed by the monetary commutation of wages become a kind of sexual promiscuity rather than a modicum of choice for laborers as to when, where, for whom, and for how much they will work. The allegory thus applies misogyny to labor outside fealty: it transfers its description of the promiscuous sexual nature of women both to wage labor and to fee-for-service working arrangements in the professions.

The tension between Conscience's two kinds of meed is ultimately a ten-

---

Universitetsforlaget, 1979) and *Economics in the Medieval Schools: Wealth, Exchange, Value, Money and Usury according to the Paris Theological Tradition, 1200–1350* (Leiden: E. J. Brill, 1992). On usury, see John T. Noonan, Jr., *The Scholastic Analysis of Usury* (Cambridge: Harvard University Press, 1957).

44. The issue of wage-labor is further explored in the episode of the plowing of the half-acre (Passus VI); see Baldwin, *Theme of Government*, 61 and Simpson, "Spirituality and Economics," 97–101.

sion inherent in economic exchange. Two commodities can only be made equivalent to each other by an act of interpretation and convention, and never in an absolute sense: corn is never absolutely measurable by potatoes, or by money. There is no inherently equal exchange, no way of insuring that a measureless meed will not be involved in service transactions or in purchases. Like sexual behavior, the determination of just price is ultimately an issue that involves subjective intention as well as social effect. As we shall see in chapter 3, the problem of defining value is necessarily enmeshed in the definition of person.

How does Conscience use his strange distinction between the two kinds of meed to win a victory over Mede? When Mede fights back with her own Latin, Conscience ridicules her:

> "I leve wel, lady," quod Conscience, "that thi Latyn be trewe.
> Ac thow art lik a lady that radde a lesson ones,
> Was *omnia probate*, and that plesed hire herte—
> For that lyne was no lenger at the leves ende.
> Hadde she loked that other half and the leef torned,
> She sholde have founden fele wordes folwynge therafter:
> *Quod bonum est tenete*—Truthe that text made."
>
> (III.337–43)

This diagnosis returns us to the comparison between Mede and Holi Chirche in Passus II. The Latin maxim *omnia probate quod bonum est tenete* [But prove all things; hold that which is good (1 Thessalonians 5:21)] logically complements the refrain with which Holi Chirche closes Passus I: "Whan alle tresors ben tried, Treuthe is the beste" (I.207). Mede has the negative capability to try everything, acting exactly like the economic general equivalent (e.g., money), which tries, or measures, all other commodities. In associating her with measurelessness, Conscience's rhetoric distinguishes her goods (as a promiscuous and, finally, only relative measure of value) from what is good (truth), thus bringing a closure to the sexual competition between Mede and Holi Chirche.

The C text moves away from the entire contractual model of marriage, away from the sexual competition of Passus II, and away from the measurable/measureless distinction with which Conscience subdues Mede in the B text, perhaps because the distinction does not work as well as the author wished it to work. Instead, Conscience develops an elaborate grammatical metaphor into a model of an agency relation in which an alignment of wills is accomplished by attention to "case" and "agreement."[45]

45. See also Maureen Quilligan, "Langland's Literal Allegory," *Essays in Criticism* 28 (1978): 95–111.

The C text performs a less acute analysis of the money economy and meed, yet the questions of measure and the determination of value come back to haunt the dreamer in a new and lengthy passage added to Passus V. Here Reson and Conscience rebuke Will, causing him to face questions about the compensation of his own labor. What is his work justly worth? One of the ways that he resolves this question is by attempting to ground that difficult distinction between just reward and surplus in his own biological body. He defends himself with the claim that he takes no money but only meals along his way, meals that are precisely measured by the carefully equilibrated measuring cup of his own stomach: "on this wyse y begge / Withoute bagge or botel but my wombe one" (C.V.51–52).[46]

In *Policraticus* V.15, John of Salisbury discusses "what pertains to the sacred calling of proconsuls, governors and ordinary justices, and to what extent it is permitted to reach out for gifts." His general rule is to avoid excess: "All duties should be freely performed so that nothing is either demanded or received beyond the fixed amount. But perhaps you ask what the fixed amount is. It is contained in the people's ordinance that none who governs is to accept a present or gift, except of food or drink, and this also is to be used in the days immediately following."[47] John takes his topic from Justinian's *Digest* 1.16.6. The movement from the question of excess to the determination of a "fixed" amount by what the body can use is exactly the logic applied by Will to his own case. He attempts to control avarice by translating it into an appetite that has a physical limit or container, the stomach. Despite the C text's movement toward grammatical metaphor and the analysis of language, the epistemological problems presented by the imbricated ideas of value and person still occupy the narrative: we might call the philosophical motive of *Piers Plowman* not the problem of other minds, but the problem of other "wombs," of needs, appetites, and interests outside what is present to the will.

Political Agency: Constitutional Monarchy and the Marriage of Males

The plot of the Mede episodes is a legal process that turns on the question of how meed should be measured. When the dreamer first sees Mede

---

46. On this rich passage, see especially Middleton, "William Langland's 'Kynde Name'" and Anne Middleton, "Acts of Vagrancy: The C Version 'Autobiography' and the Statute of 1388," in *Written Work*, 208–317; and Ralph Hanna, "Will's Work," in *Written Work*, 23–66.

47. John of Salisbury, *Policraticus: Of the Frivolities of Courtiers and the Footprints of Philosophers*, trans. Cary J. Nederman (Cambridge: Cambridge University Press, 1990), 96–97.

he wonders whose wife she is. In order to measure someone's actions against a legal doctrine, it must be clear that the standard of behavior elaborated in that doctrine properly applies to her social person; so the entity must be measured in terms of a legal person—in this case the bride and wife. Mede is the personification of compensation, a principle that represents a structure of social relations and a set of economic behaviors and actions. Mede's marriage and habitus are judged in the king's court—and so, by means of the allegory, economic policy is judged in terms of the legal person that is constructed by marriage law. Langland's thought experiment argues for a newly strong central control of the economy.

It makes this argument by employing the moral analysis of agency that is already developed in the complex legal discourse surrounding marriage, kinship, and sexuality: a discourse in which the primary category is gender. The conclusion of the Mede section of the text, as we shall see, paradoxically manages to retain unity of person as a model for contract while emptying it of gender difference or, more specifically, of the female.

Mede's capacity for consent has been established as notoriously promiscuous and vacuous. The pervasiveness of the sexuality created by the structure of coverture is so powerful that it precedes the state of marriage. If women are brought up to be agents of other principals, to be obedient to the will of others, then with what free will do they consent? Their consent is impoverished by being produced by an endless consent they are brought up to give. Further, consenting to marriage is, in this model, consenting permanently: consenting to give up the capacity to consent, consenting to life in a constant condition of what, as we have seen, the chancellor Robert Stillington calls coercion and dread. Can such consent be meaningful? Should one be capable of giving up one's capacity to consent? Many arguments against slavery say one should not, as do many arguments for divorce. Mede's consent is not meaningful; in fact, it is dangerous in its lack of intention and will. Thus the ability to consent to marriage that the church assigned to women and men equally is both tremendously important and simultaneously severely circumscribed not only by familial, social, and financial pressures, but also by the very form of the agency relation, under law, that marital consent incorporated. The lack of will in Mede's agency, its detachment from moral intentionality, prompts the king to match her with a conscience in marriage, but also fatally undermines the very notion of her capacity for contract. As Leaute proclaims in public:

> Whoso wilneth hire to wyve, for welthe of hire goodes—
> But he be knowe for a cokewold, kut of my nose!
> (IV.163–64)

Thus it is necessary to exclude Mede from the polity, to banish women's agency from unity of person and the political contract.

Indeed, the closure of the marriage plot takes place without women. The interrupted, prevented marriages of Mede are finally replaced, at the end of Passus IV of the B text, by an alternative exchange of vows *per verba de praesenti*, a mock marriage that Conscience arranges between the king and Reson:

> "And I assente," seith the Kyng, "by Seinte Marie my lady,
> Be my Counseil comen of clerkes and of erles.
> Ac redily, Reson, thow shalt noght ride hennes;
> For as longe as I lyve, lete thee I nelle."
> "I am al redy," quod Reson, "to reste with yow evere;
> So Conscience be of oure counseil, I kepe no bettre."
> "And I graunte," quod the Kyng, "Goddes forbode he faile!
> Als longe as oure lyf lasteth, lyve we togideres!"
>
> (IV.188–95)

Passus II through IV, the entire section of the text concerning Mede, progresses from the topic of the control of sexuality through marriage and its carefully institutionalized gender relations, to a picture of economic civil society, and finally to an agreement between men resulting in government. Perhaps it seems strange that this sequence resembles the contract theory of seventeenth-century political philosophers, who typically move from a story of disputes over women to a purely fraternal contract that places consent at the origins and center of the constitution of government. But an emphasis on consent in the constitution of government is not uncommon in earlier political theory.[48]

To make the analogy between kingship and marriage that Langland makes, however, is rare before the fourteenth century. John of Salisbury makes it briefly: "Varro asserts: 'The vices of a spouse are to be either removed or endured. He who removes the vices is a preferable spouse; he who tolerates them makes himself a better person.' Thus, the vices of princes and subjects are to be either endured or removed; for in fact their confederation either equals or surpasses conjugal affection."[49] While it

48. E.g., Magna Carta, Marsilius of Padua in the *Defensor Pacis* (c. 1325), Duns Scotus in *Opus Oxoniense* (c. 1300), William of Ockham in *Dialogus* (c. 1340). See Brian Tierney, "Hierarchy, Consent, and the 'Western Tradition,'" *Political Theory* 15 (1987): 646–52. For discussion of the relation between gender relations and the political constitution in early modern contract theory, see Carole Pateman, *The Sexual Contract* (Stanford: Stanford University Press, 1988) and Mary Lyndon Shanley, "Marriage Contract and Social Contract in Seventeenth Century English Political Thought," *The Western Political Quarterly* 32 (1979): 79–91.

49. John of Salisbury, *Policraticus* VI.26, trans. Nederman, 140.

compares marriage and kingship, this passage is uninterested in contract, be it sexual or political. Ernst Kantorowicz contends that the idea of marriage is transferred to "secular legal-political thought" from canon law discussions of the bishop's relation to his church, created at ordination as if through a marriage.[50] His first examples are drawn from early fourteenth-century civil law commentaries. The most elaborate fourteenth-century use of the analogy is by the Neapolitan jurist Lucas de Penna: "And just as men are joined together [*coniunguntur*] spiritually in the spiritual body, the head of which is Christ . . . , so are men joined together morally and politically in the *respublica*, which is a body the head of which is the Prince."[51] The purpose of the analogy increases the significance of its language. Kantorowicz writes: "What Lucas de Penna aimed at when enlarging on the Prince's *matrimonium morale et politicum*, was to illustrate a fundamental law: the inalienability of fiscal property. Very appropriately, therefore, he interpreted the fisc as the dowry of the bridal *respublica*, and explained that a husband was entitled only to *use* the property of his wife, but not to alienate it."[52] Lucas de Penna employs his extended metaphor (or allegory) in order to transfer the conditions of one estate to another. Similarly, *Piers Plowman* attempts to characterize the relationship between the king and the money economy (not the fisc, or royal treasury) as custodial by suggesting various kinds of kinship. According to Theology, Mede may kiss the king as a cousin if she likes; the king treats her as a kind of ward. The allegorical marriage plot, however, is transferred to two men, despite the fact that Reson could have been female.[53]

Like Liberum Arbitrium, the allegory places its agency relations simultaneously inside and outside social persons. The exchange of consent between the king and Reson is both a bond within faculty psychology, "interior" to the king, and a political bond between the king and his council. While the allegory stresses the king's decision-making process as relational, as proceeding out of his function as an agent who interprets and acts upon reason and conscience, the reader is free to see those characters either as subjective capacities belonging to an individual king or as privy councilors with institutional positions and interests of their own. "Conscience" and "reason" refer the reader to faculty psychology; but these

50. Ernst H. Kantorowicz, *The King's Two Bodies: A Study in Mediaeval Political Theology* (Princeton: Princeton University Press, 1957), 212.

51. Quoted in and trans. Kantorowicz, *King's Two Bodies*, 216. Lucas is discussing the *Tres Libri* of Justinian's *Code*.

52. Kantorowicz, *King's Two Bodies*, 217.

53. Indeed, we would expect Reson to be female according to the gender of the Latin *ratio*, *intelligentia*, *mens*. For a general assessment of Langland's personifications and proof that their gender does not depend on grammar, see Helen Cooper, "Gender and Personification in *Piers Plowman*," *Yearbook of Langland Studies* 5 (1991): 31–48.

terms also refer directly to the developing jurisprudence of the king's courts. William Gascoigne, Chief Justice of the King's Bench, is reported to have argued in 1406 that "the king has committed all his judicial powers to various courts," a notion that argues against a purely absolutist interpretation of the allegory.[54] The intellectual history of the king's law courts which are presided over by his councilors is imbued with such notions as reason and conscience, notions that are intimately intertwined: conscience is often called natural reason. Chancery, the chancellor's court, is especially associated with equity and becomes known as the court of conscience.[55] Law is often regarded as founded in reason, despite common law's origins in custom rather than in an intellectual system.[56]

Langland's political allegory pulls, therefore, in two directions. It makes strong moral demands upon both the more absolutist and the more conciliarist readings one might give it, requiring the king who feels that he embodies the law (as did Richard II) to listen to his advisers and to the requirements of jurisprudence, and also requiring ambitious advisers to personify moral faculties issuing from the king. The narrative is so skeptical about the ability of any particular institutional arrangement to ensure justice and the common welfare that it insists that any action or institutional process must be governed by ideal purposes and principles. The institution that neglects the governing agency of reason, that strays from its proper intentional source in conscience, harms the society and corrupts the souls of its members. Further, the moment of contract itself is of great importance. The last scene of Passus IV, as we have seen, depicts a new constitution of the polity according to unity of person:

54. *Chedder v. Savage* (1406), quoted in Baker, *Introduction*, 112. According to Baker, *The Reports of Sir John Spelman*: "the story of Gascoigne C.J., Prince Henry, and King Henry IV, published by Elyot in *The Governour*, was a popular story even with Henry VIII's chief justices" (2:140–41).

55. See note 10 above. On equity and notions of justice in *Piers Plowman*, see especially William J. Birnes, "Christ as Advocate: The Legal Metaphor of *Piers Plowman*," *Annuale Mediaevale* 16 (1975): 71–93, and Myra Stokes, *Justice and Mercy in "Piers Plowman": A Reading of the B Text Visio* (London: Croom Helm, 1984).

56. See Norman Doe, *Fundamental Authority in Late Medieval English Law* (Cambridge: Cambridge University Press, 1990), 108–31, including 112, n. 18, which cites a phrase from the Year Books propounded by Stonore J: "*ley est resoun*" (18 and 19 Ed. III [RS] 379). The notion of reason's coincidence with the common law, which flowers in later theorists such as St. German, may be partly due to the influence of the civilian concept of *ratio legis*. Thus, there may also be civilian as well as Thomistic undertones to the figure of Reson in *Piers Plowman*. The character Cyvylle, however, is as corrupt as his friend Symonye, showing Langland's preference for theory over practitioners (II.67–68). In Conscience's utopic prophecy there will be no conflict of laws: "Kynges court and commune court, consistorie and chapitle—/ Al shal be but oon court, and oon burn be justice: / That worth Trewe-tonge, a tidy man that tened me nevere" (III.320–23).

"And I assente," seith the Kyng, "by Seinte Marie my lady,
Be my Counseil comen of clerkes and of erles.
Ac redily, Reson, thow shalt noght ride hennes;
For as longe as I lyve, lete thee I nelle."
"I am al redy," quod Reson, "to reste with yow evere;
So Conscience be of oure counseil, I kepe no bettre."
"And I graunte," quod the Kyng, "Goddes forbode he faile!
Als longe as oure lyf lasteth, lyve we togideres!"

(IV.188–95)

The stress in these lines falls upon the quality of the agency relation it-self rather than upon which particular constitutional arrangement is achieved.[57]

The overlay of potentially contradictory models of monarchy—abso-lutist in the allegory of faculty psychology, conciliarist in the allegory of legal institutions, and consensual (however compromised) in the allegory of marital contract—thus shifts the weight of the argument from the ques-tion of specific institutional arrangements to their conditions.[58] At the same time, the combination of potentially contradictory constitutional forms in one polity is consonant with the Aristotelian and Thomistic mode of thinking that sustains John Fortescue's fifteenth-century treatise *The Governance of England*.[59] The linchpin of the book is Fortescue's descrip-tion of England as embodying a peculiar form of mixed constitution that he terms *dominium politicum et regale*. While he cites authorities from biblical Kings to Thomas Aquinas to Giles of Rome, his interpretation of this mixed dominion is ingeniously designed to reconcile political philoso-phy to the English political settlement.[60] An organic model and a consen-

---

57. For a different interpretation of political thought in *Piers Plowman*, see Baldwin, *Theme of Government*.

58. On a related problem, in which two powers are first compared in theology, beginning with Albertus Magnus and Thomas Aquinas (*potentia dei absoluta et ordinata*), and then transferred to discussions of kingship, see Francis Oakley, *Omnipotence, Covenant, and Order: An Excursion in the History of Ideas from Abelard to Leibniz* (Ithaca: Cornell University Press, 1984).

59. John Fortescue, *The Governance of England: Otherwise Called the Difference between an Absolute and a Limited Monarchy*, ed. Charles Plummer (Oxford: Clarendon, 1885). Fortescue was a prominent lawyer, Chief Justice of the King's Bench, and a Lancastrian supporter. A manuscript copy of *The Governance of England* is included together with a text of *Piers Plowman* in Bodleian Library MS. Digby 145 thought to be compiled early in the 1530s by Adrian Fortescue, John's descendent. On the manuscript, see Anne Middleton, "The Audience and Public of *Piers Plowman*," in *Middle English Alliterative Poetry and its Literary Background*, ed. David Lawton (Cambridge: D. S. Brewer, 1982), 101–23.

60. See also Nicolai Rubinstein, "The History of the Word *Politicus* in Early-Modern Europe," in *The Languages of Political Theory in Early-Modern Europe*, ed. Anthony Pagden (Cambridge: Cambridge University Press, 1987), 49–52.

sual model are combined in Fortescue's history of English kingship. In the ancient world, he tells us, kingship was divine and can be described by the legal maxim "*quod principi placuit, legis habet vigorem.*" An English improvement inaugurates the next historical stage:

> But aftirwarde, whan mankynde was more mansuete, and bettir disposid to vertu, grete comunaltes, as was the felowshippe that came in to this lande with Brute, willynge to be vnite and made a body pollitike callid a reawme, hauynge an hed to gouerne it;—as aftir the saynge of the philisopher, euery comunalte vnyed of mony parties must nedis haue an hed;—than they chese the same Brute to be ther hed and kynge. And thai and he vpon this incorperacion, institucion, and onynge of hem self in to a reaume, ordenyd the same reaume to be ruled and justified by suche lawes as thai all wolde assent vnto; wich lawe therfore is callid "polliticum," and bi cause it is ministrid bi a kynge, it is callid "regale." *Policia dicitur a* "poles," *quod est plures, et* "ycos," *scientia; quo regimen politicum dicitur* "regimen plurium scientia siue consilio ministratum."[61]

The social person ("body pollitike") of the realm is constituted both by personification—the fellowship and Brute's "incorperacion, institucion, and onynge of hem self in to a reaume"—and by common election, will, and assent. The rest of *The Governance of England* shows the two aspects of this mixed dominion holding each other in check. It is not good to have magnates that too powerfully limit the king's power; it is not good to have a commons that is impoverished and cannot stand up to the king. The model embodies a kind of balance wrought from the conflict between the absolute and the contractual ideas.

Perhaps this balance is the effect that Langland has in mind. Just before the king and Reson exchange their vows, the king has been ranting about the judgement to which Mede will be subject, and the "commune" is mentioned by Conscience:

> Quod Conscience to the Kyng, "But the commune wole assente,
> It is ful hard, by myn heed, herto to brynge it,
> And alle youre lige leodes to lede thus evene."
> "By Hym that raughte on the Rood!" quod Reson to the Kynge,   cross
> "But if I rule thus youre reaume, rende out my guttes—
> If ye bidden buxomnesse be of myn assent."   obedience
>
> (IV.182–87)

It is in connection with the commons, then, that consent is first brought into the final scene of the passus. Its consent and obedience become a con-

61. Fortescue, chap. 2 in *The Governance of England*, 112.

dition of the contract between the king and Reson, just as it is in Fortescue's description of the historical creation of the English constitutional monarchy. But in *Piers Plowman* it is not the entire body politic but the king's councilor, Reson, upon whom the role of the king's spouse falls. According to legal argument, the depositions of Edward II and Richard II both turned upon the hinge of the oath of office of the monarch, in which he vowed to listen to his council: not necessarily to obey them, but to hear them—in a sense, as Langland's king puts it, to live together. The charge of not hearing counsel could bring down a king, and perhaps it is not surprising, after exploring the significance of sexuality in *Piers Plowman*, that charges against Edward II were coupled with rumors of sexual depravity. Perversions of the relations of agency that supported the political contract in which the king participated were grounds for its invalidation.

When the bride—Reson—becomes male, coverture is disrupted and neither partner appears to experience any degree of civil death in the marriage. The picture of unity of person between the king and his chancellor, and between the king and the law, imports into government the consensual foundation and the mutuality of the entrance into marriage (embodied in their exchange of vows) but disallows the king the particular dominion of the husband. At the end of a lengthy attempt to marry the privy councilor Conscience to the economic agency personified in the promiscuous maid Mede, in hopes of thereby saving the kingdom (and especially the service economy of the Westminster courts) from corruption, the king had faced Conscience's refusal. That refusal constituted a failure of what had been the project of the allegory throughout the Mede episode: to secure economic justice by drawing on a specific model of agency, found in marriage law, in order to reform the less well theorized and moralized relations of agency found in the economy. With the marriage of Reson and the king, civil death is banished and a robust consent defines proper political relations in the body politic.

Piers Plowman links the doctrine that had grown up around the social person of marriage (unity of person) to two other ideas—that of just price and that of constitutional monarchy—in order to inaugurate the analysis of agency in social bonds at all levels of society. Moreover, these models of agency are brought together through a particular rhetorical form: personification allegory makes it possible to test these discourses against each other, assembling a more complete set of standards and conditions. The economic model of bonds lacks a sophisticated concept of impediments to meaningful consent, but offers the useful notions of just price, necessity, and price controls. The marriage model of bonds gives a refined description of consent in the entrance into an agency relation but confines its notion of incapacity to individuals and severely disables the capacities of the wife during the life of the coverture. Models of contract that ground social relations in the human body, like faculty psychology, can represent fine details of agency, but tend to promote absolutism, because they assert consent as natural and necessary without providing for a process. The grammatical model of social bonds that will be introduced by Conscience's speeches in the C text personifies parts of speech in a peculiar, magical way that is suggestive of social cooperation but similarly lacks a mechanism of legitimate consent or dissent.

The author draws conclusions from his examination of medieval society that I would not. For example, he portrays the government as a marital contract that ought to exclude women on moral grounds. The insight that derives from his analysis of social relations is nevertheless important and is reinforced in later passus, where Langland decries the impediments that invalidate the consent of the poor to economic contract.[62] Legal theory allows that duress, fraud, and incapacity prevent legitimate voluntary entrance into social relations, but *Piers Plowman* goes further. The poem reveals as inherently unjust all forms of social relations that produce duress or fraud and thus corrupt the will's capacity for virtuous agency. Thus the evaluation of the forms of social person in which bonds are embedded depends not only upon the conditions of entrance into those forms, but upon conditions that preserve meaningful agency during the tenure of the relations. In short, the allegory takes the conditions by which we evaluate the inception of contract and applies those conditions to the entire life of social bonds.[63] Despite the banishing of feminine agency recommended by the plot, then, the text produces an overriding defense of agency that urges the resurrection of those subjected to civil death.

Moreover, the text's critique of civil death is not accomplished by means of methodological individualism, that crucial tool of nineteenth- and twentieth-century political theory in its extension of the rights of full citizenship to the poor, women, and the non-white; rather, the critique derives from the allegory's representation of agency as relational. Its personifications ask to be interpreted not as individuals but as social processes. It treats social persons as personifications of social bonds. It interprets social institutions themselves as such personifications: the three passus devoted to Mede develop the understanding of government as a representation of the various bonds between people, beginning with sexual relations. Like Liberum Arbitrium, the human principal in this contract theory is neces-

---

62. On the text's treatment of the poor, see Derek Pearsall, "Poverty and Poor People in *Piers Plowman*," in *Medieval English Studies Presented to George Kane*, ed. Edward D. Kennedy, Roland Waldron and Joseph S. Wittig (Woodbridge, Suffolk: D. S. Brewer, 1988), 167–86 and Aers, *Community, Gender, and Individual Identity*, 20–72.

63. It bears pointing out how inimical this is to Hobbesian views.

sarily an allegorical sign for a network of relations between people, a figure at some distance from the independent, property-owning, male head-of-household who is the dominant social person for early modern political theorists. Rather than valuing the preservation of the rights and liberties of these particular men above all, *Piers Plowman* values the moral soundness of social bonds. It evaluates the polity by thinking about the processes that effect civil death, and about the loose ends as well as the center of the social world: beggars, the sexually promiscuous, thieves, the starving, itinerant preachers, poor widows. Often Will's vacillating self-identification, and thus the primary epistemological standpoint of the allegory, lies with them.[64]

A deeply conservative fidelity to traditional social arrangements pervades *Piers Plowman*, yet the fictional representation of those arrangements is animated by such imaginative power that everything is changed. The form of this transformative imaginative power is, in its essence, personification. The free, fluid, sometimes surreal placing of character, the representation of person, in a myriad of changeable positions in the stuff of the social fabric opens up that arranged world of descriptions and doctrines to analytical tools that can question and evaluate it closely, that can measure its consequences against its promises and ideals.

64. See Lawton, "Subject," 26.

⟳ Chapter Three ⟳

The Temporality of Social Persons: Value in "The Tunnyng of Elynour Rummynge"

I have shown, I hope, that the important role played by social persons in the structuring of intention and agency is a matter for both intellectual history and the history of institutions.[1] Notwithstanding that historical focus, I have tended to treat social persons themselves as relatively stable in time. In this chapter it will be my task to give the richest possible account of the temporal qualities of the social person. We shall see how its temporally sensitive nature poses grave difficulties for scholars just as it provides poets with opportunities for hilarity. A sense of how a text acts over time will help to thicken our account of social persons as both consensual and contested, both redolent of completed actions and still capable of acting upon and through us, the living audience, in surprising ways.

Our case is a curious one. John Skelton's raucous "Tunnyng of Elynour Rummynge" (c. 1517–1521)[2] is like an architect's folly in which the gingerbread ornament of misogyny overwhelms a barely-recognizable structure of ideas. Though it has always been viewed as a piece of exuberant but realistic description of an alewife, I will show that, through a complex of careful allusion, the poem brings together several learned discursive traditions (all far from modes of realism) in order to serve ambitions well beyond those we have perceived.

It is a revealing fact that Skelton's critics have been distracted by the ex-

---

1. See the Introduction for my term "social person," which is central to the argument here and complicated enough to require introduction.

2. *John Skelton: The Complete English Poems*, ed. John Scattergood (New Haven: Yale University Press, 1983), 449. All references to the poem will be to Scattergood's edition by line number.

travagance of the poem and have neglected its argument. If we cannot see (as critics of the poem have not seen) literary character as constructed by reference to social persons, we ignore its specific historical arguments and cannot discover how it works. By their nature, which lies in convention, social persons claim a kind of stable permanence that is instrumental to the power of society to reproduce itself and persist over generations. Yet in order to remain powerful as the forms of social life change, the social person's structures of use, reference, and meaning must adapt. Take the virulent and ornate misogyny that animates the character Elynour Rummynge. Misogyny is so distasteful, amusing, inhuman, and banal that it hardly seems to have a history. Can misogyny ever be interesting when it is so familiar and transparent?[3] On the other hand, if we are content to describe merely the general ideological function of misogyny—that its social force is to subordinate women—we will succumb to its apparently intractable presence in human culture and fail to see the twists and turns of its history as misogyny imperfectly adapts human beings to changes in social structures. If we think life would be better if women were not subordinate, we need to be able to appraise misogyny's actions and strengths. What happens when the institutions served by misogyny are radically transformed? Pursuing this question is one of the ways we can begin to make a more general inquiry about all propositions embodied in social persons: as ideas survive historical change, in what form do their meanings persist?[4]

As we shall see, the misogyny of Elynour's portrait provides a significant intellectual clue. We shall discover that the references to social persons built into her character reveal her origins in literary tradition, economic thought, and clerical antifeminism. As the institutions that generate these modes of representation shift and buckle throughout the later middle ages, the meaning produced by their social persons shifts and buckles too. We shall see how Skelton takes advantage of that process to compose a critique of economic thought and its theory of value. Like Chaucer and Langland, Skelton produces a meta-disciplinary commentary on social persons and topoi drawn from ecclesiastical, sexual, economic, and political sources. Tracing its arguments will allow me to extend our philosoph-

---

3. The social historian Judith Bennett stresses the importance of seeing misogyny as a powerful kind of social action throughout her work on women in the late medieval brewing industry. See Judith M. Bennett, *Ale, Beer, and Brewsters in England: Women's Work in a Changing World, 1300–1600* (New York: Oxford University Press, 1996).

4. J. G. A. Pocock argues that language must be specified in time for a history of ideas to work in "The Concept of a Language and the *métier d'historien*: Some Considerations on Practice," in *The Languages of Political Theory in Early-Modern Europe*, ed. Anthony Pagden (Cambridge: Cambridge University Press, 1987), 19–38. I want to add the point that in order to be understood, language must be specified in terms of the current state of the social institutions—including categories of the person—within which it works.

ical inquiry, which so far has treated intention and agency, to consider theories of value and their relation to the person.

The case of Skelton's poem will also allow us to continue our account of how conventional modes of literary characterization themselves can become social persons, and thus offer a technology for producing paradigmatic representations of the person. "The Tunnyng" represents a key facet of Skelton's literary achievement both with respect to his forbears and to the devotional and amorous sonneteers of the later sixteenth century. I shall argue that Skelton's poems are important technical experiments in which he begins to tinker with the machinery of personification, the dominant medieval form of characterization, as if it needed to be disassembled in order for the English lyric to take a Petrarchan, personal, psalm-like shape and begin its reign over later Tudor letters.

Seeing Through Character

Though Skelton's reputation has varied precipitously in the centuries since his death, critics have been unanimous on the particular merits of "The Tunnyng of Elynour Rummynge." Nearly five centuries of readers have invoked terms like "realism" in persistent celebration of the poem's visual qualities. Yet more historically minded critics have routinely ignored the poem because it lacks reference to the courtly and ecclesiastical themes emphasized by Skelton's biographers.[5] The "Tunnyng" portrays a working alewife and her female clientele; they, of course, are what Skelton has been credited for visualizing so realistically. An early eighteenth-century editor called the poem "a just and natural Description of those merry Wassail Dayes"[6]; in 1844, *The Quarterly Review* compared the poem to a painting:

> It is a low picture of the lowest life—Dutch in its grotesque minuteness: yet, even in the description of the fat hostess herself, and one or two other passages, we know not that we can justly make any stronger animadversion than that they are very Swiftish. But it will further show how little (of course excepting cant words) the genuine vulgar tongue and, we may add perhaps, vulgar life is altered since the time of Henry VIII. Take the general concourse of her female customers to Elynour Rummin, uncontrolled by any temperance societies.[7]

5. Richard Halpern draws a suggestive analogy between Skelton's poetics and the Marxist theory of the economic mode called primitive accumulation, though he does not comment on "The Tunnyng": *The Poetics of Primitive Accumulation: English Renaissance Culture and the Genealogy of Capital* (Ithaca: Cornell University Press, 1991). A list of generic sources and analogues for "The Tunnyng" is given by Arthur Kinney, *John Skelton: Priest as Poet: Seasons of Discovery* (Chapel Hill: University of North Carolina Press, 1987), 168–87.

6. *Skelton: The Critical Heritage*, ed. Anthony S. G. Edwards (London: Routledge & Kegan Paul, 1981), 74.

7. Quoted in *Skelton*, ed. Edwards, 111.

Here, as elsewhere, the assertion of Skelton's pictorialism stands as evidence of the poem's social realism. In 1936, G. S. Fraser argues that "Skelton's figures are . . . portraits, not caricatures. Eleanor Rumming, regrettably, exists. . . . Every detail (and the details grow more and more unsavoury) adds to her reality."[8] C. S. Lewis complains that the poem is *too* close to life: it is "disorder in life rendered by disorder in art."[9]

Stanley Fish continues this tradition, deriving the poem's social "realism" from the poem's "visual" technique. He elaborately identifies the poem with painting: "*The Tunning of Eleanor Rumming* is a picture, a verbal painting—and designedly nothing more. . . . to read the poem is to see a canvas prepared before (or through) your very eyes. . . . indeed the sophist Hermogenes might be describing *Eleanor Rumming* when he writes 'An ecphrasis is an account in detail, visible as they say, bringing before one's eyes what is to be shown. . . . The virtues of the ecphrasis are clearness and visibility; for the style must . . . operate to bring about seeing.' "[10] While Fish's metaphors bring out the experimentalism of the poem, they lead us away from its primary formal features and its overriding tone of disgust and enthusiastic opprobrium. The poem's virulent disapproval of its female characters makes it difficult to concur with Fish's description of the poem's moral and philosophical neutrality:

> As the "pryckemedenty" rises from her seat, the poet steps forward to make the one value judgment in the poem,
>> She was not halfe so wyse,
>> As she was pevysshe nyse, [588–89]
> and dispatches the offender with a couplet:
>> We supposed, I wys,
>> That she rose to pys. [594–95]
> By including himself in the scene ("We"), he serves notice to his characters and his readers that no moral or philosophical considerations will be allowed to disturb the surface (there is after all nothing else) of his tableau.[11]

The metaphor of the painting works to convey the idea (through the word "surface") of a form with no content, no meaning, and "no moral or philosophical considerations." In conjunction with this assertion, Fish concludes, in line with his predecessors, that the result is a kind of docu-

8. Ibid., 190.

9. *English Literature in the Sixteenth Century Excluding Drama* (Oxford: Oxford University Press, 1954), 139.

10. Stanley Eugene Fish, *John Skelton's Poetry* (New Haven: Yale University Press, 1965), 251–55.

11. Ibid., 252.

mentary: "Skelton has done nothing more nor less than portray in words the chaos and confusion of a sixteenth-century 'still.' "[12]

Yet "The Tunnyng of Elynour Rummynge" demonstrates little ecphrastic rhetoric; it is vivid, yet not primarily visual. In fact, painting that can be described as "a mood piece," or in which "no space on [the] canvas remains unfilled" with visual detail does not appear in England until much after the 1520s; the contemporary visual arts tradition is heavily symbolic and moral.[13] Skelton's descriptive mode relies on incongruous juxtaposition. The prologue-like portrait of Elynour, for example, is impossible to imagine visually unless, like the Italian painter Arcimboldo (to whom the epithet "realist" is seldom attached), we can picture a body made up of roast pig's ear, rope, a sack, egg whites, a jetty, buckles, a trowel-like tool, and a crane:

> Her face all bowsy,
> Comely crynklyd,
> Woundersly wrynklyd,
> Lyke a rost pygges eare,
> Brystled with here. . . .
> Her skynne lose and slacke,
> Greuyned lyke a sacke . . .
> Jawed lyke a jetty; . . .
> The bones of her huckels
> Lyke as they were with buckels
> Togyder made fast.
> Her youth is farre past;
> Foted lyke a plane,
> Legged lyke a crane.
> (17–21, 31–32, 38, 45–50)

This poetry is brilliantly evocative, but its mode is not "visual realism." If I were to seek an analogy from the visual arts, it would serve the poem better to call to mind the paintings of Skelton's contemporary Hieronymus Bosch or the grotesques of late medieval manuscript illustration.[14]

---

12. Ibid., 254.

13. The quotations are from Fish, *John Skelton's Poetry*, 254.

14. Mikhail Bakhtin's work has inspired a spate of essays on Skelton's grotesquerie: Bernard Sharratt, "John Skelton: Finding a Voice—Notes After Bakhtin," in *Medieval Literature: Criticism, Ideology and History*, ed. David Aers (Brighton: Harvester, 1986), 192–222; Peter Herman reads the poem as an example of (a somewhat oxymoronic) "grotesque realism" in "Leaky Ladies and Droopy Dames: The Grotesque Realism of Skelton's *The Tunnynge of Elynour Rummynge*," in *Rethinking the Henrician Era: Essays on Early Tudor Texts and Contexts*, ed. Peter C. Herman (Urbana: University of Illinois Press, 1994), 145–67; John C. Kelly stresses English carnival in "A Perfect Feast of Fools and Plenty: Carnival in John Skelton's Poem 'The Tunning of Elinor Rumming,' " *English Studies in Canada* 22 (June 1996): 129–148.

However, "The Tunnyng" makes no reference to painting; Skelton's instruments are a series of carefully referenced *poetic* techniques, and the poem is a complaint crossed with the genre of the gossip or alewife dialogue.[15] Elynour's portrait is an anti-blazon, and stands in the scurrilous and ingenious ranks of such poems as Marot's "Du laid Tetin" (1535). But while Marot narrowly concentrates on the breast, producing a grotesque, Skelton careens across Elynour's body, top to bottom and up again, framing each part in a different diction. The connections between her parts are so loose that she is in the process of falling quite apart: her hips have to be fastened together by buckles. Her nose is continually leaking egg whites. Her body appears to exude, even to manufacture, an odd assortment of commodities.

The introduction of Elynour, then, is hardly the document of visual realism it has been taken for. Nor is the poem a picture in a more complex and social sense: it does not document social history (the "vulgar life") in any direct, visual way. The incidental detail about ale-making and commercial exchange is, upon closer inspection, of little value to a historical anthropologist or a social historian. As for a picture of brewing:

> Than Elynour taketh
> The mashe bolle, and shaketh
> The hennes donge awaye,
> And skommeth it into a tray
> Where as the yeest is,
> With her maungy fystis.
> And somtyme she blennes
> The donge of her hennes
> And the ale togyder,
> And sayth, "Gossyp, come hyder,
> This ale shal be thycker,
> And floure the more quycker;
> For I may tell you,
> I lerned it of a Jewe,
> Whan I began to brewe,
> And I have found it trew."
>   (195–210)

What we learn about the process of brewing is that hen's dung is dropped into the mashfat, separated from it in the mashbowl, skimmed into a tray

15. On the Tudor complaint, see Lawrence Manley, *Literature and Culture in Early Modern London* (Cambridge: Cambridge University Press, 1995), 63–122, especially 97 on the affinity of "additive, serial structures and a residue of other oral devices" for economic invective. Skelton's poem bears comparison with William Dunbar's "The Tretis of the Tua Mariit Wemen and the Wedo." For instances of the genre, see *The Poems of William Dunbar*, ed. James Kinsley (London: Oxford University Press, 1979), 260–61.

with the yeast, and judiciously blended into the ale. While the status of this reportage as an accusation may be "representative" in a narrow sense (as we shall see, frequent charges as to the quality of their product were brought against brewers in this period), when we take it as information about brewing—the tunning—we are clearly in the territory not of realistic documentation of "vulgar life," but of parody.

In fact, the products of this parodic "brewing" suggest that the parody may be not only of brewing, but of something larger and perhaps even more pervasive than the ale business, if anything in sixteenth-century England can have been. These lines begin to suggest what is more explicitly dramatized in the course of "The Tunnyng": that the poem's concerns are economic and sexual. The process of Elynour's "brewing" produces thicker ale, quicker flour, and a younger and sexier countenance (213–22), kinds of usurious profit that Elynour tells us she learned to make from a Jew. A prominent character in early economic thought, the Jew is identified with proscribed financial practices such as usury (loaning money at profit) that were considered ruinous to society. The significance of the transfer of habitus from the Jew to Elynour is reinforced by the structure of the poem. After brief descriptions of Elynour and the brewing process, as above, the bulk of the poem—some four hundred lines—is devoted to the portrayal of sales.

What Skelton does in "The Tunnyng" is to set forth a relation between character and plot that is dependent upon the social persons evoked by Elynour's portrait and that embodies a particular contention about how the feminine is linked to economic value. This ideological contention is embedded in the formal design of the poem, which is best understood, I think, by contrasting "The Tunnyng" with its sources. Perhaps a pun on Langland's word "meed," which can mean both drink and profit, suggested the primary conceit of "The Tunnyng"; like Langland, Skelton employs a commercial plot, belabors the incontinence of women, and divides his text into sections called "passus."[16] But he also inherits his combined discourse from Chaucer's *Canterbury Tales*: the General Prologue's description of the Wife of Bath (which he cites in lines 71–72), the Wife's prologue, and the Shipman's Tale.

While Chaucer's Shipman's Tale is hardly celebratory of the connection between commerce and female sexuality, it is less bitter than *Piers* and "The Tunnyng." Like Langland, Skelton implies that women cannot be redeemed. In both texts women are abjured (as Conscience refuses to marry Mede), but Skelton also repudiates the workings of commerce. In this

16. Gail Kern Paster discusses Elynour Rummynge and the figure of the incontinent woman in *The Body Embarrassed: Drama and the Disciplines of Shame in Early Modern England* (Ithaca: Cornell University Press, 1993), 46–47. At least two earlier poems imitate the passus of *Piers Plowman*: *Richard the Redeles* and *The Wars of Alexander*. A fuller discussion of the character Mede appears above in chapter 2.

sense Langland's reluctant conclusion is Skelton's starting place. As Theologie explains, Mede in herself is not by definition immoral. But Skelton's women readily display their immorality. More often than not, that immorality simply is the female body itself:

> There came an old rybybe;
> She halted of a kybe,
> And had broken her shyn
> At the threshold comyng in,
> And fell so wyde open
> That one might se her token.
> The devyll thereon be wroken!
>   (492–98)

The antifeminist historical tradition gives a theological context for Skelton's attitude, beginning with the fall of mankind through Eve's sin. Hotly repeated throughout the middle ages, this history provoked Chaucer to the arguments of the Wife's prologue and scholars such as Christine de Pizan to elaborate rebuttals. Though of three different classes, Mede, the Wife of Bath, and Elynour are all built by animating the arguments of Church Fathers such as Tertullian and Jerome in order to evoke the paradigmatic social person created by clerical antifeminism.

Misogyny is integral to clerical antifeminism, which grew out of the patriarchal gender arrangements of the medieval church. Yet the avowed cultural function of clerical antifeminism in the late middle ages was perhaps curiously not so much the oppression of women (though it served that function effectively) as the consolidation of an estate of men who were to live without legitimate sexual ties to women. The segregation of the sexes was required in the church's administrative hierarchy: to be an unmarried male was a prerequisite for all official positions of power, and men studying for church careers had to be carefully taught to avoid women and their vices. Or, to put it another way, it was a professional advantage for ambitious men to learn the lesson of misogyny—for example, men like Skelton, who was an ordained priest and tutor to the future Henry VIII. The social persons developed by the legal and theological notion of unity of person suggest, as we have seen in *Piers Plowman*, that women need to be controlled by marriage and that men need to repudiate women if they want to serve the just commonwealth.[17] Antifeminist discourse employs misogyny to accustom men to its sexual habitus and to suit them for positions in ecclesiastical institutions; its effects on women are perhaps more interesting (as Chaucer shows in the Wife) but equally clear. Clerical misogyny habit-

17. Holi Chirche may seem an exception only if one forgets that she is the bride of Christ.

uates women to subordinate positions and, by means of suspicions and ac-cusations, to stricter behavioral assessments.[18]

Like antifeminism, Skelton's poem is a discourse about women designed for men. In "The Tunnyng" all the figures are female and the speaker and the implied audience emphatically male. The colophon purports to invite women to listen to the poem, but it "addresses" them in the third person, moreover in Latin (a language reserved nearly entirely for men), and it proposes not to reform them but to record their deeds:

> Omnes feminas, que vel nimis bibule sunt, vel que sordida labe squaloris, aut qua spurca feditatis macula, aut verbosa loquacitate notantur, poeta invitat ad audiendum hunc libellum, & c.

> Ebria, squalida, sordida femina, prodiga verbis,
>   Huc currat, properet, veniat! Sua gesta libellus
> Iste volutabit: Pean sua plectra sonando
> Materiam risus cantabit carmine rauco.

> Finis

> Quod Skelton Laureat

[All women who are either very fond of drinking, or who bear the dirty stain of filth, or who have the sordid blemish of squalor, or who are marked out by garrulous loquacity, the poet invites to listen to this little satire. Drunken, filthy, sordid, gossiping woman, let her run here, let her hasten, let her come; this little satire will willingly record her deeds: Apollo, sounding his lyre,

18. Regarding antifeminist writing and misogyny in the vernacular and in Latin, medieval to renaissance, see *The Riverside Chaucer*, ed. Larry D. Benson, 3d ed. (Boston: Houghton Mifflin, 1987), 864; R. Howard Bloch, *Medieval Misogyny and the Invention of Western Romantic Love* (Chicago: University of Chicago Press, 1991); John Peter, *Complaint and Satire in Early English Literature* (Oxford: Clarendon, 1956); Robert A. Pratt, "Jankyn's Book of Wikked Wyves: Medieval Antimatrimonial Propaganda in the Universities," *Annuale Medievale* 3 (1962): 5–27; Francis Lee Utley, *The Crooked Rib: An Analytical Index to the Argument about Women in English and Scottish Literature to the End of the Year 1568* (Columbus: Ohio State University Press, 1944); Katharine M. Rogers, *The Troublesome Helpmate: A History of Misogyny in Literature* (Seattle: University of Washington Press, 1966); Joan Smith, *Misogynies* (London: Faber and Faber, 1989); *Wykked Wyves and the Woes of Marriage: Misogamous Literature from Juvenal to Chaucer*, ed. Katharina M. Wilson and Elizabeth M. Makowski (Albany: State University of New York Press, 1990); Linda Woodbridge, *Women and the English Renaissance: Literature and the Nature of Womankind, 1540–1620* (Urbana: University of Illinois Press, 1984); Katherine Usher Henderson and Barbara F. McManus, *Half Humankind: Contexts and Texts of the Controversy about Women in England, 1540–1640* (Urbana: University of Illinois Press, 1985). See too the renovation of the study of misogyny by Judith M. Bennett, "Misogyny, Popular Culture, and Women's Work," *History Workshop* 31 (1991): 166–88. Bennett rightly treats "The Tunnyng" as "a slanderous attack on female brewers and their trade" (171).

will sing the theme of laughter in a hoarse song. (trans. Scattergood in Skelton, *Complete English Poems*, ed. Scattergood, 452)]

In these last lines Skelton authorizes the poem with the Latin apostrophe of a cleric and a humanist, placing his work firmly in the tradition of antifeminism engaged by the Wife of Bath.

"The Tunnyng" is part of a last wave of medieval clerical antifeminist rhetoric insofar as the genre's importance in England coincides with the dominance of that vast multi-national corporation, the medieval church. As the Reformation took hold, there were fewer motives for the English church's production of such systematic propaganda against women and their charms: priests who practiced cohabitation, as Skelton did, were urged to marry rather than to repudiate their sexual partners.[19] In its capacity as a powerful social tool, antifeminist rhetoric became less relevant to the English church's needs. As this occurred, "The Tunnyng of Elynour Rummynge" would necessarily have become less intelligible as satire. When the renunciation of women lost its privileged status as a clerical imperative during the reformation of the English church, the analogy upon which the "Tunnyng" rests would have become obscured.

To turn back to the poem from the intellectual ground of its analogy between female sexuality and commerce is to make recourse to the literary technology that employs the analogy. At the risk of misrepresenting the two lesser-known poems ("The Tunnyng" and *Piers Plowman*) by fastening on descriptive moments—set-pieces, really—in what are deeply narrative structures, let me compare the three passages that introduce Chaucer's Alice, Skelton's Elynour, and Langland's Mede. Here is part of the General Prologue's portrait of the Wife of Bath:

> In al the parisshe wif ne was ther noon
> That to the offrynge bifore hire sholde goon;
> And if ther dide, certeyn so wrooth was she
> That she was out of alle charitee.
> Hir coverchiefs ful fyne weren of ground;
> I dorste swere they weyeden ten pound
> That on a Sonday weren upon hir heed.
> Hir hosen weren of fyn scarlet reed.[20]

19. See Henry Charles Lea, *History of Sacerdotal Celibacy in the Christian Church* (London: Watts, 1932); Roman Cholij, *Clerical Celibacy in East and West* (Leominster, Herefordshire: Fowler Wright, 1988).

20. Lines 449–56. All quotations of Chaucer's works have been taken from *The Riverside Chaucer*, ed. Larry D. Benson, 3d ed. (Boston: Houghton Mifflin, 1987) and will be cited in the text by title and line number.

Skelton's prologue-like description of Elynour asks to be measured against Chaucer's lines. Elynour's headdress is equally imperious:

> And yet I dare saye
> She thynketh her selfe gaye
> Upon the holy daye,
> Whan she doth her aray,
> And gyrdeth in her gytes
> Stytched and pranked with pletes;
> Her kyrtell Brystowe red,
> With clothes upon her hed
> That wey a sowe of led,
> Wrythen in wonder wyse
> After the Sarasyns gyse.
>
>   (64–74)

It is a comparison at the level of character; the Wife of Bath and Elynour share a boisterous self-assertion and a pretension that is, at the root, economic. Elynour is not provided with the subtle psychological dimension that Chaucer will develop in the Wife's Prologue; despite Elynour's headdress and her sexual boast, the reader is not led to identify or sympathize with her. For Mede, the dreamer and the reader feel fascination and fear:

> I loked on my left half as the Lady [Holy Church] me taughte,
> And was war of a womman wonderliche yclothed—
> Purfiled with pelure, the pureste on erthe,   *trimmed, fur*
> Ycorouned with a coroune, the Kyng hath noon bettre.
> Fetisliche hire fyngres were fretted with gold wyr,
> And thereon rede rubies as rede as any gleede,   *glowing coal*
> And diamaundes of derrest pris and double manere saphires,   *two kinds of*
> Orientals and ewages envenymes to destroye.
> Hire robe was ful riche, of reed scarlet engreyned,   *fast-dyed*
> With ribanes of reed gold and of riche stones.
> Hire array me ravysshed, swich richesse saugh I nevere.
>   (B.II.7–17)[21]

As her story commences, Mede becomes a clear example of personification allegory, whereas Elynour has both a less iconic portrait and a less theologically over-determined role. However, she is given no more internal, "subjective" experience than a personification allegory. Her fabliau-like

---

21. William Langland, *The Vision of Piers Plowman: A Complete Edition of the B-text*, ed. A. V. C. Schmidt (London: Dent, 1978).

energy and thinness are designed to produce an enjoyable revulsion and allow Skelton to draw her as a grotesque.

In the Wife of Bath, Chaucer evokes the peculiar social powers of a bourgeois widow in late medieval England,[22] a person who was able to act economically on behalf of her own wealth and often allowed to conduct a business. The Wife's industriousness and financial independence are accompanied by a spirited sexual assertiveness; though Elynour is married, nonetheless she too acts directly in the economy through her position as an alewife and boasts of her sexuality. Both characterizations stress occupation and position in the economic world as the key to sexual behavior. The vicissitudes of the Wife of Bath's relations with her husbands depend upon the history of her economic power; Elynour's happy sexual relations are attributed to her ale-making in a bald piece of advertisement:

> "Drinke now whyle it is new;
> And ye may it broke,
> It shall make you loke
> Yonger than ye be
> Yeres two or thre,
> For ye may prove it by me.
> Behold," she sayd, "and se
> How bright I am of ble!   *countenance*
> Ich am not cast away,
> That can my husband say,
> Whan we kys and play
> In lust and in lykyng."
>   (211–22)

Here as elsewhere the poem subordinates the characterization of Elynour to the topic of the sale of the brew. I have already quoted the anti-blazon that expresses Elynour's body in what one might call "commodity form." Skelton veers away from the Chaucerian portrait, mixing the Wife's rowdiness with the more brittle and plot-manipulated characterization of a narrative like the Shipman's Tale.[23] There Chaucer combines the double theme of sexuality and money in a quite different way, one that is epito-

---

22. See Mary Carruthers, "The Wife of Bath and the Painting of Lions," *PMLA* 94 (1979): 209–22. For an introduction to the legal and economic position of late medieval women, see Mavis E. Mate, *Women in Medieval English Society* (Cambridge: Cambridge University Press, 1999); she discusses brewing at 38–46.

23. That the Shipman's Tale was originally written for the Wife of Bath was first argued by William W. Lawrence, "Chaucer's *Shipman's Tale*," *Speculum* 33 (1958): 56–68.

mized in the pun on "taillynge" that closes the tale.[24] In "The Tunnyng" and the Shipman's Tale, as in *Piers Plowman*, plot takes precedence over characterization.

Skelton's allusive feint at portraiture, then, serves to launch the simple and numbingly iterative plot that organizes "The Tunnyng of Elynour Rummynge." The women appear in sequence, each making an exchange of some commodity for ale. This series of transactions is the spine of the poem. Just as in the exchange each commodity undergoes a metamorphosis into ale, in the same way the women are reduced to beastly, squalid things—bodies unadulterated by spirit or mind. As they fill with ale, they empty of humanity. Incontinence is the theme throughout. There is no "tunning" of ale into tuns or barrels in this poem; instead, the ale is poured into human receptacles, and its paradoxical function is to evacuate them. Like Chaucer's Alice, the paranomastic "Ales" of "The Tunnyng" boasts of pilgrimages, but she strikes a less imperious posture:

> Than thydder came dronken Ales
> And she was full of tales,
> Of tydynges in Wales,
> And of Saynte James in Gales,
> And of the Portyngales;
>
> . . .
>
> She spake thus in her snout,
> Snevelyng in her nose,
> As though she had the pose.
> "Lo, here is an olde typpet,
> And ye wyll gyve me a syppet
> Of your stale ale,
> God sende you good sale!"
> And, as she was drynkynge,

24. The end of "The Tunnyng" echoes key phrases of the Shipman's Tale, as Skelton suggests by his emphasis on accounts that he has Chaucer in mind again:

> Suche were there menny
> That had not a penny,
> But, whan they shoulde walke,
> Were fayne with a chalke
> To score on the balke,
> Or score on the tayle.
> God gyve it yll hayle,
> For my fyngers ytche.
> I have wrytten so mytche
> Of this mad mummynge
> Of Elynour Rummynge.
> Thus endeth the gest
> Of this worthy fest.
> (611–23)

> She fyll in a wynkynge
> With a barlyhood;
> She pyst where she stood.
> Than began she to wepe,
> And forthwith fell on slepe.
>   (351–55, 363–75)

If the characters enter the poem as Chaucerian (on the model of the Wife of Bath), contact with commercial exchange transforms them into iconic, allegorical vice figures, closer to Langland's Deadly Sins than they are even to the cheerfully automated creatures of the Shipman's Tale. They become the emptied, conscience-less figures familiar in allegory: devoid of interior life and the capacity for intentional cognition, they are formally related to Langland's more elegant Mede.

The transformation of character into the plot of commercial exchange is epitomized in the fate of the words Elynour's husband uses for her in bed. In the course of the advertisement for her special recipe, cited above, she declares her husband's appreciation of her:

> "For ye may prove it by me.
> Behold," she sayd, "and se
> How bright I am of ble!
> Ich am not cast away,
> That can my husband say,
> Whan we kys and play
> In lust and in lykyng
> He calleth me his whytyng,
> His mullyng and his mytyng,
> His nobbes and his conny,
> His swetyng and his honny,
> With, 'Bas my prety bonny,
> Thou art worth good and monny.'
> This make I my falyre fonny,
> Tyll that he dreme and dronny;
> For, after all our sport,
> Than wyll he rout and snort;
> Than swetely togither we ly,
> As two pygges in a sty."
>   (216–34)

The rhyme group that makes up her husband's declaration consists of a series of epithets for Elynour—"conny," "honny," and "monny"—that are repeated after only nine intervening lines, in which the author disclaims the scene. Suddenly her customers come running with payments they wish to exchange for ale:

In stede of coyne and monny
Some brynge her a conny,
And some a pot with honny.
(244–46)

The epic list of commodities is generated, as it were, out of the characterization of Elynour.

The poem, then, is a mix of Langlandian and Chaucerian forms. Elynour is an alewife, a social type. She is a rebuttal to the Wife of Bath's prosecution of antifeminism, taking a role in the same controversy, the discourse of misogyny. Her character embodies a double valence (the commercial and the feminine), a metaphorical relation further elaborated by Skelton into a plot. In Puttenham's terms, the poem has an allegorical structure: "this manner of inuersion extending to whole and large speaches, it maketh the figure *allegorie* to be called a long and perpetuall Metaphore."[25] The metaphorical relation that ale draws between the incontinence of women and the incontinence of money is extended into narrative and therefore becomes the form of the poem itself.[26] In fact, were Elynour named "The Banker of Whitbread" or "The Brewster of Angels," the poem would be classed with Skelton's "Bowge of Courte" as a fair example of personification allegory. If Elynour seems transparent, if her characterization seems to lack moral and philosophical weight, it is not because Skelton is portraying some human being realistically, but because he is interested in the larger meanings of the social person of the incontinent female within his culture. Yet, following neither Langland nor Chaucer, the poem acquires a title with a "real" name, one that could have belonged to an alewife and, in fact, did.

The Alewife and the Economic Order

In 1946 John Harvey found a reference to an "Alianora Romyng" (the spelling is rich) in the Court Rolls of the Manor of Pachenesham in County Surrey:

> The Ale-Taster's presentment at the Court held on August 18, 1525 (Surrey County Muniments, S.C.6/15), runs, in translation:—
> "Robert a Dene Ale-Taster there comes and being sworn presents that Richard Godman and John Nele Thomas Snellyng and John Romyng are

25. George Puttenham, *The Arte of English Poesie* (1589, facsimile Kent, Ohio: Kent State University Press, 1970), 197.

26. Cf. Howard Bloch, commenting on Tertullian's misogyny: "The affinity between gold, the product of excess labor, 'the arts,' and women constitutes an economic nexus taken as a given; their natures, by definition conceived to be inessential and antinatural, attract each other because they partake in a scandalous excess that offends" (*Medieval Misogyny*, 43).

common brewers of ale and also keep common hostelry and in the same sell divers victuals at excessive price, therefore are they in mercy Also he presents that Alianora Romyng (fine 2d.) is a common Tippellar[27] of ale and sells at excessive price by small measures, therefore she is in mercy."[28]

The trespass recorded here is against the notion of just price. The poem makes the same accusation: Skelton's Elynour has diluted and adulterated her ale with dung, lowering its value, and charged outrageously for it, the sum of her takings in rings, pots, honey, rabbits, and the like. Price is not merely excessive in the poem, it is arbitrary or (perhaps best) whatever the customer can pay, and then some. The conversion of valuable commodities to waste by the figure of the alewife allows Skelton to place central issues of economic policy and theory before his readers. Ultimately, at issue in the social person of the incontinent female is her culture's ability to measure value.

The regulation of ale prices and quality much antedates the sixteenth century, yet it was far from absolutely effective. Then, as now, the difficulties inherent in the control of trade by legislation were formidable.[29] A clause in the 1215 Magna Carta set out a standard measure for ale, which as a staple was one of the first commodities to be regulated. The Charter required the uniformity of weights and measures throughout the realm, yet local measures for ale continued to be prevalent long after Skelton's time. True measures were set in 1267 for the brewers of London: the gallon, potel, quart and tun became set quantities and required the seal of the city aldermen.[30] Yet in addition to the variations in price charted by surviving records, measures themselves continued to vary in at least three ways: in the quantity that makes up a standard unit (e.g., a "barrel" is twenty-seven gallons in 1405 in the Countess of Warwick's account, and fifteen gallons in 1408 at Windsor); in the local terms and units of mea-

27. I do not have the original text, which is presumably in Latin. But R. E. Latham, *Revised Medieval Latin Word-List: From British and Irish Sources* (London: Oxford University Press, 1965), contains the following entry: "tip/ulator 1391, 1553, -lator 1539, -pilator 1603, 'tippler', retailer of ale and wine; +tirpillatrix, ale-wife 1547; domus -ulatoria, alehouse 1661; -lo 1371, -ulo 1507, to 'tipple', keep an ale-house" (485).

The Oxford English Dictionary (2d ed.) defines "tippler" as "a retailer of ale and other intoxicating liquor; a tapster; a tavern-keeper. Obs." It lists this 1478 entry in the records of the borough of Nottingham: "Fines pro licencia merchandizandi Alicia Bult, tipler, iiij d."

28. "Eleanor Rumming," *Times Literary Supplement* (26 Oct. 1946): 521.

29. It is not until 1603 that inquisitions by an official called the "Clerk of the Market" begin to survive in printed blank form, setting a list of commodities against spaces for filling in prices, though surely sporadic accounts were kept before the 1603 proclamation by James I requiring systematic reports (STC 8315). The clerks of the market themselves are mentioned as early as 16 Richard II. See James E. Thorold Rogers, *A History of Agriculture and Prices in England: 1259–1793* (London: Oxford, 1882), 4:203.

30. Mia Ball, *The Worshipful Company of Brewers: A Short History* (London: Hutchinson Benham, 1977), 14.

sure, such as the Pershore cestra, the Salisbury coule, the common kilderkin, firkin, pipe, and hogshead, the Beverley panyers, hopir, modius, firthindal, etc.; and in strength, that is, the quantity of malt employed per volume of water.[31] Meaningful regulation of price depends on the standardizing of measures, a normalizing that the crown, the cities and towns, the guilds, and the manor courts were unable to implement decisively in the centuries that followed Magna Carta.

For the measuring of ale involves a rich variety of factors. While measure and price may be thought of as indices of the same phenomenon (value), their relationship holds true only if quality is standardized. Elynour's brewing procedures, which rely on dilution by hen dung, aptly illustrate the controlling role of quality. Both the choice of ingredients and also the ratios of their volumes are variables in the struggle to regulate brewing. The important 1267 Assize of Bread and Ale, introduced by Henry III, set out formulae for calculating the locally-regulated price of ale according to the price of malt; tying the prices of malt and ale together is a tacit acknowledgment of cost as a fair contribution to price. Ale-tasters were employed by many authorities to attempt to judge quality before newly brewed ale was sold to the public, yet they must often have had difficulty covering the enormous numbers of brewers within their jurisdictions.[32] Indeed, the wide geographic extent of the economy was an impediment to efficient control of the trade. James Rogers finds prices paid at inns to have been "generally double" those paid elsewhere, basing this claim on records for the year 1507.[33] However, I cannot find evidence of any legal toleration of this practice, and indeed innkeepers regularly appear on the lists of wrongdoers.

Even if all these variables could have been monitored efficiently, the problem of the unit of price would have remained. Not dissuaded by the image of the hen dung in Elynour's mashbowl, Henry VIII debased the currency in 1527. Early modern writers were well aware that the value of money is not immutable, even when stabilized by law.[34] Commodity prices in general rose steadily in the first decades of the inflationary six-

31. Rogers, *History of Agriculture*, 4:547 and L. F. Salzman, *English Industries of the Middle Ages* (London: Oxford University Press, 1923), 288.
32. The standardized measure was regulated by many different police: justices of the peace and sheriffs' escheators as well as official ale-tasters are commissioned in 9 Henry V, statute 2, cap. 8 (cf. Rogers, *History of Agriculture*, 4:203).
33. Rogers, *History of Agriculture*, 4:549.
34. Nicole Oresme's tract on the origins of money (c. 1360) is a good example of the political anxiety produced by money's unstable value and of the threat of royal debasements of currency. "On the First Invention of Money," in *Early Economic Thought: Selections from Economic Literature Prior to Adam Smith*, ed. Arthur Eli Monroe (Cambridge: Harvard University Press, 1927), 79–102.

teenth century, in contrast to the immediately previous forty years during which commodity prices stayed "exceptionally low."[35] Such economic upheaval could well have stimulated Skelton's heightened sense of the artificiality of price. And, of course, enforcement of legally set standards presented its own problems. English archival records suggest that infringements of the pricing regulations for ale were so common as to render the fines "practically . . . licensing dues": "The same names are found, where any series of rolls exists, presented at court after court for breaking the assize in one way or another, and it is clear that a strict observance of the laws was difficult, it being more profitable to break them and pay the small fines extorted."[36] Alianora Romyng's fine, 2d., would probably have been equivalent to less than a gallon of her own ale: it seems unlikely that such a penalty would be truly preventative.

Not only were the brewers regulated by the assizes, but guilds had their own processes of self-regulation. The memoranda books of the Company of Brewers record many infractions similar to that recorded against Alianora Romyng in 1525. A typical example of a list is headed like this: "These be thoo persones that dede selle her ale with outen mesur yn the tyme of the seid William Crowmer mayr the wheche persones dede make dyvers ffynes as it sheweth afterward."[37] The lists include many entitled "The Wiffe of . . ." In a typical year (1487), at least five out of fifteen fine-payers are women.[38] While women never form the majority of the fine-paying constituency, they consistently form a substantial proportion.

The number of wicked alewives, tapsters, tipplers, and tavern hostesses who appear in verse and drama (leaving aside sermons) makes it clear that such women formed an image larger than life, a widely recognizable social person emblematic of financial corruption. In *Piers Plowman* the wicked Rose-the-regrater brews and sells ale deceitfully, according to the confession of her husband, none other than the deadly sin Couetyse.[39] Among her marvelous number of false starts, Margery Kempe takes up brewing

35. Rogers, *History of Agriculture*, 4:736.

36. Salzman, *English Industries*, 287.

37. Guildhall Library MS. 5440 fol. 114r in the archives of the Worshipful Company of Brewers, City of London.

38. Guildhall Library MS. 5440 fol. 120r.

39. William Langland, *Piers Plowman*, B text V.215–23; C text VI.225–33. Regraters, forestallers, and engrossers were condemned by both advocates of the poor and those who wished to dominate markets throughout the middle ages and early modern period. They are enterprising "middlemen" (figured as female here), though not in the obvious sense: James Rogers in his extensive survey did not find that prices varied with quantity (i.e., there was no difference between "wholesale" and "retail" price). Buyers who bought goods for resale in the same market (regraters), who secured commodities in advance of market arrival (forestallers), or who bought up the entire supply of one commodity in order to corner a market (engrossers), produced profits at the expense of the consumer.

under the aegis of the same sin: "Sche wold not be war be onys chastysyng ne be content wyth the goodys that God had sent hire, as hir husbond was, but euyr desyryd mor & mor. And than, for pure coveytyse & for to maynten hir pride, sche gan to brewyn & was on of the grettest brewers in the town."[40] In the Harrowing of Hell episode of the Chester cycle of mystery plays (XVII), Christ allows the devil to keep one soul—that of a brewster. Acted by the cooks' guild, and probably also "Tapsters, Hostlers, Inkeapers," the play ends with an alewife scene thought to date from early in the sixteenth century.[41] Satan welcomes the alewife Mulier as a "dere daughter," and the second demon promises to wed her, marking the symbolic importance of her gender. Like Elynour, Mulier has perpetrated the offense of dilution, though her wrong is primarily characterized in terms of financial infractions:

> Of kannes I kept no trewe measure.
> My cuppes I sould at my pleasure,
> deceavinge manye a creature,
> thoe my ale were nought.
>
> (289–92)

> Tavernes, tapsters of this cittye
> shalbe promoted here with mee
> for breakinge statutes of this contrye,
> hurtinge the commonwealth,
> with all typpers-tappers that are cunninge,
> mispendinge much malt, bruynge so thinne,
> sellinge smale cuppes money to wynne,
> agaynst all trueth to deale.
>
> (301–8)[42]

The effects of her greed are not so much personal but national, because such false business dealings hurt the commonwealth and find promotion in hell. Shakespeare's Mistress Quickly suggests the persistence of the bad reputation of alewives, a disrepute epitomized by Celia's words in *As You Like It*: "Besides, the oath of [a] lover is no stronger than the word of a tapster; they are both the confirmer of false reckonings."[43]

40. *The Book of Margery Kempe*, ed. S. B. Meech, Early English Text Society O. S. 212 (London: Oxford University Press, 1940), 9. Characters silently regularized.

41. *The Breviary of Robert Rogers* (d. 1595): see *The Chester Mystery Cycle: Essays and Documents*, ed. R. M. Lumiansky and David Mills (Chapel Hill: University of North Carolina Press, 1983), 200, 265, 45–47.

42. *The Chester Mystery Cycle: Volume I, Text*, ed. R. M. Lumiansky and David Mills, Early English Text Society S. S. 3 (London: Oxford University Press, 1974).

43. III.iv.30–32. *The Riverside Shakespeare*, ed. G. Blakemore Evans (Boston: Houghton Mifflin, 1974).

Fraud was associated not only with women who traded in ale, since the reputation of brewing itself was also suspect. The Company of Brewers was never one of the premier livery companies of London. Many of the most powerful associations trafficked in more luxurious and controllable commodities such as gold. But in the public imagination, as Judith Bennett has shown, the bad reputation of brewing is especially associated with the image of the female brewer.[44] In an infamous episode in the infamous mayoralty of Dick Whittington, the Lord Mayor attempted to extort money from the brewers after examining the city's women retailers ("Hukesters") about the prices they had paid to the brewers.[45] The City Letter Book of 1288 registers a complaint against brewsters for dressing "after the manner of reputable women" in hoods "furred with gros veer and minever."[46] The female membership of the Worshipful Company of Brewers (which excluded hucksters) was unusually high, as many as thirty-nine in 1417.[47] There were women members of the Company throughout the fifteenth and sixteenth centuries (many widows, no doubt, but not all). From the account and memoranda books that survive, it is clear that women were intimately involved in the conduct of the business of male brewers, paying dues, answering to fines, attending dinners, and generally present in the many rosters of the records.

Part of the reason that the brewster became such a prominent type of economic person lies in the fact that, though the organized brewers had been granted a charter of incorporation by Henry VI on 22 February 1437/8, of course the making and drinking of ale also remained an operation of households and inns, where the housewife, innkeeper, or tapster continued her small-scale production.[48] Women sold ale in two economic positions intermediate to the household and inn: as retailers who themselves did not brew—the hucksters and tavern hostesses, such as Shakespeare's Mistress Quickly, who sold ale purchased from a brewer—and as alewives who owned their own alehouses and occasionally, though infre-

44. Judith Bennett's history of female brewers makes an important contribution to our ability both to link and to distinguish representations and social history. She shows how the notoriety of brewing is especially associated with the brewster in *Ale, Beer and Brewsters*.

45. Guildhall Library MS. 5441 fol. 27 ff., and see Ball, *Worshipful Company*, 62. The word "hucksters" became a pejorative term that could include regraters, engrossers, and other misdoers.

46. Here "brewster" is the feminine form of the noun, but according to Toulmin Smith: "the word 'brewester' is usually stated, in glossaries, to mean a female brewer. But it is expressly put down, in the *Promptorium Parvulorum*, as used for either male or female brewer" (355n). *English Gilds: The Original Ordinances of More than One Hundred Early English Gilds Together &c.*, ed. Toulmin Smith, Early English Text Society (London: Oxford University Press, 1870), 355n.

47. Ball, *Worshipful Company*, 62.

48. The charter of incorporation is Guildhall Library MS. 5425.

quently, conducted wholesale business.[49] (Skelton's Elynour is best termed an alewife, since she brews her own ale.) In short, women in the business of making and selling ale were highly visible throughout England.

Women's conspicuous role in the selling of ale linked them to a myriad of societal sins. Despite the fact that the language of the guild's records describes the short-changing of customers, the formulaic phrase "with outen mesur" classes the crime as incontinence, as if false-bottomed potels were somehow gluttonous.[50] It is precisely the stupefying effect of greed that structures Skelton's poem, giving avarice a floating place; it is attributed to individuals, attributed to the class of the female and fairly poor, but simultaneously attributed to the brewing of the ale itself.

Such evil could afflict not just individuals and classes, but a whole race or nation. Andrew Boorde, in the early sixteenth-century *Dyetary of Helth*, gives the following ingredients and qualities as properties of ale: "Ale is made of malte and water; and they the which do put any other thynge to ale then is rehersed, except yest, barme or godesgood, doth sofystical theyr ale. Ale for an Englysshe man is a naturall drynke. Ale must haue these propertyes: it must be fresshe and cleare, it muste not be ropy nor smoky, nor it must haue no weft nor tayle. . . . Barly malte maketh better ale then oten malte or any other corne doth: it doth ingendre grose humoures; but yette it maketh a man stronge."[51] This association of ale and nationalism is not isolated, but is part of trade competition generally: English ale against Dutch beer and French wine. English dominance in ale-making, and thus its national identification, is well established by the middle of the twelfth century.[52] It also has class connotations. In Dunbar's poem, "The Dregy of Dunbar Maid to King James the Fowrth being in Strivilling," ale appears as the rations of the "hell" that is the countryside, whereas the Scottish court drinks wine in "paradise." Outside of the context of international markets, ale retains its function as a vehicle for the ethnic racism of Boorde's *Dyetary*:

> Iche cham a Cornyshe man, al[e] che can brew;
> It wyll make one to kacke, also to spew;
> It is dycke and smoky, and also it is dyn;
> It is lyke wash as pygges had wrestled dryn.
>
> (122)

49. Ball, *Worshipful Company*, 62.

50. See chapter 2 for a related discussion of measure and economic analysis in *Piers Plowman*.

51. Andrew Boorde, *A Compendyous Regyment or A Dyetary of Helth*, ed. F. J. Furnivall (1542; London: Early English Text Society, 1870), 10:256.

52. Salzman, *English Industries*, 285.

Cornwal is a pore and very barren countrey of al maner thing, except Tyn and Fysshe. . . . there ale is starke nought, lokinge whyte & thycke, as pygges had wrasteled in it,

> smoky and ropye,
> and neuer a good sope,
> in moste places it is worse and worse,
> pitie it is them to curse;
> for wagginge of a straw
> they wyl go to law,
> and al not worth a hawe,
> playinge so the dawe.
>
> (123)

In a passage that is closely related to "The Tunnyng," here Boorde lapses into Skeltonics. Indeed, Skelton's poem itself also has an ethnic and national register, though it is muted in comparison with such poems as his "Agaynst the Scottes," "Against Dundas," or "Chorus de Dys contra Gallos." One of the tales that drunken Alice brings to the other gossips of "The Tunnyng" (351–62) refers to the Evil May Day riot of 1517 in which Italian, French, and Flemish merchants and diplomats were assaulted in the City of London by a mob of possibly two thousand apprentices who blamed foreigners for the economic recession.[53] "The Tunnyng" registers ale's place as a commercial giant, floating yet sustaining an image of the national body politic.

Both the topic of ale and the figure of the alewife, then, bring us to the unstable center of early economic thought. Though "The Tunnyng" opens with the portrait of Elynour as a pastiche of objects, it moves quickly into an account, almost an accounting ledger, of her sales by customer and proceeds. In the course of seven passus a queue of women brings a wild assortment of commodities to Elynour as payment in kind for ale. In the logic of the poem, ale is at first merely one in a series of commodities of which equal exchanges are made, but with repetition it is elevated to being the one commodity that stands as the fate and measure of all the rest. It is the symbol of conversion into value of any thing, and the one solvent of all value as well. "Instede of coyne and monny," according to the Tertius Passus:

> Some brynge her a conny,
> And some a pot with honny,

---

53. See Scattergood's note to lines 355–62 (p. 451) and *The Calendar of State Papers: Foreign and Domestic, Henry VIII*, 2:2.1031.

> Some a salt, and some a spone,
> Some their hose, some their shone;
> Some ranne a good trot
> With a skellet or a pot;
> Some fyll theyr pot full
> Of good Lemster woll.
>
> (244–52)

In these lines, not only is Elynour's character reduced to commodity form (the first commodities in the list are the affectionate names for Elynour that her husband uses in bed), but money itself is reduced to being just another commodity; it has given over its privileged status to ale. Not only such household items as spoons and skillets but things that belong specifically to the characters' husbands are offered up, and as the ale progressively dissolves the drinkers' ties to the traditional social fabric, one character cashes in her wedding ring.

In a mock-heroic process of elevation, Skelton's ale achieves the status of the economic "universal or general equivalent," the one commodity that is selected to be the marker of value in all others.[54] According to economic historiography, the rise of a general equivalent accompanies the commercialization of an economy and the process of its saturation with money. As if undoing the process that Marx describes in the "Fetishism of Commodities" section of *Capital* (written under the blue dome of the British Library), Skelton projects the behavior of commodities back on the human agents of commodity exchange. According to Marx, in a market economy commodities appear to act as (what I would call) personifications of the social relations of the human agents involved: "To [the producers], their own social action takes the form of the action of objects, which rule the producers instead of being ruled by them."[55]

But in "The Tunnyng" women begin to act as if they are personifications of behavior associated with commodities. They become as adulterated, incontinent, bestial, and filthy as Elynour's ale is described as being. The depreciation of the value of the "typpet," the "brasse pan," or the bacon, when each is turned into ale, is made known to us through the actions of its former owner, who embodies that depreciation in our eyes.

> Maude Ruggy thyther skypped:
> She was ugly hypped,
> And ugly thycke-lypped
> Like an onyon syded,

---

54. The economic principle of the general equivalent is discussed in chapters 1 and 2.

55. Karl Marx, *Capital: A Critique of Political Economy*, trans. Samuel Moore and Edward Aveling, ed. Frederick Engels (1867; New York: International Publishers, 1967), 1:75.

Lyke tan ledder hyded.
She had her so guyded
Betwene the cup and the wall,
That she was therewithall
Into a palsey fall;
With that her hed shaked
And her handes quaked.

(467–77)

In came another dant,
With a gose and a gant.
She had a wyde wesant;
She was nothynge plesant;
Necked lyke an olyfant;
It was a bullyfant,
A gredy cormerant.

(515–21)

Than sterte forth a fysgygge
And she brought a bore pygge.
The fleshe thereof was ranke,
And her brethe strongely stanke,
Yet, or she went, she dranke,
And gat her great thanke
Of Elynour for her ware,
That she thyder bare
To pay for her share.

(538–46)

The women have an automatic quality, an inhuman lack of moral intent. Significantly, like their goods, they appear fully alienated from their social context: the commodities appear apart from the process of labor that produced them and the use to which they are put; the women arrive shorn of kinship, of occupational status, and of membership in associations and social hierarchies. In Chaucer's Shipman's Tale the husband is promised a usurious sexual profit from his (unwitting) loan of his wife to the monk, and the peculiar behavior of money in usury is enacted by the wife; she and it can be used and not used up but increased. Similarly, in the Skelton poem the women act out ale-like behavior. Their social existence is dissolved along with their humanity. Above all, they are emptied of their productive capacity and become merely dissolute, depreciated, consumed. If ale is the general equivalent, it reduces all things to its meaningless self, its empty signification. Infinitely desirable, it is infinitely perishable as well.

The corruption of the market and the corruption of women act as evidence for one another: swindle, inflation, and compulsiveness are summed up in what the poem says is the fleshly incontinence of money.

> We supposed, iwys,
> That she rose to pys;
> But the very grounde
> Was for to compound
> With Elynour in the spence,
> To paye for her expence.
>
> (594–99)

More famously, of course, Langland also deplores the money economy's power to corrupt. While the Mede sections of *Piers Plowman* describe a crisis in the determination of value, as we saw in chapter 2, Langland locates the crisis in the provision of services rather than of products, and offers graft and bribery as the primary form of corruption. In Skelton's poem the locus of crisis is the unstable value of the commodity and of money: the depreciation and adulteration of their value; the opportunity for injustice in exchange. The incontinent social person constructed by clerical antifeminism provides each poem with the technical tool it needs to make its argument. Langland portrays the king's courts as beset by the incontinent female; Skelton asks us to place her social person into action within the topos of the market, the scene of exchange so beloved of economic thought.

Gender and Money

If Skelton's poem seems transparent, if the topos of brewing seems to be a realistic description of a social world, it is because we have retained the important function played by the social person of the incontinent female in fitting human beings to parts of the polity. Nevertheless, we have lost her specific pre-Reformation institutional contexts, and that makes the poem obscure. Without a church that dissuaded men equally from women and from financial speculation, the saturation of the poem with allusions to economic theory becomes invisible. Skelton draws upon the similarities between the clerical discourses against women and commerce in order to claim the superiority of the incontinent female in the role of economic person. The primary consequence of that argument lies in the relation between economic person and value. How does changing the gender of economic person matter? It changes the definition of what the paradigmatic economic act is, and it changes the theory of value.

Both Skelton and Langland rely on their double subject in a fundamental way: in each the sexual is constituted in economical terms, and the economic is construed in sexual terms. While the economic plot has been neglected by critics describing "The Tunnyng," Mede's critics have caught the economic satire but tended to neglect the marriage plot and Langland's sophisticated use of gender. As chapter 2 argues, Mede, an allegorical personification, is the type of an aggregate of human behavior—she represents the habitus of a social class rather than that of an individual. The feminine gender is particularly useful to Langland, because he needs a figure that will analyze agency, one that will help differentiate between the intending subject and the performer of the act. We have noticed how within the doctrine of unity of person in marriage, English law was capable of making a distinction between principal and agent by gender, because not only in criminal law but in law regulating business transactions and contracts, women were often considered not intentional centers of subjectivity or authority but potentially authorized agents for their husbands.[56] In effect, Mede's gender helps Langland to illustrate the need for her marriage, and thus the need for royal control of the money economy.

As we saw in chapter 2, allegorical personification in Mede's case reinforces a view of women as the opportunity for corruption; however, when we turn to the characterization of Elynour, we find that a notion of the feminine as the locus of corruption coincides with the flattening of personification into social caricature. A less allegorical figure is one we hold more responsible for her actions. Elynour Rummynge does not stand for the agency of the economy; she is herself an agent in the economy. Like the other women of the poem, she is an origin and agent of corruption. The characters share this agency with ale, which seems to be powerfully vicious in itself; more than merely the opportunity for the vice enacted by the women, it seems actively to provoke corruption. The poem locates economic value in commodities: when the customers bring their solid pots and pans to Elynour and exchange them for slippery, vanishing ale, their value is consumed and lost. The process of consumption is brought vividly before us. Labor, to the contrary, is invisible in Skelton's poem. The customers are extricated from their roles in productive labor, and Elynour's work is portrayed as being as passive and corrupting as the fall of the hen dung into the vat.

In contrast, Langland's emphasis on value as "personal," something thought about by means of personification, coincides with a labor-oriented representation of value. His era witnessed changes that brought the theoretical basis of labor and wages into question, and the well-circulated

---

56. See Mary Carruthers, "The Wife of Bath." Carruthers emphasizes how much room there is for women's volition in actual economic and legal practice. For a bibliography on this topic, see Mate, *Women in Medieval English Society*, 101–11.

manuscripts of *Piers Plowman* may have even made an important contribution to social consciousness of that basis. In the late middle ages, the value of labor became increasingly less "naturalized" in England because of the accumulated losses of the plague, which were greater among laborers than in the landholding classes. The repeated enactments of the Statutes of Labourers as well as the 1381 rising bear witness to the alteration of the value of labor in English society. The increase in the mobility of workers, the spiritual movements for voluntary poverty, the invention of clocks—all such things make the determination of wages less inevitable and natural, less reasonably based on a worker's birth and station.[57]

The determination of labor's value vexes the whole of *Piers Plowman*, where it is treated among the spiritual and social obligations that accrue with special respect to the person. However, the similarity between the concepts of wage and price was little recognized in early economic thought. Work is commodified and takes on a value in money when compensation is commuted to money; thus wages are a species of price in the service economy with which Langland surrounds Mede. No clearly articulated theory claiming that labor is the primary locus of the production of value appears before the eighteenth century. Early economic theorists go only so far as to imply that labor can be part of the cost of producing a commodity, and to allow in certain cases that such cost contributes in a more or less mysterious way to price or at least to the right to profit.

In "The Tunnyng," as we have seen, the priority *Piers Plowman* accords to labor is transferred to bodily decay and corruption: moreover, the very type of the body, as in so much antifeminism, is female. This notion is part of a larger theological tradition surrounding the figure of Eve, a tradition that associates women with the flesh—the beastly, corrupt, and sexual aspect of human nature. In Genesis, the two different kinds of labor that define the human condition (agricultural and child-bearing) are punishments that find their origin in Eve's sin.

Rather than resuming Langland's trial of labor as an approach to the analysis of value, Skelton sets consumption at the heart of his inquiry. On the topic of value, he seems to turn directly to the theorists. There are a number of ways to treat economic value; it is a matter of fundamental consequence whether it is derived from price, use, exchange, labor, costs, god, alchemy, or nature, whether from the point of view of the buyer, the seller, the estates, or the state. The adoption of any of these positions di-

---

57. See Lester K. Little on the relation between economic change and the growth of religious mendicancy and voluntary poverty in *Religious Poverty and the Profit Economy in Medieval Europe* (Ithaca: Cornell University Press, 1978). On clocks, see Jacques Le Goff, *Time, Work and Culture in the Middle Ages*, trans. Arthur Goldhammer (Chicago: University of Chicago Press, 1980).

rectly recasts the structure of theories of political economy and requires a different model of social person.

Although only the modern portrayal of the market as a special object of knowledge allowed the constitution of economics as a separate discipline, theories of value are elaborated in a tight canon of economic texts stemming from Aristotle.[58] No complete theory of the production, origin, or nature of economic value had been thoroughly worked out by Skelton's time; indeed, no single theory of value has managed to secure authority for itself up to the present day.[59] Yet the early writers have the merit of normatively considering economic topics (wealth, usury, just price, money) in the context of a discussion of justice, part of the overlapping discourses of moral philosophy, jurisprudence, and theology. Theories of value are always, I would argue, theories about how the polity is constituted; they imply or openly insist upon a structure of relations between people. In poetry as well as in an economic tract or economic legislation, concepts of value are strongly tied to models of person and thus should be considered by combining the analysis of ideas and characterization.

In "The Tunnyng," for example, the familiar economic story of one commodity's rise over the others to assume the status of the general equivalent becomes a satire: money is attacked in the guise of ale through its special association with wasteful, incontinent female consumers. As I noted in chapter 1, the consumptibility of the general equivalent is a favorite topic of early economic thought. In fact, it is conventionally argued by an analogy with wine. One of the most quoted passages in the late medieval and early modern canon of economic thought is the *quaestio* on usury by Thomas Aquinas, whether it is a sin to take usury for money lent. Following Aristotle, Thomas treats drink and grain (in contrast to houses) as a category of things whose use and consumption are identical.

Reply: Making a charge for lending money is unjust in itself, for one party sells the other something non-existent, and this obviously sets up an inequality which is contrary to justice. To understand this, one has to realize

58. *The Nicomachean Ethics* was first translated into Latin by Robert Grosseteste in the thirteenth century and has been avidly read and commented upon by English readers ever since. Book v includes the core of Aristotle's economic thought. See Odd Langholm, *Price and Value in the Aristotelian Tradition: A Study in Scholastic Economic Sources* (Bergen: Universitetsforlaget, 1979), *Wealth and Money in the Aristotelian Tradition: A Study in Scholastic Economic Sources* (Bergen: Universitetsforlaget, 1983), and *Economics in the Medieval Schools: Wealth, Exchange, Value, Money, and Usury according to the Paris Theological Tradition, 1200–1350* (Leiden: E. J. Brill, 1992) for a good account of medieval European economic theory.

59. A good introduction to the issues involved can be had in *The Value Controversy*, ed. Ian Steedman (London: Verso, 1981). For the most part modern economics avoids the questions surrounding value by simply collapsing it into price.

that there are some things the use of which consists in their being consumed, in the way in which we consume wine by using it for drinking and consume corn [*triticum*] by using it for eating. We should not, therefore, reckon the use of such things apart from the things themselves. For, instead, when we grant to someone the use by that very fact we grant also the thing, and for this reason to lend things of this kind is to transfer the ownership, so that somebody who wanted to sell wine and the use of wine separately would be selling the same thing twice over or be selling something non-existent. And this would obviously be to commit the sin of injustice. By the same token, however, somebody commits an injustice if he lends corn [triticum] or wine and asks for a twofold recompense—not merely the restoration of some equivalent but also a charge for its use, which is what usury strictly is.[60]

This pair of consumables, wine and corn (an old word for "grain" generally, used here to translate *triticum*, a wheat that yields flour for bread), is not randomly coupled, but has iconographical value. Like ale and bread in the England of 1520, these are the stuff of survival, the staves of life, the staple commodities. Government more easily sees a need to interfere in prices of such goods on behalf of the community: I have already noted that the Assize of Bread and Ale was one of the first English instances of price control. Scholastic writers tend to disapprove of price regulations in cases other than those involving staples.[61] In fact, brewers (and bakers) were periodically forced to resume stalled production because of community need, "even when they considered that new ordinances or a rise in the price of malt would make their trade unprofitable."[62] To place money in such a category is to give it a special ethical force, to suggest that economic transactions, by virtue of their status as binding together the political community, should respond to needs. Aristotle argues that transactions, while voluntary, should respond to social desires (not need, though need sometimes seems to be subsumed in his description of demand).

When Thomas returns to the tenor of his metaphor (money) from his vehicle (drink and grain), he cites Aristotle's two most famous texts on economic issues, which explain the origins of money in a topos we shall take up more explicitly in the next section. Like Skelton, Thomas stresses the special association of money with consumption: "Now money, however, according to Aristotle, was invented chiefly for exchanges to be made, so that the prime and proper use of money is its use and disburse-

60. Thomas Aquinas, *Summa theologica*, 2.2.78.1 (Cambridge: Blackfriars, 1964–76), 38:234–35. I shall refer to this Latin-English edition as Blackfriars.
61. Cf. Raymond de Roover, "The Concept of the Just Price: Theory and Economic Policy," in *Economic Thought: A Historical Anthology*, ed. James A. Gherity (New York: Random House, 1965), 23–41, especially 33.
62. Salzman, *English Industries*, 293. Salzman cites fifteenth- and sixteenth-century cases in Oxford, Leicester, and Gloucester.

ment [et ita proprius et principalis pecuniae usus est ipsius consumptio] in the way of ordinary transactions. It follows that it is in principle wrong to make a charge for money lent, which is what usury consists in. Similarly a man is just as much bound to restore money earned in this way as he is to make restitution for any other ill-gotten gains."[63] The tight relation between money and consumptibility offers Skelton the connection between money and women that structures the poem. Consumptibility and incontinence are an explosive combination; together, they become a great factory for the dissolution of value.

For the women who patronize Elynour's shop, money or, more precisely, value is indeed highly consumable, even fragile: their payments are dissolved into ale, then into urine and vomit. The loss they suffer is oddly moving when imbued with the occasionally liturgical overtones of Skelton's verse.[64] When Alice is passively evacuated of piss, and then of emotion, Elynour ministers to her:

> [Ales] pyst where she stood.
> Than began she to wepe,
> And forthwith fell on slepe.
> Elynour toke her up
> And blessed her with a cup
> Of newe ale in cornes.
> Ales founde therin no thornes,
> But supped it up at ones,
> She founde therein no bones.
>
> (373–81)

The dissolution of value in consumption is a comic, debased transubstantiation that leaves its victims blissfully stupefied, but the reader disturbed and perplexed. As character becomes indistinguishable from commodity—Alice and ales are one and the same—we may learn much about our usual dependence on the way social persons feed patterns of commodification.

For money, the economists asserted, begets nothing on its own. As we saw in connection with Chaucer's Pardoner in chapter 1, money is sterile. This is a consequence of the Aristotelian distinction between commodities that are consumed in their use (like wine and grain) and those that admit of usufruct (houses or land):

> There are two sorts of wealth-getting, as I have said; one is a part of household management, the other is retail trade: the former is necessary and hon-

63. Thomas Aquinas, *Summa theologica*, 2.2.78.1, Blackfriars, 38:234–37.
64. See Kinney, *John Skelton*, for a liturgical reading of the poem.

ourable, while that which consists in exchange is justly censured; for it is unnatural, and a mode by which men gain from one another. The most hated sort, and with the greatest reason, is usury, which makes a gain out of money itself, and not from the natural object of it. For money was intended to be used in exchange, but not to increase at interest. And this term interest, which means the birth of money from money, is applied to the breeding of money because the offspring resembles the parent. That is why of all modes of getting wealth this is the most unnatural.[65]

The two spaces that in modern times would be gendered female (the household) and male (the retail market) are reversed for Aristotle. Nevertheless, the feminine signifies vice. Aristotle uses the special association of women's bodies with birth to make usury seem vicious. (Skelton reinforces this point by citing Elynour's tutelage by a Jew.) Not until the fifteenth century was Aristotle's view of money's natural sterility subjected to a serious attack.[66] It came from Antoninus (1389–1459), Archbishop of Florence, who began to develop the idea of the productivity of money capital. But it caught on rather slowly, and defenses of the Aristotelian view persisted for several centuries. Skelton adheres to this old line by associating money with drink (not wine, but the less noble ale). He portrays no accumulation of capital in the setting of Elynour's small enterprise; indeed, what capital can be assembled in an open-air alehouse?

The doctrine of the sterility of the general equivalent is graphically illustrated in the all-female cast of characters, who should, as women, be bursting with natural, fleshly fertility, yet are rendered impossible sexual objects by drink and greed.

> Ones hed wold have aked
> To se her naked.
> She dranke so of the dregges,
> The dropsy was in her legges;
> Her face glystryng lyke glas,
> All foggy fat she was;
> She had also the gout
> In all her joyntes about;
> Her breth was soure and stale
> And smelled all of ale.
> Such a bedfellaw
> Wold make one cast his craw.
> (478–89)

65. Aristotle, *Politics*, i.10; 1258a39–1258b7, in *The Complete Works of Aristotle: The Revised Oxford Translation*, ed. Jonathan Barnes (Princeton: Princeton University Press, 1984), 2.1997. All quotations of Aristotle will be similarly cited by title, chapter and part, Bekker page and line number, and volume and page number of the Barnes edition.
66. Joseph A. Schumpeter, *History of Economic Analysis*, ed. Elizabeth Boody Schumpeter (New York: Oxford University Press, 1954), 105n.

Not only does the male narrator prefer not to see such a woman as a sexual object, the very idea makes him want to vomit. Thus ale and women, it would seem, provoke the same result.

Producing physical revulsion is a familiar tactic of medieval writers on vice. Innocent III claims that avarice, like hell, consumes but does not digest; Skelton uses avarice and gluttony to describe the production and consumption of ale as a similarly endless and fruitless practice.[67] This is not a necessary connection between the two deadly sins; Chaucer associates avarice with lust rather than gluttony in the Shipman's tale, with results that differ markedly, in the relation between the sexes. Yet the association of avarice and gluttony is a common medieval theme, vividly portrayed in the Pardoner's Tale and in sermons, visions, and manuscript illustrations such as those that show the avaricious punished in hell, forced to continually eat and vomit burning coins, or that picture money as the feces of men, monsters, and apes.[68] Lester Little argues that such scenes accompany the rise of the money economy in the cultural imagination; in contrast, he shows that the aesthetics of an earlier era display a characteristic affection for money. The image of coins as treasure frequently decorated the margins of early medieval texts in a celebratory rather than cautionary mode.

Money had its late medieval and renaissance defenders. The fourteenth-century theorist Nicole Oresme tried to separate it from association with avarice: "Riches, i.e. gold and silver, which are dug from the bowels of the earth, are the mockeries and deceits of wicked men, for many evils are caused by them, including numberless murders, as men have seen in days gone by and see to-day. This results from the perverse greed of wicked men, and not from money itself; for it is very helpful and necessary to human life, and the use of it is a very good thing."[69] The benefits of money are a familiar topic among early economic writers, who trace its origins in those benefits. The list became standardized: money's ease of portability; its use in storing and preserving perishable value; its convertibility into any commodity; its provision of a standard unit of account in order to transform evaluation from a subjective endeavor to an objective one. Skelton's picture of money as ale debits this list on every count. The poem shows that the general equivalent is indeed portable yet consequently tears people from their places in the social network; it claims that money, rather than acting as conserver and preserver of value, provokes avarice and en-

67. For Innocent III on avarice, see Little, *Religious Poverty*, 36.
68. Ibid., 34–40.
69. Oresme, "On the First Invention of Money," 82. On the question of whether avarice was a property of money or only of persons, see John W. Baldwin, "The Medieval Theories of the Just Price: Romanists, Canonists, and Theologians in the Twelfth and Thirteenth Centuries," *Transactions of the American Philosophical Society*, n.s., 49, pt. 4 (1959): 32, 59.

courages the spendthrift; it depicts money's convertibility as a powerful force consuming the goods of society and draining away its wealth; and finally, the poem argues that the standardizing effect of money objectifies value injuriously, transforming the human subject into a demoralized object of the economy.

Skelton brings us back full circle to the Aristotelian distinction emblematized by the story of Midas, the distinction between value and its representation.

> Indeed, riches is assumed by many to be only a quantity of coin, because the arts of getting wealth and retail trade are concerned with coin. Others maintain that coined money is a mere sham, a thing not natural, but conventional only, because, if the users substitute another commodity for it, it is worthless, and because it is not useful as a means to any of the necessities of life, and, indeed, he who is rich in coin may often be in want of necessary food. But how can that be wealth of which a man may have a great abundance and yet perish with hunger, like Midas in the fable, whose insatiable prayer turned everything that was set before him into gold?
>
> Hence men seek after a better notion of riches and of the art of getting wealth, and they are right. (*Politics*, i.9; 1257b7–19; 2.1995)

Money, the sign of value, has no value to human life outside of its social function, which is represented by Aristotle as exchange. Money's sign in "The Tunnyng," the satirical ale, is a debased and feminine form of value. It facilitates not human relations but the exchange of useful goods for a useless, avarice-producing flow of dissolution.

Social Persons and the Topos of the Market

In order to understand the radical effects of Skelton's fictional thought experiment about economic person, we need to understand not just the connection between gender and money, but also the importance of social persons in the larger matrix of the traditional analysis of exchange.[70] The topos of market exchange is normally peopled by continent, rational, male manufacturers of commodities. The *locus classicus* of the scene of exchange, repeated by numerous medieval and modern economic thinkers, is found in Aristotle's *Nicomachean Ethics*. The purpose of the scene of exchange is to work out the relationship between justice and value as they function in society: they are principles and processes both. First Aristotle considers distributive justice with respect to persons:

> The just, then, must be both intermediate and equal and relative (i.e. for certain persons). . . . The just, therefore, involves at least four terms; for the

70. For more on thought experiments, see the Introduction.

persons for whom it is in fact just are two, and the things in which it is manifested, the objects, are two. And the same equality will exist between the persons and between the things concerned; for as the latter—the things concerned—are related, so are the former; if they are not equal, they will not have what is equal, but this is the origin of quarrels and complaints—when either equals have and are awarded unequal shares, or unequals equal shares. (*Nicomachean Ethics [EN]*, v.3; 1131a15–16, 18–24; 2.1785)

The relations between persons become manifest in the interactions among objects; this manifestation allows objects to become a criterion for assessing just social relations: "Awards should be according to merit; for all men agree that what is just in distribution must be according to merit in some sense, though they do not all specify the same sort of merit, but democrats identify it with the status of freeman, supporters of oligarchy with wealth (or with noble birth), and supporters of aristocracy with excellence. The just, then, is a species of the proportionate" (*EN*, v.3; 1131a24–29; 2.1785). The analogy between the proportion among things and the proportion among persons is a way of codifying the principles and institutional arrangements of a society. This process continually generates the measurement of value and, in that measuring, produces society itself.

The topos of the market also produces a special myth of origins for money. The connection of the market with money provides, as we have seen, a central trope for Skelton; this scene is rehearsed throughout the economic canon and may seem so natural to us that alternatives are unimaginable. But money could have been invented by a king as a reward, by a fairy as a treasure, or by merchant sailors as a kind of lingua franca. In the economic imagination, it belongs instead to the tradesmen. Here is the version of money's invention in the *Magna Moralia*, attributed to Aristotle:

> But since the work which the housebuilder produces is of more value than that of the shoemaker, and the shoemaker had to exchange his work with the housebuilder, but it was not possible to get a house for shoes; under these circumstances they had recourse to using something for which all these things are purchasable, to wit silver, which they called money, and to effecting their mutual exchanges by each paying the worth of each product, and thereby holding the political communion together.
>
> Since, then, the just is in those things and in what was mentioned before, the justice which is concerned with these things will be an habitual impulse attended with choice about and in these things. (*Magna Moralia*, i.33; 1194a19–28; 2.1889)

The ability of money to hold the political communion together is predicated on its invention by versions of the same social person; builders and shoemakers are just that—the same representation of economic person.

Virtuous, autonomous, continent, laboring, productive, capable of rational choice, and male, this economic person is a far cry from the vicious, incomplete, incontinent, consuming, sterile, mentally incompetent, and female person imagined by clerical antifeminism and mobilized by Skelton.

Although differences between persons are depicted very narrowly in the traditional topos of the market, they embody real obstacles to social cohesion that must bridged by money and by exchange:

> This proportion [between awards and merit] is not continuous; for we cannot get a single term standing for a person and a thing. (*EN*, v.3; 1131b14–16; 2.1785; my insertion).
> For it is not two doctors that associate for exchange, but a doctor and a farmer, or in general people who are different and unequal; but these must be equated. This is why all things that are exchanged must be somehow commensurable. It is for this end that money has been introduced, and it becomes in a sense an intermediate; for it measures all things . . . The number of shoes exchanged for a house [or for a given amount of food] must therefore correspond to the ratio of builder to shoemaker. For if this be not so, there will be no exchange and no intercourse. (*EN*, v.5; 1133a16–24; 2.1788)

The commensurability of unequal persons is produced by money; the doctor, the farmer, the builder, and the shoemaker make up an economy and a polity in which production and consumption are alienated from one another. The market topos pretends to represent difference in its depiction of economic person, but it is a difference that denies class and inherited wealth, gender, race, and religion—the kinds of difference that, since ancient times, most determine the distribution of wealth and most threaten to divide and dissolve political society. "For it is by proportionate requital that the city holds together. Men seek to return either evil for evil—and if they cannot do so, think their position mere slavery—or good for good— and if they cannot do so there is no exchange, but it is by exchange that they hold together" (*EN*, v.5; 1132b33–1133a2; 2.1788). In a given society it is likely that tradesmen participate less often in exchanges with each other than with the class that controls most of the wealth (and is least likely to make shoes or houses). Notwithstanding, the topos of the market depicts tradesmen in commerce with one another, not with the controllers of land or capital. In this scene lies the ancient history of the idea that the market is inherently democratizing, a faulty notion founded on the radically argumentative representation of social person made by economic theory of the market.

In the face of this narrow but powerful representation of social divisions and tensions, money has an enormous role: it is expected to represent and absorb those divisions, turning them into social bonds. What is money? It is the general equivalent, which measures all things, but it also represents a peculiar attribute of the market, a human intentional state come unstuck from any particular body. "And this proportion [between awards and merit] will not be effected unless the goods are somehow equal. All goods must therefore be measured by some one thing, as we said before. Now this unit is in truth demand, which holds all things together . . . ; but money has become by convention a sort of representative of demand; and this is why it has the name 'money' . . . because it exists not by nature but by law . . . and it is in our power to change it and make it useless" (*EN*, v.5; 1133a24–31; 2.1788; my insertion). By means of this inherently mystical notion of demand, the process of consumption and its relation to value are acknowledged as a kind of engine, but one that has already been relegated to some uncharted offstage area. "There will, then, be reciprocity when the terms have been equated so that as farmer is to shoemaker, the amount of the shoemaker's work is to that of the farmer's work. . . . Now in truth it is impossible that things differing so much should become commensurate, but with reference to demand they may become so sufficiently" (*EN*, v.5; 1133a32–33, 1133b18–20; 2.1788–89). The equation of demand, money, and social bonds covers much sleight of hand. It hides important parts of the relation that it claims to reveal between persons and things. For instance, the topos of the market entails, for Aristotle and his followers, an alienation of intentional states from labor: there is no way of accounting, in the traditional scheme, for what may happen if everyone wants to make shoes not for profit, but because they like the work of shoe-making. The model neglects demand for work in favor of demand for products. But the demand for a product has no necessarily just relation to the labor it represents or to the merit or estate of those who produce it; the traditional assessment of justice does not hold itself accountable to these criteria with respect to demand.

This omission allows Skelton to unmask demand for products as mere fleshly avarice—a demand capable of corrupting the social order and incapable of reflecting value. Similarly, the traditional analysis alienates consumption from the description of value, but consumption is more than simply the receiving end of a sale, because its persons can produce further value or destroy it. Skelton is able to show how consumption does the latter and becomes a great engine for waste rather than for production. In this view, money does not effectively bind society together and does not reflect value.

Skelton also takes advantage of the fact that any representation of person that intends to define value precipitates a strangely unstable ontological state in which persons and things are less than distinct. Value produces a kind of mixed form. Augustine speaks of this in the *City of God*:

> There are, however, other standards of value that vary according to the proper use of each created thing, and by this system we rank certain things that lack sensation above certain sentient beings. We go so far in such cases as to wish, if we had the power, to banish the latter from nature altogether, either because we do not know where they naturally fit or because in spite of our knowledge we still put our own interests first. For who would not rather have bread in his house than mice, or money rather than fleas? But why should this surprise us? When it comes to evaluating men themselves, who surely rank very high in nature, a horse often brings a higher price than a slave, or a jewel more than a servant girl.
>
> So in point of freedom of judgement, the rationality of a thoughtful man is poles apart from the necessity felt by a man in want or the calculus of pleasure applied by one who is ruled by desire.[71]

In Augustine's analysis of economic value there is a strong impression of the violence of the workings of the social estimation of value upon the natural value of sentient and insentient beings. The "just price" that economic thought defined as a common estimate seems almost impossible here, where those in want and those desiring pleasure come to cross-purposes.

The importance for value and justice of the difference between persons is a recurrent problem for economics and moral philosophy. Aristotle's analysis of economics proper is centered in the topos of the household economy, unlike his analysis of justice, which unfolds in the topos of the market and its "unnatural" retail trade. Under the pressure of the question of value, persons and things vacillate in status within the household:

> Thus it is clear that household management attends more to men than to the acquisition of inanimate things, and to human excellence more than to the excellence of property which we call wealth, and to the excellence of freemen more than to the excellence of slaves. A question may indeed be raised, whether there is any excellence at all in a slave beyond those of an instrument and of a servant—whether he can have the excellences of temperance, courage, justice, and the like; or whether slaves possess only bodily services. And, whichever way we answer the question, a difficulty arises; for, if they have excellence, in what will they differ from freemen? On the other hand, since they are men and share in rational principle, it seems absurd to say that they have no excellence. A similar question may be raised about women and children, whether they too have excellences; ought a woman to

71. Augustine, *De civitate dei contra paganos*, 11.16, *The City of God Against the Pagans*, trans. David S. Wiesen (Cambridge: Harvard University Press, 1968), 3:488–91.

be temperate and brave and just, and is a child to be called temperate, and intemperate, or not? So in general we may ask about the natural ruler and the natural subject, whether they have the same or different excellences. (*Politics*, i.13; 1259b17–34; 2.1999)

Aristotle unsatisfactorily resolves his dilemma by means of what we might call decorum (a woman's excellence consists in the courage of obeying rather than the courage of commanding, etc.), and flat contradiction (a slave has "no deliberative faculty at all"). In the *Politics*, as elsewhere, a thorough investigation of the theory of value and exchange necessarily precipitates fundamental questioning of social constructions of the person.

Skelton, it should now be clear, turns the topos of the market inside out by peopling it with the social person of clerical antifeminism rather than with its indigenous character, the tradesman. The incontinent woman brings with her many things the topos excludes: desire, appetite, consumption, and sex all appear in central roles in Skelton's version of this venerable scene. Commodities are not products of labor in "The Tunnyng." Therefore, they are brought to commercial exchange not by laborers who have produced them but by consumers who intend, literally, to liquidate them. The connection between things and persons that seems so natural in the market topos—the connection between shoes and shoemakers—is dissolved. Trade is no longer an adjunct to production and a process by which the value supplied by labor is ratified by demand. Instead, trade consumes the wealth of the polity by wasting it. Rather than the distribution of wealth that glues society together, trade is depicted by Skelton as the dissolution of wealth, the unraveling of the ties that bind the social fabric. Pots and pans, wedding rings—they all disappear into the great brimming maw of the tun. The general equivalent is no protector of value, but the supreme agent of its ruin.

A fight about the relation of person to value arose, in early modern times, out of the revived and championed doctrine of the sterility of money. Is a merchant class of speculators to be allowed to accumulate wealth at the expense of the rest of the community? If so, on what basis? The idea of the sterility of money argues for class stasis by censuring the "portability" or mobility of wealth in the body politic. Land is naturally "fertile," but other kinds of wealth should not be allowed to reproduce themselves. The politics of the natural attachment of wealth to the gentry (the home of "desert" and "worth") and to agricultural labor (naturally productive) go hand in hand in the war waged against commerce, trade, and business. This politics claims that trade is devoid of worth, on the one hand, and of productive labor, on the other—two claims that measure trading activity precisely against the landholding class and against the class that provided its agricultural labor. These are two naturalized models of the relation of value to person fashioned in the work of medieval thinkers by reference to the "merits" of blood and political status, and of manual labor. As models, they should be seen in their mutual political contingency: the mutuality that has been called the ideology of feudalism. Though he is certainly no champion of the bourgeoisie, Skelton anticipates two aspects of the dominant scene of market exchange in modern theory: its alienation from both the claims by blood of the landholding gentry and the claims by labor attached to the agricultural peasantry.

When later thinkers fashion a discipline out of the study of the market, the epistemological veil between a buyer or seller and what is happening "in the market" becomes the assurance that the greater workings of the market are socially just, insofar as the freedom of choice of individual buyers and sellers is preserved. At stake in Skelton's poem is the corruption of choice and free agency by the commodity of money itself. In his view, the confrontation with commercial value has transformative power over people and social persons. The process of evaluation in economic terms, enacted in market exchange, transforms character into a compulsive plot; alienates personal agency to a corrupt social, economic form; and creates an inhuman, sterile object out of a fertile subject. The concept of false consciousness elaborated by Marxist thought—just one turn of the screw from the Aristotelian notion of effeminate incontinence—is already present here, portrayed in the drunkenness of the women.[72] They are inebriates of the agency of money, possessed by an agency that has replaced their own. In the confrontation of economic person with value, it is value that is the agent, corrupting the moral capacities of the person, and making what might have been a subject—running to make her choice in the market—into the depreciated object of the workings of money itself. Whereas in the Shipman's Tale the wife becomes a kind of productive commodity, in "The Tunnyng" Elynour and her customers become consumed, decayed commodities, used up by the economy and thrown away by the poet like putrefying corpses.

Though I have translated the effects of Skelton's thought experiment into a kind of propositional economic paraphrase, no propositional treatise could make those arguments as convincing as does Skelton's poem. Only in fiction can the social person developed by clerical antifeminism find its way into the economists' topos of the market. Fictional representation allows such metadisciplinary moves; we recognize the features of the different fields as they cross one another's tracks. Only by blending such

---

72. On incontinence, see Aristotle, *Magna Moralia* i.33 and *Nicomachean Ethics*, vii.

responsibility and irresponsibility, such heaviness and lightness, can Skelton require us to hold one field to the standards of the other. This is the stratagem that produces his scathing critique.

Literary and Other Social Forms in Time

So what is the worth of this poetry? Skelton does not go so far as to compare his poem to an architectural folly, as I have, but he does call it a trifle. He claims it is "no foly" to use such a trifling mode when in the "Garlande or Chapelet of Laurell" he brings the "Tunnyng of Elynour Rummynge" into his *curriculum vitae*. Occupation reads the list of his works to the Queen of Fame, and reaches his tutorial of the young King Henry VIII:

> The Duke of Yorkis creauncer whan Skelton was,
> Now Henry the viij, Kyng of Englonde,
> A tratyse he devysid and browght it to pas,
> Callid *Speculum Principis*, to bere in his honde,
> Therin to rede, and to understande
> All the demenour of princely astate,
> To be our kyng, of God preordinate.

> Also the Tunnynge of Elinour Rummyng,
> With Colyn Clowt, Johnn Ive, with Joforth Jack;
> To make suche trifels it asketh sum konnyng,
> In honest myrth, parde, requyreth no lack;
> The whyte apperyth the better for the black,
> And after conveyauns as the world goos,
> It is no foly to use the Walshemannys hoos.
>
> (1226–39)

With characteristic modesty Skelton uses a word for "tutor" that looks like "creator" and has a primary meaning of "creditor."[73] By 1500, "creauncer" was both the common English and the technical, law-French word for creditor.[74] Skelton's agency takes syntactical primacy over God's: though God placed Henry, Skelton lettered him. This high claim (inspired in part by the tone proper to the genre of advice to princes) runs abruptly into lowly Elynour. There is a chasm between these stanzas, bridged by the fragile "also." It is a chasm that runs deeply in Skelton's work, where, as critics have often noted, "high" and "low" matters are deployed in concert.

The poem partly assimilates the juxtaposition of such opposites by the

73. *Oxford English Dictionary*, 2d ed.
74. John H. Baker, *A Manual of Law-French*, 2d ed. (Hants, England: Scolar Press, 1990).

stable relation of white and black, and by the reciprocity between the hand of the monarch and the feet of the poet. The poet's feet are covered in Welshman's hose—the form of the trifling poems. He either wants to walk a long way in those socks, or to sell them: the meaning of "conveyauns" is double. Do not think honest mirth is meaningless, the lines say; decorum is observed by the choice of appropriate form. A trifle can be an important part of one's bibliography. An ideologically flexible contention may sell to a larger audience. But is Skelton's trifle flexible?

In Skelton's "Collyn Clout" (which Scattergood dates from the same period as "The Tunnyng") the Welshman's stockings reappear in the midst of virulent estates satire:

> But men say your auctoryte
> And your noble se
> And your dygnyte
> Shulde be imprynted better
> Then all the freres letter.
> But yf ye wolde take payne
> To preche a worde or twayne,
> Though it were never so playne,
> With clauses two or thre,
> So as they myght be
> Compendyously conveyed,
> These words shuld be more weyed,
> . . .
> Than a thousande thousande other
> That blaber, barke, and blother,
> And make a Welchmans hose
> Of the texte and the glose.
>   (758–79)

This use of "conveyance" glosses the earlier one. The word signifies the verbal communication of meaning, a primary definition that the passage from the "Garlande" extends into pun. The stockings of the Welsh, though they are made to fit all shapes of leg, have here become the corrupt and indecorous interpretation covering an authoritative text and gloss. In Skelton's politics, the exercise of higher authority should contain such practices. The interpretation of ecclesiastical texts, many legal texts among them, is of much importance in the world of "Collyn Clout." Here, then, Skelton chastises priests who make Welshman's hose of scripture. It seems that this negative use of the term is the usual one. Dyce cites a parallel use of "shipman's hose" in Jewel's *Defence of the Apologie, &c.*: "Hereunto they adde also a Similitude not very agreeable, how the Scriptures be like to a Nose of Waxe, or a *Shipmans Hose*: how thei may be fashioned, and plied al manner of waies, and serue al mennes turnes."[75]

John Hardyng addressed Henry VI in 1457 with the claim that if "mayntnanse," or the gentry that supported "Ryotours" against the peace were to be allowed to plead before the law for offenders, then in such a case "the lawe is lyke vnto a Walshmannes hose / To eche mannes legge that shapen is and mete."[76] Hardyng promotes strict controls, urging the king to smash all signs of opposition:

> Wythstonde, gode lorde, begynnyng of debate,
> And chastyse well also the Ryotours
> That in eche shire bene now consociate
> Agayne youre pese, and all thair mayntenours.[77]

One might say the chronicler Hardyng was like a pair of such socks himself; he had a career of spectacular shifts in allegiance, and was instrumental in an important forgery of legal documents that "proved" Scotland's submission to English overlordship.[78] At the time he expressed this moral outrage about the pliability of the law, he was making efforts to be paid for providing the forged documents.[79] In fact his entire chronicle might be seen as the means of his repeated bids for reward. According to Hardyng and Skelton, then, such authoritative texts as scripture and law must not be stretched to fit any intention (though it seems that specially-authorized intentions may properly be fitted with fabricated texts). Poems such as the "Tunnyng," however, are profitably stretched into nasty shapes in order to suit their topic. They are trifles, yet these poems merit as much space and defense in the poet's "Garlande of Laurell" as the treatise Skelton wrote for Henry, a mirror in which the prince was meant to read his ideal self.

In "The Tunnyng" nasty women are invited to "hear" themselves: it is precisely misogyny, the "carmen raucum," that is the poem's conveyance. And as the poem's conveyance, misogyny works out Skelton's economic

75. *The Poetical Works of John Skelton*, ed. Alexander Dyce (London: Thomas Rodd, 1843), 2:289. He gives the reference for the 1567 *Defence*, from 465.

76. The parallel is identified by Scattergood, 475.

77. "Extracts from the First Version of Hardyng's Chronicle," ed. C. L. Kingsford, *English Historical Review* 27 (1912): 740–53, 749.

78. For discussion of the forgeries see "Extracts," ed. Kingsford, 740–53, on the basis of Palgrave's *Documents and Records Relating to Scotland*, 376.

79. "In [1457], a rupture being expected with Scotland, the ministry of the time seem to have had it in contemplation to renew the claim of homage. Among the same deeds in the Exchequer, from which a copy of king James's safe-conduct [to Hardyng] has been already given, is an indenture between Hardyng and the earl of Shrewsbury, dated November 15th, 1457, for delivering into the Treasury such instruments relating to the homage as were still in his possession." *The Chronicle of Iohn Hardyng*, ed. Henry Ellis (London: privately printed, 1812), xi–xii.

thought in an important way. It has made the poem both more and less accessible—taken in itself, misogyny has not ceased to be provocative. The trouble with such a poem for feminists is that its misogyny is so bald and virulent that at first we may find ourselves with nothing intelligent to say about it. It is merely shocking, or it is exaggerated and witty enough to amuse us. What is the meaning—both historically and for us—of antifeminism in "The Tunnyng"? The old answer, "realism," no longer rings true. Judith Bennett's important work has shown how misogyny's power can be marshaled in the distribution of work and wealth.[80] It is clear from the standpoint of the social historian as well as the intellectual historian that the poem does not present either a transparent picture of women or a transparent picture of an unchanging misogyny.

Over time, "as the world goos," misogyny has managed to obscure Skelton's economic satire because the feminine has come to function differently from the way it does in clerical antifeminism. Despite the importance of women in retail trades and as consumers, when the scene of the market later came to hold the center of the emerging discipline of modern economics, economic person, was not female. The story of the corrupt feminine origins of labor was discursively marginalized, and Skelton's tirade against the monetary measurement of value in the mechanism of exchange lost all but its "surface" value: it has been taken not as the indictment of a threat to moral agency and to the body politic, but as a picture of vicious woman. Had this rival picture of economic person become dominant, the role of the feminine in it might have become naturalized. During the modern period, the market has increasingly come to represent public life, and the feminine has become its domesticated, private opposite. In unpacking some of the social history embedded in "The Tunnyng of Elynour Rum-

---

80. Bennett, *Ale, Beer and Brewsters*. See the thoughtful response to her work by Ralph Hanna III, "Brewing Trouble: On Literature and History—and Alewives," in *Bodies and Disciplines: Intersections of Literature and History in Fifteenth-Century England*, ed. Barbara A. Hanawalt and David Wallace (Minneapolis: University of Minnesota Press, 1996), 1–17. Hanna writes, "In this mimetic reading strategy, Bennett operates as if representations of alewives might be detached and treated discretely from complicated and intertwined medieval representations. These typically emphasize broader social institutions of which alewives form but a part—drinking and the tavern" (6). It seems to me that Skelton's poem depends precisely on the detachability of representations of alewives from the tavern—the portability of both social persons and topoi is grist for the poet's mill. Hanna's main point, that representations must be situated not only in topoi but also in discourses, is surely right; the point is acknowledged to my satisfaction by Bennett, who sees images of alewives within clerical antifeminist discourse. We should be guided by the details of the representation itself when we judge what level of subtlety is required in our descriptions of discursive contexts. Certainly clerical antifeminism "is" complex; whether Skelton calls upon its complexity or its unity when he represents Elynour is the question that most concerns our treatment of the alewife.

mynge," I hope to have shown that characters as they appear in poems are not mere objects for realistic or unrealistic portrayal; rather, when situated among social persons, they are arguments about ideals, values, processes, and institutions.

"The Tunnyng" constructs character, then, in a way that demonstrates the usefulness of the concept of the social person. Skelton's character is not a metaphor or an allegory, and it is more than an individualized type or role. The poem constructs a notion of an aggregate class: all the characters in the poem are women, all occupy the same standpoint in the network of the economy, and all are agents in sales transactions. Their portraits conjure up the incontinent social person of clerical antifeminism; their acts conjure up the topos of the market and standardize the characters, reducing them to a common denomination and setting that figure in the place we expect to see economic person. "The Tunnyng" does not effect the subtle probing of sexual politics that Chaucer accomplishes in the Wife of Bath's Prologue and Tale, nor does it wage the sophisticated legal critique mounted by Langland's plot. Using fragments of Langlandian and Chaucerian representations of the person within the specially concentrated acid of the satire of value, Skelton manages nonetheless to create a mode of characterization that can argue powerfully about the effect of commercial life on social agency.

Yet that is to put my point too neutrally, for social agency has a violent, gendered charge throughout his work. To brilliant effect, Skelton takes advantage of his model of the imperfect female subject, and of the less-than-human characters of birds, in poems such as "Ware the Hauke," "Phyllyp Sparowe" and "Speke Parott." Skelton is experimental about the representation of person in such poems partly because the material allows him to be: these poems are about women, children, and animals—partial subjects to whom the culture does not accord full intentional capacity. His poetic personae are not the nightingale or the lark but the Phoenix-out-of-ashes (in the riddle of "Ware the Hauke," 239–45); the ventriloquist Parott who speaks in gobbets and macaronics; and the lad dressed in rags, Collyn Clout. In these poems, the liberation of voice from its earlier conventional poetic embodiments accomplishes all the characterological schizophrenia that is promised by the narrative fever of "The Tunnyng of Elynour Rummynge."

Skelton's work precedes the formation of a new dominant literary form of person in the devotional and Petrarchan sonnets of the 1580s and 90s. It was not Wyatt or Sidney who found something useful in Skelton, but Spenser and his more narrative imagination: Skelton's negative logic suited Spenser's own indirection and obsession with experimentation and the forms of person. Skelton's achievement lies in his profound curiosity about the question of person and his new technical approach to the representation of the person in letters. He is a poet of *bricolage*: it is as if we watch him dismantling full-blown personification allegory in order to see what he can do with pieces of it. In moments like the confrontation of the literary person with the question of value, dramatized in "The Tunnyng of Elynour Rummynge," he leaves the old cast of medieval characters lying dead around the stage. If the poem is an architectural folly, we can call it a chantry chapel, a memorial erected at the site of the funeral of residual forms. It is left to Wyatt and Surrey to take up the task left incomplete by Chaucer: the rearranging of personification into persona; it is left to Spenser to reanimate personification as a social form particularly suited to a heterogeneous body politic, one that Aristotle and Thomas Aquinas could not envision.

It is important to acknowledge that the technical forms of characterization used by poets have their own momentum and internal scope of reference as well as their anchors in the forms taken by the larger cultural life around them. But my study cannot follow the history of literary techniques for long if it is to focus on the general principles that characterization reveals about the cultural work of representations of the person. Skelton's poem demonstrates the way social persons are used as a measure of value that generates social differentiation, exchange, and the continual fitting of human beings into the processes that distribute and dissolve wealth and power. The next chapter will concern the ways that representations of the person can make arguments about the political constitution and its place in the international world.

Chapter Four

Architectonic Person and the Grounds of the Polity in *The Faerie Queene*

Corpus intelligi sine loco non potest.
—Cicero

W hen John Skelton engineers his character Elynour Rummynge so that clerical antifeminism corrects economic thought, he demonstrates the use of character to give a tendentious order to the disciplines, to place them in relation to one another. We have seen Chaucer use his Pardoner and Langland use his Mede to similar effect: the very construction of literary character from the material of social persons puts forth arguments about the nature of contemporary institutions and their attendant modes of thought.[1] I shall call such uses of fictional character "architectonic," because they implicitly order kinds of knowledge according to a sense of subordinate and superordinate pursuits and ends. It is axiomatic that all verbal representations of the human figure can be analyzed for social content, since their intelligibility depends upon social persons. But some poets exercise this capacity of representation more thoroughly than do others. Edmund Spenser was the first poet in English to theorize the architectonic nature of fictional characterization. As we shall see, his technical accomplishments superbly develop and extend its practice so that character becomes a brilliant means of assessing and reimagining the very foundations of social life: the volatile forms of per-

1. See the Introduction for the first extended discussion of the term "social person," which is central to my argument here.

son, the creation of social bonds in contract or conquest, the geographical and cultural landscapes of political realms, and the constitutional fit between peoples and governments.[2]

Spenser's theoretical treatment of architectonic character builds upon what a number of his near contemporaries were thinking about the capacities of poetry. Under the influence of Aristotle, Philip Sidney writes in *An Apology for Poetry* that the poet has the best claim to practicing "the mistress knowledge, by the Greeks called *architectonike*."[3] Poetry, according to Sidney, is the queen of the disciplines, the practice that contains ethics, political philosophy, and all the other "serving" sciences. The "*architectonike* . . . stands (as I think) in the knowledge of a man's self, in the ethic and politic consideration, with the end of well doing and not of well knowing only," asserts Sidney, recognizing poetry as an ethical process (rather than an ethical proposition), a process that accomplishes its purpose through its habituation of the reader to virtuous action, "the end of well doing." By these direct allusions to the opening pages of the *Nicomachean Ethics*, Sidney is asserting that poetry has the status of Aristotle's *politike*: it is the highest form of practical inquiry, one that aims at the highest good for the individual and the polis.[4] Despite the fact that the im-

---

2. See David Galbraith, *Architectonics of Imitation in Spenser, Daniel, and Drayton* (Toronto: University of Toronto Press, 2000), for Spenser's ordering of the relations between poetry and history through imitation, rhetoric, and genre.

3. Philip Sidney, *An Apology for Poetry*, ed. Forrest G. Robinson (Indianapolis: Bobbs-Merrill, 1970), 23. On Sidney, see Kathy Eden, *Poetic and Legal Fiction in the Aristotelian Tradition* (Princeton: Princeton University Press, 1986), 157–75.

4. The modern translation of the term *politike* is nearly always given as "political science," but that phrase is a late invention. *Politike* is the object of ethics. Although Sidney draws a conclusion that is not drawn in the *Ethics* (that poetry is the queen of the disciplines), he is interpreting rather than contradicting Aristotle. "Political science" and "poetry" did not have independent compartments in the sixteenth-century curriculum, as they have in ours, and Sidney interprets *politike* not as itself another discipline but as the occupation and aim *of poetry*. The anonymous author of the Bodleian Library's 1578 English translation of the *Nicomachean Ethics* (MS. Bywater 6) translates "politike" as the "science of ciuilitie." The Dubliner Lodowick Bryskett calls it the "discourse of civill life"; the phrase gives him the title of his 1606 book, in which his friend Spenser is depicted reading from *The Faerie Queene*. The term "courtesy" too purports to identify this mode of knowledge. Spenser's book of courtesy, *The Faerie Queene*, Book VI, speaks about government in these "architectonic" terms (and returns to Book IV's image of the rivers in the last stanza of the proem). Proem 4 reveals the spatial metaphor for the ordering of knowledge necessary to the notion of the architectonic:

> Amongst them all growes not a fayrer flowre,
> Then is the bloosme of comely courtesie,
> Which though it on a lowly stalke doe bowre,
> Yet brancheth forth in braue nobilitie,
> And spreds it selfe through all ciuilitie.

The Faerie Queene, ed. A. C. Hamilton (London: Longman, 1984), VI.Proem.4. All references to *The Faerie Queene* (by book, canto, stanza) and the letter to Ralegh (by page) will be to this edition.

portance of the category of the person is already implicit in the phrase "knowledge of a man's self," and despite his attention elsewhere to ideal personages as soliciting imitation, Sidney does not, as Edmund Spenser will, theorize characterization as especially capable of architectonic ordering and the deliberative and creative process it can engender.

Renaissance authors are able to think of poetry as achieving large ordering functions when they think of the art, in the tradition of Chaucer, Langland, Gower, Lydgate, Hoccleve, and others, as supremely compendious. In 1591, the year after the first three books of *The Faerie Queene* appeared in print, John Harington's preface to his translation of one of Spenser's sources, Ludovico Ariosto's *Orlando Furioso*, defines poetry as a tradition of gathering together the fruits of the disciplines:

> The ancient Poets haue indeed wrapped as it were in their writings diuers and sundry meanings, which they call the senses or mysteries thereof. First of all for the litterall sence (as it were the vtmost barke or ryne) they set downe in manner of an historie the acts and notable exploits of some persons worthy memorie: then in the same fiction, as a second rine and somewhat more fine, as it were nearer to the pith and marrow, they place the Morall sence profitable for the actiue life of man, approuing vertuous actions and condemning the contrarie. Manie times also vnder the selfesame words they comprehend some true vnderstanding of naturall Philosophie, or somtimes of politike gouernement, and now and then of diuinitie : and these same sences that comprehend so excellent knowledge we call the Allegorie, which *Plutarch* defineth to be when one thing is told, and by that another is vnderstood.[5]

Harington's "meanings" or "senses" of the allegory systematically correspond to different disciplines, all comprehended "in the same fiction." His example includes what we would now call history ("the litterall sence . . . they set downe in manner of an historie"), ethics ("the Morall sence profitable for the actiue life of man, approuing vertuous actions"), science ("naturall Philosophie"), political philosophy ("politike gouernement"), and theology ("diuinitie"). When we understand the specifically disciplinary reference of these phrases and their interchangeability ("manie times . . . or somtimes . . . and now and then") according to the purposes of the poet, we begin to recognize a quite different theory of allegory than those proposed by modern readers of medieval and renaissance poems, one which deserves elaboration.[6] Harington understands

5. Sir John Harington, *A Preface, or rather a Briefe Apologie of Poetrie, and of the Author and Translator*, prefixed to Harington's translation of *Orlando Furioso* (1591), in *Elizabethan Critical Essays*, ed. G. Gregory Smith (London: Oxford University Press, 1904), 2:201–2.
6. Compare the important discussion of this passage of Harington in Thomas P. Roche, Jr., *The Kindly Flame: A Study of the Third and Fourth Books of Spenser's "Faerie Queene"*

how poetry can position and map modes of thought, providing readers with access to different ideas and visions of the very architecture of knowledge. The tensions among these modes of thought instigate the practice of deliberation and the process of ethics.

Edmund Spenser's letter to Walter Ralegh, published with the first installment of *The Faerie Queene*, makes it clear that he too follows this Aristotelian mode of poetic analysis and practice. As we shall see in an extended discussion of the letter below, Spenser's theoretical contribution is to identify character as the primary technical tool for producing architectonic effects. He cites history, ethics, and politics as the source of characterization in the line of tradition that runs from Homer to Tasso, and he particularly claims the "twelue priuate morall vertues, as Aristotle hath deuised" as the source of his portrait of Arthur before he became king; the "polliticke vertues" are the frame for his character after coronation.[7] Arthur's coming to kingship plays no role in the plot of the poem as we have it, and scholars have been mystified by what Spenser could have meant by the "twelue" Aristotelian virtues. But the "Methode" of characterization described here corresponds well to the architectonic ambitions of Sidney and Harington. The two great themes of the letter to Ralegh are, first, the notion of poetry as habituating a reader to a larger structure of modes of knowledge and, second, the idea of literary character as a means to such an end.

The letter to Ralegh announces not only this advanced mastery of the capacities of character, but also the ambition of the poet "historicall," as Spenser calls himself, to show something of the structure of society: "In that Faery Queene I meane glory in my generall intention, but in my particular I conceiue the most excellent and glorious person of our soueraine the Queene, and her kingdome in Faery land" (737). Both architectonic character and the living polity itself are his objects. The "Faery Queene" and "Faery land" are two images for the real and imagined space that the British realm constitutes: the shapes of its disciplines and social relations. In this most ambitious English poem, Spenser strives to see character's architectonic map of knowledge in the light of large-scale institutions such as country, commonwealth, and empire. His representations of the human figure test such social and political configurations by the ideals embodied in the order of the disciplines that he proposes. This chapter concentrates on Spenser's techniques of characterization and spatialization. It proposes to treat their inextricability and artistry as a demonstration of the capacity

---

(Princeton: Princeton University Press, 1964), 5–15, which exemplifies a metaphysical understanding of allegory. For a brief discussion of theories of allegory, see the Introduction.

7. Edmund Spenser, the letter to Ralegh, in *The Faerie Queene*, ed. Hamilton, 737.

of human figures made out of words to make claims about the orders and kinds of space that constitute the world.

Persons and the Polity

As Spenser practices allegory in *The Faerie Queene*, the poem's ordering of knowledge becomes increasingly about the architecture of social space from which modes of knowledge derive and to which they contribute. In the Aristotelian metaphor of the architectonic, the great intellectual and practical pursuits of societies are arranged in such a way that their internal relations are represented as political. Sidney, living under a queen and following the traditional gendering of the disciplines as female, calls the *architectonike* the "mistress knowledge" and all others the "serving sciences." Today we find Aristotle's term translated as the "controlling science" or "ruling science" in a current edition by Terence Irwin,[8] whose glossary gives "origin" as the meaning of *archē* and "craft" as that of *technē*.

In Spenser's work, this metaphor of disciplinary dominion interpenetrates with perceptions of social space . There were many modes of social space available to Spenser, and an amazing number and range appear in his poem. When he posits "Faery land," he draws on folk traditions that grow out of a local and potent anti-national notion of space. In other aspects of the poem, he draws upon nationalist, colonialist visions of Ireland, as well as upon the New World that was familiar to the Elizabethan court. He draws on a map belonging to a religious militarism that refigures the old territorial opposition of chivalric romance as Protestant against Catholic, rather than merely Christian against Saracen. He draws on an epic construct of space that frames action and character according to its places for exile, encounter, and territorial redemption. He draws on the scientific and natural philosophical views of space as generative, fateful, miraculous, cosmographic, and atomistic. He draws on an Ovidian mythography that assigns space the features of etiology, human passion, and politics.

My list here is far from an exhaustive account of Spenserian modes of representing space, yet the most extraordinary thing about the orders of space in *The Faerie Queene* is their combination of such utter discontinuities. There is a formal insistence that these multifarious modes of space are present together. By "together," I mean something complicated that

---

8. Aristotle, *Nicomachean Ethics*, trans. Terence Irwin (Indianapolis: Hackett, 1985), 2. Unless otherwise indicated, my quotations of the *Ethics* are taken from this edition. Where appropriate, I shall cite passages by title, chapter, and Bekker page and line number.

requires us to consider both the representation of person in the poem and the poem's shaping of its uses by readers. We have seen in earlier chapters how characters are composed of multiple social persons—those dominant social representations of the person that I have been concerned to define. A further consequence is that the representation of space around them takes on a similar multiplicity of social meanings. Because of the intensely social qualities of space, Spenser proposes to understand it through persons, and I hope to show how it is with this method that he fashions *The Faerie Queene* to confront the foundational issues of the English constitution of his day. By means of fictional character, he is able to frame the issue of dominion—that hybrid of persons and places—in an allegory, rather than a treatise, on the ethical and political virtues.

It may be surprising to speak of allegory as a genre capable of broaching constitutional issues; without Spenser's example, one might not allow the proposition. But, as we have seen in Sidney's and Harington's writings, the comprehensiveness of poetry makes it suitable to such philosophically large ambitions. Though we think of them primarily as poets, Sidney, Spenser, and even Harington wrote political treatises on Ireland as well as epic romances and were well versed in the political philosophy of their time. Before turning back to Spenser's letter to Ralegh and its technical description of the poem's uses of person, let us turn to an important constitutional treatise that was read by Spenser before 1579, according to the gloss to the poem for January in *The Shepheardes Calender*.[9] To help us explore the relation between persons and social space in fiction, the treatise will illustrate the conventions of their relation in political thought.

Thomas Smith wrote the learned anatomy of the government of England, *De republica Anglorum,* in the years 1562–65; it is cited by Spenser in the *Calender,* but it was not published until 1583. Like the poets, Smith studied (and taught) the ancients and modeled his work upon Aristotle's example. "*Aristotle,*" he writes, "of all writers hath most absolutely and methodically treated of the division and natures of common wealthes."[10] Smith defines a commonwealth or polity as "a society or common doing

9. The glossator of *The Shepheardes Calender,* E. K., claims in the gloss to January to have consulted *De republica Anglorum* in manuscript some years before its first publication: "couthe) commeth of the verbe Conne, that is, to know or to have skill. As well interpreteth the same the worthy Sir Tho. Smitth in his booke of goverment: wherof I have a perfect copie in wryting, lent me by his kinseman, and my verye singular good freend, M. Gabriel Harvey: as also of some other his most grave and excellent wrytings." Edmund Spenser, *The Shepheardes Calender,* in *The Yale Edition of the Shorter Poems of Edmund Spenser,* ed. William A. Oram, Einar Bjorvand, Ronald Bond, Thomas H. Cain, Alexander Dunlop, and Richard Schell (New Haven: Yale University Press, 1989), 33.

10. Thomas Smith, *De republica Anglorum,* ed. Mary Dewar (Cambridge: Cambridge University Press, 1982), 54.

of a multitude of free men collected together and united by common accord and covenauntes among themselves, for the conservation of themselves aswell in peace as in warre."[11] This definition assimilates England to
Aristotle's notion of the *polis*. Indeed, the polity is the most important and
largest social space imagined by the political philosophers of early modern
England. How do they imagine the polity? It is revealing that the rubric
"persons" provides Smith with one of the main structural "divisions,"
"parts," or "parties" of his topic, and that a full two thirds of the book are
explicitly devoted to what I have been calling social persons.

After an introductory definition of politics by recourse to philology, history, principle (justice), and authorities such as Aristotle, Smith turns to
his larger purpose, the exposition of the English commonwealth. This requires him to describe its constituent social persons in turn: there are
chapters on Gentlemen (*nobilitas major* and *nobilitas minor*), Esquiers,
Citizens and Burgesses, Yeomen, and laborers ("the fourth sort of men
which do not rule"). It is interesting to note that women, children, and
bondmen are not what he calls "parties" to the polity, though females and
children may on occasion accede by blood to positions in the nobility, becoming princes, and so forth. There are no female social persons in
Smith's English government, though women may be the bearers of its male
social persons. Chapters on these persons round out Smith's first of three
books; the second considers English institutions—comprised of a different
order of social persons such as parliament, monarch, courts, chancellor
and chancery, judges, sheriffs, juries ("the xij men"), shires, justices of the
peace, coroners, and constables. The third and last book, though it posits
the functions of yet more social persons, is organized largely by actions at
law and jurisdictions rather than persons. The form of Smith's book conveys its quasi-jurisprudential nature: following Justinian, comprehensive
western legal treatises typically begin with a section on the "law of persons" and follow with the law as it concerns things and legal actions.

Social persons (including legal persons) are not only a way of thinking
about what it means to be human but, like a kind of interface, they join
human beings to the polity. As we have seen in earlier chapters, and especially chapter 1, figures of the person—including literary character—habituate human beings to social persons. Here I shall describe more particularly how social persons in turn habituate human beings to the polity. If
the social persons of a particular polity seem natural to us, so too will its
constitution. The social person of "the queen," for instance, was an interface or a bit of glue between the body of Elizabeth Tudor and the polity of
late sixteenth-century England. Representations of queenship habituated

11. Ibid., 57.

their audiences to all the positions in the polity that interlocked in various ways with monarchy: to *queen*, certainly—but also to *knight, citizen, yeoman*, and so forth, as well as *parliament, jury, chancery, shire*.[12] Social persons constitute the polity in a profound conceptual sense that entirely differs from the sense in which society is said to be constituted of human beings.

As Smith's treatise shows, the catalog of a society's dominant forms of social person describes not only its members but also its constitutional shape, because persons are fit to each other and to the institutional arrangements of the polity. In chapter 2 I argued that legal persons, like other social persons, are best understood as personifications of social relations, as abstractions of social bonds that have been elaborated and given discursive life. Their primary reference is not to their occupants but to a position in the network of social relations they personify. This is why, in order to demonstrate the shape of the polity, Smith's authoritative constitutional treatise provides us with a roster of carefully ordered social persons. Fiction, of course, has more various uses for person.

It is easy to see that fiction always puts forth visions of social structure and place that are highly charged with argument: Chaucer's pilgrimage from Southwark to Canterbury becomes, by the time of the Parson's Prologue, a journey to a celestial destination; Langland's view from the Malvern Hills quickly becomes a survey of a broad landscape of social practices and estates; Skelton's ale-making takes place in a conceptual setting that we recognize as the market, but are urged to view from clerical antifeminism's stance against consumption; and Edmund Spenser's *Faerie Queene* presents, we shall see, a richly various allegorical landscape that, rather like weather, continually precipitates uncanny scenes—drawn at once from the disciplines and from the contemporary political world. Two examples of such scenes will be part of my discussion: the marriage of the rivers Thames and Medway (IV.xi–xii) and the trial of Mutability before Nature (the so-called book VII). These two episodes employ personifications that test the identification between geographical space and political space. Other sections of this chapter will consider the status of social persons in English colonial activity in Ireland, in order to give a context for the peculiar forms of person found in *The Faerie Queene* when it treats the relation between the polity's constitution and its geography.

No doubt Spenser's own experience of persons and polity was especially complex because he worked as an English colonial official in Ireland,

---

12. Stephen Orgel is particularly good on this process in the Jacobean court entertainments. See Stephen Orgel, *The Jonsonian Masque* (Cambridge: Harvard University Press, 1965).

where he was resident (save for a few visits to England) from 1580 until just before he died in January of 1599. In 1580 he was in his late twenties, which means that the nearly twenty years in Ireland cover most of his adult life and therefore his poetic production. During the time that he composed *The Faerie Queene* and *A Vewe of the Present State of Irelande*, his native archipelago was especially volatile both as a geographical territory (because cartography was changing, as were uses of land and modes of its ownership) and as a set of constitutions or collections of political institutions and ideals. What happens when Aristotle's "political animal" lives in a geographical space that is claimed by competing societies, competing languages, images, and ideas about the person?[13] What is the relation between literary representations of the person and the history of constitutional and geographical struggles? How do people use and respond to social categories of the person during conflicts among antagonistic forms of political space? Spenser develops a fictional mode that raises these questions by placing characters in such a multiply organized space.

In the previous chapter, temporal change held our attention as we investigated literary characterization in the light of evolving economic and clerical representations of the person. Here, another kind of alteration requires investigation: alteration in place. Even after considering the abstract, conceptual place of Elynour Rummynge's tunning, we may believe that cultural forms retain a geographical unity. Yet for each of our conceptions of social space—bodily, domestic, disciplinary, vocational, urban or rural, ecclesiastical, courtly, jurisdictional, regional, linguistic, continental—there are competing and collaborating social forms. It hardly helps us to think of social space as constant when these territorial disputes and agreements produce so many ideas about the person.

Of course such competition is, to a greater or lesser degree, the usual state of affairs, because social forms at different scales constantly conflict, because language is made up of place-derived dialects, because images are responsive to many visual traditions, and so forth. Yet we shall see that late sixteenth-century Ireland presents a special case of cultural conflict that exacerbates the processes of interaction in revealing ways, because it shows how the social forms of different cultures change as they are pressed into comparison, estrangement, mutual engagement, and antagonism. When the gap between polity and geography is revealed by war, as we shall see in the final section of this chapter, the articulation of dominion in social persons becomes paramount. Like Langland's social criticism, Spenserian jurisprudence attempts to find a simultaneously local and Archimedean place from which the poem can put forth social persons as

13. Aristotle, *Nicomachean Ethics*, i.7; 1097b11.

measures of dominion. In other words, it is important to consider Spenser's techniques of personification not only as literary events, but also as a means of thinking about the polity and other social forms in distress.

The letter Spenser addressed to Walter Ralegh, published as an appendix to the first three books of *The Faerie Queene* in 1590, is very much concerned with government. It is also one of the earliest and most elaborate English analyses of how characterization produces meaning. In the letter, we learn to interpret the intertwined concepts of person and polity and so to read the complex embodiments of their social forms in *The Faerie Queene*. Spenser describes himself as emulating Greek, Roman, and Italian "historicall" poets in his use of "persons":

> I haue followed all the antique Poets historicall, first Homere, who in the Persons of Agamemnon and Vlysses hath ensampled a good gouernour and a vertuous man, the one in his Ilias, the other in his Odysseis: then Virgil, whose like intention was to doe in the person of Aeneas: after him Ariosto comprised them both in his Orlando: and lately Tasso disseuered them againe, and formed both parts in two persons, namely that part which they in Philosophy call Ethice, or vertues of a priuate man, coloured in his Rinaldo: The other named Politice in his Godfredo. (737)

How can characterization provide a way of thinking about "Politice"? Spenser goes on to propose his Arthur as exemplary and his other knightly protagonists as "patrones" of the virtues that concern each of the poem's books.

Yet this exemplarity of character is confusing. In fact, the knights are perhaps more frequently in error than in the right. They do not experience the moral development that is undergone, for instance, by Will in *Piers Plowman*. Neither does Spenser's narrator grow in moral or political understanding, and while it is to be hoped that the reader may experience such growth, the poem itself never makes that process explicit. Still, something involving exemplarity must take place between the characters of the poem and the "gentleman or noble person" whom Spenser posits as the ideal reader, something that his letter to Ralegh calls "fashioning" "by ensample" rather than "by rule." Indeed, Spenser proposes to "ensample" the topic of "Politice" by writing "historicall fiction" (like Xenophon's *Cyropedia*) about exemplary men, rather than legislation (like Plato's *Republic*) about principles and ideals. The element of character is clearly designated as central to the poem's rhetoric and pedagogy.

Let us spend a moment puzzling out the letter and its references to person and character. Throughout the letter there is an emphasis on the word "person": Spenser uses it eleven times in short space. On five of these occasions we could substitute the term "literary character" for "person" without too much strain. Homer is said, for instance, to "ensample" a good governor and a virtuous man in the "persons" of Agamemnon and Ulysses. Yet by using the term "persons," Spenser includes all that the reader might know of these characters from sources *outside* Homer. Unlike "literary character," which refers to a figure's specific appearances in a work or works of literature, this "person" is consubstantial with the human being who lived and died, with his appearance in historiography, and with the full range of his meanings in human memory, including his literary depictions. The word "person" invokes Ulysses' status as a topos in itself: this rich sense of the figure of Ulysses is included in Spenser's "person," but mostly gone from our "literary character."[14]

Another of Spenser's uses could be translated by our notion of character as "the sum of the moral and mental qualities which distinguish an individual": he describes Arthur as "most fitte for the excellency of his person" to be chosen for the poem, meaning largely that Arthur is of good character—is virtuous—and is a suitable choice for an exemplary hero.[15] The phrase also embraces Arthur's office, his kingship, what would have been called his "honor" and "dignity," though we have since lost the special legal resonance of these early modern terms. Arthur is a suitable choice because of his exalted position. This subordinate sense of "person" is best defined as "social person," because we need a term that points to Arthur's place among others rather than merely to qualities that inhere in him. This use appears again when Spenser speaks of what he may do in later books if the first are successful: "I may be perhaps encoraged, to frame the other part of politicke vertues in his person, after that hee came to be king" (737). The anticipated books will show what accrued not merely in the Arthur so far depicted but in the newly acceded King Arthur—a monarch, the monarch.

Arthur is not the only figure distinguished by a kind of personhood that refers to a social position: the phrase "gentleman or noble person" names one (or rather two) that cannot be satisfactorily translated in literary terms as "characters." Throughout the letter, in fact, Spenser conjures a slew of social persons—poet, knight, king, etc.—but it is in reference to the queen that he acknowledges personhood to require the description I have been giving the term "social person" in this book.

> In that Faery Queene I meane glory in my generall intention, but in my particular I conceiue the most excellent and glorious person of our soueraine

14. For examples of work that teases out the rich meanings surrounding the figures of such classical persons as they are passed among renaissance poets, see the Introduction, note 7.

15. *Oxford English Dictionary*, 2d ed., s.v. "character," sense 11.

the Queene, and her kingdome in Faery land. And yet in some places els, I
doe otherwise shadow her. For considering she beareth two persons, the one
of a most royall Queene or Empresse, the other of a most vertuous and beautifull Lady, this latter part in some places I doe expresse in Belphoebe, fashioning her name according to your owne excellent conceipt of Cynthia,
(Phoebe and Cynthia being both names of Diana.) (737)

Spenser's sense of "person" in this passage is clearly indebted to the legal
theories of monarchy expounded by the law reports of Edmund Plowden
(and made familiar in this century by Ernst Kantorowicz) in which the
queen mystically has both corporate and natural bodies.[16] Here, however,
Elizabeth's natural body bears two social persons, not one. "Queene" and
"Lady" are both figures that refer to cultural categories rather than to a
human body. The phrase a "vertuous and beautifull Lady" refers to a
specific figure of Elizabethan social life, albeit one whose habitus is written intimately upon the queen's natural person. The term "lady" desig-
nates both rank and training (in ethics, manners, grooming) and confers a
set of capacities and restrictions that is entirely distinct from that of
queenship.[17]

Throughout the paragraph's examples of persons, as we have seen,
Spenser makes a distinction between "Ethice" and "Politice," the fashioning of persons and of polities. Neither ethics nor politics is limited to the
natural person, the body that can be a bearer of social persons. Ethics are
the "vertues of a priuate man," but such privacy is in Spenser's world intensely civil, referring to the precincts of the court rather than those of the
state. As Spenser "shadows" the sovereign in his allegorical characters, he
makes clear that she bears a range of social categories. She is identified
with many social persons, and the poem is concerned with their interplay:
ethics in the "Lady" of the court, and politics in the "Queene or Empresse" of the state.

The most difficult use of the word "person" in the letter to Ralegh lies
in Spenser's alignment of his poem with Xenophon against Plato: "For this
cause is Xenophon preferred before Plato, for that the one in the exquisite
depth of his iudgement, formed a Commune welth such as it should be,
but the other in the person of Cyrus and the Persians fashioned a gouernement such as might best be: So much more profitable and gratious is doc-

16. Ernst H. Kantorowicz, *The King's Two Bodies: A Study in Mediaeval Political Theology* (Princeton: Princeton University Press, 1957). See Marie Axton, *The Queen's Two Bodies: Drama and the Elizabethan Succession* (London: Royal Historical Society, 1977), and see
David Lee Miller, *The Poem's Two Bodies: The Poetics of the 1590 "Faerie Queene"* (Princeton: Princeton University Press, 1998), on Spenser's imaginative use of this juridical notion.
17. On the title "lady," see Smith, *De republica Anglorum*, 69.

trine by ensample, then by rule. So haue I laboured to doe in the person of Arthure" (737). How can a government, a polity, be fashioned "in the person" of Cyrus and the Persians? The phrase confuses both by number and by action. In one sense, this is a case that reverses the idea of the human being who bears two persons, the Empresse and the Lady: here, the government bears the person of Cyrus and the Persians. In what sense can a government be a bearer of persons?

These questions have broad implications throughout *The Faerie Queene*; Spenser urges us to interpret literary characters as modeled on persons *extricated* from their bearers. The obliquity of this method of characterization is remarkable—every reader of *The Faerie Queene* feels "clowdily enwrapped in Allegoricall deuises" when attempting to make sense of Spenser's personifications. Yet the references to Plato and Aristotle should help remind us that the abstract quality of the poem's characterization is well suited to its philosophical mode of thought. Indirection, here, is not simply an invitation to decode a character by finding its "particular" intention in a historical figure, but rather is an instruction to work out a complex notion of ideal government.

The government bears the person of Cyrus, and the sovereign bears the person of the Lady; *The Faerie Queene* will forcefully elaborate the place of character in depicting the constitution of a polity. The representation of person in the poem is part of an interlocking system of social representations and relations that take their effects through figures. We will see how Spenser invents a personification allegory that can treat "Politice" in ways that connect reader, character, polity, and social categories (those I will continue to call social persons) and connect them indeed with sometimes dangerous intensity.

In the 1596 publication of the full six books of *The Faerie Queene*, Spenser's letter to Ralegh is not reprinted; even in the original edition the strain between its description of the poem and the poem's text is already severe. Thus (as with Chaucer's Retraction) reasoning from the author's stated "general intention" is a tenuous business. Nevertheless, I feel confident in writing that the letter describes an aim pursued urgently in the second half of the poem: to set out a moral philosophy that is comprised of both "Ethice" and "Politice," that connects *person* with *polity*. Appearing for the first time in the 1596 edition, Books IV (friendship), V (justice), and VI (courtesy) are named by virtues that have expansive significance in both ethical and political discourse. The rubrics of friendship and justice are drawn directly from categories in the *Nicomachean Ethics*, where friendship covers a much wider range of social bonds than it does today, including those of economic exchange, which, according to Aristotle, knit the polity together and become the basis of political structures.[18] And courtesy has, in addition to its reference to the ethics or manners of the court (much emphasized in the proem to Book VI), a further political significance lost to modern usage: in jurisprudence it is another English word for the anglicized Latin *comity*, the principle upon which conflicts of laws are decided.[19] Like consent (the principle of friendship tested throughout Book IV) and equity (the principle of justice tested throughout Book V), comity is a principle and a practice that extends through jurisprudence into political philosophy. It provides an ideal diplomatic relation between polities as it indicates a practice through which conflicts between jurisdictions are settled. Book VI has an intercultural concern that rescues the meaning of courtesy—the "roote of ciuill conuersation" (VI.i.1)—from its narrow (and maligning) definition as the flattery and voyeurism of the courtier. The conflicts between the values encoded in chivalric romance and in pastoral, conflicts that motivate the plot of Book VI to move among various generic and political spaces, raise questions about the status of customary or local law, and explore the problems of comity.

My discussion of the titular virtues of the second half of *The Faerie Queene* is necessarily brief here, but as we now turn to a discussion of key passages of the poem, it should serve to remind us of Spenser's continuous concern with both ethics and politics, with the two projects of fashioning a gentleman or noble person and of fashioning a people, a commonwealth, a polity.[20] Spenser reinvents personification allegory as a tool that

18. Early modern political philosophers (prominently, Jean Bodin) habitually used "friendship" with this larger meaning. Lorna Hutson, *The Usurer's Daughter: Male Friendship and Fictions of Women in Sixteenth-Century England* (London: Routledge, 1994), traces the economic theme of friendship.

19. *Black's Law Dictionary* defines *comity* as "Courtesy; complaisance; respect; a willingness to grant a privilege . . . In general, principle of 'comity' is that courts of one state or jurisdiction will give effect to laws and judicial decisions of another state or jurisdiction." *Black's* gives related definitions for "comity of nations," "judicial comity," and also the Latin "comitas," which begins "Courtesy; civility; comity"; *Black's Law Dictionary*, 5th ed., s.v. "comity," "comitas." The *Oxford English Dictionary*, 2d ed., cites Joseph Story's succinct negative expression of the concept in his classic *Conflict of Laws* (1834): "It has been thought . . that the term comity is not sufficiently expressive of the obligation of nations to give effect to foreign laws when they are not prejudicial to their own rights and interests"; s.v. "comity." For a good short introduction to renaissance notions of courtesy, see the discussion of Thomas Elyot's *The Governour*, Castiglione's *The Courtier*, and Shakespeare's Hal and Hotspur in G. M. Pinciss, "The Old Honor and the New Courtesy: '1 Henry IV'," *Shakespeare Survey* 31 (1978): 85–91. For courtesy, see Richard C. McCoy, *The Rites of Knighthood: The Literature and Politics of Elizabethan Chivalry* (Berkeley: University of California Press, 1989). For philological study of the pervasive legal diction of the poem, including "courtesy," see the forthcoming work of Andrew Zurcher.

20. The nationalism of the poem has been discussed by many critics, including Richard Helgerson, *Forms of Nationhood: The Elizabethan Writing of England* (Chicago: University of Chicago Press, 1992); Andrew Hadfield, *Literature, Politics and National Identity: Refor-*

can help us measure the fit between these two projects. In the following sections, we shall see how the forms of person imagined by renaissance poets and political philosophers such as Spenser and Smith were developed under pressure from the changing shapes and spaces of polities.

Proteus' House and the Grounds of the English Constitution

The topic of person and polity in Spenser requires me to turn to the two culminating cantos (xi and xii) of Book IV of *The Faerie Queene*, in which the poet's subject is the shape of the English polity and its constitutional principles. These cantos take place in the house of Proteus, where the marriage of the rivers Thames and Medway is celebrated by a global cast of characters marching toward the hall while, in a cave below, Proteus tortures the captive Florimell until he is forced to release her. The plot of cantos xi-xii is simple, but its form is extraordinarily complex. The doubled architectural space (hall and cave) and the doubled ceremony (marriage and rape) proceed according to antithetical principles (consent and conquest) and are joined to a doubled genre.[21] Spenser interlaces a version of the ancient poem of marriage, the epithalamion, with the ancient Ovidian and Chaucerian poem of "pleynt" or complaint.[22] The specificities of these paired forms are combined in a larger, modal doubleness: the rape has the texture of mythographic romance, and the marriage that of chorography, an epic catalog or systematic description of landscape popular with Elizabethan and Jacobean writers, historians, and cartographers.[23] As we shall see with special reference to the polysemous character

mation to Renaissance (Cambridge: Cambridge University Press, 1994); Claire McEachern, *The Poetics of English Nationhood, 1590–1612* (Cambridge: Cambridge University Press, 1996); Christopher Highley, *Shakespeare, Spenser, and the Crisis in Ireland* (Cambridge: Cambridge University Press, 1997).

21. Chaucer's Knight's Tale was clearly on Spenser's mind in these cantos: V. A. Kolve's treatment of the image of the conjoined garden and prison displays the iconographical tradition to which belongs the image of Proteus's conjoined festival hall and torture chamber. See V. A. Kolve, "The Knight's Tale and its Settings," chap. 3 of *Chaucer and the Imagery of Narrative* (Stanford: Stanford University Press, 1984).

22. On the renaissance epithalamion, see Heather Dubrow, *A Happier Eden: The Politics of Marriage in the Stuart Epithalamium* (Ithaca: Cornell University Press, 1990).

23. On the episode as a philologically inventive epic catalog, see Gordon Braden, "riverrun: An Epic Catalogue in *The Faerie Queene*," *English Literary Renaissance* 5 (1975): 25–48. On dating the composition of the episode, see Charles G. Osgood, "Spenser's English Rivers," *Transactions of the Connecticut Academy of Arts and Sciences* 23 (1920): 66–108, who argues that the influence of Camden's *Brittania* (1586) requires us to view the Spenser episode as post-1586. See Jack B. Oruch, "Spenser, Camden, and the Poetic Marriages of Rivers," *Studies in Philology* 64 (1967): 606–624, for a comparison of the poems. For renaissance chorography, see Helgerson, "The Land Speaks" in *Forms of Nationhood*, 105–48, and Arthur F. Kinney, "Imagining England: the Chorographical Glass," in *Soundings of Things Done: Essays in Early Modern Literature in Honor of S. K. Heninger, Jr.*, ed. Peter E.

of Thames, all is held together by the flexible glue of an architectonic personification allegory. The complexly formal nature of the cantos underwrites their philosophical portrayal of public ceremony and generates their deliberative politics.

It is less surprising that the ornate personification of these cantos carries the weight of an argument about the foundational principles of the English constitution when one considers how prominent a role the human figure plays in early modern descriptions of the nation.[24] Chorographical descriptions of the landscapes of political regions often involved complex personification in which natural landmarks speak of their political histories. We have already considered political philosophy and jurisprudence in Smith's *De republica Anglorum*, where social persons perform the largest organizational role. Parliamentary representation personified shires in its members, and the class system generally, as audiences of Shakespeare will remember, provided geography as a means of referring to the nobility. Thus, for example, the name of Lear's faithful Kent signifies the title of personal address and title to property at once—place and dominion are inextricably linked within the social person of the earl. Despite its more severe abstraction, the science of early modern cartography also came to incorporate figures: a catalog of human couples appears in the framing ornament of the tradition of English maps initiated by the Flemish Londoner Jodocus Hondius. His 1590 map, entitled "Typvs Angliae" and dedicated to the Earl of Essex, depicts England, Wales, Ireland, and parts of France, Scotland, and Holland in an oval space topped by an oval portrait of Queen Elizabeth. In the four corners, men on the left and women on the right, are full-length oval portraits of a noble English couple and, below them, a London couple, each figure gazing out toward its sexual counterpart. Two years later, Hondius produced another influential map that mentions one of Spenser's literary sources, Camden's *Britannia*, in its title. The genealogical and mythological aesthetics of Spenser's episode are shared by the map. Hondius features an enormous genealogical table, in botanical form, that explains Elizabeth's dynastic claims, and the sea is ornamented with ships, monsters, a fine Triton, and a divine figure, apparently Neptune, carrying a crowned coat of arms. No nymphs appear here, but they are a familiar ornament on the cartouches of other maps of the

---

Medine and Joseph Wittreich (Newark: University of Delaware Press, 1997). For traditions of description both verbal and visual, see Lawrence Manley's learned *Literature and Culture in Early Modern London* (Cambridge: Cambridge University Press, 1995), especially 131–67.

24. Lawrence Manley treats urban personification as primarily a gendering act (*Literature and Culture*, 143–44). It is interesting that Spenser does not personify London.

period.[25] Painting too linked the human figure with the landscape of the nation. The famous Ditchley portrait of Elizabeth I now in the National Portrait Gallery in London represents dominion cartographically beneath her human figure, which stands on a map of England. Similarly, if less exotically, many contemporary portraits of lesser but landed mortals represented their bodies in front of views of their property. As they compete for explanatory power, all such forms of representation tie geography and topography to the polity and its social persons, making the social and legal fictions of their relations seem natural, visible, and consequential.

In order to discover how Spenser's technique of architectonic characterization can produce its own political impact, let us look carefully at the character Thames, a central figure in the vast dynastic pageant of persons that unrolls before the reader of Book IV. Details of Thames's characterization are designed to evoke social persons, and those persons, like all those we have perceived in the analyses undertaken by this book, set up a circuit of deliberative thinking and feeling for the reader that generates the figure's meaning. Literary scholars have recognized Thames's sources in earlier river-processions written by John Leland (*Cygnea cantio*, 1545) and William Camden (*De connubio Tamae et Isis* [1586] in *Britannia* [1610]).[26] Later examples of the genre include Michael Drayton's great, Spenserian *Poly-Olbion* (1612). Spenser's Thames rewards careful comparison with the other personified rivers. But rather than use the notion of the social person to rehearse familiar literary arguments about how character produces meaning through source, allusion, and genre, let us add to our stock of analytical procedures by deriving the non-literary (cartographic, etc.) social persons at Spenser's disposal.

To state that a personified river combines place with a human figure requires no argument, but even here geographical place needs interpretation before we can understand it as a social representation. What, then, does the name "Thames" mean? As a designation for a river, the term is part of the discourse of cartography. There the Thames plays a longstanding, important role as the major English route of traffic and trade: it was both interregional highway and international port. In the earliest printed maps, which contain only a few features of the island, the Thames is prominently marked; no doubt this is because of its provision of access, on the outgo-

---

25. For the Hondius, see Rodney W. Shirley, *Early Printed Maps of the British Isles: A Bibliography, 1477–1650*, rev. ed. (London: Holland, 1980), plate 36. For nymphs, see especially the Humphrey Lhuyd and Abraham Ortelius map published in Antwerp (1573), Shirley's plate 25.

26. Osgood, "Spenser's English Rivers" and Oruch, "Spenser, Camden, and the Poetic Marriages of Rivers."

ing tack, to the sea and, on the incoming tack, to London, Westminster, and the interior, where it serves as the boundary for a large number of important shires.[27] The choice of the Thames emphasizes both the edge and the interior of the island, and thus England's relation to other nations, as well as the arrangement of its internal regions. The choice of a river rather than a city, landmark, or other built feature of the landscape reflects the usefulness in the poem of the Thames's status between such things, both boundary and transport, both link and divider. Moreover, the political import of the river's position is military. The Thames meets the river Medway, personified by the poem as his bride, at the latest possible place in his journey—in the waters of the estuary where both rivers combine in salt water. That placement may remind us that the Thames carried the diplomatic and military fleets that emanated from and approached the crown's palaces and halls of government and that the Medway was a theater for naval exercises.[28] In Spenser's time, English military power was overwhelmingly water-based, and indeed Elizabeth's proudest military action had been the naval repulse of the Spanish Armada in 1588. Water, particularly that of these two rivers, epitomizes early modern Britain's international power. In cartography and in economic and military history, then, the Thames is an important agent, if not usually a human figure, in ways that strengthen the poem's constitutional reference, as well as broaden its encomiastic tone. All of this information is conveyed by the proper name "Thames" itself, a nominative metonymy as powerful as today's "Wall Street" or "Fleet Street."

The details of Spenser's description of Thames invite us to mix cartographic and constitutional thinking with quite different modes of perception. The fantastic nature of the river's clothing reminds us that the event before us is ritual, even mystical, in its ability to transform persons and re-

27. Shirley describes the principal lines of development of the map of the British Isles as deriving from the Ptolemaic tradition, sea charts, medieval land-maps, and Roman itineraries (6). In all of these traditions, whose manuscript maps issue in printed cartography in the late fifteenth century, the Thames is reported. See especially the relatively bare maps of Benedetto Bordone (Venice, 1528, Shirley, *Early Printed Maps*, plate 7), Pietro Coppo (Venice, 1528, plate 8), and Martin Waldseemueller (Vienne, 1541, plate 5), in the sea chart tradition, and that of Sebastian Muenster (Basle, 1538, plate 9), derived from the medieval English Gough map. Lawrence Manley observes that the large foreground of most panoramas of early modern London is dedicated to the Thames (*Literature and Culture*, 145).

28. On the Medway, see Alastair Fowler, *Spenser and the Numbers of Time* (New York: Barnes and Noble, 1964), 172–75. Gordon Braden points out the geographical lateness and incompleteness of the union of the rivers: "One of the Medway's two mouths empties directly into the North Sea; the other empties into the Thames at a point where that river is already so wide that Camden refers to it as an estuary, and the town on the opposite bank is today called Southend-on-Sea" ("riverrun," 38). Topographically, then, Spenser's choice of bride is surprising.

lations. The wedding costume of Thames consists of a robe of eye-fooling artistry. It is of "watchet" hue. Richard Hakluyt describes mariners wearing cloth of this "skie colour," so we can understand the robe's color as expressing water's ability to reflect sky.[29] The magic of optics also motivates the addition of ambiguous, crystal-seeming waves to the robe. The reader who imagines this figure is dazzled and at the same time aware that the celebratory glitter is not transparent, that optics is a science of illusion, not substance. The lines invite us to look carefully, as well as with excitement, at the images evoked. Thames wears a little crown-like headdress set with towers and castles that is, Spenser explains, a city:[30]

> And on his head like to a Coronet
> He wore, that seemed strange to common vew,
> In which were many towres and castels set,
> That it encompast round as with a golden fret.
>
> Like as the mother of the Gods, they say,
> In her great iron charet wonts to ride,
> When to *Ioues* pallace she doth take her way:
> Old *Cybele*, arayd with pompous pride,
> Wearing a Diademe embattild wide
> With hundred turrets, like a Turribant.
> With such an one was Thamis beautified;
> That was to weet the famous Troynouant,
> In which her kingdomes throne is chiefly resiant.
> (IV.xi.27–28)

Both fancy dress and headgear are a familiar costume of weddings, hence pointing Thames out as a bridegroom, but they also expand into magical props.[31] The gorgeous description of these stanzas confuses and awes the reader with impossibilities of scale, material, and workmanship. Spenser awards the coronet its own epic simile, a mythological comparison to Cybele's exotic turban upon which a hundred turrets form a battlement (and an allusion to Vergil's *Aeneid*). The turban came in and out of fashion for both men and women through the late medieval and early modern periods; it alluded to the Turk or Saracen, and thus to heathen eastern autoc-

---

29. Richard Hakluyt, *The Principall Navigations, Voiages, and Discoueries of the English Nation* (1589), 282, cited in *Oxford English Dictionary*, 2d ed., s.v. "watchet."

30. A. C. Hamilton's edition of the poem cites the iconic crown that marks chief cities on Elizabethan maps, reminding us again of the cartographic register of the portrait.

31. For marriage costumes, see David Cressy, *Birth, Marriage, and Death: Ritual, Religion, and the Life-cycle in Tudor and Stuart England*, (Oxford: Oxford University Press, 1997), 362–63.

racy, though the allusion was perhaps muted by familiarity.[32] Architecturally, the turban's hundred small buildings form a single castle, just as many families banded together make one defensible fortified town. The constitutional theme reappears in miniature on the head of Thames.

Epic similes that include human figures make explicit the dynamic of identification and contrast that is inherent in characterization's every recourse to social persons. Because of the similarity of their headdress, Thames is a kind of Cybele; yet the comparative logical structure of the simile incites the reader to find the limits of this identification (is he female? is he a god?). In the reflective shuttling between the figures of Thames and Cybele we select the social persons they might share and, in rejecting the ones we deem inappropriate, create Thames's character, along with a shadow set of kinds of person that are present though negated. Through this process of expanding and limiting identification, epic similes provide a rhetorical form for deliberation. Spenser augments this deliberative form throughout the portrait in his free use of the comparative with verbs that stress appearance ("seemed") and judgement ("weenen"). To this rhetorical, grammatical, and thematic activity, Spenser adds a moral dimension. Glittering through the images of fabulous accoutrements in these stanzas are, as readers have often noticed, little questions that threaten to become bigger: are the robe's waves "false or trew"? Does the coronet represent "pompous pride," as does Cybele's array? Does the turban suggest tyranny? These glimpses of moral issues are designed to heighten the affective and ethical intensity of the reader's deliberative response.

The epic simile is a momentary change of register that marks a larger change in style. The air of mysterious illusion and grandiosity that animates Thames's ornate clothing is at odds with the vernacular diction of the preceding chorography, which has moved us easily from folk-voiced descriptions of his parents to their simply "fresh and iolly" son. At the center of the newly elevated register is Troynouant itself, the city on Thames's hat. Spenser carefully designs Troynouant to have the kind of vacillating meaning that intensifies deliberation. As a fabulous literary and chronicle term for London derived from the chronicler Geoffrey of Monmouth's "Troia nova" (I.xi.xvii), "Troynouant" or "new Troy" is a way of claiming the lineage of *translatio imperii* for England's chief place of power.[33] The name also derives, however, from the British tribe "Tri-

---

32. For instance, see Mary G. Houston, *Medieval Costume in England and France: The 13th, 14th and 15th Centuries*, rev. ed. (New York: Dover, 1996), 161–66.

33. See S. K. Heninger, Jr., "The Tudor Myth of Troynovant," *South Atlantic Quarterly* 61 (1963): 378–87; Manley, *Literature and Culture*, 173–200; and Galbraith, *Architectonics of Imitation*, 52–74.

nobantes," who are found on many early maps to occupy the land north and west of the Thames estuary. In the annals of Tacitus (14.29–38), their revolt for freedom from the Roman empire is described. Thus "Troynouant" calls up both imperialist and anti-imperialist histories. Yet, because in Spenser's Book IV the image of the city is generated by a chorographical description of the country's rivers, I believe we should understand the poem's view of the sources of English political power and authority as local and civic rather than national, royal, or Tudor.[34] In the 1580s, John Stow quotes a political philosopher saying, "Cities and great townes are a continuall bridle against tyranny . . . not onely in the Aristocritie, but also in the lawfull kingdome or iust royalty."[35] Much later (1623), in the frontispiece of Edmund Bolton's *Nero Caesar*, a treatise on monarchy "depraued"; the personification of London wears a burning city on her head and stands under a cartouche portraying the warrior queen Boadicia. Bolton, at least, read the convention of the London headdress to be opposed to tyranny.[36] Of course the name "Troynouant" carries with it an entire historiography that might occupy its own chapter of explication. Here, though, let us be content with a connection internal to *The Faerie Queene*.

Troynouant's origins have been described in Book III by the heroine-knight Britomart, who sees it during an apparently prophetic vision brought on by hearing the pathetic story of Troy:

34. Richard Helgerson excludes Spenser's epithalamion of the rivers from the genre of chorography (*Forms of Nationhood*, 140) because of the extremity of its geographical revisions; these are, however, extremes of degree and not of kind. He is right, of course, to treat Drayton's *Poly-Olbion* in terms of Spenser's example, though he emphasizes Drayton's differences from Spenser rather than the similarities that Drayton stressed. It will be clear from my general argument that I see Spenser offering the reader a deliberative exercise that sets different claims to authority in tension with each other, including both the absolutist and local kinds. Helgerson specifies these kinds as admired by Spenser and Drayton, respectively: "Clearly Drayton was far less susceptible than was even Spenser, despite Spenser's neofeudal predilections, to the humbling and exalting thrill of absolutism. His image of authority, an image determined by the genre in which he chose to write [chorography], is at once more dispersed and less personal" (142). Though I agree that Drayton's poem suits Helgerson's description, it seems to me that he learned to make "dispersed and less personal" images of authority from *The Faerie Queene*, which never provides images of its dedicatee except in dispersed and impersonal persons, many of which are markedly absent. To trump one level of the allegory with another in this way thins the dense politics of the poem. It would be more accurate to say that the chorographical form of Spenser's epithalamion of the rivers pulls in one direction, its monarchical hints (such as the coronet) pull weakly in another, and it is in the interplay between these (and other) aspects of the allegorical form that the political force of the poem is generated. "The humbling and exalting thrill of absolutism" is, I hope I have shown, systematically exposed to criticism in Spenser.

35. John Stow, *A Survey of London*, ed. C. L. Kingsford (Oxford: Clarendon, 1908), 2:206, 198–99, cited in Manley, *Literature and Culture*, 127.

36. Reproduced in Manley, *Literature and Culture*, figure 3, 147.

It *Troynouant* is hight, that with the waues
Of wealthy *Thamis* washed is along,
Vpon whose stubborne neck, whereat he raues
With roring rage, and sore him selfe does throng,
That all men feare to tempt his billowes strong,
She fastned hath her foot, which standes so hy,
That it a wonder of the world is song
In forreine landes, and all which passen by,
Beholding it from far, do thinke it threates the skye.

The *Troian Brute* did first that Citie found,
And Hygate made the meare thereof by West,
And *Ouert* gate by North: that is the bound
Toward the land; two riuers bound the rest.
So huge a scope at first him seemed best,
To be the compasse of his kingdomes seat :
So huge a mind could not in lesser rest,
Ne in small meares containe his glory great,
That *Albion* had conquered first by warlike feat.

(III.ix.45–46)

The episode from which this passage comes associates vice and abuse with the *translatio imperii*; its glories are false and tyrannical.[37] (In Book II, the Roman Caesar is drawn to "this sweet Island, neuer conquered" by his envy of "the Britons blazed fame" and the "hideous hunger of dominion" [II.x.47]). In the midst of a streak of bad judgement, impassioned by the stories of the cowardly rapist Paridell, Britomart divines the relationship between London and the Thames to be that of a mistress and slave: the city fastens her foot on the stubborn, resisting neck of the enraged river in the attitude of triumph and, like Mutability, seems to threaten the sky. The familiar pose and attitude of London is that of the triumphing conqueror, the *triumphator*, a social person much cited in the European tradition of political iconography.[38] In Book III, the historical foundation of England's power is Brute's embodiment of himself in the city. Troynouant

37. This passage is part of an exchange between Britomart and the ransacking rapist Paridell, who chases Florimell and plays a Chaucerian Damyan to Hellenore's May, making a fabliau of the tragedy of Troy. In the figure of Britomart, who is misled, we are cautioned that Minerva, the goddess of wisdom, turns too easily into Bellona, the goddess of war. In contrast, Heather Dubrow praises Britomart's response as "public and communal" (323) in "The Arraignment of Paridell: Tudor Historiography in *The Faerie Queene* III.ix," *Studies in Philology* 87 (1990): 312–27, and Galbraith sees Britomart's response as properly heroic, ignoring Book IV (*Architectonics of Imitation*, 63–65).

38. It may be that this foot-on-neck posture of the victor was attributed erroneously to the ceremonies of the ancient Greeks and Romans; while triumphal processions displaying the losers were authentically classical, Clifford Ronan suggests that "pedal humiliation" was not Graeco-Roman, but a "deeply engrained Renaissance misconception" exhibiting "a strange need to believe that Roman majesty naturally pushed onward beyond hubristic pride into sadistic, even inhuman, cruelty." Clifford Ronan, *"Antike Roman": Power, Symbology, and*

provides Brute's seat and a resting place for his "huge" mind and self-aggrandizing conqueror's glory.

This simultaneously grand and debased image of place contrasts graphically with that of Book IV in which Troynouant ornaments rather than enslaves the Thames. This new Troy is preceded by "famous founders" of powerful nations, including the eponymous founder of Albion, the English polity. He is "mightie *Albion*, father of the bold / And warlike people, which the *Britaine* Islands hold" (IV.xi.15). Though his body was vanquished by Hercules in France, Albion's immortal spirit lives still and has come to the wedding. Here is an alternative history that praises Albion rather than Brute, who is never mentioned at this feast. Rather it is Albion who is called a son of Neptune and is depicted as a legitimate inheritor of a part of Neptune's "Diademe imperiall" (xi.11). The name "Troynouant" carries with it an ominous as well as triumphal ring: Troy was destroyed because of a raptus, as we are reminded by the description of Nereus (18–19), who is said to be a virtuous teacher and to have foretold the destruction of "Proud *Priams* towne" (19). The two images of Troynouant's relation to the Thames give us radical alternatives for thinking about the internal power structures of the polity. They suggest different possible futures for that polity, depending on whether one chooses Albion or Brute, the celebrated or abject Thames, benevolent Neptune or tyrannical Proteus. The temporal origins of England, its "headedness" or form of rule, and its inheritance are all shown to be subject to competing traditions. The topic of Thames's hat, then, is the foundation of the English polity.

Our deliberation on this constitutional topic is generated and organized by the social persons attributed to the figure of Thames. The gorgeous robe and the coronet celebrate his status as a mystically transfiguring *bridegroom*, and the turban gives us an edge of worry about whether he could be a *tyrant*. The description of his attire is framed by the procession, an allegory of his social relations. True to Elizabethan ceremony, the ritual procession is designed to display the order of society. That he is a *son*, whose parents come before him, emphasizes the ordering importance of inheritance and, by their portraits, excludes him from royalty. That such a national allegorical procession does not include a monarch suggests strongly that it is republican in character, emphasizing the "mixed" rather than solely monarchical constitution favored by Smith and many other humanist thinkers.[39] Thames's vassals, to whom he is a *lord*, place him in a local feudal economy. That in stanza 30 he is the *"principall"* to his

---

the Roman Play in Early Modern England, 1585–1635 (Athens: University of Georgia Press, 1995), 116–17.

39. The question of Spenser's relationship to humanist republicanism is taken up by Andrew Hadfield, "Was Spenser a Republican?" *English* 47 (1998): 169–82.

"neighbour flouds" around the nation suggests the baronial and quasi-representative politics of parliamentary government. The description culminates in his honor as the *neighbor* of Irish rivers in "neighbourhood of kingdome nere" (40), rivers that attend him in "duefull seruice" (44), as peers do at rituals such as marriages and funerals. The steady expansion of scale moves us through a set of concentric spheres of social space: familial, feudal, national, international. Thames is subordinate to ancient customary traditions, allegorized in his parents; he is a feudal lord among other English lords, as well as among Irish lords. Perhaps this vision of the mixed constitution is best described as a hybrid of republican and feudal forms. In contrast to what we would expect of a colonial and imperial British attitude toward the island of Spenser's residence, the canto praises alliance with Ireland and speaks of it as a neighboring kingdom rather than a dependent state.

As the social persons of the portrait of Thames evoke various kinds of political entities, they also put forward the principles that undergird them. It is principles such as inheritance, fealty, and neighborhood that entitle Thames to his social persons. The deliberative tension generated by such a mix is engaging and productive, but it is not directionless. Thames's character gives an overall shape to its manifold political evocations by architectonic ordering. The social person of the bridegroom dominates the portrait and is kept in its position by the epithalamic nature of the episode. Thames is a bridegroom because Medway has, at long last, agreed to marry him. The authority of her consent is further stressed by the absence of her parents. No father or patron gives her away, though we would expect him to in customary English practice.[40] Like the female eagle in Chaucer's *Parliament of Fowls*, she is to make this decision herself. The crucial event celebrated by the canto is, of course, the union of bridegroom and bride into the legal, spiritual, economic, and sexual unity of person created by marriage, and that constitutional event proceeds upon the principle of consent.

As the principle upon which this unity of person is achieved, consent is the central motive of the episode and explains the primary parts of the allegory. Chorography is joined to epithalamion. Moreover, landscape is presented as a sexual conjunction in order to transfer the core principle of marriage, that it is created by consent, to the case of the polity. Of the many discourses and iconographic traditions the portrait draws upon, marriage doctrine and chorography are presented to us as the stuff of which political philosophy is made.[41] The principle of consent does rest

---

40. Cressy, *Birth, Marriage, and Death*, 339–42.

41. Tudor coronation pageants often included, in Lawrence Manley's phrase, "mysterious spousals" (*Literature and Culture*, 128) and so drew upon the same link between marriage doctrine and political philosophy.

somewhat uneasily next to those of feudal homage, dynastic inheritance, and neighborly obligation. The poem acknowledges serious conflicts among these social forms, conflicts I will say more about later in this section. Still, all these and more are brought together in Thames's person in the architectonic nature of Spenserian characterization, so that we can see them as ranked contributions to constitutional theory.

In placing consent at the center of political life, Spenser draws on an Aristotelian tradition in which *philia* is said to be the virtue that knits the polity together. The Early Modern English word "friendship" that Spenser uses as the title of Book IV includes all kinds of social bonds in its semantic range; "friend" could mean "spouse" in early English, and "friendship" is also the English title of an important section of the *Nicomachean Ethics* in which Aristotle describes bonds that range from sexual love to economic trade.[42] According to Thomas Smith (though not so much to Aristotle, who stressed the patriarchal household as economic unit), the conjunction of husband and wife was the very type of all political bonds:

> Then if this be a societie [the commonwealth or polity], and consisteth onely of freemen, the least part thereof must be of two. The naturalest and first conjunction of two toward the making of a further societie of continuance is of the husband and the wife after a diverse sorte ech having care of the familie . . . And without this societie of man, and woman, the kinde of man coulde not long endure. And to this societie we be so naturally borne that the prince of all Philosophers in consideration of natures was not afraide to say that [blank in all manuscripts] A man by nature is rather desirous to fellow himselfe to another and so to live in couple, than to hearde himselfe with many. Although of all beastes or lyuing creatures a man doth shew himselfe most politique, yet can he not well live without the societie and fellowship civill. He that can live alone saith *Aristotle* is either a wild beast in mans likenes, or else a god rather than a man.[43]

Smith chooses marriage as the "least part" or constitutive unit of society for a purpose, and although he could have chosen lordship or maternity or slavery or mercantile trade, he does not. Unlike these other relations, marriage has its foundation in consent. The Roman church codified marriage as consisting in the mutual consent of two qualified persons in the twelfth century, and this principle continued to be upheld by the English ecclesiastical courts after the Reformation.[44] Smith's definition of a polity emphasizes that it is made up of free men "united by common accord and covenauntes among themselves"; he elevates the reproductive and com-

---

42. For example, Bodleian Library Bywater MS. 6 (1578) translates Aristotle's "philia" as "frendship."
43. Smith, *De republica Anglorum*, 58–59.
44. For more on marriage law, see chapter 2 above.

panionate roles of women as supporting that accord among free men.[45]
(Smith may have had trouble finding a warrant in Aristotle for his political
praise of heterosexual coupling. As the quotation above shows, he left a
blank space where a bit of Aristotle is expected.) Spenser, in what we are
now in a position to identify clearly as a version of the social contract,
goes further and places the contract of marriage, instead of that of frater-
nity, in the prime position. The result is a fundamental constitutional role
for women and a "common accord and covenaunt" that draws on the
body of custom and jurisprudence surrounding the marital vow. When
Spenser chooses marriage and the epithalamion for his description of the
English constitution, opposing it to Proteus's tyranny, he chooses a particularly sexual consent as constitutive of the polity.

Like other examples of chorography in maps and narrative surveys cited
by Helgerson (many of which imitate Spenser explicitly and reverently),
the epithalamion of the rivers is anti-absolutist and surprisingly non-
monarchical.[46] While the queen's blood and virtues entitle her to rule (see
VI.proem.7), in Book IV the foundation of idealized contemporary English power does not lie in the person of the conquering ruler. As we have
seen, Albion, rather than Brute, comes to the wedding with the other
founders "Of puissant Nations" (IV.xi.15). If England's power had its
source in royal succession, Spenser might have interpreted its seat as Westminster or even Greenwich (both, of course, on the Thames—and Greenwich closest to the Medway), but he sets the seat of the kingdom in London, and, through the human figures with which he endows the rivers, he
conveys the sense that the source of rule lies in English landed and civic
power, ornamented by its urban civilization.[47] The natural and the civic
aspects of the characterizations combine to people a doubled land- (and

45. Smith, *De republica Anglorum*, 57. After identifying marriage as the basic unit of society, Smith's next step in building the polity is to describe how the family "oikonomia" increases and multiplies by generation: "So by this propagation or provining first of one, and
then another, and so from one to another in space of time, of many howses was made a
streete or village, of many streetes and villages joyned together a citie or borough. And when
many cities, boroughes and villages were by their common and mutuall consent for their conservation ruled by that one and first father of them all, it was called a nation or kingdome"
(*De republica Anglorum*, 59). Notice how thoroughly Smith specifies the importance of consent at each level of the social world.

46. See the chapter "The Land Speaks" in Helgerson, *Forms of Nationhood*. For some
specific relations of *The Faerie Queene* to contemporary cartography, see Joanne Woolway,
"Spenser and the Culture of Place" (Ph.D. diss., Oxford University, 1997). Bruce McLeod
treats the topic of Spenser and Irish space thematically in "Thinking Territorially: Spenser,
Ireland, and the English Nation-State," *The Geography of Empire in English Literature,
1580–1745* (Cambridge: Cambridge University Press, 1999), 32–75.

47. John Erskine Hankins, among others, stresses Spenser's treatment of London and
Westminster as separate cities (Troynouant and Cleopolis, respectively) in *Source and Meaning in Spenser's Allegory: A Study of "The Faerie Queene"* (Oxford: Clarendon, 1971), 55.

water-) scape that celebrates voluntary and mutually celebratory political union.

The episode of the marriage of Thames and Medway ceremoniously asserts the voluntary contractual and reciprocal basis of British national power, yet while this very celebration takes place above ground, something horrible and quite opposite—conquest or *raptus*—threatens below. In this large interlacing of plots that links cantos xi and xii, Spenser builds a tension between two constitutional principles.[48] Smith's use of marriage never contemplates its non-consensual opposite, rape, but the briefest glance at later constitutional discourse will turn up prominent citations of the rape of allegorical figures. For instance, a female Liberty is frequently under sexual assault in the debates that produce the rhetoric of the American constitution.[49] Slavery, Spenser's "thraldom," is another pervasive metaphor for civil death of the kind the American founders were intent on minimizing (though sadly, of course, actual women's and slaves' civil rights were not protected for generations).

What Spenser constructs by interlacing the plots of marriage and rape is a larger version of what we saw in the epic simile, with its cognitive shuttle among social persons. He produces an engine of deliberation that draws the reader, in its first stage, to puzzle out logical explanations for appositions and oppositions. In its second stage, deliberation invites the reader to seek out the underlying principles of comparison. Finally, deliberation moves the reader to respond affectively and deepen that response with ethical and political judgement. Similar effects are produced by the poet building a number of other devices into the poem. For instance, I might cite the familiar Spenserian gesture of drawing our attention to the unreliability of appearances with verbs like "seems"; the sudden apostrophes that exhort, such as stanza 22 to the Amazons; the slippery allusions that seem to work against the prevailing moral wind, like Cybele's "pompous pride" (IV.xi.28); the momentary appearances of the poet in the poem, like those at IV.xi.34 ("My mother Cambridge") and IV.xi.41

---

48. Though Lawrence Manley does not notice this ordering conflict, he makes an interesting and perhaps compatible argument that Spenser's poem combines class interests in a "creative tension": "the chivalric milieu of the poem simultaneously links the sphere of epic action to its royal Tudor patron and the epic theme of *translatio* to bourgeois aspirations of London's citizen class." Further: "In its vision, this work of a London journeyman's son not only 'translates' culture over time and space, but effects the emergence of the English state by negotiating the liminary relations between bourgeois and aristocratic tendencies within the neofeudal synthesis," *Literature and Culture*, 182, 174. This is a more occasional and less philosophical and processual view of the poem than mine, but it has the virtue of tying together aesthetics and class politics through historical evidence.

49. See *Pamphlets of the American Revolution, 1750–1776*, ed. Bernard Bailyn et al. (Cambridge: Harvard University Press, 1965).

("And Mulla [an Irish river] mine, whose waues I whilom taught to weep"); and the reuse of images in an opposite register, as the relation of Troynouant to Thames is dramatically altered when we compare the images of III.ix.45 and IV.xi.28.

Spenser's affection for "seem" and the like may be compared to Aristotle's use of the Greek verbs "phainesthai" ("appear") and "dokein" ("seem"). In rhetoric, these moves are recognized as the accommodation of enthymemes—a mode of enlisting the reader in a course of thought that will develop and criticize such received wisdom. Terence Irwin writes that "when Aristotle reports what appears, or sets out the appearances . . . only by context can one decide whether he endorses or rejects (e.g. [*Nicomachean Ethics*] 1113b1) or neither." Further, "translation may mislead if it suggests that Aristotle is necessarily being tentative or non-committal in his assertion; this may, but need not, be true (just as what is apparent may, but need not, be misleading or dubious)." He also points out that such uses of appearances include "the commonly accepted beliefs which Aristotle takes as the material for arguments."[50] Spenser's frequent lapses into oddly assertive or disavowed depictions of appearances, together with his fondness for mixing sudden aphorisms, ordinary speech idioms, concocted anachronisms, and aggressively conflicting ideological statements, all seem to me to be of a similar kind and function. They are usually set off from the surrounding narrative by pronounced rhetorical shifting of gears, and they prompt us to deliberate on the Aristotelian model.

Critics know well how these Spenserian practices of building in oppositions frustrate the process of making literary arguments. When writing about Milton, who clearly learned from Spenser how to build cognitive process into poems, one nevertheless feels the helpful collaboration of the poet ever augmenting one's arguments; when writing about Spenser, one walks across a minefield where no matter how carefully one follows the instructions of the poet in finding the path of his argument, contradictions and negations are apt to explode underfoot every few paces. Unlike Miltonic antitheses, these Spenserian counter-points often refuse to reinforce their opposites and synthesize dialectically. To some extent, this is because Spenser does not, as Milton does, attribute voice to person. In traditional romance fashion, the voice of *The Faerie Queene* slides complexly, and often imperceptibly, among points of view quite unconstrained by character—even the incipient character of the narrator.

I was addressing the large-scale tension between the marriage and the raptus, between the positions of Medway and Florimell. The interlacing of the plots of these cantos, the architectural juncture of their settings, and the

50. Aristotle, *Nicomachean Ethics*, ed. Irwin, 387.

many antitheses of their construction require the reader to consider them together. The spatial qualities of the characters in the wedding of canto xi allegorize the political constitution in its geographical extent. As we move to canto xii, we move out of the geographical politics of the constitution and deeper into its basis in legal action. Canto xi is a scene that belongs to contract theory. The following, final canto of the book also belongs to that tradition, but its status is that of a long caveat, a conditional clause that develops the suspicions and hesitations of the "seems" that, as we have seen, pervasively open up in the very midst of the idealizing mode of canto xi.

There is a strong commitment through these final cantos to value consent and denigrate conquest. The reader has been prepared for these attitudes by canto x, which relates Scudamour's story of his raptus of Amorett from the Temple of Venus. I have argued elsewhere that the episode in the Temple of Venus both airs and reproves the glorification of conquest by setting the narrative in Scudamour's voice and, at the same time, clearly deploring his praise of conquest.[51] In a glance at the condemnation of conquest pursued there, we would note Arthur's promulgation of franchise for women in ix.37;[52] Amorett's explicit unwillingness to be taken (reported but euphemized by Scudamour's personification allegory); the Chaucerian allusions of the end of canto ix, which signal an unreliable narrator; the tension between epic and romance modes of landscape and plot; Scudamour's ethical failures here and elsewhere in the poem; the action of raptus itself; the pattern of Petrarchan gestures; and more. As we have seen, in canto xi the marriage itself glorifies consent. In canto xii, by means of a contrast that serves to emphasize the legitimacy of consent, raptus is again used to condemn conquest.[53] The condemnation in canto

<hr/>

51. On the episode of the Temple of Venus, see my "The Failure of Moral Philosophy in the Work of Edmund Spenser," *Representations* 51 (1995): 47–76.

52. In Arthur's declaimed principle, ladies' freedom includes both negative and positive liberties: it opposes "thralldom" or slavery, and it endows women with the capacity and right to choose their futures. The risks of franchise have been demonstrated by Books II and III, where raptus is shown to erode the human capacity to choose. At the end of Book II, enchanted by animal life and the personified vice *akrasia*, a man who had become a pig has chosen to remain one. The debased version of the Troy story in Book III demonstrates not the glories of conquest but the risk that women and men allowed franchise may degenerate to an animal life: after running off with her Paris, Hellenore becomes the sexually satisfied common property of a band of satyrs. Conquest is to blame for precipitating an erosion of the will in these cases, and the risks of franchise are presented as small compared to the injuries perpetrated in the triumphs of conquest.

53. One important exception to the cantos' antagonism to conquest is the famous stanza on the Amazon women (IV.xi.22). This immediately precedes the groom and is carefully designed to raise the issue of conquest within the controlling context of marital consent. The Americas and Ireland were the two places where the notion of consent at the center of the English constitution was contradicted by English colonial plans and activity, and the Amazon stanza is matched by the stanzas on the Irish rivers that immediately precede the bride.

xii is largely effected by the gothic description of Proteus's cave, much explicit declaiming of his tyranny, and the episode's constant appeals to pity and terror.

Why not end the Book of Friendship with canto xi and its ideal picture of social contract? Why show the contract occurring in the house of a man who is simultaneously torturing a captive woman under the very floorboards that support the constitutional wedding? How does a celebration of consent transform so easily into a distressing scene of force? Here, the fragility of consent seems to lie in the tendency of power to become tyrannical and to need restraining by law. In canto xii, that restraint is not positive legislation criminalizing tyranny, but rather what legal historians call the "forms of action at common law"—modes of taking action before the law in order to correct a present state of affairs. The forms of action (many medieval in origin) were supported by a system of writs that persisted until the nineteenth century.[54] In the early 1580s, Spenser was Clerk of Faculties in the Irish Court of Chancery in Dublin. This was the English court that issued writs establishing what form of legal action could be taken before what common law court with what plea and procedure and what support from sheriff or bailiff. Spenser turns to the forms of action as a remedy for constitutional flaws arising in the midst of a scene of social contract that places Ireland in the tail of the groom's party, immediately before the bride, when the criterion of genuine consent is most strongly felt.

The legal actions of canto xii concern the character of Florimell, the victim of *raptus*. Marinell's mother, Cymodoche, is able to dispossess Proteus, the tyrant, by means of a complaint addressed to Neptune, the sover-

---

The Amazon conquest is a topos Spenser takes from Chaucer's Knight's Tale: the war between the sexes that Theseus wins with "chivalry" is there shown to be an impoverished foundation for society. See my "The Afterlife of the Civil Dead: Conquest in The Knight's Tale," in *Critical Essays on Geoffrey Chaucer*, ed. Thomas C. Stillinger (New York: G.K. Hall, 1998), 59–79. On Amazons, see Kathryn Schwarz, *Tough Love: Amazon Encounters in the English Renaissance* (Durham: Duke University Press, 2000). The opposition of Spenser's poem is not to empire, but to tyranny and proceeding without consent. So Spenser briefly revives Scudamour's point of view, but within a topos (marriage) that squashes it. The rich stanzas on the Irish rivers (which include the poet placing himself in Ireland on the Mulla) show them not as vassals, colonials, or tributaries, but as peers in "kingdome nere," consenting voluntarily to celebrate the bridegroom. The rhetorical question ("Why should they not likewise in loue agree, / And ioy likewise this solemne day to see?" IV.xi.40) plaintively leaves room for refusal. It may be that a consensual, republican empire (though that may now seem impossibly contradictory) is the best representation of Spenser's political ideal in modern terms; the theory of the mixed constitution accommodates those contradictions.

54. For a lively introduction to the history of the writ system, see F. W. Maitland's 1909 lectures, *The Forms of Action at Common Law*, ed. A. H. Chaytor and W. J. Whittaker (Cambridge: Cambridge University Press, 1969).

eign of the oceans.[55] She seeks a warrant for Florimell's release, claiming that, by holding Florimell, Proteus has tyrannically condemned Marinell to die. It is the first of a series of complicated legal fictions that Neptune's reply encourages:

> To whom God *Neptune* softly smyling, thus;
> Daughter me seemes of double wrong ye plaine,
> Gainst one that hath both wronged you, and vs:
> For death t'adward I ween'd did appertaine
> To none, but to the seas sole Soueraine.
>
> (IV.xii.30)

In response to his urging her to reveal the name of the offender, Cymodoche suggests two specific forms of action, the actions of replevin and trover:

> To whom she answerd, Then it is by name
> *Proteus*, that hath ordayn'd my sonne to die;
> For that a waift, the which by fortune came
> Vpon your seas, he claym'd as propertie:
> And yet nor his, nor his in equitie,
> But yours the waift by high prerogatiue.
> Therefore I humbly craue your Maiestie,
> It to repleuie, and my sonne repriue:
> So shall you by one gift saue all vs three aliue.
>
> (IV.xii.31)

Replevin is an action that concerns goods wrongly "distrained," here as if Proteus had taken Florimell (like a lot of furniture or cattle, for example) in order to force Cymodoche to pay some alleged debt (most often rent in cases of replevin, but in this instance her son's life).[56] The framework of

---

55. The complaint, in its literary and legal forms, opens up the narrative possibilities for rescue and rebirth in this canto. Florimell's literary complaint (IV.xii.6–11), in true Chaucerian mode, engenders pity in Marinell and, with pity, the sharing of her civil death. Pity is a strongly political passion. Here, as in the Knight's Tale, pity interferes with the triumphs of conquest and tyranny and opens up the opportunity for the reform of tyrannical conquerors and for the rebirth of the civil dead. Like the thought experiment embodied in John Rawls's "original position," pity allows one to occupy other social persons and their positions in the polity (John Rawls, *A Theory of Justice*, rev. ed. [Cambridge: Harvard University Press, 1999], 15–19 and elsewhere). No mere emotion is imagined by Spenser; instead Marinell nearly dies by participating in Florimell's civil death and is saved only when Proteus is legally dispossessed. The literary complaint (Florimell's) is remedied by the legal complaint (Cymodoce's).

56. A. C. Hamilton's gloss makes use of the first definition for the verb "replevy" in the *Oxford English Dictionary*, 2d ed., which is "To bail (a person), or admit to bail." However, Cymodoce is not requesting bail, and the object of her verb is not a person, but property.

the action of trover depicts Florimell as a sea-wrecked "waift" (our "waif") or bit of lost property that, according to common law, belongs to the sovereign, unless the owner claims the goods within a year and a day after their discovery. The notion of "waift" and its common-law remedy help to tie the two plots of cantos xi and xii together, because the Elizabethan justification of the crown's right to such property involved the great expense of maintaining English naval power.[57] A transformation by the fiction of trover brings Florimell under the special right and title to wrecked treasure given to Marinell by Nereus in III.iv.21–23. Instead of being rendered to him upon discovery, the waif has been unlawfully kept by Proteus. Though no choice is specified among these forms of action, Neptune issues and properly seals Cymodoche's warrant for Florimell's release, and Proteus, though "grieued to restore the pledge, he did possesse," gives up Florimell into Cymodoche's possession without legal argument.[58]

These remedial actions are based, in their legal fictions, on tort rather than on contract, and we can now see Spenser's jurisprudence distributing constitutional thought across the two fields of contract (canto xi) and tort (canto xii). Because they are capable of powerfully transforming social persons, the forms of action can be clever strategies for using the common law against injustice.[59] Cymodoche and Neptune declare that Proteus has injured them (rather than, for instance, injuring Florimell) and that this is the basis of their claim on Florimell. In order to create civil health for Florimell, Marinell, and Cymodoche herself, the fictions paradoxically run to Florimell's treatment as chattel. Such fictions of tort complement and begin to complete the contract at the heart of Spenser's treatment of the constitution, because they appear to be capable of creating liberties in persons (such as Florimell) by means of the system of legal remedies instigated by the writs. Here, the fictions actually create the rights: first, a right of ownership is created in Neptune and Cymodoche, and then civil personality begins to be created in Florimell as Neptune and Cymodoche are willing to give her to Marinell, who is willing to give himself to her. This kind of freedom, supported by the social ties around Florimell and Marinell (and reminiscent of Chaucer's thinking in, say, the Franklin's

---

Thus the second definition is the right one: "To recover (cattle or goods) by replevin," the action at law. Spenser's lines are appropriately cited under definition 2b, together with several other instances, as a transferred sense: "Of the sheriff or bailiff: To recover for, or restore to, the owner by replevin."

57. J. H. Baker, *An Introduction to English Legal History*, 3d ed. (London: Butterworths, 1990), 438–39. He cites *Constable v. Gamble* (1601).

58. Florimell is a "pledge" in the action of replevin, where the distrained goods are a pledge for the debt.

59. Writs could not run against the king, as the maxim went, so the forms of action could not directly constitute a strategy to contain a tyrannical monarch.

Tale and the Physician's Tale), allows the lovers to begin to turn from civil death, recover habitus, and grow toward civil health.

We must not lose sight here of the constitutional context of Proteus's wrongdoing; this is not merely a private sexual tyranny, but a clandestine political corruption. The actions of canto xii clarify two conditions of the constitutional consent idealized in the union of the Thames and Medway. The propositional form of those conditions might read something like the following. First, whether or not consent is genuine depends upon the civil capacities of social persons, but since their fictions may either underestimate or overestimate those capacities, stronger diagnostic tools are needed to ensure justice. What kind of tools? Spenser offers political theory the rich thinking in canon law about impediments to marital consent. He does this by means of his allegory, which tropes the social contract as a wedding (just as Langland does), providing a supplemental diagnosis of civil health. We saw in chapter 2 that Langland banishes women from the social contract in order to avoid the legal flaw introduced by their partial civil death. In contrast, Spenser, like Chaucer, stresses the theoretical importance of placing impaired agents (such as women) inside the scene of contract. This is where the second condition of the Spenserian view of consent appears. Canto xii proposes that the civil health of the contracting agents should be assessed not merely by their social persons, whether partly or fully occupied, but by the network of social relations produced by those social persons before, during, and after contract. For contract is a legal action that transforms social persons as other forms of legal action do, expanding and reducing the civil capacities of its parties. The paradox of Florimell's release by reduction to lost property is that it effectively redresses her civil death by increasing it. Other repairs to her person must follow, but what is demonstrated is that accession to social persons has an environment and a plot in time that offer better indices of civil health than can any single social person. The assessment of civil status in action gives us a yet more accurate picture of the value and strength of the social persons positioned within their networks of bonds. This networked environment is what Spenser calls "friendship"; it is another important consequence of the polysemous variety of the social persons attributed to a figure like Thames.

Such an anti-individualist notion of the person is bound to seem a strange description of rights to twenty-first century readers, but it offers an appealingly rich account of civil health. The space of the polity is, in Spenser, a climate of legal actions that provides the conditions of civil death and life for those acting within it. Further, the general principle put forward by the sequence of these last constitutional cantos of the book is that the well-being of social contract should be measured in part by the status of the weakest parties to it. The reader is put in a position to take this view of political theory by the sequence beginning with the Irish rivers. From here, the center of the scene of contract, the poem tails off to describe the bride, the nymphs, the thrall (slave) whose story has been put off too long (IV.xi.1), and her transformations to female chattel and female "waift." As central as he is, Thames says nothing. The most prominent voices are those of the thrall (in Florimell's haunting complaint) and of the mother (in the maternal suit to repair the constitutional flaws). This is a very different social contract than those of such successors to Spenser as Robert Filmer, Thomas Hobbes, or John Locke.[60]

The transformation of social persons through various states of unity and conflict with others makes up the plots of the Book of Friendship and gives us an important interpretive key to the legal and characterological strategies of *Two Cantos of Mutabilitie*, as we shall see in the last section of this chapter. For the legal fictions of the poem are not merely fanciful ways of expressing thoughts, but ethical and political explorations of social forms—persons, marriage, polity, dominion—that had tremendous force in Spenser's culture and still survive, albeit changed, in those many parts of the world that have received aspects of Roman civil law and English common law.

As we have seen, legal actions often accomplish their goals by recategorizing social relationships in a new set of social persons. The *thrall* Florimell is released from civil death and given to Marinell by means of her successful definition as *waift*, a change argued by Cymodoce's legal fiction and authorized by the seas' *sovereign*, Neptune; Medway moves from *maid* to *bride* by consent and ceremony; Thames similarly becomes a *bridegroom* and ratifies, in his wedding costume, a new genealogy for the newly recreated constitution—of Albion—that the marriage represents. In such rituals, characters are "created" in social persons new to them, and the place around them is recreated as their relations are transformed. Thomas Smith insists upon the simultaneously ethical and political qualities of such changes: "In common wealthes which have had long continuance, by diversities of times all these maners of rules or government hath

---

60. See Carole Pateman, *The Sexual Contract* (Stanford: Stanford University Press, 1988) for an analysis of the fate of women in contract theory; see *The Quality of Life*, ed. Martha C. Nussbaum and Amartya Sen (Oxford: Clarendon, 1993) for an introduction to contemporary thought about measuring the well being of nations. For compatible accounts of the strong effects of sexual forms and stories on political cognition, see Roland Greene, *Unrequited Conquests: Love and Empire in the Colonial Americas* (Chicago: University of Chicago Press, 1999) and Victoria Kahn on romance narrative in "Margaret Cavendish and the Romance of Contract," *Renaissance Quarterly* 50 (1997): 526–66.

been seen . . . For the nature of man is never to stand still in one maner of estate, but to grow from the lesse to the more, and so to decay from the more againe to the lesse, till it come to the fatall end and destruction, with many turnes and turmoyles of sicknesse and recovering, seldome standing in a perfect health, neither of a mans bodie it selfe, nor of the politique bodie which is compact of the same."[61] Growth and decay are more than a natural metaphor; this passage recognizes the identity between the "maners of estates" and the constitution of the polity. The natural body's changes of state are only as real as the changes of category into which the "politique" body also grows. Similarly, Spenser's aim "to fashion a gentleman or noble person in vertuous and gentle discipline" is a project of habituation that concerns both the fit between the human animal and the social person ("vertuous discipline" or ethics) and also the place of the social person in the polity ("gentle discipline" or politics). These two kinds of fit derive from the fundamental architectonic quality in characterization that Spenser describes in the letter to Ralegh: the ethical and political nature of his fictional characters.

Book Four's legal actions release Florimell and Marinell from tyrannical "estates" that were impediments to the consensual constitution of society that is idealized in the chorographical marriage of the English rivers, but the book does not depict their union or resolve the threat that conquest presents to the ideal of a voluntary and "friendly" affiliation between the neighboring kingdoms of England and Ireland. Perfect fits among social persons and the constitution of the polity are precariously achieved, if and when they are achieved, and the criterion of consent reminds us that fitting social persons to people—the desperate task of Cymodoce—can be a challenge indeed. Late sixteenth-century English society is now often thought to be rigid, but the plasticity of human beings, social persons, and polities was very apparent to thinkers like Thomas Smith and Edmund Spenser. Decay and growth are the "nature" of political man for Smith, and alteration is as frequent a theme in *De republica* as it is in *The Faerie Queene*, where it forms, of course, the main theme of the coda-like *Two Cantos of Mutabilitie*. Capable of tending toward good or evil, change is both natural and artificial—and it is susceptible to engineering by many means. Like Cymodoce's legal actions, the engineering of social person risks much, but, as it shapes political institutions, it is a process that is necessary to ensure justice and peace. The crucial jurisprudential point here is the primacy of consent and the urgent insufficiency of our understanding of its conditions. The crucial literary achievement is Spenser's building of an ar-

61. Smith, *De republica Anglorum*, 51.

chitectonic mode of characterization that, through embodying a complement of social persons, can assess constitutional ideals and geographical
space at once.

The Criterion of Fit and the Creation of Persons:
Jurisprudence in Tudor Ireland

If social persons are Spenser's tools for assessing the polity, it must be
said that his government was very interested in tools like Cymodoce's that
enabled it to fashion the forms of person as a way of shaping people. To
what was the polity responsive in such engineering? Social persons differ
from place to place, and must encounter local customs and character,
habits, beliefs, social practices, and all the things usually included in our
present uses of the word "culture." Early modern English philosophers
formulated a clear principle: there should be a close fit between persons
and political institutions.[62] It was a commonplace of political thought that
the form of government should be matched with the nature of the people
of a given place. For example, Thomas Smith entitles a section of *De republica Anglorum*, "That the Common Wealth or Policie Must Be According to the Nature of the People":

> And that according to the nature of the people, so the commonwealth is to it
> fit and proper. And as all these iii. [the Aristotelian] kindes of common
> wealthes are naturall, so when to ech partie or espece and kinde of the
> people that is geaven which agreeth as ye would putt a garment fyt to a
> man's bodie or a shoe fyt to a man's foot, so the bodie politique is in quiet,
> and findeth ease, pleasure and profit thereby. But if a contrary forme be
> given to a contrary maner of people, as when the shoe is too litle or too great
> for the foote, it doth hurt and encomber and letteth the convenient use
> thereof, so that free people of nature tyrannized or ruled by one against their
> willes, were he never so good, either faile of corage and wexe servile, or
> never rest while they either destroie their king or them that would subdue
> them, or be destroyed themselves.[63]

Early modern constitutional theorists like Smith have in mind colonial enterprise as much as the domestic problems of Westminster, though the importance of this colonial interest has been little recognized by historians of

---

62. For fit with respect to the history of the disciplines, see my "Failure of Moral Philoso-
phy"; for fit and the transformation of social persons in other works, see my "The Rhetoric
of Political Forms: Social Persons and the Criterion of Fit in Colonial Law, *Macbeth*, and the
Irish Masque at Covrt," in *Form and Reform in Renaissance England: Essays in Honor of
Barbara Kiefer Lewalski*, ed. Amy Boesky and Mary Thomas Crane (Newark: University of
Delaware Press, 2000), 70–103.

63. Smith, *De republica Anglorum*, 62–63.

constitutional thought.[64] Smith's version of political fit—a kind of decorum—has implications for England's colonists in Ireland, because the constitutional ideals so often cited to justify the crown's actions in Ireland might themselves require reform of its colonial government.

Smith's prescription for the fit between the people and the law says that it should proceed in one particular direction: that the law should fit the people and not the other way around. The constant changes of "nature" and law that European peoples experienced throughout this period made the direction of the fit a particularly urgent problem. Irenius, the most single-minded speaker in Spenser's prose dialogue, *A Vewe of the Present State of Irelande* (1596), addresses the colonial violence in Ireland with the principle of fit in mind:

> I see *Eudox*: That youe well remember our firste purpose and do rightelie Continewe the Course theareof/ ffirste thearefore to speake of lawes since we firste begane with them I doe not thinke it Conveniente (thoughe now it be in the power of the Prince) to Chaunge all the Lawes and make newe for that shoulde brede a greate trouble and Confusion aswell in the Englishe theare dwellinge and to be planted as allsoe in the Irishe for the Englishe havinge bene trayned vp allwaies in the Englishe Gouernement will hardelie be inevrde vnto anye other, and the Irishe will better be drawen to the Englishe then the Englishe to the Irishe gouernemente, Therefore sithens we Cannot now applie Lawes fitt to the people as in the firste institucion of Comon wealthes it oughte to be we will applie the people and fitt them to the Lawes as it moste Convenientlye maye be.[65]

64. Smith's own plan for a colony on the Ards peninsula of northeast Ireland was privately financed by joint-stock subscription in 1572, but objections by the lord deputy and by the local power, Sir Brian O'Neill of Clandeboye, caused Elizabeth to withdraw the grant. Most of the colonists were dispersed to other projects. Backed into Carrickfergus by O'Neill's resistance, the project failed soon after Thomas Smith junior was killed by his Irish household servants, boiled, and served up to the dogs. Smith's book about the project was perceived by Elizabeth and her privy council as a threat to royal prerogative according to Mary Dewar, *Sir Thomas Smith: A Tudor Intellectual in Office* (London: Athlone, 1964), 157–59.

65. Edmund Spenser, *A Vewe of the Present State of Irelande* in *Spenser's Prose Works: Discoursed by Way of a Dialogue between Eudoxus and Irenius*, ed. Rudolf Gottfried (1596, Baltimore: Johns Hopkins, 1949), 199. The text is a philosophical dialogue; among a library of sources and analogues, perhaps the most important is the jurisprudential dialogue *Doctor and Student* (1523–30) by Christopher St. German, which considers different notions of justice in the comparison of several kinds of law (the Doctor's canon law and the Student's common law). "Convenient" is a law-French word that has lost some of its force in modern English. It means "suitable, meet, fitting [L. conveniens]" vs. "**enconvenient**, absurd, unfitting, logically inconsistent, unnecessary, undesirable [L. inconveniens]," according to John H. Baker, *Manual of Law-French*, 2d ed. (Hants, England: Scolar Press, 1990). An "inconvenience" is a legal harm that is distinguished from a "mischief" by being public rather than private. A synonym for decorum, convenience is related to "convention." For the notions of convention and decorum throughout various early modern disciplines, see Lawrence Manley,

In his provision of excuses, Irenius, or at least Spenser, seems conscious of contradicting Smith's prescription for the direction of the fit between laws and people. Both military violence and Aristotelian ethics are implied in Irenius's position, and they look incompatible, as Spenser gives him a metaphor that works against him: clothes are cut to fit the person and not the person to fit the clothes.

The language of "applying" and "fitting" the people invites us to think about the most familiar dilemma of English colonial policy—whether to "reform" or "reduce" people in another place—in terms of the principle of fit between the people and the laws. The expression "trayned vp" clarifies the metaphor of clothing (or "habit") by drawing on the Aristotelian notion of habituation: the process by which bodies become fit for social persons.[66] An important interest of Spenser's, declared in his letter to Ralegh, the notion of habituation is much complicated by a colonial setting.

One may easily address the question of fit in relation to a hypothetical commonwealth and its native inhabitants considered as "a people" and having a kind of natural closure by virtue of geography, race, custom, or culture. But such an address is harder to make if the inhabitants are substantially divided. The population of Ireland, though bounded by water, was politically and culturally riven by dozens of regional lordships, by disparities in status and levels of subsistence, and by the results of centuries of ethnically various invasions. John Davies claimed that the descendants of English colonists in 1612 outnumbered the population of the "ancient natives" (who were "so many war-like nations, or septs") in the time of Henry II and Gerald of Wales.[67] As the *Vewe* points out, England was equally mixed in its "racial" composition. But the legal centralization begun by William the Conqueror in the eleventh century had been widely successful by the sixteenth so that the status of England as a nation was conceptually defensible on the grounds of national institutions that had accommodated or vanquished extreme variances of custom. Unlike Ireland, for instance, Wales had submitted to settlement within the system of English law and government by the 1530s.

What could it mean, in Irenius's words, to "applie" the people of a given

---

Convention: 1500–1750 (Cambridge: Harvard University Press, 1980). On "inconvenience" in Spenser see Judith Anderson, " 'Better a Mischief Than an Inconvenience': 'The Saying Self' in Spenser's View: Or, How Many Meanings Can Stand on the Head of a Proverb?" in *Worldmaking Spenser: Explorations in the Early Modern Age*, ed. Patrick Cheney and Lauren Silberman (Lexington: University Press of Kentucky, 2000), 219–33.

66. See the Introduction and chapter 1 on habituation.

67. John Davies, *A Discovery of the True Causes Why Ireland Was Never Entirely Subdued and Brought Under Obedience of the Crown of England Until the Beginning of His Majesty's Happy Reign*, ed. James P. Myers, Jr. (1612, Washington, D.C.: The Catholic University of America Press, 1988), 70–71.

place and "fitt" them to the laws of another? The project is strangely
suited to the English language's premier allegorist, because it relies upon
the personification of "the Irish," an easy (to us now) collective locution
that nevertheless covers, as the *Vewe* continually reminds us, a multitude
of difficulties.[68] The ethical or military metamorphosis of the Irish called
for by Irenius must confront an ideal expressed, or perhaps merely con-
ceded, in the same passage: "Therefore sithens we Cannot now applie
Lawes fitt to the people *as in the firste institucion of Comon wealthes it
oughte to be . . .*" The recommendation of an ideal relation between the
form of the laws and the character of people is the commonplace that Irenius's concession implies it is, yet the political conclusions that writers
draw from such an axiom vary. Irenius feels it would be unsuitable (he offends by using the technical term "inconvenient") to fit the laws to the
people and resolves to reform the people by measure of the law.

Calling for this direction of fit is not new with Irenius, though his
speeches make its violence explicit: the English government continually attempted to manipulate concepts of person in order to establish control
over the populace. Such a procedure could be quite literal. As Artegall's
android Talus (that personification of executive power) reminds us only
too graphically in Book V of *The Faerie Queene*, Irish people, like Grantorto, had their heads chopped off (V.xii.23) and (like Pollente) pitched
upon poles as "mirrour[s] to all mighty men" (V.ii.19); like Munera, they
had their hands cut off and nailed up (V.ii.26); and like Malengin, they
were disemboweled and left for beasts and birds (V.ix.19). Though these
criminal penalties were also dispensed in England (if less freely), special
penalties were invented for Ireland with a specifically cultural object, and
they had been in place for quite a while. For example, the notorious fourteenth-century Statutes of Kilkenny sought to establish a stable social hierarchy through the regulation of marriage, custom and culture, spoken language, and clothing ("habit") in Anglicized Ireland, but upon the grounds
of an incipient racial model of the person, rather than the class and gender
categories formulated by English sumptuary laws.[69] The failure of such

---

68. Peter Stallybrass and Ann Rosalind Jones write that in the 1590s the "whole enterprise [of the New English] depended upon the *denial* that Ireland was 'wholly together one
body,' governed by English common law"; this position, they argue, allowed the New English to claim that the Irish were not capable of assimilation and therefore should be reduced
by force to submission; "Dismantling Irena: The Sexualizing of Ireland in Early Modern England," in *Nationalism and Sexualities*, ed. Andrew Parker, Mary Russo, Doris Sommer, and
Patricia Yaeger (New York: Routledge, 1992), 158. See also Nicholas Canny, chap. 6 in *The
Elizabethan Conquest of Ireland: A Pattern Established 1565–76* (Hassocks, Sussex: Harvester Press, 1976).

69. For the Statutes and an introduction to early modern Irish history, see Canny, *Elizabethan Conquest*; Steven G. Ellis, *Tudor Ireland: Crown, Community and the Conflict of*

legislation is apparent in the complaints about Irish customs recorded by English authors over several centuries.[70]

Sixteenth-century English courts are known to have accommodated Gaelic culture as well as to have fought it, extending something like the principle of comity, and nowhere is this more evident than in the Irish Chancery—the court where Spenser held a clerkship for seven years after the departure of his employer, Arthur Grey, fourteenth Baron of Wilton, from Ireland. Here, in the court known as the "court of conscience" and the "equitable jurisdiction," Brehon law was often treated as customary law, to be preserved when it did not directly contradict common law. In practice it was sometimes preserved even when it did so contradict.[71] Bills of complaint surviving the 1922 fire, now housed in the National Archives in Dublin, frequently cite the custom of gavelkind in formal complaints and petitions sometimes signed by, and presumably drawn up with the help of, the solicitor general.[72] While we cannot trace the result of every suit or determine the patterns of reasoning used by the Court of Chancery, it is amply established by these records that the argument by gavelkind was viable through the time of Spenser's death. By the legal fiction that imagined the relation between colonial law and Brehon law as if it were like the relation of the king's law to local English custom, the court could fit itself to some aspects of local Gaelic social persons as it made some adjustments to the Irish chieftains and their Brehon lawyers.

John Davies, the attorney general for Ireland under James I, uses marriage (with a sea nymph) as a trope to suggest how difficult conquest was in the face of the lack of symmetry between English and Irish structures of governance. In Davies' account, early attempts at conquest come to particular grief over conflicts in the law of persons:

Cultures, 1470–1603 (London: Longman, 1985); Brendan Bradshaw, *The Irish Constitutional Revolution of the Sixteenth Century* (Cambridge: Cambridge University Press, 1979); and David Beers Quinn, *The Elizabethans and the Irish* (Ithaca: Cornell University Press, 1966).

70. For a literary discussion of the politics of English descriptions of Irish clothing, see Ann Rosalind Jones and Peter Stallybrass, "Dismantling Irena," and *Renaissance Clothing and the Materials of Memory* (Cambridge: Cambridge University Press, 2000).

71. See K. W. Nicholls, "Some Documents on Irish Law and Custom in the Sixteenth Century" *Analecta Hibernica* 26 (1970): 103–43, and Margaret McGlynn, "Equitable Jurisdiction in the Irish Chancery Court," (M.Phil. thesis, National University of Ireland, University College, Dublin, May 1990). McGlynn shows that Gaelic marriage customs were sometimes enforced in Chancery. I am grateful to Dr. McGlynn for providing expertise and advice in Chancery matters.

72. E.g., Ancient Pleadings of Irish Chancery, Parcel A, Item 76, National Archives of Ireland, Dublin. Ellis defines gavelkind as the "system of partible inheritance prevailing in Kent but extended in English usage to denote the system of joint and equal inheritance among males found in Ireland and Wales" (Ellis, *Tudor Ireland*, 322).

The better to assure this inconstant sea-nymph (who was so easily won), the pope would needs give her [Ireland] unto him [Henry II] with a ring: *conubio jungan stabili, propriamque dicabo*. But as the conquest was but slight and superficial, so the pope's donation and the Irish submissions were but weak and fickle assurances. For, as the pope had no more [ownership] interest in this kingdom than he which offered to Christ all the kingdoms of the earth, so the Irish pretend that by their law a tanist [the designated successor of an Irish chief] might do no act that might bind his successor. But this was the best assurance he [Henry II] could get from so many strong nations of people with so weak a [military] power.[73]

Who is in a position to give Ireland away? How can conquest and contracts be settled when the legal persons involved consist of such different powers and obligations? The "so many strong nations" proved themselves to be skillful lawyers and fighters, so that English legal strategists who were trying to make the Irish accept their government had to generate complicated mixtures of accommodation and force.

One suggestive example of such a mixture is the transformation of the person enacted in the strategy that historians call "surrender and regrant."[74] Anthony St Leger, lieutenant of Henry VIII in Ireland through most of the early 1540s, extracted a number of indentures of submission from both Gaelic lords and Old English families (descendants of the twelfth-century conquerors) who were considered to have "degenerated" into native customs. In negotiation, the lords gave up their Gaelic titles and agreed to hold their land from the king in knight service. In June 1541, St Leger opened the parliament that declared the crown's title to Ireland altered from "lord" to "king" ("an acte that the kinges Majestie shalbe king of the realme of Irland"[75]). This act was for Henry one of both concessions and gains, and he would soon repudiate some of his concessions when he realized that the revenues were largely impossible to collect.

In recognition of the new English lordships, over the next few years a number of powerful men were entertained at Henry's court and created earls, knights, and barons according to the terms of their indentures. They

73. Davies, *A Discovery*, 74–75. For Davies's career and an ambitious argument about his legal strategies in Ireland, see Hans S. Pawlisch, *Sir John Davies and the Conquest of Ireland: A Study in Legal Imperialism* (Cambridge: Cambridge University Press, 1985).

74. Surrender and regrant is the "modern name for the process whereby Henry VIII and his successors regularized titles by Gaelic law to land" as defined by Ellis, *Tudor Ireland*, 324. The term describes a process whereby submission to the crown was exchanged for a particular English legal status and negotiated privileges. My sketch of the policy is based on Canny, *Elizabethan Conquest*; Bradshaw, *Irish Constitutional Revolution*; and Ellis, chap. 5 in *Tudor Ireland*.

75. Quoted on p. 157 of David Beers Quinn, "The Bills and Statutes of the Irish Parliaments of Henry VII and Henry VIII," *Analecta Hibernica* 10 (1941): 71–170. See Ellis, *Tudor Ireland*, 146, and Bradshaw, *Irish Constitutional Revolution*, 201–5, 233, 264–5.

were expected to promote English law, education, agriculture, and religion in their lordships. In ceremonies at the royal court they were given, among other things, English clothes.[76] Like the related transformation declared (if not fully effected) by parliament's metamorphosis of "lord" to "king," surrender and regrant was a legal strategy for bringing Irish elites (Gaelic, Old English, mixed) into English courts and legal relationships. The policy involved perhaps equal parts of symbolic, legal, and financial machination. If it worked, it would raise revenue for the crown, but it often failed, in part because of the asymmetry between English and Irish legal persons. In the Irish political, legal, and familial corporation—known as the "clan" (its branches are "septs"), and, in Davies, the "nation" or "country"—the leader was succeeded by his "tanist." As Davies describes: "In every one of these countries there was a chiefe lord or captaine and under him a tanist which was his successor apparent, Both these were ellected of the country whoe commonly made choice of such as were most active and had most swordsmen and followers dependinge upon them."[77] If the leader of a clan surrendered, becoming an earl and agreeing to hold his property in tenure from the crown, how did that affect the tanist or his rivals? In Brehon law (the system used in Gaelic areas), lordship was not passed on at death to the oldest male heirs of the lord's body, as it was in English primogeniture. The tanist might argue (as Spenser's *Vewe* and Fynes Moryson later observe) that according to custom he was not bound by his predecessor's contracts and could make claims according to what he thought strongest grounds.[78] Confusing the case further was the English administration's occasional preference for a tanist over a weak heir.[79]

Submission would not be binding unless it were representative, unless a newly-minted "earl" truly carried with him the network of English social relations he was meant to personify. Indeed, surrender was not binding in a significant number of sixteenth-century cases that embarrassed and eroded the position of the English crown, the privy council, and the various English lords deputy of Ireland. The English government wanted individual acts of submission to be permanently and generally binding to the clan. Yet a legal person such as an "earl" was not a representation of an

76. English habit was a royal incentive long attempted in Ireland: Richard III sent English clothing and a gold collar to the Earl of Desmond on the condition that he abandon Gaelic dress (Ellis, *Tudor Ireland*, 67).

77. John Davies, "Lawes of Irelande," ed. Hiram Morgan, *The Irish Jurist*, n.s., 28–30 (1993–95): 307–13; quotation at 310–311.

78. Spenser, *A Vewe of the Present State of Irelande*, 49–50. See Pawlisch, *Sir John Davies*, 62.

79. On the example of Shane O'Neill, see Canny, *Elizabethan Conquest*, 33–34, and Ellis, *Tudor Ireland*, 142.

individual human being but the personification of relations between people; it did not take effect unless they were able to subinfeudate his followers and dependents and transform his rivalries and alignments. The creation of an earl out of a Gaelic lord was the attempt to retrofit an agnatic, territorial, and political group of people into alien forms of kinship, property, and polity.

The customary social persons of Gaelic culture could not be transformed, of course, merely by translating the names of legal persons into their rough English equivalents; the English had to find ways of penetrating the social bonds underneath the language, the networks embodied in the persons. Surrender and regrant was only one experiment among many in the prosecution of English conquest, but it is important as a particularly graphic case of the colonial attempt to transform social persons. Like Spenser's constitutional allegory, the river marriage, the success of colonial transformations of Irish social persons depended upon a robust notion of consent; like Cymodoce's task, they also depended upon legal actions designed to preserve that consent.

Tudor government in Ireland struggled with its own social persons too. John Davies, for example, was both agent and object of personifications crucial to Irish rule. By assigning eighty-four seats to the colonial plantations in Munster and Ulster, Davies engineered a Protestant majority for the crown in the Irish parliament that opened in 1613. King James then chose Davies as his candidate for speaker, but the appointment was opposed by John Everard of the Old English faction, a recusant whom Davies had ousted from his position as Second Justice of the King's Bench. When the election appeared to be even, Everard was placed in the chair, and in a matching move the "corpulent" Davies was simply placed in Everard's lap until crown supporters were able to oust Everard out from underneath Davies.[80] Control of political personification is, of course, more than symbolically important: contests such as that over the speaker's chair influence the future course of justice in the most material ways.

Davies' term in the speaker's chair added to a prominent career in colonial government. He was an experienced lawyer and had been solicitor general and attorney general for Ireland under James. As his speeches to parliament show, he was also a learned historian and constitutional theorist. Davies' treatise, *A Discoverie of the True Cavses why Ireland was neuer entirely Subdued, nor brought Vnder Obedience of the Crowne of England, vntill the Beginning of His Maiesties Happie Raigne,* had been published in 1612. In it, he claims that the conquest of Ireland was delayed by two faults on the part of English governance: lack of military

80. Pawlisch, *Sir John Davies*, 31.

commitment and reluctance to extend the benefits of the common law to the Irish.

> For that I call a "perfect conquest" of a country which doth reduce all the people thereof to the condition of subjects; and those I call "subjects" which are governed by the ordinary laws and magistrates of the sovereign. For though the prince doth bear the title of "sovereign lord" of an entire country (as our kings did of all Ireland), yet if there be two-third parts of that country wherein he cannot punish treasons, murders, or thefts, unless he send an army to do it; if the jurisdiction of his ordinary courts of justice doth not extend into those parts to protect the people from wrong and oppression; if he have no certain revenue, no escheats or forfeitures out of the same, I cannot justly say that such a country is wholly conquered.[81]

Here Davies treats the need for military force as an indication of the absence of the deep social support—both financial and political—that is required by the legal person "the subject" no less than by its counterpart "the king." Davies' writing revives the constitutional issues that concerned St Leger in the 1540s: he repeatedly stresses that the condition of "the subject" must be extended to the inhabitants of Ireland. Such an extension is a matter of legal personification as well as political importance. Davies recognizes that the title "sovereign lord" personifies the relation between ruler and subject and thus depends for its efficacy on the condition of subjects.

The extension of the legal person "subject" is also a matter of distributive justice. Davies is an unreliable witness as to whether his policy produced an improvement in the status of people in Ireland, but at least he bases his argument on a standard of such improvement. In previous centuries, people stranded between legal persons, under the military overview of English law but without recourse to its principles, had certainly suffered. Davies writes: "It is evident by all the records of this kingdom that only the English colonies and some few septs of the Irishry, which were enfranchised by special charters, were admitted to the benefit and protection of the laws of England, and that the Irish generally were held and reputed aliens, or rather enemies, to the Crown of England; insomuch as they were not only disabled to bring any actions, but they were so far out of the protection of the law as it was often adjudged no felony to kill a mere [native] Irishman in the time of peace."[82] Davies is no enemy of class privilege, but he complains repeatedly that the status of subject was not extended to the less powerful "mere" Irish. The rich could at least purchase denization in

81. Davies, *A Discovery*, 71–72.
82. Ibid., 125–26.

the form of a charter: "That the mere Irish were reputed aliens appeareth by sundry records wherein judgment is demanded if they shall be answered in actions brought by them, and likewise by the charters of denization, which in all ages were purchased by them."[83] Davies frequently championed second-order leaders of septs against the great lords in an effort to extend the government's influence and to procure land for English colonists. He claims a principled English opposition to tyrannical overlords, repeating a motto of earlier administrations even in the face of the skepticism with which those who had lived through years of the crown's consolidation of power might respond to such well-worn promises.

Despite its class politics, of course, Davies' policy of extending the status of the subject to the Irish was explicitly designed to further their assimilation to English rule. On another front, Davies engineered the extinction of the traditional (if limited) recognition by English courts of Brehon law as a legitimate form of local customary law, although it had been a venerable common law practice of tolerance that worked well in other parts of the realm. Throughout *A Discovery*, Davies recognizes the impossibility of bringing English governance to Ireland without bringing with it English forms of social person, but insofar as this requires the suppression of Irish customary forms, his ideals of legal endowment remain those of military conquest.[84]

When we see Smith and Davies wrestle with the difficulty of fit it is clear how the questions and methods of ethnography became urgent during this period, which is often identified as the beginning of modern anthropology. One motive of ethnographic writing in the period is the project of making a coherent *collective person* (a "people," "race," or "nation" in the early modern meanings of those words) out of populations in order to constitute a unified object of study.[85] The intellectual motive went along with the political fact that a group of people who were not perceptible as a unit, who were not susceptible to personification as a singular "people," could not submit to conquest. Once "the Irish" becomes intelligible as a personification that can justly include the "so many strong nations" of the various Gaelic clans, "the Irish" can take political actions as a group through

83. Ibid., 126.

84. John Davies, *A Discovery* and *Le Primer Report des Cases in les Courts del Roy* (Dublin, 1615). For a deeper understanding of Davies' legal strategies, see Pawlisch, *Sir John Davies*.

85. On early modern race, for example, see *Women, "Race," and Writing in The Early Modern Period*, ed. Margo Hendricks and Patricia Parker (New York: Routledge, 1994); Kim Hall, *Things of Darkness: Economies of Race and Gender in Early Modern England* (Ithaca: Cornell University Press, 1995); and Valerie Babb, *Whiteness Visible: The Meaning of Whiteness in American Literature and Culture* (New York: New York University Press, 1998).

the fiction of the collective locution. The form of that personification establishes what counts as an action by specifying who has authority to act for the group. If this personification is a military project, it is also an imaginative project that takes place in language. At the turn of the sixteenth century, the island had a number of important groupings, including those the English sometimes called the "Old English" (largely recusant descendants of twelfth-century colonists), the "mere Irish" (Irish speaking "natives"), lords who were confusing mixtures of Irish, Norman, and English birth and breeding (some well-connected at court, many going "in" and "out" of loyalty to the crown), Anglican church officials, Jesuit priests trained on the Continent, English planters, crown soldiers who sometimes became colonists (including mercenaries from outside Britain), and English officials (largely Protestant and working in the area around Dublin controlled by the English government and known as the Pale). Since the Old English, the officials, the lords, and those who recognized the Pope's authority were usually at odds with one another as well as the English privy council, it is important to realize how vexed collective locutions were—and are.[86]

The ethnographic opinions of Spenser's dialogue contribute to a unifying framework for understanding Ireland by making it possible to think of it as a single body. A personification such as the character Irena in *The Faerie Queene* Book V is a figure for Ireland who can be rescued from the Irish—whose unification is imaginatively an already accomplished fact. Like many later makers of political tracts, cartoons, and maps, Spenser conjures a personification of a whole and single island that does not represent (and may be the victim of) the indigenous peoples. Their unification and ability to surrender can thus be rendered as natural. But it is the genre of the treatise that develops the ethnographic description and reasoning necessary for making it possible to think of Ireland as a single body. In the tradition of the twelfth-century *Topographia hibernica* and *Expugnatio hibernica* of Giraldus Cambrensis (Gerald of Wales), a number of writings on Irish peoples and customs appeared in Tudor and Jacobean times, including important works by not only Spenser, but Andrew Boorde, Edmund Campion, Philip Sidney, Richard Stanyhurst, Barnabe Rich, Rich-

86. Nicholas Canny's work has paid sustained attention to the formation of identity in this period. See especially chap. 1 in *Elizabethan Conquest*; "Identity Formation in Ireland: The Emergence of the Anglo-Irish," in *Colonial Identity in the Atlantic World, 1500–1800*, ed. Nicholas Canny and Anthony Pagden (Princeton: Princeton University Press, 1987); and "Edmund Spenser and the Development of an Anglo-Irish Identity," *Yearbook of English Studies* 13 (1983): 1–19. On the use of the words "Norman" or "English" for the colonists of the twelfth century, see John Gillingham, "The English Invasion of Ireland," in *Representing Ireland: Literature and the Origins of Conflict, 1534–1660*, ed. Brendan Bradshaw, Andrew Hadfield, and Willy Maley (Cambridge: Cambridge University Press, 1993), 24–42.

ard Beacon, William Herbert, Thomas Churchyard, Fynes Moryson, John Dymmok, John Harington, John Derricke.[87] Spenser's prose had a notable influence upon John Davies and his development of policies in the years after Spenser's death.[88]

In the *Vewe*, Spenser pursues a deliberative political philosophy without "colouring" it, as he had said in the letter to Ralegh, with the "darke conceit" of narrative allegory. The *Vewe* has two speakers who take different standpoints: one is oriented toward principle and is positioned "outside" Ireland, whereas the other is oriented toward practice and has experience "inside" Ireland. The work is generally organized into four parts for the exposition of "evils" in positive law, customary law, religious law, and finally their cures.[89] Under each kind of law, the discussion includes forms of person, habitus, language, social bonds, and political institutions; as we have seen, the dialogue is animated by a recognition of the criterion of fit between the nature of the people and the government.

The Book of Justice in *The Faerie Queene*, on the other hand, works its political deliberation on Ireland by a case method. Episodes are strung together on similar topics and designed to be as controversial as possible. Yet this is not merely provocative, because the episodes are carefully chosen to display the difficult subtleties of the principles at stake. For instance, the choice between reform and spilling the "principall" that is central to the discussion of the *Vewe's* speakers gains an immediate international context when Arthur and Artegall are suddenly plunged into quests against the tyrants who have usurped sovereignty in a series of nations. Larger than the *polis*-like commonwealths of the middle part of Book V, these realms seem to carry clear historical references: they belong to characters named Belge, Sir Burbon (who courts Flourdelice), and, fi-

87. A good introduction to the early modern English literature on Ireland is *Strangers to That Land: British Perceptions of Ireland from the Reformation to the Famine*, ed. Andrew Hadfield and John McVeagh (Gerrards Cross: Colin Smythe, 1994).

88. For the *Vewe's* influence on Milton, see Willy Maley, "How Milton and Some Contemporaries Read Spenser's *View*," in *Representing Ireland*, 191–208.

89. By emphasizing the dialogism of Spenser's *Vewe of the Present State of Irelande* I do not wish to suggest that either speaker presents anything defensible as an Irish point of view. The interpretation—literary, historical, and moral—of the *Vewe* is a matter of persistent difficulty and requires, I think, a more thorough understanding of its generic and allusive structure than we have yet produced. For the beginnings of such an understanding, see Patricia Coughlan, "Some Secret Scourge Which Shall By Her Come Unto England: Ireland and Incivility in Spenser," in *Spenser and Ireland: An Interdisciplinary Perspective*, ed. Patricia Coughlan (Cork: Cork University Press, 1989), 46–74; David Lee Miller, "The Earl of Cork's Lute," in *Spenser's Life and the Subject of Biography*, ed. Judith Anderson, Donald Cheney, and David A. Richardson (Amherst: University of Massachusetts Press, 1996), 146–71; and Andrew Hadfield, "Who is Speaking in Spenser's *A View of the Present State of Ireland*? A Response to John Breen," *Connotations* 4 (1994–95): 233–41.

nally, Irena. Artegall's primary task in the Book of Justice is to restore Irena's claim to sovereignty over a "saluage Iland" (xi.39). Her country suggests Ireland: it lies across a channel from the Faery Queene's court and is a day's sail, in good wind, from the religiously vexed territory of Sir Bourbon and Flourdelis. Artegall is given his task by the Faery Queene in canto i, when Irena appears at court seeking aid; by the last stanzas of Book V when he is recalled to court, he has restored Irena to power but has not completely reformed "that ragged common-weale" (xii.26).

Despite the directness of the allusion to Ireland (indeed critics have complained of its transparency), Artegall does not establish the Faery Queene as sovereign of the savage island, nor does the poem suggest in any way that Irena is not native. Usurped by her enemy Grantorto, whose name suggests a cartoon drawn from a legal textbook on torts, Irena seeks assistance from the Faery Queene, but does not render homage:[90]

> Wherefore the Lady, which *Irena* hight,
> Did to the Faery Queene her way addresse,
> To whom complayning her afflicted plight,
> She her besought of gratious redresse.
> That soueraine Queene, that mightie Emperesse,
> Whose glorie is to aide all suppliants pore,
> And of weake Princes to be Patronesse,
> Chose *Artegall* to right her to restore;
> For that to her he seem'd best skild in righteous lore.
>
> (i.4)

Gloriana helps Irena because she is a patron of weak princes: this clearly identifies Irena as sovereign in her own right, though in need of military assistance to defend that right. She does not take Gloriana as her feudal lord. The Irish episode is set in parallel, not in contrast, to English support of Henry IV's France and of self-rule in the Low Countries against the Spanish crown, yet Grantorto has no links, whether by blood, military alliance, or spiritual doctrine, to Geryneo, though he might easily have been so portrayed. It is foreign to received notions of Spenser's colonial project, but Book V supports an English defense of a self-sovereign, monarchical commonwealth in Ireland.[91]

90. Contrary to A. C. Hamilton's note, which suggests that Irena "attends Mercilla, as ideally a peaceful Ireland should pay homage to Elizabeth" in Spenser, *The Faerie Queene*, ed. A. C. Hamilton. On Grantorto, see W. Nicholas Knight, "The Narrative Unity of Book V of *The Faerie Queene*: 'That Part of Justice Which is Equity,'" *Review of English Studies* 21 (1970): 267–94.

91. Andrew Hadfield argues that Irena is a personification of Elizabeth's sovereignty over Ireland in *Edmund Spenser's Irish Experience: "Wilde Fruit and Savage Soyl"* (Oxford: Clarendon, 1997), 151; later in the argument, Nature and Cynthia each join the ranks as "yet another figure for Elizabeth" (189). These identifications, as so often in Spenser criti-

The great, wrongful power Grantorto is singular, not a large mix of warring chieftains and rebelling lords; as an allegory he is conceptual (from the legal "tort") rather than collective. Book V itself is introduced by a proem which seems to bewail ambition, war, and the present state of political thought. Spenser warns the reader of his own, conservative revisions to ethics and political philosophy:

> Let none then blame me, if in discipline
>   Of vertue and of ciuill vses lore,
>   I doe not forme them to the common line
>   Of present dayes, which are corrupted sore,
>   But to the antique vse, which was of yore,
>   When good was onely for it selfe desyred,
>   And all men sought their owne, and none no more;
>   When Iustice was not for most meed outhyred,
> But simple Truth did rayne, and was of all admyred.
>   (Proem.3)

"All men should seek their own, and none no more" is not an obviously imperial or colonial motto. If the primary quest of the book's protagonist is restoring indigenous, inherited rule in Ireland, then it is bound to end unsatisfactorily, and is a quite different treatment of justice than has been recognized. We have misunderstood its topicality; and we have also misinterpreted its principles. The kind of attention Paul Alpers urged Spenserians to give to the "surface" of the poetry in *The Poetry of "The Faerie Queene"* needs now to be turned to the raw materials of character.[92] We must devote specific attention to the way the details of character call upon social persons drawn from different topoi, institutions, and discourses, and to how Spenser invites us to deliberate about their relative merits, rather than to make exclusive identifications. When I claim Spenser is using a case-study method here, I mean to point out that the poem is an unsatisfactory chronicle of political history in part *because* of its status as political philosophy.

Spenser accomplishes extraordinary alterations of place in his fictional hash of landscapes terrestrial, otherworldly, historical, topographical, and literary; this mixture provides some general and particular points of reference for character as human figures move within the parameters of the so-

---

cism, allow fruitful connections among episodes, but, as attributions, too easily become so general as to be beyond argument.

92. Paul Alpers, *The Poetry of "The Faerie Queene"* (Princeton: Princeton University Press, 1967). My emphasis on political philosophy here follows, I believe, the strengths of the poem, but it remains true that much work still needs to be done on Spenser's historical references.

cial spaces conjured by the fiction.[93] The hybrid legal, political, and social state of Ireland appears most intensely in the *Two Cantos of Mutabilitie*, and I shall devote the final section of my argument to them. We shall see how social persons give us an analytical tool that can be used to assess the indebtedness of his technique of personification allegory to the vexed political space of colonial war.

Architectonic Character and Dominion in *Two Cantos of Mutabilitie*

The 1596 version of *The Faerie Queene* breaks off after six books; the fragmentary *Two Cantos of Mutabilitie* were first published, as part of a seventh book, by Matthew Lownes after Spenser's death. In the *Two Cantos*, Spenser turns from moral philosophy to jurisprudence, leaving the scheme of the virtues and their ethical and political aspects behind. Like *A Vewe of the Present State of Irelande*, the *Two Cantos* are structured around a comparison of different kinds of law. More explicitly than in the episode that combined the river marriage with the story of Florimell, Spenser makes dominion the topic of the legal allegory of the *Two Cantos*.[94] The poem tells the story of a dispute about dominion and sets that story simultaneously in a colonial backwater and at the center of power. In other words, while the *Two Cantos* begin in the heavens at the court of Cynthia (Ralegh's figure for Elizabeth, complete with her black and white colors), and then climb to the higher imperial court of Jove, in time we discover that a yet higher court, that of Dame Nature, convenes on a terrestrial hill that was visible from Spenser's home at Kilcolman, a land forsaken by the goddess Cynthia/Diana.

The protagonist of the *Two Cantos* is Mutability, a character who deserves a much more careful analysis than she has yet received. Returning again to the explicatory method of the Introduction, I shall consider her here in terms of seven social persons that provide much of the essential material of her creation. First, her name places her in the philosophers' tradition of female personifications of abstract nouns. From Boethius's Lady Philosophy to the chaste lady Liberty of the American constitutional

93. Anne Fogarty makes a suggestive connection between Spenser's landscapes and Foucault's concept of the heterotopia in "The Colonization of Language: Narrative Strategy in *A View of the Present State of Ireland* and *The Faerie Queene*, Book VI," in *Spenser and Ireland*, 91. See also Willy Maley, chap. 4 in *Salvaging Spenser: Colonialism, Culture and Identity* (New York: St. Martin's, 1997).

94. This is the argument I advanced in "The Failure of Moral Philosophy." Space as *political estate* is closely associated with genre throughout Spenser. See Paul Alpers on the "demesne" or "domain" of lyric in "Pastoral and the Domain of Lyric in Spenser's *Shepheardes Calender*," *Representations* 12 (1985): 83–100.

debates, these figures are instructional and suasive. As we saw in chapter 2 in the person of Langland's Mede, their gender invites the reader to take up an intentional state toward them that becomes, if developed as intended, constitutive of social and political obligations.

The name Mutability may seem an odd choice for such a character until we understand in what way her discursive origins are indeed philosophical. In his emphasis on mutability, Thomas Smith follows the scholastics, as well as Aristotle; he echoes Thomas Aquinas, who devotes a question of the *Summa theologica* to "De mutatione legum," the reasons for and the limits of the mutability of human law (*lex humana*).[95] This section is central to Thomas's discussion of kinds of law and their relative scope and powers, and it answers the earlier discussion of the relative immutability of natural law (1.2.94.5). The theme of mutability is prominent in Smith's *De republica Anglorum*, as we have seen; it is the nature of both "a mans bodie it selfe" and "the politique bodie." Smith writes that it is natural for the "fashions of governement" (i.e., democracy, aristocracy, monarchy, and their variants) to change and mutate in a commonwealth over time.[96] His sense of the plasticity of the polity is acute: "for never in all pointes one common wealth doth agree with an other, no nor long time any one common wealth with it selfe. For al chaungeth continually to more or lesse, and still to diverse and diverse orders, as the diversity of times do present occasion, and the mutabilitie of mens wittes doth invent and assay newe wayes, to reforme and amende that werein they do finde fault."[97] This view of polities changing in time from monarchies to aristocracies, etc., depends in part upon the standard view English political philosophers adopted (from Aquinas) of their own polity as a "mixed constitution," the form set out most influentially by John Fortescue in the fifteenth century. The title of Smith's treatise calls England not a monarchy, but a republic; the notion of the mixed constitution explains why this did not amount to political heresy.[98]

95. Thomas Aquinas, *Summa theologica*, 1.2.97 (Cambridge: Blackfriars, 1964–76), 28:142–43.

96. Smith, *De republica Anglorum*, 51, 62.

97. Ibid., 67.

98. Patrick Collinson draws attention to Smith's use of the term "absolute" for the character of England's monarchy (in *De republica*, 85), claiming that "Smith failed to define England as a mixed monarchy, but on the contrary reported that it enjoyed no other government than that of 'the royal and kingly majesty,'" in his 1989 lecture *De Republica Anglorum: Or, History with the Politics Put Back* (Cambridge: Cambridge University Press, 1990), 19, 23. Yet Smith's description of the polity belies that view, as I hope I have indicated, and of course Smith did know the Latin word for "monarchy" and chose not to use it in his title. Still, Collinson energetically makes room for our seeing "quasi-republican modes of political reflection and action" in Elizabethan figures such as Smith, modes that he believes (as I do) have been underestimated (23).

One main source of the polity's mutations is the failure of the nobility to habituate its offspring to virtue. He traces the cause of degeneration to mutability:

> But as other common wealthes were faine to doe, so must all princes nec-essarilie followe, where vertue is to honour it: and as vertue of auncient race is easier to be obtained, for the example of the progenitors, for the abilitie to give to their race better education and bringing up for the enraced love of tenants and neybors to such noblemen and gentlemen, of whom they holde and by whom they doe dwell. So if all this doe faile (which it is great pitie it should) yet such is the nature of all humaine things, and so the world is subject to mutability, that it doth many times faile.[99]

Out of this failure grows the need newly to create knights, barons, and gentlemen. The extinction and creation of social persons in the polity is part of the mutable nature of the world:

> But when it [education] doth [fail], the prince and common wealth have the same power that their predecessors had, and as the husbandman hath to plant a new tree where the olde fayleth, to honour vertue where he doth find it, to make gentlemen, esquiers, knights, barons, earles, marquises, and dukes, where he seeth vertue able to beare that honour or merits, to deserve it, and so it hath always bin used among us. But ordinarily the king doth but make knights and create the barons and higher degrees: for as for gen-tlemen, they be made good cheape in England.[100]

Ethical virtue gives a kind of root to social persons in the face of the muta-bility of governments and family lines. Mutability is why the criterion of fit is so important: fit is a less mutable criterion of justice than those ideals which derive from the particular kinds of government. "By this processe and discourse it doth appeare that the mutations and changes of fashions of gov-ernement of common wealthes be naturall, and do not alwayes come of am-bition or malice: And that according to the nature of the people, so the com-monwealth is to it fit and proper."[101] Mutability is a quality of constitutions that threatens the appropriateness of their very ideals; the prominence of the term in constitutional thought brings the issues we encountered in the mar-riage of the Thames and Medway back into the poem in full force.

Philosophy of politics and law, then, is the source of the social person we attach to Mutability's personification of an abstract quality. This ex-

99. Smith, *De republica Anglorum*, 71.
100. Ibid., 71–72.
101. Ibid., 62.

plains the stress throughout the cantos on law. It also explains the details of her checkered past:

> For, she the face of earthly things so changed,
>   That all which Nature had establisht first
>   In good estate, and in meet order ranged,
>   She did pervert, and all their statutes burst:
>   And all the worlds faire frame (which none yet durst
>   Of Gods or men to alter or misguide)
>   She alter'd quite, and made them all accurst
>   That God had blest; and did at first prouide
> In that still happy state for euer to abide.
>
> Ne shee the lawes of Nature onely brake,
>   But eke of Iustice, and of Policie;
>   And wrong of right, and bad of good did make,
>   And death for life exchanged foolishlie:
>   Since which, all liuing wights haue learn'd to die,
>   And all this world is woxen daily worse.
>   O pittious worke of *MVTABILITIE*!
>   By which, we all are subiect to that curse,
> And death in stead of life haue sucked from our Nurse.
>
>   (vi.5–6)

Mutability, an inherent quality of many kinds of laws, is here imagined as abstracted from them and disordering and perverting them from "outside." The mutability of persons and polities destroys the very frame of the world, its order and estate, and its very fitness. In this effect, an effect compared to the fall, mutability causes just and good laws to have evil results quite opposite to their original, intended good. The philosophical convention of her gender here invites us to interpret the character's dislocation from the larger political framework of social bonds as part of the same painful and pathetic problem of fit.

Let us return to enumerating the references of Mutability's characterization. The second social person that provides Spenser with material for her is the personification of a conquered *race*, the "antique race," Spenser calls it, of the Titans:[102]

> She was, to weet, a daughter by descent
>   Of those old *Titans*, that did whylome striue

---

102. Gordon Teskey interprets Mutability's genealogy in Nietzschean rather than legal terms in "Mutability, Genealogy, and the Authority of Forms," *Representations* 41 (1993): 104–22 and "Spenser's *Mutabilitie* and the Authority of Forms," in his *Allegory and Violence* (Ithaca: Cornell University Press, 1996), 168–88.

> With *Saturnes* sonne for heauens regiment.
> Whom, though high *Ioue* of kingdome did depriue,
> Yet many of their stemme long after did surviue.
>
> (vi.2)

She is not the only surviving Titan:

> And many of them, afterwards obtain'd
> Great power of *Ioue*, and high authority;
> As *Hecaté*, in whose almighty hand,
> He plac't all rule and principality,
> To be by her disposed diuersly,
> To Gods, and men, as she them list diuide:
> And drad *Bellona*, that doth sound on hie
> Warres and allarums vnto Nations wide,
> That makes both heauen and earth to tremble at her pride.
>
> (vi.3)

The legal action here is familiar to those with some sense of Irish history: it is the policy of surrender and regrant discussed earlier, now extended by Jove to the personifications of hell and war. It is terrifying to find that hell and war are in charge of the distribution of political sovereignty and possession, in charge of the investment of nations with dominion (Hecate has been granted something like an Irish palatinate lordship). The personifications depict the strife and accommodation that conquest involves as evil indeed. The racial social person, Titan, allows Spenser to extricate the conquered and accommodated states of the Gaelic earldoms from their bearers, and to suggest that the devastation of colonial war is caused by a kind of tragic and corrupt legal license given by the conqueror to direct the conquered's revenge toward ordinary citizens.

Mutability's racial character has its most powerful effect in the issue of genocide, an act even Jove hesitates to commit. He responds to Mutability's challenge with violent rage, but is stayed by her beauty and, significantly, by the thought of genocide:

> He staide his hand: and hauing chang'd his cheare,
> He thus againe in milder wise began;
> But ah! if Gods should striue with flesh yfere,
> Then shortly should the progeny of Man
> Be rooted out, if *Ioue* should doe still what he can:
>
> (vi.31)

The *Cantos* contain a parallel scene in the Ovidian subplot: there "*Cynthia's* selfe" and her nymphs refrain from gelding the offending Actaeonfigure Faunus, because "that same would spill / The Wood-gods breed, which must for euer liue" (vi.50). This limit case serves as an etiological myth explaining the withdrawal of the virgin goddess from Ireland, her parting curse, and the ensuing plague of unrest. The possibility of genocide recurs throughout Spenser's thinking about Ireland, an unwanted end that his reasoning tends toward and yet must ward off.[103] Spenserian jurisprudence characteristically navigates precariously between two dangers, his Scylla and Charybdis: first, the threat that genocide might prove to be the most logical, effective, and efficient version of reduction and reformation, and second, the opposite threat of assimilation, devolution, and "degeneration"—that the colonial government be altered to suit a barbaric culture and be ruined in the attempt. Extricating "race" from "Irishness" allows Spenser twice to raise the spector of genocide as an indisputable limit to violence.

The racial characterization of Mutability is (perhaps curiously) sympathetic; yet there are other positive social persons evoked by her portrait. Related to her status as a Titan, for example, is a third social person, that of the *heir*. The dynastic genealogy of the Titans positions Mutability as the heir to "heauens regiment" (vi.2). As an heir, she has expectations of succession that give her a strong claim on our legal attention.

> I am a daughter, by the mothers side,
> Of her that is Grand-mother magnifide
> Of all the Gods, great *Earth*, great *Chaos* child:
> But by the fathers (be it not envide)
> I greater am in bloud (whereon I build)
> Then all the Gods, though wrongfully from heauen exil'd.
>
> For, *Titan* (as ye all acknowledge must)
> Was *Saturnes* elder brother by birth-right;
> Both, sonnes of *Vranus* : but by vniust
> And guilefull meanes, through *Corybantes* slight,
> The younger thrust the elder from his right:
> Since which, thou *Ioue*, iniuriously hast held
> The Heauens rule from *Titans* sonnes by might;
> And them to hellish dungeons downe hast feld:
> Witnesse ye Heauens the truth of all that I haue teld.
>
> (vi.26–27)

English common law is largely oriented by principles of devolution and succession that bind what happens to government to what happens to property in families. Shakespeare was able to justify the deposition of

---

103. The term "genocide" was coined after World War II, but it is clear from these passages of Spenser's writings that the concept far predates the word.

Richard II mainly by describing Richard's interference with the inheritance of Henry Bolingbroke. The portrayal of Mutability as an apparently entirely legitimate heir (we hear of no brothers) is rather positive and powerful in comparison, for instance, with the largely vicious construction of the quality of mutability by the political philosophers.

The *heir* is the basis for the appearance of the fourth and fifth social persons, also legal persons, through which we understand Mutability. Her action makes her a legal *appellant*, a claimant of her rights, and according to Jove at least, a *rebel in rising*. One within the legal systems set up by government, the other "out," both act to alter their legal status and are acted upon by legal strategies designed to redress or revenge the interests of the government's justice. We have seen Mutability give her credentials as an heir; the same utterance is a legal speech act by which she claims heaven, astonishing her audience of gods. When Jove denies her (suggesting she might instead surrender and receive a regrant, which she refuses[104]), she mounts her appeal:

> So, hauing said, she thus to him replide;
> Ceasse *Saturnes* sonne, to seeke by proffers vaine
> Of idle hopes t'allure mee to thy side,
> For to betray my Right, before I haue it tride.

> But thee, O *Ioue*, no equall Iudge I deeme
> Of my desert, or of my dewfull Right;
> That in thine owne behalfe maist partiall seeme:
> But to the highest him, that is behight
> Father of Gods and men by equall might;
> To weet, the God of Nature, I appeale.
> There-at *Ioue* wexed wroth, and in his spright
> Did inly grudge, yet did it well conceale;
> And bade *Dan Phoebus* Scribe her Appellation seale.
>
> (vi.34–35)

Jove must suffer her appeal because natural law trumps both legislated and customary law. But why is her rising not subject to punitive action?

The action of attainder was frequently taken by the crown's privy council against those important lords it refused to accommodate and declared rebels. This opposite of "creation" involved the legal (if not always possible to effect) escheat of the lord's property to the crown (i.e., its seizure by the crown's deputy and distribution to favorites). It also produced a civil death that disrupted inheritance entirely, as well as death by bodily

---

104. An opposite response can be found in Ben Jonson's "Irish Masqve at Covrt," where Irishmen are quick to welcome James's transforming presence. See Fowler, "The Rhetoric of Political Forms."

execution if that could be arranged. Spenser's own property at Kilcolman was part of the Munster plantation that was engineered upon lands seized by the crown following the attainder of the Earl of Desmond. Attainder was an immediate and drastic transformation of legal person. The action of attainder is available to Jove and to Nature in the *Two Cantos*, because Mutability is clearly portrayed as "rising"; yet it is interesting that neither takes it against her. Though the vertical register of her action ("rising") represents the movement that defined rebellion, and though she is "put downe" in vii.59, she is neither ordered to accept surrender and regrant, nor attainted. Nature's judgments are not like those issued by the privy council, and Mutability, despite her rebellious acts, is allowed to continue in her old dominion.

The sixth social person that seems relevant to Mutability's character is that of *emperor*, a ruler who claims an increasingly expansive dominion of nations and races. Insofar as her claims are imperial, the poet invites us to see Mutability in the same category as Jove and Elizabeth Tudor. When it is extricated from Elizabeth, the social person of the emperor usually receives a negative depiction in the *Faerie Queene*. Empire is unnatural according to the judgement of nature upon Mutability's title and rights:

> Cease therefore daughter further to aspire,
> And thee content thus to be rul'd by me:
> For thy decay thou seekst by thy desire
> (vii.59)

To be thus ruled by natural law is consonant with Spenser's view of the golden age:

> the antique vse, which was of yore,
> When good was onely for it selfe desyred,
> And all men sought their owne, and none no more;
> When Iustice was not for most meed outhyred,
> But simple Truth did rayne, and was of all admyred.
>
> For that which all men then did vertue call,
> Is now cald vice; and that which vice was hight,
> Is now hight vertue, and so vs'd of all:
> Right now is wrong, and wrong that was is right,
> As all things else in time are chaunged quight.
> Ne wonder; for the heauens reuolution
> Is wandred farre from where it first was pight,
> And so doe make contrarie constitution
> Of all this lower world, toward his dissolution.
> (V.Proem.3-4)

As Spenser turns to the stars, the anti-imperial sentiment reminds us of Mutability's characterization as the *personification of a natural force*, a principle of natural philosophy. This is the seventh in our gallery of social persons invoked by her character. She is associated with the moon because Aristotelian physics divided the universe into mutable and immutable parts at the sphere of the moon. All below the moon was thought to be mutable; all above immutable. The personification of force in Mutability's character is inseparable, then, from place—from the way that science imagined the space of the universe. Mutability's ascent and challenge to Cynthia is represented in the poem as an eclipse. When combined with Christian theories of history, the astronomical level of the allegory naturalizes the failure of Mutability's suit and the putting "downe" of the rebel below the moon's sphere. Yet natural philosophy also gives some credence to Mutability's arguments, because of the eccentricities of the planets' motions and science's inability to master their description.

The seven representations of person I have sketched here have different effects on our assessment of Mutability; each raises strong presuppositions and offers a different set of criteria for judging her. Her character calls upon a string of disciplines and discourses that give it the metadisciplinary quality that Sidney claims for poetry when he calls it, as we saw in the first section of this chapter, *architectonike*. Only a careful measuring of these social persons and, thus, the templates provided by their sources in knowledge and practice can bring us to an understanding of her meaning for the poem. Let us now turn to the allegory of the trial, the larger formal structure that directs our understanding.

Critics have tended to treat Mutability as if she were on trial, and as if Jove were not. But this is not a criminal trial, it is a property suit. Mutability argues that she, not Jove, is the proper lord of the realm of the heavens. She makes two claims: first, that she is rightful ruler of the heavens by inheritance, a claim in line with the precepts of English common law (the third and sixth persons described above), and second, that she is rightful ruler because of the inherently mutable natures of all things heavenly and earthly, a claim of a weak sort of possession by natural law (the sixth and seventh persons).[105] In rebuttal comes Jove's claim that he was invested by right of conquest and by the fact of his current "fated" possession of the heavens:

---

105. I say "weak" because legal possession of property lies in the act of holding it, not in a similarity between the nature of property and the nature of the claimant. The latter is a strong claim in early modern physics and astronomy, though the term "possession" is not special to their lexicon.

But wote thou this, thou hardy *Titanesse*,
   That not the worth of any liuing wight
   May challenge ought in Heauens interesse;
   Much lesse the Title of old *Titans* Right:
   For, we by Conquest of our soueraine might,
   And by eternall doome of Fates decree,
   Haue wonne the Empire of the Heauens bright;
   Which to our selues we hold, and to whom wee
Shall worthy deeme partakers of our blisse to bee.
                              (vi.33)

As a kind of cure for what he regards as her defects, being a Titan (second) and a rebel (third), Jove then offers her a version of surrender and regrant that her kinswomen Hecate and Bellona, the goddesses of hell and war, already enjoy. He formulates this offer as if his state were a meritocracy, and he begins with a dig ("gerle") that intends to disqualify her from being an heir, a ruler, or even an appellant (vi.34). But a bribe holds no appeal for Mutability, who insists on trying her claims as heir (third) and as natural force (seventh) before a higher court than Jove's. This further aggrandizes her role as the appellant (fourth) in the hope that she will be invested as an emperor (sixth). The seven social persons that provide Spenser with the raw cultural material for the figure of Mutability are built into the plot in conflict with one another.

The gorgeous ceremony of the trial tends to overwhelm its simple structure as a clash of claims and principles. Like the marriage of the rivers, the trial includes an elaborate procession of iconographically complex figures; these require us to recall Mutability's effects as conventions out of constitutional philosophy and natural science, the most abstract social persons of her makeup, in the sense that they are least able to be occupied by human beings. The four elements are cited ("the which the ground–work bee / Of all the world, and of all liuing wights," vii.25), and Mutability asks Nature to call "The rest which doe the world in being hold" (vii.27). Rather than English places, Mutability's witnesses are aspects of the cosmos, and especially of time—time as a figure for the domain of the heavens and its stately procession around the earth. We see the seasons, months, day and night, hours, and death and life. Like the rivers of Book IV, each of these temporal figures comes before us in a human form whose details spell out dominion: the quality and range of its power. After twenty stanzas of this procession, Jove objects that he and his pantheon rule Time itself (vii.48); Mutability counters that the gods change too, and goes on to describe the eccentric paths of the god-planets, the stories of their births on earth, and the altering effects that they have upon one another's courses. The total effect is to direct our attention to the investment of figures with social persons, and thus dominion, as a philosophically complex process that takes place in time and space.

The cases are clear. Inheritance and nature are argued on Mutability's side, and conquest and possession on Jove's. The subject for the reader's deliberation is the justice of those claims and their relation to a temporally charged space. The *Two Cantos* frame this issue of the grounds of dominion in the same way that Book IV frames the issue of the grounds of the constitution: by fashioning a topically multiple fictional space that acts as a context for the reader's responses to the characters. In the *Two Cantos*, Spenser instructs us to imagine a place that is simultaneously local and cosmic, a place in which to bring our deliberation of abstract principles and ideals to bear on a specific political entity. The place is Arlo Hill, and there the heavens touch the earth above Spenser's own estate, Kilcolman castle, in the Munster plantation in southern Ireland, just as the map of the globe touches the map of England in the rivers' wedding. There too, eternity touches a moment at the end of the sixteenth century. But his conjunction is not a product of a transcendental idealizing of Spenser's world, as earlier generations of scholars might have led us to expect.

Remember that the consensual marriage of the Thames and the Medway takes place above a cave in which the unwilling Florimell is tortured by Proteus. As we have seen, this doubled space of contradictory sexual institutions represents the English polity and its constitutional ideals of consensus, voluntarism, and feudal reciprocity, which require robust supporting processes of legal endowment and limitation. The *Two Cantos* refocus the issues of the epithalamion, turning slightly from the relationships and social institutions in which social persons are created and have their being (such as marriage and raptus), toward the claims of social persons to place—what English writers called the "estate," "honor," or "dignity" of persons. These terms represent substantive legal fictions that are the properties of social persons, not mere quaint honorifics. They can be summarized in the capacity of social persons to endow their bearers with dominion, the intellectual key to this chapter's conclusion.

The form of power that Mutability claims has been stolen from her by Jove, dominion (Latin *dominium*) is a fundamental concept of medieval and early modern political philosophy and yet it is perhaps the most contested of all such concepts. From the investiture controversies of the high middle ages to the fourteenth-century conflicts over religious poverty, from the cultural, military, and commercial crises of early modern European expansion to the Reformation, and from the depositions of rulers to every crisis of succession, the topic of dominion lies at the center of the most important debates in European jurisprudence. Theories of dominion consider the sources, limits, institutions, and justification—in a word, the constitution—of power in persons.[106] The right of Christian Europe to jurisdiction over other cultures became urgent in the context of the Crusades and was ruled upon by Pope Innocent IV, who declared that infidels had *dominium*—the right to possess property and be self-governing—and that they did so by virtue of natural law: the very principle Spenser personifies to preside over the trial of Mutability's right.[107]

Christian conquest and dispossession of other cultures requires justification, and an important part of the legal writing of the following centuries devotes itself to this project. Kinds of justification under Innocent's decrees include proof that the non-Christians occupied territories previously held by Christians, or that they participated in the violation of natural law (for example, through sexual perversity or idol-worship—favorite Spenserian themes). But dispossession of people on the basis of sin is tricky. It was particularly difficult during the early modern era because of the long-standing effort to defend the rights of officials in both church and state to hold property and exercise their duties and prerogatives, despite the state of their own souls, against such assaults as Wyclif's doctrine of dominion by grace. Spenser draws on the curious double role of controversies about dominion, the crucial position of its theorization both in the colonial wars at the territorial margins of European culture and in the contests of power at the very centers of the West. He grapples with the jurisprudence of conquest by writing both a chivalric romance and a dynastic national epic; he elaborates an English political philosophy in a setting that is sometimes a folktale otherworld, sometimes the dominions of Elizabeth Tudor, and sometimes Ireland.

In the *Two Cantos*, I have said, space becomes double according to different configurations of dominion, different claims of social persons to place. The legal issue—inheritance vs. conquest—is raised in the poetic space of the heavens, as Spenser takes much of his matter from Ovid's tales

---

106. Introductions to these debates may be found in John Gilchrist, *The Church and Economic Activity in the Middle Ages* (New York: St. Martin's Press, 1969), and in the work of Brian Tierney: *The Crisis of Church and State, 1050–1300* (Toronto: University of Toronto Press, 1988); "Hierarchy, Consent, and the 'Western Tradition,'" *Political Theory* 15 (1987): 646–52; *Medieval Poor Law: A Sketch of Canonical Theory and its Application in England* (Berkeley: University of California Press, 1959); and *Religion, Law, and the Growth of Constitutional Thought, 1150–1650* (Cambridge: Cambridge University Press, 1982).

107. On these issues in the context of Spanish conquest in the new world, see Anthony Pagden, "Dispossessing the Barbarian: The Language of Spanish Thomism and the Debate over the Property Rights of the American Indians," in *The Languages of Political Theory in Early-Modern Europe*, ed. Pagden (Cambridge: Cambridge University Press, 1987), 79–98, and more generally, Pagden's *The Fall of Natural Man: The American Indian and the Origins of Comparative Ethnology*, 2d ed. (Cambridge: Cambridge University Press, 1986).

of the classical gods. The higher space is the cosmos; Spenser folds into this space a second one that tells a separate story in a separate form. This is the Ovidian epyllion that explains the origin of Cynthia's curse upon Arlo Hill and of the unity of two of its rivers, Fanchin and Molanna.[108] This myth is the story of a locality, elicited by the convening of Nature's court there for "triall of . . . Titles and best Rights" of "all, both heauenly Powers, and earthly wights" (vi.36). Cynthia, Ralegh's figure for Elizabeth (as Spenser himself notes in the letter to Ralegh), has a prominent role in both stories, pursued by Mutability in the heavens and on Arlo Hill by Faunus, a wood god, satyr, and spy.

The double space of Proteus's house had allowed Spenser to assert the ideal of consent in the English polity while searching, in the more mythical and archetypal space of the Florimell story, for an ongoing remedy to the injuries and impediments that were presented by conquest. The double setting of the *Two Cantos* allows Spenser to question the status of conquest in Ireland while reaching for the abstract principles of jurisprudence with a cosmic opening and ending. We do not find Jove raping maidens in his basement, but when his position is challenged from below, he does firmly attest to his conqueror's nature, a nature of long standing poetic convention, already well evoked in Busirane's tapestries and elsewhere in the poem. What is law for, if not to protect legitimate but fragile rights from naked "might"? The two spaces, cosmic and local, settle neatly into two topoi that guide our readings of character. The heavens are imagined as an imperial court, its planets personified as courtiers and gods. Arlo Hill is imagined as a prelapsarian paradise, its woods and rivers personified as satyrs and nymphs who attend Cynthia/Diana, the goddess of the moon, chastity, and the hunt, as well as a conceit for the Queen. The heavens and the earth, the court and the country, the empire and the paradisal colonial wilderness, the dynastic struggle and the river courtship all exemplify a pervasive opposition that comes together in a single setting for the second ("seventh") canto, when the trial itself combines the cosmic and the local in an allegory of jurisprudence upon Arlo Hill.

The trial scene on Arlo Hill derives from Chaucer's *Parlement of Foules*

---

108. The Fall plays a prominent part in Christian theories of dominion. See, for example, Brian Tierney's discussion of Jean Gerson, "Conciliarism, Corporatism, and Individualism: The Doctrine of Individual Rights in Gerson," *Cristianesimo nella storia* 9 (1988): 104–6. Gerson derives a complex theory of kinds of human dominion from the persistence after sin of some of Adam's natural dominion (notably, his liberty and right of self-preservation). The *Cantos* offer the culminating example of how Spenser elevates Ovid and Chaucer in order to critique the promotion of conquest that he ascribes to Vergil and Petrarch. Note that wolves, which mark Diana's curse of Arlo Hill, are associated both with the wild Irish and with Rome—and thus imperial pillage.

(circa 1380), itself indebted to the natural law deliberations of Alanus de Insulis in *De planctu naturae* (circa 1160–70). Chaucer's poem is an allegory of the political constitution, an allegory driven by the role of consent (again imagined as the consent of the female to marriage). The plot appears to give precedence to rank, but the end makes clear that the issue is process—franchise itself—the opportunity to take counsel and have a "choys al fre."[109] The female's endowment with franchise by nature is here the paramount condition of the highest political good, which Chaucer calls "commune profyt" (47). It makes possible the creation of social bonds "By evene acord" (668). This topos, the allegorical trial by a personified judge, is also taken up by John Fortescue, in the second part of the fifteenth-century *De natura legis naturae*, where Justice presides over another case of disputed dominion involving a question of female sovereignty.[110] The sources of Spenser's topos reinforce our reading of the *Two Cantos* as an allegory of constitutional jurisprudence.

It is important to stress the difference between an allegory of jurisprudence and a legal allegory. The parties' claims derive from different legal sources. Mutability's claim by inheritance is a common-law claim, and thus it applies the customs of English property law. Jove's claim by conquest, however, would be regarded by renaissance thinkers as a Roman law claim. Further complicating matters is the identity of the mysterious judge, Nature, who personifies a third body of law—the law of nature— often drawn upon by early modern debates about colonial activity.[111] The qualities of Arlo Hill as a social space, so well established in the preceding canto, make it clear that the dominion at issue in the trial is dominion in Ireland. Spenser is not interested in telling us *who* should have dominion, and so Mutability, Jove, and Diana represent motives and modes of pos-

---

109. Geoffrey Chaucer, *The Parlement of Foules*, in *The Riverside Chaucer*, ed. Larry D. Benson, 3d ed. (Boston: Houghton Mifflin, 1987), 649. All quotations of Chaucer's works are taken from this edition and cited by title and line number.

110. John Fortescue wrote the allegory in support of Lancastrian claims; it must have been particularly noxious to Elizabeth. See the edition and "Remarks" by Thomas (Fortescue) Lord Clermont, *Works of Sir John Fortescue, Knight, Chief Justice of England and Lord Chancellor to King Henry the Sixth* (London: 1869), reprinted in Sir John Fortescue, *De Natura Legis Naturae*, ed. David S. Berkowitz and Samuel E. Thorne (Garland: New York, 1980): "the writer's intention is evident, and is fully admitted in his *Declaracion made by John Fortescue Knight upon certayn wrytings sent out of Scotteland ayenst the Kinges title of the Roialme of Englond*, in which he calls it 'a booke which I wrote in Latin to enforce myne intent,' namely, 'that no woman ought sovranly or supremely to reynge upon man' " (337).

111. Natural law is often drawn upon by poets as well; for arguments about its influence on renaissance literature, including *The Faerie Queene*, Book V (though not, oddly, the *Two Cantos*), see R. S. White, *Natural Law in English Renaissance Literature* (Cambridge: Cambridge University Press, 1996).

session rather than specific agents such as Irish chieftains, English military governors, or the crown. His trial is about the relative merits of the claims to dominion embodied in the social persons that make up these characters.

Conquest, the right that Innocent IV had deliberated and limited in his doctrine of *dominium*, is one of the main arguments for Elizabeth's sovereignty in Ireland. The implications of Innocent's ruling were elaborated by successive waves of colonial theorists, particularly in Spain and the New World. For Richard Hooker, Francis Bacon, John Davies, and Edward Coke, the right of conquest intends to establish absolute power, so that no consent of the people is necessary for government. However, English constitutional theory prides itself on its opposition to absolute rule, often going so far as Hooker, for example, who claims that William the Conqueror came to power by succession, but pretended to conquest mainly in order to be able to change some laws. Despite England's status as a monarchy, Hooker regards the power of making laws to be invested in the commonwealth, rather than in the king alone.[112] The assertion of William's accession by inheritance allows one to trace the ancient customary law of England in an unbroken line forward from some primeval consent. Absolute rule is reviled as corrupt and tyrannical both in histories and in popular sixteenth-century English arguments against Spain. As we have seen, conquest conflicts with the ideal form of commonwealth described by political philosophy. What moral justification do the English have to offer for instituting their law in Ireland if the primary benefits of English law must be suspended in order to be established?

It is interesting and important that Nature does not rule for Jove's claim by conquest but merely defers to the fact of his possession. Neither does Nature rule upon Mutability's strong claim by inheritance, which the poem assures us is valid from the very beginning. Spenser, the sometime Clerk of Chancery in Dublin and Clerk of the Council of Munster, describes her lineage as he found it "registred of old, / In *Faery* Land mongst records permanent" (vi.2). The judge does rule, however, against the claim of Mutability to a kind of natural or inherent possession—the claim that because things are mutable, she already has some power over them. In a judgement of fact rather than law, Nature finds that things "by their

---

112. Richard Hooker, *Of the Laws of Ecclesiastical Politie* (London, 1593–), VIII.6.1. This view is supported by medieval chroniclers. For Hooker's view of political law as growing out of general consent, see I.10.4; on custom, see IV.5.1. See Annabel Patterson, *Reading Holinshed's Chronicles* (Chicago: University of Chicago Press, 1994), for Holinshed and his colleagues' assessment of the legal consequences of conquest (105–07), and pervasive emphasis on parliamentary consent. On the persistent importance of custom, see J. G. A. Pocock, *The Ancient Constitution and the Common Law: A Study of English Historical Thought in the Seventeenth Century: A Reissue with a Retrospect* (Cambridge: Cambridge University Press, 1975).

change their being doe dilate," so that all things—*not* only the gods, as Jove claimed—rule over change and "maintaine" their "states" (vii.58).

Dominion is a state—really, an estate—of persons and it is conferred together with social persons, especially with that of the *sovereign*. Although her ruling leaves "*Ioue* confirm'd in his imperiall see" (vii.59), Nature does not endow anyone with anything. After the trial, both parties to the litigation look bad. Each of their claims is insufficient. Mutability's principle of inheritance does not guarantee virtue or desert. Jove's principle of conquest "depriues" others of their rights and, by means of surrender and regrant, sets up local agents of damnation and destruction. The only glimmer of constitutional hope is the hapless, scorned Molanna, punished by Cynthia and locals alike and left to wriggle out under the stones into the bed of her lover. This more miserable river marriage echoes the constitutional allegory of the Thames and the Medway, and so it holds the Irish polity to the same criteria of consent and voluntary unity of person. Like Florimell, Molanna is a character who needs protection from the injuries of conquest in order to form the joint social person idealized by the legal notion of marriage and its unity of person. The poem ends on a tragic note, in full cognizance of having exposed the contradictions and legitimately conflicting ideals of English constitutional jurisprudence.

Spenser's personification allegory dramatizes the power of social persons to establish the nature of place; it also acknowledges the power that polities exert upon the forms of social person. Eudoxus marvels, "Lorde how quicklye dothe that country alter mens natures" (210), an Alteration (as Mutability is called) that turns the people away from English law, in the opposite direction from that prescribed by Irenius. As we have seen, English people could not import their social persons intact into the different social and political spaces of Ireland. The Elizabethan "application" of colonial law did not prove to be morally tenable; nor did it succeed in its project of justly altering "mens natures," bringing them to "fit" and embrace the virtues of the English commonwealth. Spenser's writing shows, though, that these struggles over social persons and their investment with dominion did prove to be an important test for the ideals of English constitutional law and its practices. In coming to understand them, such difficult histories of person require us, and such a difficult poem explicitly invites us, to develop the deliberative standards by which we can measure and recreate polities—the places of social persons—against their own, and our own, ideals.

Conflicts among competing political factions or regimes proceed according to power, but they also open up ideological contests that may or may not be decided along the lines of force. Like the jousting knights of medieval romance, social orders experience the trial not only of their physical strength, but of their spiritual or ideological strength as well. In Chaucer's Pardoner, Langland's Mede, Skelton's Elynour Rummynge, and Spenser's Mutability, we see the contradictory and yet convergent shapes of character acting within the texture of social institutions and practices. Can the social persons of political authority be justified in terms of distributive justice and in terms of the relationships they intend to personify? Are the structure of our polity and the body of its customary and statutory laws responsive to the human beings who bear its social persons? In *De oratore* II.87.357, Cicero writes, "corpus intelligi sine loco non potest." Nor can we understand the human figure in words without a robust notion of place as social and political. Assessing social persons is a way to test the fit between people and polity; calling for the criterion of fit gives scope to our ability to sustain that testing in both directions and to suit the shapes of social persons, and the institutions and ideals of government, to justice.

∞ *Afterword* ∞

The Obligations of Persons

I believe we scholars have an occasional obligation to reinvent the strengths of our specialties in ways that offer method and knowledge to fields and disciplines outside our own. That task requires us to find the intersections between our most specialized technical expertise and the urgent concerns of outside worlds. I have felt such an obligation press itself upon me throughout the course of work on this book, though I cannot estimate whether I have fulfilled it. That right belongs to those outside my fields, just as other gauges of my work's success belong to those inside. Disobeying a number of urges, I have here kept faith with my training in medieval and renaissance English literature, and I hope that whatever utility this book's ideas may have for historians, feminists, legal theorists, theologians, moral and political philosophers, or historians of art, it is increased rather than diminished by my resisting the urge to write essays on the application of my ideas to others' fields before I had properly developed them in my own. Literary study is especially good at the analysis of fictions, which are crucial but largely unrecognized in other fields (as this book demonstrates). The law runs a close second. In this use of the term "fiction" I am not making the argument that all objects of study are socially constructed and have little basis in material nature. I intend, instead, to draw attention to the subjunctive and hypothetical nature of many important premises, concepts, and modes of procedure across the humanities and sciences. Especially, of course, I mean the nature of their models of the person.

Still, in a somewhat underground way, the book is driven by concerns I share with other fields. For instance, thinkers as diverse as Catharine

MacKinnon, Judith Butler, and Tipper Gore have noticed that we need a better account of the injuries that images and words can perpetrate. Developing our sense of the process of habituation and the role of social persons in that process, as Geoffrey Chaucer and I begin to do in chapter 1, gives us a means of understanding the relation of visual and verbal fiction to action that might help us grapple with the enormous social and legal challenge presented by violence and representation. In the twentieth century, high art turned away from figuration, and so did art historians. Feminism—in the form of New York's Guerilla Girls, for instance—gave us one of the first reasons to turn back to thinking about the human figure. Yet 1970s and '80s work by feminists resulted in a kind of theoretical dead end for the figure, and feminist theory turned to gender and away from character. Returning now to a more theoretically and historically able treatment of the female or African figure in terms of social persons would allow us to fatten our rather thin sense of how painters participated in the explosive constructions of modern sexuality and race. The visual conventions of these figures were a means of engaging in arguments like those that surround the social persons treated in chapter 3, where antifeminist discourse is mobilized by John Skelton as a system of signs that enables him to make intellectually serious forays into the basis of economic thought. I suspect that the social person offers art history a tool for connecting feminist analysis with a newly rigorous history of ideas.

In another area, despite the enormous civil rights gains that individualism has made possible in the last two centuries, it seems to me a matter of current importance that legal personality be redesigned so as to remedy its injuries. We need a more powerful recognition of the gap between individual rights and civil health than current models of the person allow; the social person of the individual copes inadequately with pregnant women, race, and other joint or corporate persons that are not designed merely to protect shareholders from liability. Chapter 2 demonstrates the analytic power of avoiding methodological individualism by using social persons, as William Langland does, to assess civil incapacities and their effects on social bonds. We need to reimagine the process of political representation in a way that justly recognizes the corporate social persons (of race, gender, class, religion) that dominate the contemporary experience of citizens. We need accordingly to reimagine policies of opportunity in education, health care, and employment with stronger models of corporate entitlement. Chapter 4 treats the responsiveness of social persons, especially legal persons, to issues of group justice. Like Edmund Spenser's, our own institutions and processes of dominion—government, property rights, civil obligations, entitlements—need to be adjusted by continual and robust assessment of social persons. Citizenship and the polity both need constant reinvention as we cope with the increasingly multicultural obligations of geography and government in today's interdependent, transnational, transcontinental world. The criterion of fit that is the focus of the second half of chapter 4 develops the social person as a tool for assessing and producing justice as it pertains to both peoples and governments.

The constitutional questions treated in chapter 4 grow in part out of my perception that the critique of social contract in law and political philosophy is an urgent labor. It requires, I believe, a complex analysis of social persons if it is to strengthen its account of consent and grapple with the problems of incapacity, durability, revocability, and gender. Chapters 2 and 4 are perhaps most explicit in their orientation toward the project of contract theory. There it is clear, I hope, how historical material from the early centuries of thinking about the inception and life of social bonds could deepen our current thinking. In all these cross-disciplinary challenges to our joint project of imagining social life, the history of social persons and their fates in past societies provides an enormous legacy and resource. Before the modern era, the world faced these familiar problems in unfamiliar, productive, ingenious, and sometimes disastrous ways that we do well to recover and understand.

It now seems to me that the most apparently arcane and specialized knowledge often has the capacity to offer the widest utility. Thus this book reverses the order of much of my graduate training, which demonstrated the application of large theories developed in other fields (anthropology, history, linguistics, philosophy, psychoanalysis) to literary texts. I reverse this order not by applying literary theory to the materials of other fields (though I do treat such material often) but by developing a literary account of traditionally literary materials that is sufficiently thorough and theoretical to be profitably used in any discipline or discourse that represents the human figure. Early in the project I felt the need to reconcile my account of character in poetry with a recognition that it is a literary instance of the representation of persons more broadly construed. Subsequently that insight revealed a sturdy bridge between literary artifacts and their places in cultural history. Interpretation of character by means of social persons satisfies my need for a formal analysis that opens immediately and necessarily onto historical and political analysis. I hope you will find it so in your own work.

A book on reading and its ability to form the social world must acknowledge the way its own readers are likely to use it. I expect a number of you will read the conclusion alone, or at least first, and so it is appropriate to summarize, in its barest form, what I have argued. We have seen, in chapter 1, how verbal figurations of the human, including literary character, provide a cognitive and affective exercise or thought experiment that habituates the reader to social persons; part of this process is to train the human animal to become a political animal and (for better or worse) to use the language, the images, the ideas about the polity that are the common coin of its social environment. Chapter 2 stresses the complexity of conventional figures of the human or social persons, especially their status as personifications of social relations. Chapters 3 and 4 extend the analysis of how meaning is produced by characterization's constant reference to social persons. The problem of reading archaic forms of person through the cognitive screen of later forms (especially those that purport to be ahistorical, like gender) provides the topic of chapter 3. Then, in the last chapter, I take up the problem of discontinuities of social space, drawing out the political consequences of the mixed nature of social forms, their uneven geographical reach, their colonial transformations.

This book identifies, describes, and gives examples of the social person in action: a conceptual constituent of the business of making the human figure in words. Perhaps it is appropriate here to say something more about what I have not done. I have not written a history. As I have been working on this study and explaining it to my colleagues, many have initially understood it as an essay in the history of subjectivity. It is not. However, the study of social persons is crucial for historians of subjectivity in several ways.[1] In order to understand the history of emotional experience, of bodily and sensual experience, of the passions, of spiritual experience, of agency, and of psychological experience in general, it is necessary, I think, to delineate the cultural forms and practices that were available to people as modes in which to own or to practice that subjectivity. Social persons are paramount among such modes and intimately involved in perhaps all practices of subjectivity. They work together with the genetic, biological, and material conditions of a people's existence to shape subjectivity. The history of subjectivity is contingent upon the history of social persons.

Neither have I written a history of social persons. In the history of English language culture, as in western culture at large, there are a number of models of person that attain successive dominance, originating in one discipline and gaining explanatory power in many. The "self," for example, emerges as a dominant construction of person only during the early modern period. In Old and Middle English, the term "self" is largely confined

---

1. In *Subjectivities: A History of Self-Representation in Britain, 1832–1920* (Oxford: Oxford University Press, 1991), Regenia Gagnier acknowledges the contributions of Foucault and Althusser but credits Anthony Giddens's "duality of structure" with enabling analysis of "the reflexive, acting subject . . . and rejecting accounts that see it merely as a series of moments brought about by the intersection of the dominant signifying structures" (10); for Gagnier on the "self," which she views as profoundly intersubjective, see 11–14.

to its emphatic and reflexive grammatical functions. The concept of the self comes into its own after the Reformation, along with the Protestant practice of private prayer. These cultural impulses find literary expression in the late sixteenth-century practice of a newly personal lyric poetry, one that takes both devotional and amorous forms. In the *Oxford English Dictionary*, Spenser's 1595 use is among the earliest citations of a newly substantive "self": "and in my selfe, my inward selfe I meane, / most lively lyke behold your semblant trew" (*Amoretti* 45).[2]

In contrast, it is wholly modern to think of the person as first and foremost "the individual," a term that was used in a nearly opposite sense in early modern times.[3] The first citation in the *Oxford English Dictionary*, 2d ed., is dated 1425, and in it "individual" is found only as an adjective, with a meaning close to the modern "indivisible." The word has nearly reversed its meaning. Though the emergence of the idea of the individual person in late seventeenth-century English society was not unequivocally progressive, it became a conceptual foundation upon which much in philosophy, psychology, and law stands today. It is difficult to grasp the details of seemingly transparent and natural ideas such as "the self" and "the individual" because they are so much a part of our contemporary experience. The attempt to make sense of pre-modern ideas of person offers, I hope, a way of categorizing and distinguishing them that will help us to understand our present assumptions about the person.

In the social sciences, a late-twentieth-century awakening of interest in what Marcel Mauss called "the category of person" coincided with the increasing cross-disciplinary attempts to write the histories of subjectivity

2. Edmund Spenser, *Amoretti*, in *The Yale Edition of the Shorter Poems of Edmund Spenser*, ed. William A. Oram, Einar Bjorvand, Ronald Bond, Thomas H. Cain, Alexander Dunlop, and Richard Schell (New Haven: Yale University Press, 1989). For a teaching-oriented discussion of the relation of the sixteenth-century "self" to the arts, see my "Chaucer and the Elizabethan Invention of the 'Selfe,' " in *Approaches to Teaching Shorter Elizabethan Poetry*, ed. Patrick Cheney and Anne Lake Prescott (New York: Modern Language Association, 2000), 249–55. Because it lacks a robust historical understanding of such notions as the self and the soul as social persons that exist within important institutional and disciplinary frameworks that alter radically in time, Charles Taylor's important and moving *Sources of the Self: The Making of the Modern Identity* (Cambridge: Harvard University Press, 1989) fails to appreciate how radically the very purposes and natures of these social persons differ. For instance, if Augustine has a notion of the self at all, it is something to be repudiated rather than cultivated. It seems to me that an Augustinian soul is nearly diametrically opposed to what Taylor views as the self. The fact that both of these social persons imply practices of interior experience is not enough to support a historical account of the linear kind Taylor pursues, where the self is a single entity that evolves through time. I hope I demonstrate something of what I think is required for a more weighty account in chapter 1, where Taylor's chapter on Augustine was very much on my mind.

3. See Peter Stallybrass, "Shakespeare, the Individual, and the Text," in *Cultural Studies*, ed. Larry Grossberg, Cary Nelson and Paula Treichler (London: Routledge, 1992), 593–612.

and individualism.[4] This type of work has been too often limited by its readiness to conflate the different terms "person," "self," "individual," and "subjectivity," a conflation that cripples our ability to develop a more historical understanding of these figures of the human. As if to dramatize the need for greater theoretical purchase on the objects of such investigations, an opposing chorus arose to make the perfectly sensible objection (against the Shakespeareans, especially) that subjectivity exists before the English Reformation, in so-called primitive cultures, and before political theories of the individual in the East.[5]

The confined terms of this debate on the historical "appearance" of subjectivity demonstrate the inadequacy of a methodologically individualist approach to cultural criticism. Although people had and represented the experience of subjectivity before the ideology of individualism came to dominate Western culture in the modern era, the meaning of their subjectivities differs from ours because it existed within an archaic set of relations to other kinds of socially defined agents, intentions, and possible acts. Subjectivity exists, in short, in a contingent relation to dominant forms of social person. A nineteenth-century romance like *The Scarlet Letter*, for example, imagines subjectivity as the experience that escapes description by historically reigning models of person, a kind of excess of the individual. Imagine, Nathaniel Hawthorne asks his contemporary audience, how did those Puritans squeeze that big, feeling, cantankerous person we know as the *individual* into the small spaces they reserved for the characters of the *woman* and the *preacher*? The fact that person overlaps with subjectivity (and, on the other front, with human physiology) should not mislead us into thinking that they are ever synonymous. The category of social person has a history that includes but is not fully described by the various histories of subjectivity, the self, and the individual. Unless the concept of person is untangled from the narrow paradigms of individualist ideology, the logical conflicts in the pursuit of the history of subjectivity will prevent it from being written.

4. E.g., Michel Foucault, Ian Hacking, Alan Macfarlane, and, among literary scholars, Stephen Greenblatt, Linda Gregerson, H. Marshall Leicester, Jr., Katharine Maus, Colin Morris, Regenia Gagnier, Elizabeth Hanson. See *Reconstructing Individualism: Autonomy, Individuality, and the Self in Western Thought*, ed. Thomas C. Heller, Morton Sosna, and David E. Wellbery (Stanford: Stanford University Press, 1986) and *Rewriting the Self: Histories from the Renaissance to the Present*, ed. Roy Porter (London: Routledge, 1997).

5. Including, for instance, David Aers, "A Whisper in the Ear of Early Modernists; or, Reflections on Literary Critics Writing the 'History of the Subject,'" in *Culture and History, 1350–1600: Essays on English Communities, Identities, and Writing*, ed. David Aers (Detroit: Wayne State University Press, 1992), 177–202 and the sinologist Mark Elvin, "Between the Earth and Heaven: Conceptions of the Self in China," in *The Category of the Person: Anthropology, Philosophy, History*, ed. Michael Carrithers, Steven Collins, and Steven Lukes (Cambridge: Cambridge University Press, 1985), 156–89.

A good history of social persons would not chronicle the fortunes of a single idea, emblematized in the single human being (whether male, white, and property-holding, as in Thomas Hobbes, or liberalized to the atomistic subject stripped of attributes who lies at the center of John Rawls's thought experiment) but instead would reveal each model of the person as the condensation of a cultural system of classifications. The category of person is best treated as constructed "negatively," to use Theodor Adorno's term. It should be understood as a response to social problems rather than as sprung fully formed out of any Archimedean mind. The history of social persons is nothing like the orderly parade of *Two Cantos of Mutabilitie*, one allegorical figure after another, dignified and expected, all turning state's evidence. Instead, this history is like the shifting figural gestures of *Piers Plowman*: a troubled contest of epistemological frames where momentarily human-seeming figures made of language coalesce within our field of vision and just as suddenly dissolve. A good history of social persons would depend on our understanding of their nature, capacities, and uses. This book strives to provide such an understanding. I hope it will be useful to those who contribute to the history of both subjectivities and social persons.

Reading the late medieval philosophers, I realize that my subject, person, is an *impossibilia*, a missing substance that is projected by a set of accidentals. That is the way I treat it here: as an empty space that is shaped by the surrounding cloud of controversies over attributions. The power of this emptiness, though it issues from nothing but the thought experiment of the social person, is manifest in how people come to understand themselves and each other through shaping, occupying, owning, dissolving, and bringing to life that absent substance *person*. Studying the human figure in words is a most strenuous and rewarding way to strengthen our ability to assess and reinvent our own participation in social life. When Chaucer's dreamer wakes up from his thought experiment about the constitution of society that is the *Parliament of Fowls*, the birds fly away, and he says (and I say with him):

> And with the shoutyng, whan the song was do
> That foules maden at here flyght awey,
> I wok, and othere bokes tok me to,
> To reede upon, and yit I rede alwey.
> I hope, ywis, to rede so som day
> That I shal mete som thyng for to fare
> The bet, and thus to rede I nyl nat spare.
> (693–99)

Index